MYSTICS OF THE
CHRISTIAN TRADITION

From divine visions to self-tortures, some strange mystical experiences have shaped the Christian tradition as we know it. Full of colorful detail, *Mystics of the Christian Tradition* examines the mystical experiences that have determined the history of Christianity over two thousand years, and reveals the often sexual nature of these encounters with the divine.

In this fascinating account, Fanning reveals how God's direct revelation to St. Francis of Assisi led to his living with lepers and kissing their sores, and describes the mystical life of Margery Kempe who "took weeping to new decibel levels." Through presenting the lives of almost a hundred mystics, this broad survey invites us to consider what it means to be a mystic and to explore how people such as Joan of Arc had their lives determined by divine visions.

Mystics of the Christian Tradition is a comprehensive guide to discovering what mysticism means and who the mystics of the Christian tradition actually were. This lively and authoritative introduction to mysticism is a valuable survey for students and the general reader alike.

Steven Fanning is Associate Professor of History at the University of Illinois at Chicago. He is the author of *A Bishop and His World Before the Gregorian Reform, Hubert of Angers, 1006–1047* (1988), as well as almost a dozen articles on late antiquity and the Middle Ages.

MYSTICS OF THE CHRISTIAN TRADITION

Steven Fanning

London and New York

First published 2001
by Routledge
11 New Fetter Lane, London EC4P 4EE

Simultaneously published in the USA and Canada
by Routledge
29 West 35th Street, New York, NY 10001

Reprinted 2002 (twice)

Routledge is an imprint of the Taylor & Francis Group

© 2001 Steven Fanning

Typeset in Garamond by
Bookcraft Ltd, Stroud, Gloucestershire
Printed and bound in Great Britain by
Biddles Ltd, Guildford and King's Lynn

British Library Cataloguing in Publication Data
A catalogue record for this book is available from the
British Library

Library of Congress Cataloging in Publication Data
Fanning, Steven
Mystics of the Christian tradition / Steven Fanning
p. cm.
Includes bibliographical references and index.
1. Mysticism–History. 2. Mystics. I. Title.
BV5075 .F36 2001
248.2′2–dc21   00–068358

ISBN 0–415–22467–5 (hbk)
ISBN 0–415–22468–3 (pbk)

CONTENTS

——— •◆• ———

— Contents —

PLATES AND TIMELINES

———— •◦• ————

ACKNOWLEDGEMENTS

I am greatly indebted to a number of people for making this book possible. The deans of the College of Liberal Arts and Sciences of the University of Illinois at Chicago under whom I served, Sidney B. Simpson, Jr., Eric A. Gislason and Stanley E. Fish, kindly allowed me research time in the midst of my administrative duties, without which I could not have written this book. I am grateful to the library staff members of the Richard J. Daley Library at the University of Illinois at Chicago for their invaluable assistance in acquiring books from libraries in the Illinet Online system and on Interlibrary Loan. I am also very indebted to those who read the manuscript in the various stages of its incarnation and provided me with their most helpful comments, criticisms and encouragement: Annette Chapman-Adisho, Suzanne A. Wells, Carlene Thissen, and my friend and colleague at UIC, Dr. Mary Sinclair. I am especially indebted to my wife Sarah, who not only read the entire manuscript but also cheerfully carried home many books for my use from the Cudahy Library of Loyola University Chicago.

PLATES

CREDITS FOR ILLUSTRATIONS

Plates 1 (and front cover), 6: Scala/Art Resource, NY.

Plates 2, 10, 11: Yale Center for British Art, Paul Mellon Collection, New Haven, CT.

Plate 3: Valamo Society, Helsinki, Finland.

Plate 4: Brotherhood of St. Herman of Alaska, Platina, CA.

Plate 5: Art Resource, NY; plate 8: Alinari/Art Resource, NY.

Plate 7: The Julian Centre, Norwich

Plate 9: Institute of Carmelite Studies Press, Washington, DC from *The Collected Works of St. John of the Cross*, translated by Kieran Kavanaugh and Otilio Rodriguez, copyright © 1979, 1990 by Washington Province of Discalced Carmelites, ICS Publications, 2131 Lincoln Road., N. E., Washington, DC 20002-1199 USA.

Plate 1   The Desert Fathers as depicted in a fifteenth-century Italian painting by Gherardo Starnina (*The Thebaid: Hermits in the Wilderness*, Uffizi, Florence).

Plate 2   View of Mount Athos by Edward Lear, 1857 (*Mount Athos and the Monastery of Stavroniketes*).

Plate 3   A Russian monk's cell (cell of Nicholas of Valaam).

Plate 4   St. Sergius and the bear.

Plate 5 Hildegard of Bingen receives the Holy Spirit, illumination from a twelfth-century manuscript.

Plate 6   St. Francis renounces his worldly goods, detail of fresco in the Cappella Bardi, S. Croce, Florence, by Giotto di Bondone.

Plate 7   Julian's cell at the church of St. Julian, Norwich, rebuilt after bomb damage in 1942.

Plate 8 Detail of Gian Lorenzo Bernini's *The Ecstasy of St. Teresa*, Cornaro Chapel, S. Maria della Vittoria, Rome.

Plate 9 View of Crucifixion of Jesus by St. John of the Cross.

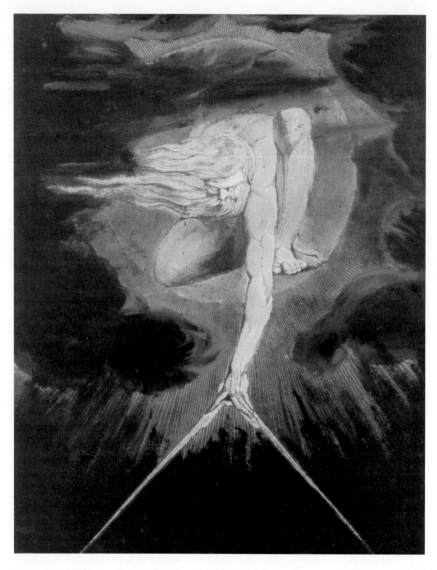

Plate 10 William Blake, The Ancient of Days, from *Europe: A Prophecy* (1794), Plate i.

Plate 11   William Blake, The Soul in the Mystical Embrace of God, from *Jerusalem* (1804), Plate 99 (*Jerusalem: 'All Human Forms identified ...'*)

PROLOGUE

———— •◦• ————

The modern Anglican priest and mystic Robert Llewelyn, former chaplain of the shrine of Julian in Norwich, wrote that there were two ways of knowing Christ: one can either know all about him or one can know him. He added that knowing Christ "is the only knowledge which ultimately matters. We Christians have a great start in being able to know about Christ from the Gospels, but if we do not know him it is as nothing."[1] This dichotomy represents the two different though intimately related Christianities that coexist uneasily within each other. One Christianity emphasizes human intellect and reason and is a theology, a set of beliefs to be accepted and rules to be followed, a creed that is proclaimed. The other Christianity is that of the mystics, who seek the experience of the God of the former and stress the inability of human reasoning to know the incomprehensible deity. These two Christianities present different means by which one can know God, either through the divine self-revelation to be found in the Scriptures and in Christian theology or through the direct revelation of the divine to the individual. Fr. Llewelyn's preference for the mystical approach as the essential aspect of Christianity fits easily with the view of Evelyn Underhill, one of the twentieth century's best-known writers and teachers on mysticism, who argued that "mysticism represents the very soul of religion."[2]

This book is concerned with the mystics of the Christian tradition, those who have gained the direct experience of the divine. However, the central problem in the study of mystics and of mysticism remains one of definition, for there is an astonishingly wide variety of connotations associated with those terms, which was pointed out from the beginning of the "modern" study of mysticism. In 1899 William Ralph Inge, later dean of St. Paul's Cathedral, London, published *Christian Mysticism*, which "almost single-handedly caused an English revival of interest in Christian mysticism."[3] In that work he wrote that no word in the English language

> has been employed more loosely than "Mysticism." Sometimes it is used as an equivalent for symbolism or allegorism, sometimes for theosophy or occult science; and sometimes it merely suggests the mental state of a dreamer, or vague and fantastic opinions about God and the world. In Roman Catholic writers, "mystical phenomena" mean supernatural suspensions of physical law. Even those writers who have made a special study of the subject, show by their definitions of the word how uncertain is its connotation.[4]

Dean Inge then provided twenty-six definitions of mysticism in a Christian context as "specimens" of the possibilities. At one extreme is the philosophical and theological concept of mysticism as a union with the divine so close that all distinction between the mystic and the divine is obliterated. At the other extreme "mystical" is sometimes regarded as a synonym for the occult or simply for the weird, or as William James said, "The words 'mysticism' and 'mystical' are often used as terms of mere reproach, to throw at any opinion which we regard as vague and vast and sentimental and without a base in either facts or logic."[5] James, however, pointed out that

> Churches, when once established, live at second-hand upon tradition; but the *founders* of every church owed their power originally to the fact of their direct personal communion with the divine. Not only the superhuman founders, the Christ, the Buddha, Mahomet, but all the originators of Christian sects have been in this case.[6]

Between these extremes is the approach of those who "focus on mysticism almost exclusively as a psychological moment of inspired rapture."[7] However, debates about the definition of mysticism, "while interesting, lend themselves to scholastic quibbling."[8]

From the various possibilities, the definition of mysticism employed in this present work is that of Evelyn Underhill, "the direct intuition or experience of God,"[9] or, to put it differently, mysticism is "every religious tendency that discovers the way to God direct through inner experience without the mediation of reasoning. The constitutive element in mysticism is immediacy of contact with the deity."[10] This definition is in wide use in the study of mysticism,[11] although when discussing mysticism in world religions, "God" is often replaced by more general terms such as "Absolute Reality," "the Ultimate," or "the One." Moreover, it also permits a very broad horizon for the investigation of mystics. If mystics are defined as those who have gained the direct experience of the divine, the term can comprise not only those who attained a distinctionless union with God but also those whose experience of the divine was less complete, for example it can include those in the constant presence of God or those within whom the Holy Spirit dwelled and who received the spiritual gifts accompanying the signs of that indwelling, such as divinely infused knowledge, clairvoyance, healing powers, as well as what are sometimes taken to be the typical mystical manifestations, visions and voices.

One can study either mysticism or mystics. Both methods are useful but they tend to have different effects and to be more valuable to different audiences. The study of mysticism is important, being concerned with phenomenology and methodology, but it also carries limitations, especially in introductory works. Inevitably examples from the writings of mystics are produced to illustrate particular aspects of mysticism; this tends to overwhelm the beginning reader with a seemingly endless series of disembodied and decontextualized quotations attributed to authors who are largely unknown, leaving one to ponder the significance of the isolated quotations. However, ideas have contexts and cannot always be judged simply at face value, for at times the historical context is vital for an understanding of mystical works. For example, the condemnations of Meister Eckhart and Marguerite Porete had a chilling effect on particular expressions of mystical ideas and shaped the framework of acceptable mystical language for two centuries to come. Or again, the devaluation of visions and voices by St. John of the Cross is often cited as if it were an abstract judgment on the matter by this acknowledged master of the mystical life while ignoring the fact that in the Spain of his day visionary mystics were being prosecuted by the Inquisition and it was vital for mystics who wished to avoid inquisitorial scrutiny to disassociate themselves from those who were considered heretics. Additionally, for those not already familiar with the authors of the quotations, the effect of the presentation of a series of excerpts from writers bearing unfamiliar and sometimes exotic names can often be bewildering and discouraging, needlessly emphasizing a mysterious and impenetrable element to mysticism. Moreover, a study of mysticism tends to present a specific mystical paradigm as a model by which particular expressions of mysticism are to be judged.

A study of mystics can produce a different effect. Attention can be drawn to the particular context in which a mystic lived and moved, influences of previous mystics can be more easily observed and the position of the mystics and their ideas in the long perspective of the mystical tradition can be discerned. The effect of a focus on mystics is to make one aware that the direct experience of the divine has come in many different ways and paths and has been expressed in a variety of forms. Thus rather than there being a favored paradigm of mysticism, one more readily sees that there is tremendous variation in Christian mysticism alongside the many areas of commonality shared by the mystics. Moreover, many find it easier to focus on individuals than on abstractions. Thus an introduction to mysticism can often be gained more profitably first by examining individual mystics before attempting to construct an Ism from their experiences.

This work is concerned primarily with mystics but not to the exclusion of the larger topic of mysticism. Its focus is to place the mystics in the context of their own lives as well as in the times in which they lived and, as much as is possible in something that is not an anthology, the mystics will be allowed to speak their own words. A particular emphasis here is the mystical experience itself, that is, on what it is like to be a mystic, which leads to considerable attention being given to mystical visions and voices. This is not to imply that mysticism is to be equated with the reception of these phenomena, for that is indeed not the case, but such manifestations have long been regarded as a certain indication that the recipient was in fact a mystic and were usually emphasized by the mystics' biographers, hagiographers and contemporaries as evidence that their subjects had in fact been graced by divine visitations. Moreover, the visions frequently were crucial, catalytic events in the mystical life of the mystics and are thus inseparable from an understanding of their lives and careers.

For the most part, the individuals considered here are mystics and not simply writers on mysticism. There are some exceptions – the unknown authors of highly influential mystical works, such as Pseudo-Macarius, Pseudo-Dionysius or the author of *The Cloud of Unknowing*. However, for the first thousand years of Christian mysticism there was a pronounced bias against claiming mystical experiences for oneself, preferring instead to attribute them to another person. Thus the assumption in this work, as in most which have considered figures such as Augustine or Gregory the

Great, is that when virtually all of authors' works are permeated with mysticism and provide exquisite descriptions of mystical experiences, they indeed were mystics.

A work intended to be a wieldy one-volume introduction to two millennia of Christian mystics necessarily entails limitations of its own. The requisite brevity mandates that each individual be discussed succinctly, to the omission of many aspects of the mystics' lives, writings and teachings. Regrettably, many mystics have been excluded, for a work twice this size could easily be produced that would still not encompass all Christian mystics. Therefore this work serves as an introduction to Christian mystics that will perhaps encourage readers to investigate particular mystics in greater depth and to take up the broader topic of mysticism with more profit. For those wishing to study Christian mysticism well-placed in historical context, one should consult the volumes now appearing in Bernard McGinn's outstanding series *The Presence of God, A History of Western Christian Mysticism.*[12]

As seen,[13] William James argued that the founders of every church and Christian sect were mystics, as were the great founders of three of the world's great religions, Christianity, Islam and Buddhism. Indeed, the claim of the mystics to immediate contact with the Transcendent is to be found in virtually all of the world's religions and commonly is the source of those religions:

> Not only has mysticism its fount in what is the raw material of all religion, but also all the most profound insights of religious truth have their origin in the mystical experiences of those who have led the spiritual progress of the human race.[14]

Perhaps the figure of the shaman making spiritual journeys into the other world on behalf of individuals as well as the community is the oldest type of mystic, a figure who has been traced back to the paleolithic period: "The lifeway of the shaman is nearly as old as human consciousness itself, predating the earliest recorded civilizations by thousands of years."[15] Among the Plains Indians of North America, the vision quest, the individual's search for direct contact with a guardian spirit, was "the most characteristic feature of North American religions outside the Pueblo area" and "provided an opportunity for direct contact with the supernatural."[16]

The religions and philosophies of the East are marked strongly by mysticism. It has been remarked that in the religion of the subcontinent of India "mystical experience holds a central place" and that in Hinduism in particular there is the appeal "to the soul's immediate knowledge and experience of God."[17] The founder of Buddhism, Siddhartha Gautama (ca. 563 to ca. 483 BC), "both at his enlightenment and death ... attained to a unifying vision and passed through trance states before the final peace of Nirvana,"[18] and Nirvana has been described as "the core of Buddhist mysticism," which is "an immediate apprehension of supreme Reality."[19] In China, the Taoists sought union with the Tao, which is the Infinite and Eternal, that is, Supreme Reality. When Buddhism reached China in the first century AD, it blended with Taoism to produce Zen Buddhism, whose goal is enlightenment (*satori*) – "Zen's version of the mystical experience, which, wherever it appears, brings joy, at-one-ment, and a sense of reality that defies ordinary language."[20]

In the ancient Greek world, contact with the divine could be achieved through intermediaries, such as the famous oracle at Delphi, who were important channels of communication between the two worlds, as "seers and oracle mongers were omnipresent."[21] Moreover, as will also be seen in the next chapter, at the same time the widespread and increasingly popular mystery cults of the Mediterranean world offered individuals unmediated personal access to communion as well as union with the gods. The Jewish world of antiquity was also familiar with mystics, such as the Essenes who will be discussed in the next chapter, and in medieval and modern Judaism the mysticism of the Kabbalists and Hassidists has been of profound influence on Jewish spirituality. At the same time, in the other great world religion related to Judaism and Christianity, Islam's prophet Mohammed (ca. 572–632) was the recipient of divine revelations on Mount Hira outside Mecca, including the word of God, the Qu'ran, and by the beginning of the ninth century AD the Islamic mystical movement of the Sufis had arisen. "From its origins in the Prophet Muhammed and the Qu'ranic revelation, the mystical trend among Muslims has played an extraordinary role in the public and private development of the Islamic faith."[22]

Thus in considering the Christian mystics, it is important to remember that among the seemingly myriad differences of Christian denominations and the competing claims of the world's faiths, it is in mysticism that they meet on a common ground of the experience of the divine. The Trappist monk and mystic Thomas Merton, who will be seen again in chapter V, expressed this commonality of divine revelation to the individual:

> Everywhere we find at least a natural striving for interior unity and intuitive communion with the Absolute. And everywhere we find expressions of some kind of spiritual experience, often natural, sometimes supernatural. Supernatural mystical experience is at least theoretically possible anywhere under the sun, to any man of good conscience who sincerely seeks the truth and responds to the inspirations of divine grace.[23]

The Christian mystics prove the strength and persistence of the element in Christianity that is the core, fount and energizing spirit of all religion, the direct encounter with God.

CHAPTER I

ORIGINS

— •◆• —

MYSTICISM IN THE GRECO–ROMAN WORLD

The Roman world in which Christianity arose was one steeped in mystical religion. The traditional Greco–Roman pantheon of gods had been in decline since the mid-fourth century BC when the conquests of Alexander the Great (356–23 BC) reduced the significance of the Greek city-states whose public cults were based on the worship of the state gods. Previously religion in Greece had been based on the city-state and had as its purpose the welfare of the entire community. But the Hellenistic world of the eastern Mediterranean that succeeded Alexander's empire was international and cosmopolitan, in which one's local or national identity and its associated religion were overwhelmed by the reality of belonging to large, multi-ethnic, multi-cultural states unconnected to the old civic gods. To a great extent, individuals were isolated individuals in a great sea of humanity to the diminution of a consciousness of being members of a close and clearly-defined community. Consequently, religions appealing to individuals of every ethnic or national origin were readily adopted throughout the Hellenistic world, often blending both Greek and non-Greek elements. These tendencies were strengthened by the expansion of the Roman Empire to the East in the second and first centuries BC, tending to render meaningless the previous local or national cultures that were now dominated by a state centered far away to the West.

What these new and altered religions offered was salvation from the sufferings of this world, immortality in the next world and a direct communication with salvific deities. These new and rapidly growing religions featured esoteric teachings known only to their initiates, who took the strictest oaths of secrecy, pledging never to reveal the secrets of the cult to outsiders. Hence these cults are known collectively as the Mystery Religions, with the word "mystery" etymologically related to "mysticism." Like mysticism, the Greek word *mysterion*, "mystery," was derived from *myein*, "to close," in this case indicating the closed mouth of the initiates of the cults. The adherents of these mysteries kept their oaths so well that we know almost nothing of their esoteric secrets.

The Mystery Religions arose all over the Eastern world and spread easily throughout the Mediterranean, becoming universal cults. From Greece itself the mysteries of Eleusis developed out of a local agricultural cult celebrating the deliverance of Demeter's daughter Persephone from the clutches of Pluto, ruler of the underworld. In the Hellenistic period, the religion began admitting non-Athenians and even non-Greeks, including a number of Roman emperors. The vernal renewal of life that resulted from Persephone's annual liberation was allegorized into a symbol of the triumph over death, that is, an immortality that was available to participants in the mysteries of Eleusis. The cult attached to the Greek god Dionysos, a god of vegetation and especially of wine, was also associated with the annual celebration of the return of spring, but it was too marked by orgiastic elements and wild intoxication to be widely adopted outside of Greece. The essence of the worship of Dionysos was taken over and tamed by the Orphic mysteries, which, on the basis of the rebirth of Dionysos after he was killed by the Titans, also celebrated the possibility of immortality.

The cult of the Great Mother was found under a number of names from Asia Minor to Syria and on to Mesopotamia, and at Rome she was generally called Cybele. Here, too, there was the promise of rebirth and immortality, expressed in the myth of her consort Attis, who was killed, or died after castrating himself, and was restored to life each spring. From Egypt a Hellenized version of the worship of Isis and Osiris emerged, based on the murder and dismemberment of Osiris, the search of his wife Isis for the parts of his body and his resurrection when she found them. Thus resurrection and rebirth again symbolized the promise of immortality to the adherents of the cult. All of these Mystery Religions featured a dying male figure who was mourned by the female goddess, with the male being reborn or resurrected as a symbol of new life and immortality. Very different was the religion devoted to the Persian figure Mithras, or Mithra, which was a form of sun worship. In myth, Mithras, a deity of deliverance, slew a bull from whose body and blood grew plants, herbs and crops, again linking death with life, rebirth and immortality.

These Mystery Religions all had the same purpose, the salvation of the individual in a blessed and happy immortality and, with the exception of Mithras, they shared core elements of mythological symbolism. In the Hellenistic and Roman periods they were also remarkably syncretic as elements from one cult were adopted by various other cults, making them increasingly similar over time. All of them, including Mithras, existed on two levels. One was a public side for the purpose of proselytization and evangelization by which the essentials of the cult were explained and potential initiates were recruited. At the same time there was the private aspect of the cult, wherein its inner, hidden and secret face was revealed only after the aspirants underwent elaborate ritualistic initiation ceremonies. One of the most important functions of the initiation was to bring the initiate into direct contact and communion with the deity.

Unfortunately the initiation rites of the Mystery Religions are obscure to us but it is clear that the mystical contact with the deity concerned was achieved through various means. The preparatory stages of fasting, vigils and meditation might be combined with initiation rites, usually held in darkness with dancing and music to produce a state of ecstasy whereby the initiates "leave their own identity, become at home with the gods, and experience divine possession."[1] At the same time, the believers might encounter their deity in the forms of dreams or visions, as when Isis came to Lucius in *The Golden Ass* (or *Metamorphoses*) of Apuleius, reassuring him, "I am here to take pity on your ills; I am here to give aid and solace. Cease then from tears and wailings, set aside your sadness; there is now dawning for you, through my providence, the day of salvation."[2] The rites were also intended to bring about the assimilation of the believer with the deity through a number of means. The ceremonies might lead to the initiate's being transformed into a divine being either through the bestowal of immortality or by a divine indwelling within the believer. At the climax of the initiation in *The Golden Ass*, Lucius reported,

> At the dead of night I saw the sun flashing with bright effulgence. I approached close to the gods above and the gods below and worshipped them face to face. Behold, I have related things about which you must remain in ignorance.[3]

Some of the cults featured a mystical marriage with the deity to indicate the most intimate union possible for humans, while virtually all of them offered some sort of sacramental meal of food and drink wherein one was thought actually to consume the deity and thus to be united with it. Through one or many of these means the adherent of the cult could receive the deity's direct theophany, often expressed in terms of brightness and light and the reception of unutterable revelations. Thus the Mysteries offered, and the population eagerly desired, direct contact with the divine, whether in the form of dreams and visions, the indwelling of the divine, a spiritual marriage with the deity, consuming the divine and making it one with the believer, or rebirth and assimilation with the deity. Put simply, the Mysteries "conduce to Mysticism."[4]

Very similar to the Mystery Religions was Gnosticism, whose name falsely implies a coherency and unity to what was a number of schools, movements and philosophies that shared only a basic world-view. However, ignoring the myriad of differences among the various strands of thought within the core of Gnosticism, in general Gnostics were dualists, opposing the spiritual and the good to the material and the evil. To the Gnostics, God was purely spiritual and absolutely unknowable and incomprehensible to humans and thus could not have had a direct role in the creation of the material world or of humanity. The world, including human bodies, was created by intermediary powers who placed divine light (or "the divine spark," that is, the human spirit) inside the material human body, making humans both material and divine. However, the human condition was one of absolute ignorance of the truth of the human condition and of anything of the world of the divine. As long as humans remained in that condition, they were doomed to a cycle of birth and rebirth into this prison of the corrupt, evil, material world dominated by evil powers and Fate. On their own, humans were unable to escape.

The means of salvation, therefore, must come from outside, by a divine revelation or illumination of truth providing knowledge (*gnosis* in Greek, from which word Gnosticism is derived), that is, by means of mystical experience. One text describes this illuminatory vision, "in an instant everything was immediately opened to me. I saw an endless vision in which everything became light."[5] The one who had been chosen was given knowledge of the entire human condition, of "who we were, what we became, where we were, where we have been thrown, towards what end we haste, from where we are redeemed, what birth is, and what rebirth is."[6] This *gnosis* was also the knowledge of God, which can come only by means of a revelation from the deity, and was thus a means to liberation. This salvation meant the return of the divine spark to God, "the final end for those who have received knowledge: to be made god."[7] While the Gnostics had no mythology in common with the Mystery Religions, they did share much of the basic outlook of the Mysteries, especially those of Orpheus, in teaching that a piece of the divine was trapped in the prison of the body with liberation possible only by means of a direct illuminatory revelation from the deity.

The surviving Gnostic literature is generally fragmentary and derived from a number of differing Gnostic traditions, especially from the hostile writings of their Christian and Neoplatonic opponents, making it difficult to discover the origins and early progress of the Gnostic thought. The first traces of Gnosticism appear only in the mid-first century AD and within a century there was a distinctive Gnostic form of Christianity that drew the bitter opposition of such writers as Irenaeus and Tertullian, who treated Gnosticism as an heretical Christian sect. However, there were also Jewish Gnostics as well as Gnostics outside of Christianity and Judaism, whom the Neoplatonist Plotinus attacked. The scanty information available limits our knowledge of who the Gnostics were or how widespread Gnosticism was, but it was strong enough within Christianity to be regarded as the most serious challenge to its unity and doctrine in the second and third centuries. The growth and strength of Gnosticism, with its salvation delivered as a divine gift of vision and illumination, add to the ubiquity of mystical religion in the world into which Christianity emerged.

The Mystery Religions and Gnosticism are examples of mystical religions that had mass appeal over the almost four centuries following Alexander's creation of the Hellenistic world. Plato (429–347 BC) provided a more philosophical mystical worldview that attracted many of the educated élite of the Greco–Roman cultures of the Mediterranean. His teachings had much in common with some of the Mystery Religions, especially the Orphic cult and Gnosticism, as well as with the religious communities that revered Pythagoras as their founder. While Plato was not officially a Pythagorean, he shared the core of the religious philosophy of Pythagoreanism – the divinity and immortality of the soul, which is imprisoned in the body in a series of transmigrations. Plato wrote no comprehensive treatise on his teachings and vowed never to do so; thus the general tenor of Plato's beliefs must be pieced together from a number of his works which present his thought in the form of allegories and myths. Plato appears to have posited a deity who created the universe and was so remote from human affairs that the race of humans was, in the mythology found in the *Timaeus*, put together by intermediary gods created by the deity. The intermediaries combined divine souls provided by the deity and material bodies made up of the basic elements of the universe, thus the soul is divine and immortal while remaining alien to the material body in which it is imprisoned. In the *Phaedrus*, Plato provided an additional mythology, describing how the original winged souls in the heavenly realms lost their wings due to their wrongdoing and were born into human bodies. The souls were doomed to 10,000 years of successive incarnations before they could return to their original heavenly home and, according to how they lived their lives, they could even be sentenced to incarnations as animals. But in essence the soul was divine and in time would return to its origin.

Ten thousand years are a virtual infinity in which to be trapped in a seemingly endless cycle of incarnations and for Plato, as in the Mystery Religions, the imperative was to find a means to effect an early release from the dreary cycle. In the *Phaedo* Plato argues that a person can disassociate the soul from the body by allowing none of the senses to distract it, by overcoming the body's needs and demands and living as though one were dead already, that is, by leading a life of purificatory asceticism that permits the soul to dwell by itself apart from the body. At the physical death, such a soul, no longer incumbered by the heavy, earthly body, can join the "company of the gods." The greatest obstacle to leading such a "philosophical" life is the ignorance of humans, unaware that all that is seen and known through the senses, that is, what they think they know, is but a feeble, mutable and transitory image of absolute, immutable, divine truths, and thus are completely unreliable. Humans misunderstand what is real and lead lives dedicated to satisfying the sensual, bodily demands, thinking that "nothing exists but what they can grasp with both hands."[8]

This produces a dilemma – the soul remains weighed down in bodily incarnations because it does not know the truth but it can never find truth in the illusory world in which it is encased in the body. Genuine knowledge of eternal absolute truths can only come by means of revelation from the divine, as Plato describes in the *Symposium*, and it is through contemplation that humans can prepare themselves for the divine revelation. Plato's most famous allegory for such revelation is in his story of the cave in the *Republic*, where a person is able to struggle free of the shackles of darkness and ascend to the dazzling, illuminating light of the sun.

Plato saw this divine illumination as a mystical experience and employed the language of the Mystery Religions, especially the concept of initiation in the mysteries, throughout his dialogues. He described the revelation in terms of divine possession and ecstasy and even provided what is often regarded as a personal account of such an experience, "only after long partnership in common life devoted to this very thing [philosophy] does truth flash upon the soul, like a flame kindled by a leaping spark, and once born there it nourishes itself thereafter."[9] For Plato, "salvation" was achieved through mystical revelation which a person could assist by leading a life of asceticism and contemplation.

Perhaps a far more important influence during the founding phase of Christianity were the many strands of mysticism within Judaism. On the one hand, a straightforward literal reading of the Jewish scriptures presents the original state of the ancestors of the human race as one in which they were in direct communication with God until the sin of Adam and Eve caused them to be expelled from the Garden of Eden. Subsequently a life of constant conversation with God was impossible but God continued to appear directly or through intermediaries to humans. God warned Noah directly of the coming flood and instructed him to build the ark (Gen. 6.13–14), the patriarch Abraham constantly received directions by God as well as the divine promise that his descendants, who would be innumerable (Gen. 15. 2–6), would receive the land of Canaan (Gen. 12.7), and Abraham received the three divine visitors at Mamre (Gen. 18.1–5). God gave a direct answer to Rebekah's prayer (Gen. 25.23), Jacob was addressed by God during his dream of the ladder (Gen. 28.13), renewing his covenant previously made to Abraham. In Egypt Joseph was given the ability to interpret dreams ("Are not interpretations God's business?"[10]).

Of course the arch-mystic of the Hebrew tradition was Moses, to whom God called from the burning bush (Ex. 3.4) and whom God sent on his mission to free the children of Israel from Egyptian bondage after arming him with the ability to perform miracles. On the mountain of Sinai, Moses spoke with God and received directly from God the Law, being allowed to see the back of God (Ex. 33.23–34.6). When he descended from the mountain, Moses was transformed, as his skin shone (Ex. 34.29). Of course, during the forty years of wandering in the Sinai, God was present with the Israelites, though obscured in a pillar of cloud by day and a pillar of fire by night (Ex. 13.22). Upon the death of Moses, God spoke to his successor Joshua, on whom Moses had laid his hands, as the Israelites conquered the land of Canaan. During the period of the judges, God spoke with the military leader Gideon (Jdg. 6. 11–3) and other Israelite judges either directly or through an angel, and seeing an angel was considered equivalent to seeing God (Jdg. 13.20–22).

As the Israelites slid into idolatry, "it was rare for Yahweh to speak in those days; visions were uncommon."[11] However, God did call some who were specially favored to be his messengers and prophets, such as Samuel (1 Sam. 3.10–4), Nathan (2 Sam. 7.5–16) and Gad (2 Sam. 24.11–2). During the reign of King Ahab (869–50 BC), the prophet Elijah not only spoke with God but was granted a vision of the divine. Standing on a mountain as he was directed, Elijah was sent a great wind, an earthquake and a fire, but God was not in them. Then there came "the sound of a gentle breeze. And when Elijah heard this he covered his face with his cloak and went out and stood at the entrance of the cave."[12] This was the voice of God. Elijah did not die but instead was taken up to heaven as "a chariot of fire appeared and horses of fire, coming between the two of them; and Elijah went up to heaven in the whirlwind."[13] The prophet Isaiah was called by God as the reign of King Ahaz began (735 BC), shortly before the Assyrians conquered the kingdom of Israel, and he received a vision of God:

> I saw the Lord Yahweh seated on a high throne; his train filled the sanctuary; above him stood seraphs, each one with six wings; two to cover its face, two to cover its feet and two for flying. … The foundations of the threshold shook with the voice of the one who cried out, and the Temple filled with smoke.[14]

As the kingdom of Judah fell under the shadow of the great Babylonian king Nebuchadnezzar about six hundred years before the beginning of the Common Era, Ezekiel, one of the greatest of the Jewish prophets, arose and his calling stands as one of the great visionary mystical texts of biblical Judaism. Ezekiel is made to say,

> the hand of Yahweh came on me. I looked; a stormy wind blew from the north, a great cloud with light around it, a fire from which flashes of lightning darted, and in the center a sheen like bronze at the heart of the fire.

In the center there were what seemed to be four animals, and between them "something could be seen like flaming brands or torches, darting between the animals; the fire flashed light, and lightning streaked from the fire." By each of the animals there was a wheel and "when the animals left the ground, the wheels too left the ground." Above the animals was a vault in which was something that appeared to be a sapphire throne and on the throne sat what looked like a man who shone like bronze, surrounded by fire, and "the surrounding light appeared. It was something that looked like the glory of Yahweh. I looked, and prostrated myself, and I heard a voice speaking." It was the voice of Yahweh sending Ezekiel to the Israelites to call them back from their rebellion against God.[15] Thus the Jewish scriptural tradition was one that established direct communication with God as the original human state and therefore within the human potential to achieve.

By the turn of the Eras, "early Jewish mysticism" had emerged, a term "best defined as an esoteric tendency within Second Temple Judaism (538 BC – AD 70) which was characterized by speculation about ascent into heaven and gaining a transforming vision of the *kavod* [the Glory of God]."[16] Quasi-monastic communities like the Essenes at Qumran in Palestine and the closely related sect of the Therapeutae in Egypt followed severely ascetical disciplines in part to prepare and purify themselves for an attempt to gain a vision of God, or rather, using the language of Ezekiel, a vision of the Glory of God, which would transform them into angelic or divine beings. For example, one of the Dead Sea Scroll fragments states, "I am seated in … heaven … I am reckoned with gods and my abode is in the holy congregation. … I am with the gods … my glory is with the sons of the King,"[17] which has been taken as evidence that "mystical ascents to heaven were characteristic of the Qumran sect,"[18] a community that "was already experiencing heaven on earth … living the angelic life."[19]

Jewish mysticism could also be expressed in highly Platonic terms, as with Philo of Alexandria (ca. 25 BC to ca. AD 50), whose mystical approach was far more influential in Christianity, especially with his fellow Alexandrians Clement and Origen,[20] than it was among his fellow Jews. Philo belonged to one of the leading families of Alexandria and was chosen to head a delegation of the Jews of Alexandria to the Roman emperor Caligula, but we know very little about his life. It is obvious that he was a fully Hellenized Jew who was deeply immersed in Greek philosophy. In the enormous corpus of his writings he revealed his dedication to philosophy as well as a firm belief in the truth of the Jewish scriptures as an authentic revelation from the one true God, the God of Abraham, Isaac and Jacob, best understood by means of an allegorical interpretation of the book of Genesis, a method already in wide use in the Greek world, especially by the Stoics. Philo's aim was to demonstrate that Judaism was fully compatible with and indeed superior to the highest standards of Greek philosophy. Moreover, he also found that the language of the Mystery Religions was appropriate for Judaism, properly understood, for the literal sense of the Scriptures obscured the deeper truths hidden within them from the scrutiny of the unworthy. Only by divine revelation could their hidden meanings be discerned.

Mysticism permeated the thought of Philo. The goal of those who were wise was to gain the vision of God, an almost impossible quest for humans in their natural state because of the utter transcendence and incomprehensibility of God, of whom nothing more can be affirmed than his existence. Yet humans, whose souls are divine, also have a natural yearning for God and God desires to be known by humans. Thus he makes himself known in an act of grace to those whom he chooses. Humans can prepare themselves for this gift, however, by coming to a realization of their own inferiority and worthlessness in relationship to the deity, which can be termed "illumination," followed by a turning away from all that is material and everything having to do with the world of the senses and the passions, which might or might not conclude with the vision of God, a form of union. Philo favored a personal life of moderately ascetical self-discipline and for him the Jews who most exemplified this path to direct knowledge of God were the Essenes and Therapeutae.

Prominent in Philo's works is the description of mystical ecstasy, a state of sober intoxication, of being possessed by a divine frenzy like that of the cult of the Great Mother, of having one's soul on fire, when it is "no longer in itself, but is agitated and maddened by a heavenly passion."[21] Philo also provided extraordinary detailed descriptions of mystical experiences, when the divine light illuminates the soul, and, speaking of his own experiences, he wrote:

> I have become empty and have suddenly become full, the ideas descending like snow and invisibly sown, so that under the impact of divine possession I had been filled with corybantic frenzy and become ignorant of everything, place, people present, myself, what was said and what was written.[22]

In this state, the human soul departed from the body to be replaced for the moment by the divine Spirit, "For it is not meet that mortal cohabit with the immortal."[23]

Thus for Philo, the focus of a person's life should properly be the knowledge of God, which could be gained only by means of a divine act of grace, a revelation directly from God to those who had prepared themselves appropriately by overcoming the body (the prison of the soul) and its passions by means of asceticism. He was in complete sympathy with the ascetics at Qumran and their kindred spirits of the Therapeutae, who were seeking a mystical ascent to the throne-chariot of God. Philo's language and philosophical underpinnings differed from those of the desert ascetics but his end and means to that end were the same. The life devoted to God was a mystical life, for "to be engaged on the quest for God is what matters."[24]

The destruction of Jerusalem and the Temple by the Romans in the year AD 70 transformed Judaism, ending the period of the Second Temple and beginning the period of rabbinical Judaism, in which rabbis focused on exegesis of the Scriptures, especially the Torah. Meanwhile the ascetical and mystical communities of the Essenes and the Therapeutae disappeared, extinguishing one strain of the Jewish search for a vision of God, while the same themes endured in the literature of the Rabbinic period and into medieval Judaism. Another consequence was the Jewish repudiation of the Greek Septuagint version of the Jewish scriptures in favor of a smaller canon of scriptures written in Hebrew. The works of Jews like Philo, a Platonist who probably knew no Hebrew and believed that the Septuagint was a divinely-inspired translation of the Bible, were thereby rendered irrelevant and they disappeared from the Jewish tradition. However, Philo was drawing on even older traditions of Jewish mysticism and the mysticism of the apostle Paul[25] demonstrates that Philo's Hellenized form of Jewish mysticism must have been shared by many in the Jewish Diaspora. But all of this was after Christianity had been born from the Judaism of Judea and Syria and was already spreading among Hellenized Jews and Greek-speaking Gentiles.

Whether one looks at the Mystery Religions, Gnosticism or Judaism, one finds "a world saturated in mystical thought."[26] The religions that were prospering offered their adherents direct contact with their deities at the same time that severe ascetics were ascending to visions of the heavenly throne-room and the formally educated were seeking divine revelations of truth that bring them to the knowledge of God. From philosopher to peasant, the search for direct contact with and knowledge of the divine dominated the religious concerns of the inhabitants of the Roman Empire, among whom was Jesus of Nazareth.

MYSTICISM AND THE FOUNDATION OF CHRISTIANITY

Attempting to make definitive statements about the "real" or "historical" Jesus is precarious in the extreme. Among the canonical books of the Christian New Testament are many of unsure date and uncertain authorship, frequently bearing the marks of having undergone several redactions at the hands of members of various Christian communities. Other sources are extra-canonical Christian works that share the same limitations as those in the canon. As scholars have investigated these highly problematical sources, a number of different Jesuses have emerged from the same body of evidence, leading to the suspicion that the only clear and consistent view of Jesus that can be adduced is the result of tendentious selection of data and dating of arguable sources. Alongside the mutually exclusive images of Jesus the peripatetic wonderworker, the charismatic healer, the eschatological prophet, the Cynic-sage, the political or social revolutionary gathering up the have-nots of Judea and Galilee into his Kingdom of God, or Jesus "just another Jew,"[27] one can also discern a remarkably clear outline of Jesus the mystic and mystagogue.

The Gospel accounts are unanimous in presenting Jesus as one in whom God's Spirit descended and in whom that Spirit dwelled. Jesus appeared out of obscurity for baptism at the hands of John the Baptist. As he rose from the water, the spirit of God came down from heaven and rested on him as a voice announced, "You are my Son, the Beloved; my favor rests on you," with some ancient manuscripts of the Lucan passage reading, "today I have begotten thee."[28] Jesus retreated into the wilderness for forty days to face the devil's temptation. He then returned to Galilee "with the power of the Spirit in him" and began his public life in the synagogue in Nazareth by reading the words of Isaiah, "The spirit of the Lord has been given to me, for he has anointed me." He then added, "This text is being fulfilled today as you listen."[29] The Gospel of

Matthew states that Jesus fulfilled the prophecy of Isaiah, "Here is my servant whom I have chosen, my beloved, the favorite of my soul. I will endow him with my spirit."[30]

Moreover, the Gospel presentations of Jesus's public life have him possessing all of the gifts of the Spirit that are manifested by the mystics of the Christian tradition, most especially the gift of healing. "No fact about Jesus of Nazareth is so widely and repeatedly attested in the New Testament gospels as the fact that he was a healer of people in mental and physical distress."[31] It has been calculated that "nearly one-fifth of the entire gospels is devoted to Jesus' healing and the discussions occasioned by it."[32] Moreover, Jesus considered this healing power to have been the work of the Holy Spirit, for he denounced as blasphemers against the Holy Spirit those who attributed his healings to "the prince of devils."[33] Jesus healed a variety of illnesses, not only casting out devils but also curing leprosy, paralysis, blindness, hemorrhage and the ultimate malady, death. Jesus employed a number of different methods in his healings. Sometimes he simply spoke the words and people were cured, while at other times he laid his hands on the ill, or pronounced their sins forgiven, or simply walked by as they touched him, while he "also used primitive techniques such as touching, spitting, and mud application, and recommended that individuals bathe in supposedly medicinally-effective pools."[34] At the same time Jesus also possessed clairvoyance (seeing Nathaniel sitting under a fig tree[35]), knew the thoughts of others (especially the plots of the scribes and Pharisees against him[36]), as well as the state of their souls (the Samaritan woman with five husbands[37]), and of course he had foreknowledge of events, such as his own death, Peter's denial and Judas's betrayal. Like so many other mystics, Jesus displayed advanced learning and understanding despite his lack of formal study. Like Moses on Mount Sinai, Jesus experienced a transfigured appearance as "his face shone like the sun and his clothes became as white as the light" when he was on a mountain top where he encountered both Moses and Elijah. Moreover, the accounts of Jesus walking on the water[38] could be interpreted as a manifestation, albeit exceedingly spectacular, of mystical levitation.

Of course as important as Jesus's mystical qualities and the gifts of the Spirit that he possessed was his message, the Good News of the kingdom of God, or kingdom of heaven in Matthew, which was close by or within the hearers ("you know that the kingdom of God is within you"[39]). The kingdom of God can be interpreted a number of ways, including "the power and presence of God himself,"[40] that is, the indwelling presence of the Holy Spirit. If Jesus's mission were to establish the kingdom of God, which was the reception of the Holy Spirit within a person, then indeed Jesus the mystic was a mystagogue, a conclusion confirmed by the assertion in all four Gospels that while John the Baptist had immersed in water, Jesus would immerse with the Holy Spirit and with fire. When Jesus began his proclamation of the kingdom of God, his hearers were called on to repent, an indication that the kingdom required the cleansing and transformation of one's interior state. These themes were repeated in the Sermon on the Mount, in which Jesus promised that the kingdom of heaven belonged to the poor in spirit and to those who were persecuted for the sake of righteousness, that the pure in heart would see God and the peacemakers would be called sons of God. Jesus warned that the ordinary virtue of the Pharisees who scrupulously followed the Mosaic law would not be sufficient to allow one to be in the kingdom of heaven, for what was required was moving beyond mere outward observance of commandments to an interiorization of morality, that is, not lusting in one's heart; turning the other cheek; going the second mile; loving one's enemies in order to be sons of the Father; giving alms; praying and fasting in secret; withholding judgment of others; forgiving others and, perhaps most astonishing of all, not even resisting evil. Thus it was the interior of the person that mattered rather than external observances, for a person was defiled by what came out of the mouth, what was within, not by what went into it, what was without. Thus Jesus was teaching a radically different form of religion, one that would make possible the indwelling of the Spirit.

Moreover, all three of the synoptic Gospels (Matthew, Mark and Luke) stress that Jesus taught an esoteric lore known only to his inner circle, that is, in parables that provided one message to ordinary listeners but possessed a hidden element understood only by those who were worthy. Jesus explained these "mysteries of the kingdom" to his disciples when they were alone[41] and the very term "mysteries" would have been understood by all as referring to the secret doctrines of the Mystery Religions that were revealed only to the initiates of the cults. Moreover, the Synoptics portray Jesus thanking God that these mysteries were hidden from the "learned and clever" while being known only by Jesus and those to whom he revealed them. Jesus, from the small village of Nazareth in Galilee, would have been familiar with the wider Greco-Roman culture around him and its Mystery Religions, for Galilee had one of the densest populations in the Roman Empire and Nazareth was located only three or four miles from Sepphoris, a provincial capital serving as a regional communications hub and boasting a population of 30,000 people along with all the urban amenities of the period. As a resident of Nazareth, Jesus "lived in the shadow of a major administrative city, in the middle of a densely populated urban network, and in continuity with its Hellenized cultural traditions."[42]

Jesus continued his mystagogical role by giving his disciples the same power to heal and to perform miracles that he had received from the Spirit and, after his resurrection, Jesus "opened their minds" to understand Scripture, a revelation usually considered to be a mystical gift. Moreover, Jesus is represented as constantly desiring mystical solitude and prayer, withdrawing alone into deserted, lonely places and hills so that he could spend long hours communicating with the Father in prayer. In the "Lord's Prayer," Jesus taught his disciples how to pray and he enjoined his disciples to pray constantly. The evidence for Jesus's mystagogy is so compelling that one scholar has stated forthrightly that Jesus founded a mystery cult.[43]

While the Synoptics support the view of Jesus as a Spirit-filled mystic who imparted an esoteric mystical lore to his disciples, the Gospel of John is imbued with "a mystical world view and purpose,"[44] and paints the strongest and most consistent portrayal of the mystical Jesus. In the Gospel of John, the relationship between Jesus and God is extremely intimate, bearing all the signs of mysticism. Jesus constantly referred to God as the Father, who was always with him. Jesus was himself taught by the Father,[45] he heard truth from the Father,[46] what he spoke and declared was what he heard from the Father[47] and he received his authority from the Father. The union between Jesus and the Father was so close that whoever saw Jesus also saw the Father[48] and Jesus was in the Father while the Father was in Jesus.[49]

The Gospel of John also specifies that Jesus's disciples would have the same relationship with the Father as that enjoyed by Jesus because of the complete identity of Jesus with them. They were no longer servants but rather his friends,[50] just as he was not of this world, neither were they,[51] and where Jesus was, so would be his servants and disciples. He taught them what the Father had given him. The Spirit of truth would come to them to dwell in them and to teach them,[52] the Father would make his home in them[53] and they would be in the Father. In the most graphic instance of Jesus acting as a mystagogue, after his resurrection "he breathed on them and said: 'Receive the Holy Spirit,'" and he shared his authority with them. Thus was fulfilled the earlier promise that Jesus would immerse in the Holy Spirit. The fulfillment of the immersion in fire came after the ascension of Jesus to heaven when the apostles were gathered together on the day of Pentecost. Suddenly

> they heard what sounded like a powerful wind from heaven, the noise of which filled the entire house in which they were sitting; and something appeared to them that seemed like tongues of fire; these separated and came to rest on the head of each of them. They were all filled with the Holy Spirit, and began to speak foreign tongues as the Spirit gave them the gift of speech.[54]

Thus the Christian church was founded in a mystical filling with the Holy Spirit, with the apostles forming a community of mystics. With their gifts of the Spirit, just as Jesus had done, the apostles drew crowds to them because they could cure the lame, the paralyzed, the crippled, those possessed by unclean spirits, and even raise up the dead. Being filled with the Holy Spirit was not the special privilege of the apostles, however, for it was expected to happen to those who became Christians. When the apostles in Jerusalem heard that Samaritans had "accepted the word of God" but that the Holy Spirit had not yet come down on them, they dispatched Peter and John to them to lay their hands on them so that the new Christians might receive the Holy Spirit. To the astonishment of the first Christians, all of whom were Jews, the Holy Spirit appeared to a Gentile, the Roman centurion Cornelius, who was instructed in a vision to summon Peter. Peter had been given a vision that presented symbolically the extension of the Gospel to Gentiles and he readily answered the summons and preached to Cornelius and his household. As he did, the Holy Spirit "poured out" over all of them, just as it had on the apostles.[55]

While the original apostles are portrayed as having established the Christian church after receiving the Holy Spirit on Pentecost, it can be argued that the chief organizer of the early church was Paul of Tarsus, a convert to Christianity around AD 36. Of the twenty-seven books in the New Testament, fourteen are letters attributed to the apostle Paul and another, the Acts of the Apostles, is largely concerned with his activities. Paul was the leading proponent of taking Christianity to the Gentile world and was the founder of a number of Christian communities in Asia Minor and Greece. Of him it has been said simply, "Paul is a mystic."[56]

The little that is known of the life of Paul must be pieced together from the inconsistent information gleaned from his letters and the Acts of the Apostles. He was born probably no later than AD 10, a Jew of the tribe of Benjamin but also a Roman citizen, and he was from the city of Tarsus, the capital of the province of Cilicia in southeastern Asia Minor. Paul's early education in Tarsus was no doubt superb, for the city was a cultural and educational center, whose schools were regarded as superior to those of Athens and Alexandria. The author of the Acts of the Apostles wrote that Paul, a member of the sect of the Pharisees, went to Jerusalem to study under the Jewish scholar Gamaliel, but Paul's first presence in the Acts is as a persecutor of the fledgling Christian community. As Paul was on his way to Damascus to arrest any Christians there, a light brighter than the sun came out of heaven and he heard a voice, speaking in Hebrew, which identified itself as that of Jesus, who was now choosing Paul as his servant and witness. Paul was struck blind until Ananias, acting on directions given him by Jesus in a vision, laid his hands on him, an act that restored Paul's sight and also caused him to be filled with the Holy Spirit. Jesus told Paul that he would appear to him more times in the future and in the book of Acts two additional visions of Jesus are recorded for Paul, one sending him out of Jerusalem to the Gentiles and another informing him that he should carry out his work in Rome.

Like the original apostles, Paul expected those who believed in Jesus to receive the Holy Spirit. When he was at Ephesus he found Christians who had never heard of the Holy Spirit and he laid his hands on them, whereupon "the Holy Spirit came down on them, and they began to speak with tongues and to prophesy."[57] As is evident from the letters of Paul to the Christian communities that he established and guided, those churches were pneumatic, that is, filled with the Spirit. Moreover, to Gentiles in the Hellenistic world, Paul presented Christianity as a Mystery Religion possessing its own mysteries, "the hidden wisdom of God which we teach in our mysteries." Paul declared that "it was by a revelation that I was given the knowledge of the mystery … the message that was a mystery for generations and centuries and has now been revealed to his saints."[58]

The members of Paul's churches exhibited the various gifts of the Spirit to such an extent that the communities were in danger of dissolving into factions. Paul wrote of the various gifts, preaching, healing, miracles, prophecy, the discernment of spirits, speaking in tongues and interpreting such speech, noting, "All these are the work of one and the same Spirit, who distributes different gifts to different people just as he chooses."[59] Paul fell back on his authority and commanded them to love each other and not to take pride in what was given to them, for he had a greater gift for speaking in tongues than any of them. However, some in the community were claiming divine visions and revelations and on that basis were challenging Paul's leadership of the church in Corinth, which prompted Paul to flaunt his own visionary credentials, noting that in this gift he again surpassed them all. Relating an experience from fourteen years earlier, Paul reminded them that he, whether in the body or out of it he did not know, rose up to the third heaven and then he passed even beyond it to paradise, where he "heard things which must not and cannot be put into human language."[60]

Thus when Paul wrote to his church in Galatia that he no longer lived but that

"Christ lives in me,"[61] this phrase should be understood in its literal sense, for he challenged the Christians in Corinth, "Do you acknowledge that Jesus Christ is really in you?"[62] Thereby the union of the Christian with Christ was complete, including the physical body, much as it was to Symeon the New Theologian in the eleventh century.[63] Paul had been called to his apostolate to the Gentiles directly by the risen Jesus and continued to experience encounters with Jesus after the event on the road to Damascus. (Significantly, the Gospel of Matthew recorded promises made by Jesus that he would always be with his disciples, even to the end of time and that wherever two or three gather in his name, he would be with them.[64]) Paul had received gifts of the Holy Spirit and laid hands on new believers so that they also could receive the Holy Spirit. Paul organized pneumatic churches so effectively that they were in danger of slipping out of his control. Paul, himself a mystic, faced the perennial problem with mystics – what they received in their visions and revelations might not coincide perfectly with a given orthodoxy. He warned the Christians of Galatia that they should condemn anyone preaching anything different than what they had heard from him even if the messenger should be an angel from heaven.[65]

The Christian church of the first century was a collection of individuals who were recipients of the Holy Spirit and of the gifts of the Spirit, for "the possession of the Spirit was *the* hallmark of the Christian … the earliest Christian community was essentially charismatic and enthusiastic in nature."[66] Its divine founder, whatever else he may have been, was remembered as having the closest possible relationship with God, living in constant communication with God, receiving the Holy Spirit at his baptism and imparting the Holy Spirit to the apostles. After they received the Holy Spirit the apostles were renowned for the miracles that flowed from this indwelling of the Spirit while they encountered the risen Jesus and received continuing revelations. These experiences served to authenticate the teaching of the apostles, especially when they provided a radical change of direction, as when the divine intent that the Good News be extended to Gentiles was made known to Peter in the form of a vision and to Paul in his revelations. The first-century church was a mystical body ("that the Spirit, and particularly the gift of the Spirit, was *a fact of experience* in the lives of the earliest Christians has been too obvious to require elaboration"[67]) and to Paul's chagrin it manifested the potentially disruptive consequences of that fact. A church filled with charismatic mystics necessarily invited the risk of the reception of conflicting revelations. Hence Paul, standing on his own authority that was derived from his mystical encounters with Jesus, forbade the members of his churches to believe any revelations other than those that he had taught.

Thus mysticism in an organization leads to a crisis of authority and many of the internal disputes of the first three centuries of the Christian church concerned the problem of revelations, beginning with the issue of the ministry to the Gentiles, resolved at the meeting of the apostolic founders in Jerusalem around AD 50. The New Testament closes as the first generation of pneumatic Christians, including the Spirit-filled apostles, were ending their lives. The crises for Christianity centered on the questions of whether such a mystical church could maintain unity in the face of possible conflicting revelations or fresh revelations that might be inconsistent with the traditions of the founding generation and whether pneumatic Christians could co-exist with non-pneumatics as there began to be Christians born into the faith.

THE POST-APOSTOLIC CHURCH

The second-century church continued to face potentially disruptive divisions based on revelations and individual encounters with the divinity. On the one hand there were Christian Gnostics, initiates into divine mysteries and possessors of esoteric teachings, who formed no single body and had little in common beyond their rejection of the violent and judgmental God of the Old Testament as being identical to the loving Father of Jesus. They produced cosmologies and cosmogonies that differed greatly from the account found in the Jewish scriptures and some denied that Jesus the Christ actually bore a physical, human body, and thus he could not have experienced a literal death and resurrection.

During this time, little after the year 150, there arose the charismatic and prophetic Christian movement of Montanism, named for Montanus, a convert to Christianity in Phrygia in Asia Minor. At his baptism Montanus was seized by the Holy Spirit, fell into ecstasy and began speaking in tongues and prophesying, much as was done in the New Testament church. He also gathered around him others who had similar experiences, especially the two prophetesses Prisca and Maximilla. Speaking for the Holy Spirit, they prophesied the imminent return of Jesus to earth to reign with his saints for a thousand years in the New Jerusalem that would descend from heaven to Phrygia. All that we know of Montanist teachings comes from hostile sources, which report Montanus claiming, "I am the Lord God Omnipotent dwelling in man ... I am neither an angel nor an envoy, but I, the Lord God, the Father, have come."[68] Maximilla claimed to speak as Christ, as "a revealer of this covenant, an interpreter of this promise, forced ... to learn the knowledge of God."[69] Interestingly, the prophetess Prisca was given a vision of Jesus, "Appearing as a woman clothed in a shining robe ... he put wisdom into me and revealed to me that this place is sacred and that here Jerusalem will come down from heaven."[70]

There was no doctrinal error in the Montanist teaching but there was everything wrong in its style. The reaction of the anti-Montanist Christians indicates that the mainstream of Christianity no longer experienced possession by the Holy Spirit as a normative feature of the faith. One opponent scorned Montanus's "abnormal ecstasy," claiming that he was "prophesying contrary to the manner which the Church had received from generation to generation by tradition from the beginning."[71] Moreover, the discipline of the first-century church was sliding into a more lukewarm and accommodating morality, which Montanus challenged by enjoining on his followers a strict asceticism, with severe fasting, mandatory celibacy, and a prohibition on second marriages. Significantly, the promise of the unmediated, indwelling divinity within the believer offered a means of bypassing the authority of the emerging hierarchy of bishops, who claimed to possess the authority of the apostles as well as their authoritative traditions. Moreover the prominence of the prophetesses was considered to be unseemly by the male clergy of the church who claimed that apostolic tradition. By the end of the second century, there is "no evidence for women taking prophetic, priestly, and episcopal roles among orthodox churches."[72]

Montanism flourished in the last half of the second century, spreading throughout Asia Minor as well as to Rome, Gaul (modern France) and North Africa, where it gained the adherence of the great Carthaginian theologian Tertullian (ca. 160 to ca. 225), to whom Christianity was a religion of revelation and who was attracted to the strict asceticism of Montanism. Tertullian reported the ecstatic experiences by a woman during church services and how it was regarded by the Montanist community:

> There is among us a sister who has been favored with wonderful gifts of revelation which she experiences in an ecstasy of the spirit during the sacred ceremonies on the Lord's day. She converses with the angels and, sometimes, with the Lord Himself. She perceives hidden mysteries and has the power of reading the hearts of men and of prescribing remedies for such as need them. ... One time I happened to be preaching about the soul when she became rapt in ecstasy. After the services were over and the laity had left, we asked her as is our custom, what visions she had had. (All her visions are carefully written down for purposes of examination.)[73]

The challenge of Montanism further stimulated the growth of episcopal authority in the main body of Christianity and soured it on new prophecies based on the inspiration of the Holy Spirit. Just as with Paul, the Christian community of the second century was in a bind – it both honored the continuing presence of the Holy Spirit within the church and was wary of purported revelations that challenged in any manner the authority of the ecclesiastical leaders or of its increasingly specific and narrowing orthodox faith. Such a reaction is a common pattern in religion:

> New faiths may announce their advent with a flourish of ecstatic revelations, but once they become securely established they have little time or tolerance for enthusiasm. For the religious enthusiast, with his direct claim to divine knowledge, is always a threat to the established order.[74]

Nonetheless, as will be seen in the next chapter, the third century amply illustrates that for some in Egyptian Alexandria, Christianity continued to be a mystical religion. They continued to advocate asceticism as the path to the direct experience of God.

CHAPTER II

THE EASTERN CHURCH

—— ·•· ——

THE ALEXANDRIAN ASCETICS

The first Christian successor to the mystical and ascetical tradition of Philo of Alexandria, and thus not coincidentally the first Christian writer on mystical theology following the Apostolic Age, was Clement of Alexandria (Titus Flavius Clemens, ca. 150 to ca. 216). Only the barest outline of his life is known to us. He was a convert to Christianity and thought to have been either Athenian or Alexandrian in origin. As a seeker of wisdom he traveled around the eastern Mediterranean until he reached Alexandria and found the Christian teacher Pantaenus. He settled there and began teaching in Pantaenus's school for cathechumens, eventually succeeding his master in charge of the school. Clement's surviving works are concerned with explaining and defending Christianity to non-Christians in Alexandria, one of the centers of Greco–Roman culture in the ancient world. Drawing upon Greek literature and philosophical works, Clement argued that the best of Greek philosophy was consistent with Christian teachings, even allowing that some of the philosophers, especially Plato, had indeed glimpsed divine truths. Greek religion, however, was a different matter entirely, which he denounced for its moral corruption.

In the course of his exposition of Christianity, Clement revealed an essentially Platonic and thus mystical understanding of his faith, which he saw as an effort to know God and to understand divine mysteries, taking it as granted that "the knowledge of God is the most important of all things. ... And he who knows God is holy and pious."[1] The Christian who gained this knowledge (*gnosis*) was the true Gnostic, thus adopting and Christianizing the essential framework of Gnostic teaching that was so popular in contemporary Alexandria. While Clement revered the Scriptures for their divine origin, it was not through their study that one came to this knowledge, for not all Christian truths were committed to writing. To Clement, divine truths were generally not taught openly but rather were hidden and veiled lest they be misunderstood by those not ready to receive them. These divine truths were to be found in the Scriptures, but, of course, with their sense hidden:

> For many reasons, then, the Scriptures hide the sense. First, that we may become inquisitive, and be ever on the watch for the discovery of the words of salvation. Then it was not suitable for all to understand, so that they might not receive harm in consequence of taking in another sense the things declared for salvation by the Holy Spirit. Wherefore the holy mysteries of the prophecies are

veiled in the parables – preserved for chosen men, selected to knowledge in consequence of their faith; for the style of the Scriptures is parabolic.[2]

In order to discover the concealed truths in the Scriptures, Clement adopted Philo's allegorical method of Biblical interpretation, especially concerning the Old Testament and to a lesser extent the New Testament.

Knowledge of God comes as a revelation received directly from God: "We are 'God-taught.' We have been educated in a course which is really holy by God's Son."[3] The image chosen by Clement for this infusion of divine knowledge was budding, the form of grafting in which a bud is cut out of one tree and inserted in an area of the same size on another.[4] God can be known only through direct revelation because, in the overriding theme of Clement's works, God is transcendent. God is unknowable, he is simply Being, of whom "it is not possible to speak" in its divine nature.[5] He is the God of the universe, "who is above all speech, all conception, all thought, can never be committed to writing, being inexpressible even by His own power."[6] God is incapable of being taught and cannot be the subject of discourse, but can be known "only by His own power."[7] The senses are of no use in knowing God, who cannot be portrayed or represented in any manner,[8] for "God is invisible and beyond expression by words."[9] God is without form or name and while we can use names for God (the One, the Good, the Father, etc.), none of them truly expresses God but rather they only point collectively to the power of God.[10]

Because all words and concepts about God are inadequate and capable of revealing only limited aspects of the essence of God, Clement was free to develop a theme that would become familiar again in the Middle Ages, the feminine attributes of God:

> God Himself is love; and out of love to us became feminine. In His ineffable essence He is Father; in His compassion to us He became Mother. The Father by loving became feminine: and the great proof of this is He whom He begot of Himself; and the fruit brought forth by love is love.[11]

At the same time, in an expression of the eternal mystical paradox, the ineffable, transcendent God is also an immanent God:

> But this same ruler, distant as he is, has, marvelous to relate, drawn near. "I am God at hand," says the Lord. In his essential being he is distant – how ever could a creature subject to birth draw near to the unborn and uncreated? – but very close by the exercise of that power which has enfolded all things in its embrace.[12]

Knowledge of God can come only from God as a divine gift given to those capable of understanding, for it is "handed down by tradition according to the grace of God, is entrusted as a deposit to those who show themselves worthy of the teaching."[13] However, this knowledge is also an assimilation to God which can be received only by one's becoming like God in the manifestation of his Word, that is, Christ, one "become like his Teacher in impassibility," in ridding oneself of all passions of the soul.[14] Thus,

> he who holds intercourse with God must have his soul undefiled and absolutely pure, having raised himself to a state of perfect goodness if possible, but at any rate both making progress towards knowledge and longing for it, and being entirely withdrawn from the works of wickedness.[15]

Clement was unrelenting on this point, those who were still driven by their passions could never attain the knowledge of God. "Therefore they cannot attain the salvation they hope for as they have not obtained any knowledge of God. It is absolutely impossible at the same time to be a man of understanding and not be ashamed to gratify the body."[16]

Thus for Clement, the goal of the Christian life was direct, that is, mystical, knowledge of God that was given by God to those who had made themselves worthy by overcoming their passions and their bodily appetites, thereby becoming "equal to the angels."[17] This was essentially the same aspiration as that of the adherents of the other Mystery Religions, but the Christian God was the true God, just as Christianity comprised the best of Greek philosophy and the truest Christian was the best Gnostic. Clement was comfortable in applying the technical language of the Mystery Religions, such as mysteries, illumination and *gnosis* to Christianity, and, as in the Mystery Religions, he posited differing levels of understanding of Christianity, one for ordinary people and another, esoteric teaching for the Christian Gnostic who had been initiated into the divine Christian mysteries.

Just as Clement's early life is obscure, so is its wane. Upon a renewal of Roman persecution of Christians in 202–3 he departed Alexandria for Cappadocia, in eastern Turkey, and had died by the year 215. Unfortunately for Clement's general reputation in the Christian Church, some of his theology was left outside the boundaries of orthodoxy by the theological definitions of the great church councils of the fourth and fifth centuries. But equally damaging to Clement's legacy was the even greater influence of his successor as head of the catechetical school of Alexandria, his own pupil Origen (ca 185–253), perhaps the greatest figure of the third-century church. Origen subsumed the core of Clement's teachings into his own works and mediated them to succeeding generations.

The persecution that drove Clement out of Alexandria claimed as one of its victims Origen's father and Origen, hoping for the glory of martyrdom, was ready to rush out and proclaim his Christianity. However, his rashness was checked by his mother when she hid his clothing from him. The bishop of Alexandria named Origen, only eighteen years old, to succeed Clement in the school for catechumens, an indication of Origen's tremendous intellect and his outstanding classical Hellenistic education, which was "almost unrivaled among the [Church] Fathers."[18] He was instructed by Clement as well as Ammonius Saccas, the pre-eminent Platonist of Alexandria who was also the mentor of Plotinus, the founder of Neoplatonic philosophy. At the same time, Origen gained a mastery of both the Hebrew scriptures and the Christian New

Testament and was devoted to the allegorical method of biblical interpretation championed by Philo and taught him by Clement.

For Origen, all of the scriptures existed on several levels simultaneously – the literal, historical meaning, which was intended for simple believers of a simple mind who did not possess the spiritual maturity to understand deep spiritual truths and a hidden, esoteric meaning for those who were capable of comprehending the deeper meanings. The teachings of Jesus and of his apostles, whether written or oral, always existed on these multiple levels. The literal meaning was milk for babes while the hidden, deeper spiritual meaning was meat for adults.

Like Clement, Origen conceived of the purpose of Christian life as the immediate knowledge of God by the believer, a goal hampered by the natural inability of humans to comprehend God, for "God is incomprehensible, and incapable of being measured … whose nature cannot be grasped or seen by the power of any human understanding, even the purest and brightest."[19] Thus knowledge of God is "beyond the power of human nature to take in" and God "arranged that the things concerning Him should be unknown and beyond the grasp of knowledge."[20] Nonetheless, the situation was not hopeless, for God sent his divine Logos, his Son, as a mediator to instruct humans in the knowledge of divine matters. Through the teachings of Jesus, who appeared in order "to make known and reveal the Father,"[21] knowledge of God was given at both the literal and the esoteric levels. One form of this knowledge was through the Scriptures when understood properly in their hidden meanings, an understanding that came by means of inspiration as a gift from God. However, the Scriptures were insufficient because they "are to be understood as most meager elements and the briefest introductions, even when they are understood entirely accurately."[22] Origen used St. Paul's description of his mystical ascent to make the point that what the apostle saw and heard were "above Scripture" because "it is not possible to write as Scriptures"[23] such things. Scripture was only an introduction to the knowledge of God and one must go beyond them and "ascend to Jesus"[24] for further, immediate knowledge. This continuing inspiration, also seen as the dwelling of the Holy Spirit within the believer, whose purpose is to enlighten holy souls, is necessary to the Christian, for "no soul can arrive at perfection in knowledge in any other way than by becoming inspired by the truth of divine wisdom."[25] Thus while "human nature is not sufficient in any way to seek for God and to find Him in His pure nature," it could do so by the help of God.[26] God in his nature was as transcendent and unknowable to Origen as he was to Clement, but Origen allowed that through divine enlightenment humans can gain some knowledge of God, "Since knowledge is disclosed to them that are worthy in the present life 'through a mirror' and 'in a riddle,' but is revealed hereafter 'face to face.'"[27]

The indwelling of the Spirit of God is a gift, but humans are not completely passive in its reception, for "God is always giving us a share of His own Spirit to those who are able to partake of Him."[28] Moreover, just as in the Mystery Religions, one should not speak freely of what is seen and heard during this communication with God, but one "will necessarily have frugality of mouth, since he knows to whom, when, and how he should speak of the divine mysteries."[29] The Holy Spirit comes only to those who are worthy and the principal means of becoming worthy, just as for Clement, was "by renouncing the world and everything in the world,"[30] and to separate one's "soul from the earthly body but also from everything material,"[31] that is, through asceticism, self-denial and despising all that is visible and corporeal. Necessarily such a path was not for all, for "the experience of the knowledge of God comes to men on rare occasions, and is to be found by very few people."[32] Origen was himself on the severely ascetical path, for he ate only minimal food, slept on the floor, never in a bed, and followed the injunction of Jesus not to keep two coats or wear shoes. Moreover, in one of the best-known episodes in his life, he read the words of Jesus that some had made themselves eunuchs for the sake of the kingdom of heaven, followed by the command, "He who is able to receive it, let him receive it."[33] Origen was able to receive it and had himself castrated.

Thus Origen, like Clement, saw two levels of believers in the Christian Church, the perfect few who experienced God and were given an understanding of the divine mysteries because they were pure, and the ordinary believers, children in the faith, who gained only a little knowledge of God because of their "more defective capacities" and were helped to "live a better life, so far as they can, and to accept doctrines about God such as they have the capacity to receive."[34] Again, like Clement, Origen did not hesitate to equate Christianity with the Mystery Religions, for in it, just as in the mysteries, only one "who is pure not only *from all defilement*, but also from what are regarded as minor sins," could be "initiated into the mysteries of the religion of Jesus which are delivered only to the holy and pure."[35]

Accordingly, Origen saw Christianity essentially as a mystical religion. Even the name "Israel," which Christians had appropriated for themselves, he defined mystically as "the mind seeing God."[36] As one of the first Christian writers to devote himself to the mystical understanding of Christianity, Origen developed some of the major themes and images that were adopted by later figures in the church. He developed at length the Platonic concept of the mystical Christian life as an ascent and allegorized the forty-two stages of the movement of the children of Israel out of Egypt to the promised land as expressing the stages of the soul's progressive ascent to God. Moreover, he saw the three books of the Hebrew Bible attributed to Solomon (Proverbs, Ecclesiastes and the Song of Songs) as representing the progression of the soul through the three stages of illumination, purgation and, finally, union with God. Regarding the Song of Songs, Origen may have been the first to see the book as an allegory of the individual soul, the bride, and its union with God, the bridegroom. He also was the first to discuss the problem of the role of ecstasies ("a time when the mind is struck with amazement by the knowledge of great and marvelous things"[37]), visions, apparitions and voices in the mystical experience, issues to vex writers on mysticism from his time forward. These phenomena were an integral and expected part of the mystical ascent to God, divine charisms given to the soul, but at the same time "visions usually involve temptation. Sometimes an angel of wickedness disguises himself as an angel of light. And so you must beware and exercise great care in order to discern with knowledge the kinds of visions."[38] On the topic of mystical visions, it has been suggested that "Origen speaks with such clearness that he must have realized their purpose and value from his own experience."[39]

As brilliant a figure as Origen was, his life in the church was marked by constant controversy. Demetrius, the bishop who appointed him over the catechetical school, grew jealous as Origen's reputation widened and, also because Origen had not been ordained, began to oppose his preaching. When Origen was ordained a presbyter by the bishops of Jerusalem and Caesarea, Demetrius protested, claiming that they were interfering in his diocese and that Origen was barred from ordination because of his self-castration. In the end, Origen left Alexandria permanently for a similar position in Caesarea, where he spent the last twenty years of his life, but not in peace. In 250 the emperor Decius initiated another persecution of Christians in the Roman Empire and Origen was arrested and tortured severely. He survived and was released but his health was broken and he died at Tyre in 253.

Controversy followed Origen's teachings long after his death. As with Clement, the progression of Christian theology in the fourth, fifth and sixth centuries left behind much of his theology and some of his Platonic base. He taught a first creation before the creation of the material world, the pre-existence of souls before their eventual bodily incarnation, the salvation of all beings and the subordination of Christ to God the Father, while denying the resurrection of the physical body. The fourth-century condemnations were a serious blow to his reputation, while his censure at the fifth ecumenical council in Constantinople in 553 left him posthumously branded as a heretic and many of his works were destroyed. Nonetheless, his influence on Christian mysticism is immense. His allegorical interpretation of scriptures and his mystical view of the Song of Songs became standard among Christian spiritual writers, and, along with Clement of Alexandria, he was the founder of the exaltation of Christian asceticism as necessary preparation for mysticism that produced the monastic movement in the deserts of Egypt at the beginning of the fourth century.

THE DESERT FATHERS

The view of Clement and Origen that Christianity existed on two levels – an inner, higher, mystical Christianity concerned with receiving the knowledge of God given only to those who had freed themselves of their passions (a state of *apatheia*, passionlessness), and ordinary Christianity concerned with instructing the masses in the moral teachings of the faith – continued to dominate the church and attained its most extreme expression at the beginning of the fourth century with the appearance in Egypt of the Desert Fathers and Mothers. Flight from the cities and villages was a familiar feature in Egypt as an escape from the tax-collector and the military conscriptor and, for Christians, from the persecutors of the last half of the third century. By about the year 300 the Christian ideal of withdrawal from the world took a more literal expression when great numbers began to leave their homes and families and move out into the desert to live their lives in "solitude." (See plate 1.) Three types of monastics ("those who live alone") came to be found in the desert, hermits who truly lived apart from others, those who lived in *laurae*, collections of huts where the monks of the community lived alone but met together in a common church where the monastics would meet on Saturdays and Sundays for services, and *cenobia*, where the monks and nuns lived communally in barracks.

While the terms "flight" and "withdrawal" suggest that monastic life was an escape, it actually represented spiritual combat with oneself in a struggle to overcome the body and its passions and appetites in a life of asceticism, a term derived from the Greek word *ascesis*, "discipline." This was not asceticism for its own sake but rather for its reward, living in the presence of God and gaining knowledge of God, which was the life of the angels – a foretaste of the heavenly life. "God's athletes" the monastics were often called, signifying their being in training for this contest. By spurning the world and its falsity, one could focus on the only contest that mattered, the struggle to overcome one's passions and appetites, but at the same time one would be tested severely as demonic forces sought to overcome the ascetics.

St. Anthony the Great was by no means the first Christian monastic, but he was the first to gain great renown, owing to the tremendously popular biography written about him by Athanasius, the patriarch of Alexandria and champion of orthodoxy, which established Anthony as the paradigm for all future monastics. In the patriarch's work Anthony (ca. 250–357) was an Egyptian from a well-to-do although not well-educated Christian family. When he was about twenty, after both his parents had died, Anthony decided to follow the Scriptures literally, by obeying the commands of Jesus and imitating the Christians of the New Testament. He sold all his family's considerable possessions and gave the money to the poor, committing his sister to the care of nuns in a convent and henceforth devoting his life to *ascesis*. As he heard of the ascetic acts of other hermits he was determined to equal or surpass them and thus he slept little and then usually on the ground, ate only bread and salt and drank only water. Anthony's life was one devoted to prayer and discipline, "for the sake of which he dwelled in the mountain, and he rejoiced in the contemplation of divine realities."[40] Asceticism, however, must be accompanied by the cultivation of virtues and Athanasius has Anthony say that the virtues of the monks that combat demonic temptations are "their fasting, the vigils, the prayers, the meekness and gentleness, the contempt for money, the lack of vanity, the humility, the love of the poor, the almsgiving, the freedom from wrath, and most of all their devotion to Christ."[41]

After twenty years of such discipline, Anthony was, in the words of Athanasius, "led into divine mysteries and inspired by God."[42] Anthony was favored with divine gifts, with frequent divine visions, the ability to know the future, clairvoyance, the discernment of spirits and the ability to heal. He was caught up into trances and ecstasies like that of Paul which he related for the benefit of his disciples so that "they would learn that the discipline yields good fruit, and that the visions frequently take place as an assuagement of the trials."[43] However, while visions, voices and apparitions were considered to be among the divine charisms and were the reward for the ascetic life, it was recognized that some visions were of demonic origins, sent to tempt the monks into sin. Athanasius has Anthony warn his disciples that the demons were capable of taking on various shapes and of sending visions, which should be ignored even if they foretold the future or urged the monks to pray or to fast, for they did this not "for the sake of piety or truth, but so that they might bring the simple to despair, and declare the discipline useless, and make men sick of the solitary life as something burdensome and very oppressive."[44] Anthony related his own demonic visions that came "having the appearance of a light,"[45] to which he simply closed his eyes. Thus Anthony's biography introduced one of the great conflicts of mysticism, for divine gifts such as visions and apparitions bestowed by God were thought to be rewards for genuine asceticism and virtue, but sometimes they were of demonic origin, intended to mislead, and should be disregarded. The continual problem for church authorities was how to extol such manifestations as evidence of genuine mysticism while also discouraging a false, demonic imitation of mysticism that might lead one away from orthodoxy. In Anthony, Athanasius saw the mystical as well as the monastic exemplar. His Anthony counseled against boasting "not in virtue but in signs,"[46] was devoted to the Scriptures and, especially important to the bishop of Alexandria, "he honored the rule of the Church with extreme care, and he wanted every cleric to be held in greater regard than himself."[47] Thus humility and obedience were hailed as the greatest of the monastic virtues.

The pursuit of monasticism became so popular that an account of a journey to visit the Desert Fathers and Mothers of Egypt written towards the end of the fourth century described dozens of monasteries comprising thousands of men and women, and the author, with obvious hyperbole, claimed that in Egypt, "There are as many monks in the desert as there are laymen in the rest of the world."[48] One of the Fathers the visitors sought out was John of Lycopolis, who declared his objective to be God, who could be found only by making a complete renunciation of the world and being absorbed in the struggle against the passions, otherwise one "cannot see God."[49] John was especially devoted to stillness (*hēsychia*, a state of inner tranquility that was the result of the victory over the passions) and spent his days in prayer and contemplation, seeing "clear visions of a divine nature, sometimes while fully awake, and sometimes while asleep. … [H]e voluntarily kept himself in the presence of God."[50] One version of this account adds John's sermon,

> we stand before God with a pure heart and free from all the passions and vices we have mentioned, we can, insofar as this is possible, see even God, and as we pray the eyes of our heart are turned towards him and we see that which is invisible with the spirit not with the flesh: this is a learning of the mind, and not a part of the flesh. For no one can suppose that he can behold the being of God himself, but he shapes for himself some kind of appearance or image in his heart in some corporeal likeness. … I say this, provided that there is purity of mind, totally freed of voluntary stains of sin. Those who have renounced the world and are seen to follow God must make this their central occupation.[51]

Because John had denied himself, his visitors reported, "He stands unimpeded in the presence of God without any anxiety holding him back. For such a man spends his life with God, he is occupied with God."[52] To such a person, graces were granted: "He sees mysteries, for God shows him them; he foresees what belongs to the future; he contemplates revelations like the saints did; he performs mighty works; he becomes a friend of God."[53] To John's fellow hermit, the Abba Apollo, such gifts were "the beginning of the charisms of God" when one had "acquired mastery over the passions and the appetites."[54]

A similar report of the wondrous feats of asceticism and charismatic deeds of the desert dwellers was written around 420 by the Galatian monk and bishop Palladius (ca. 363 to ca. 431), who spent nine years as a monk in the desert, west of the Nile delta. Written at the request of the royal chamberlain Lausus, the *Lausiac History* describes the lives of the men and women with whom Palladius came in contact during his years in the desert, those who had taken "the journey which leads to the kingdom of heaven,"[55] whose example might encourage others to imitate their devotion to God. Sharing the didactic purpose of Athanasius's *Life of Anthony*, it promotes a similar viewpoint, exposing monks who ran shipwreck on the rocks of pride and arrogance and lack of complete renunciation of the world. Of course, the conquest of the passions was supremely important. The monks who were to be emulated, such as Father Elias, claimed that "passion comes no more to my mind"[56] while the author declared, "I have never seen a man more free from passion" than was Father Ammonius.[57] The rewards for their perfection were charisms, such as visions and power to heal, to discern spirits and to cast out demons. Some, such as Macarius of Egypt, lived in continual ecstasy. Macarius of Alexandria ordered his mind not to descend from heaven for five days. The deaconess Sabiniana "held converse intimately with God,"[58] Philoremus was given to saying, "Never do I remember being absent from God in thought,"[59] and the monk Diocles was also always with God, explaining, "Whenever the soul is concerned with a thought or deed that is pious or godlike, then it is with God."[60]

In these earliest lives of the desert saints we are confronted with one of the most difficult aspects of understanding the experiences of the monastic mystics themselves, the lack of first-hand accounts among them. If they had indeed gained the humility that was essential for their perfection, they would not boast of their gifts and powers. Accordingly, when Abba Or spoke with his visitors and informed them of his visions, "He told us of these things as if speaking about someone else because he wished to conceal his own manner of life. But the fathers who lived with him said that he was the one who had seen this vision."[61]

THE BYZANTINE CHURCH

Gregory of Nyssa (ca. 335 to ca. 395) is one of the great Fathers of the Eastern Church and one of the leading Christian figures of the latter fourth century. He was born into a remarkable family of martyrs, bishops and saints. His brother Basil, known as the Great, was bishop of Caesarea in Cappadocia, in the east central region of modern Turkey, and was one of the most important figures in the development of monasticism in the Eastern Church. His brother Peter became bishop of the Armenian diocese of Sebaste and a sister Macrina (the Younger) was leader of a community of ascetics living on a family estate. After a secular career in which he married, to his later regret,

Gregory became interested in monastic life. In 372 his brother Basil appointed him bishop of the Cappadocian see of Nyssa, which drew him into the bitter disputes over the Arian heresy[62] and for a while he suffered a brief banishment from his diocese. After the death of his brother Basil in 379, Gregory emerged as the dominant figure in the Eastern Church and was given the honor of making the opening speech at the Second Ecumenical Council of the Christian Church, held in 381 in Constantinople.

As involved as he was in secular and ecclesiastical politics, Gregory never abandoned his interest in monasticism and mysticism. In his many influential writings on asceticism, Gregory was an ardent proponent of the mystical belief found in Clement and Origen, that the nature of God is incomprehensible to our rational faculties:

> The divine nature in and of itself, whatever its essential character, lies beyond our human apprehension. It is unapproachable and inaccessible to human conjectures. There has never been found among men anyone to grasp the ungraspable with the human intelligence, nor has there ever been found a method of comprehending the incomprehensible.[63]

The vision of God, the ultimate goal for contemplatives, Gregory wrote, "is the seeing that consists in not seeing, because that which is sought transcends all knowledge, being separated on all sides by a kind of darkness," which Gregory described as "luminous darkness,"[64] where God "is hidden in the *dark cloud*" in "the realm of the invisible, surrounded by the divine darkness."[65] Gregory affirmed that his brother, Basil the Great, had often entered "into the darkness where God was. By the mystical guidance of the Spirit he understood what was invisible to others, so that he seemed to be enveloped in that darkness in which the Word of God is concealed."[66]

Following in the tradition of Philo of Alexandria and Origen, Gregory saw in the Bible mystical truths and in the life of Moses he saw a paradigm of the life of a mystic. Moses first experienced God as dazzling light (the burning bush), but this was not a perfect vision, for, "none of those things which are apprehended by sense perception and contemplated by the understanding really subsists."[67] However, eventually Moses saw God in the darkness, "And the people stood afar off, while Moses drew near to the thick darkness where God was."[68] Gregory wrote:

> For leaving behind everything that is observed, not only what sense comprehends but also what the intelligence thinks it sees, it keeps on penetrating deeper until by the intelligence's yearning for understanding it gains access to the invisible and the incomprehensible, and there it sees God. This is the true knowledge of what is sought; this is the seeing that consists in not seeing, because that which is sought transcends all knowledge, being separated on all sides by incomprehensibility as by a kind of darkness.[69]

In perhaps the first of his many ascetical works, *On Virginity*, seemingly based on his own experience, Gregory extolled the celibate life as being holier, higher and better than the state of marriage, which is a "sad tragedy,"[70] for virginity allowed one to avoid the entanglements of secular life and find quiet for divine contemplation, and "no one can climb up to that who has once planted his foot upon the secular life."[71] The purpose of asceticism was to purify the heart, which led to the vision of God, something with which Gregory would appear to have been familiar:

> What people normally experience when they look down from some lofty promontory upon some mighty sea, that is the experience of my mind as I peer down from the height of the lord's voice, as from some mountain peak, upon the inexhaustible depth of my thoughts.[72]

He described the encounter with God in terms of sober intoxication:

> In this way the mighty David became intoxicated and went out of himself: he saw, while in ecstasy, that divine beauty which no mortal can behold ... [Peter] experienced that divine and sober inebriation. And he went out of himself ... This then is the inebriation to which the Lord exhorts His table companions, and it is through this that the soul's divine ecstasy takes place.[73]

Roughly contemporary with Gregory of Nyssa are the homilies attributed to a certain Macarius, which are among the most influential mystical works in the Eastern Church, especially with the hesychasts,[74] but in the West they also influenced John Cassian and thus St. Benedict of Nursia and even John Wesley.[75] The author of the homilies appears to have lived in northeastern Syria in the mid-fourth century and some have suggested that Pseudo-Macarius was a certain Symeon of Mesopotamia, who is known to have been a Messalian. (The Messalians were not an organized sect but rather were ascetics who believed that the best Christian life consisted in constant prayer, while paying little attention to fasting, the sacraments or the clergy.) This life of incessant prayer would lead them to *apatheia*, a passionless state which would produce an immediate vision of God apprehended by the physical body. Messalian practices were condemned by a series of church councils in the fourth and fifth centuries but Messalianism survived into the seventh century, leaving traces in the works of Gregory of Nyssa, St. Basil the Great, as well as Pseudo-Macarius/Symeon.

The Homilies of Pseudo-Macarius do not form a treatise on mysticism but rather concern the monastic life, exhorting monks, called simply Christians, to persevere in complete renunciation of the bodily desires and in constant prayer, which will lead to the indwelling of the Holy Spirit and the deification of the soul. Thus mystical union is the ultimate goal for all true Christians. This is stated simply enough in the *Great Letter*, "Such a person shows himself to be a pure dwelling place for the adorable and Holy Spirit, from whom he receives the immortal peace of Christ, through whom he is joined and united with the Lord."[76]

In typical Eastern fashion, there is little personal testimony of the experience of the divine light of God, but the experience itself is described many times:

> Sometimes indeed the very light itself, shining in the heart, opened up interiorly

and in a profound way a hidden light, so that the whole person was completely drowned with that sweet contemplation. He was no longer in control of himself, but became like a fool and a barbarian toward this world, so over-whelmed was he by the excessive love and sweetness of the hidden mysteries that were being revealed to him.[77]

However, on one occasion the author does describe his own experience and its pro-found effects on him:

> After I received the experience of the sign of the cross, grace now acts in this manner. It quiets all my parts and my heart so that the soul with the greatest joy seems to be a guileless child. No longer am I a man that condemns Greek or Jew or sinner or worldling. Truly, the interior man looks on all human beings with pure eyes and finds joy in the whole world.[78]

The imagery of the experience of God in the soul found in the Homilies is described in terms of light and fire: "All things will become light. All are immersed in light and fire and are indeed changed."[79] The author wrote of "that heavenly fire of the Godhead which Christians receive interiorly in their hearts now in this life."[80] This experience of God is in fact the most intimate possible for a human: "As near as the body is to the soul in intimate interrelationships, so much nearer is God who is present to come and open the locked doors of our heart and to fill us with heavenly riches."[81] The author expressed the transforming power of the experience of God, which was so great that

> when a person reaches the perfection of the Spirit, completely purified of all passions and united to and interpenetrated by the Paraclete Spirit in an ineffable communion, and is deemed worthy to become spirit in a mutual pene-tration with the Spirit, then it becomes all light, all eye, all spirit, all joy, all repose, all happiness, all love, all compassion, all goodness and kindness. ... They become like to Christ, putting on the virtues of the power of the Spirit with a constancy. They interiorly become faultless and spotless and pure. Having been restored by the Spirit, how can they produce externally any evil fruit?[82]

The experience of the Spirit can produce different effects at different times. At one time "one is instructed in an understanding and unspeakable wisdom and knowledge of the unknowable Spirit through grace in matters that cannot be expressed by tongue and speech. At another time one becomes one with all human beings."[83] Pseudo-Macarius also made it clear that God appeared to different people in different forms, as was most suitable for each one:

> When God wishes, he becomes fire ... the Lord transforms himself into bread and drink ... Thus he appeared to each of the holy fathers, exactly as he wished and as it seemed helpful to them. ... To each of the saints, likewise, God

appeared as he wished so as to refresh them, to save and lead them into a knowledge of God.[84]

It is clear that in the fourth century there was a conflict between those who saw Christianity as a religion of the mind, a system of beliefs about God that was governed by the Scriptures, and those who saw Christianity as an experience of God. Pseudo-Macarius was clearly among the latter. For him, the true Christians are mystics who have "tasted the Lord."

> Such a taste is this power of the Spirit working to effect full certainty of faith which operates in the heart. ... For they are taught by God. His very grace writes in their hearts the laws of the Spirit. They should not put all their trusting hope solely in the Scriptures written in ink. For divine grace writes on the "tables of the heart" the laws of the Spirit and the heavenly mysteries.[85]

Macarius/Symeon wrote that God "has sent to men the divine Scriptures as letters. ... But if a man does not approach and beg and receive, it will profit him nothing for having read the Scriptures."[86] Those rich in the Holy Spirit "truly possess the fellowship of the Spirit within themselves. And when they speak words of truth or deliver any spiritual conference and wish to edify persons, they speak out of the same wealth and treasure which indwells within them."[87] How different this is from the one who wishes to teach without this experience, for such a one "does not possess in himself the Word of God in power and in truth. He repeats things he memorized or borrowed from some writings or from what he has heard from spiritual persons and these he organizes and teaches."[88] Those who presumed to teach on spiritual matters without having personally experienced what they expounded simply enunciate empty words: "Those who truly are wise, the brave soldiers and philosophers of God, are those directed and guided in the interior man by divine power."[89]

The legacy of the Pseudo-Macarian homilies was an uncompromising devotion to overcoming the bodily passions and unceasing zeal for constant prayer as the elements of the true Christian life. The homilies exude an unflagging confidence that these will lead to the physical experience of the light of God, which is promised to all Christians.

Little is known of the life of John Climacus ("of the Ladder," also known as the Scholastic in the Eastern Orthodox Church), but his influence on Eastern monasticism and his emphasis on the goal of attaining direct illumination of God cannot be exaggerated. Each year *The Ladder* is read in Eastern Orthodox monasteries during Lent and he is remembered on the fourth Sunday of Lent. One can state little beyond the bare facts that he lived in the second half of the sixth century and in the early seventh century. He became abbot of a monastery on Mount Sinai, where he composed *The Ladder* for a nearby monastic community to encourage and instruct the monks there in their effort to achieve the monastic goal – direct illumination by God and knowledge of God. This was attained by becoming dispassionate, that is, overcoming the body and practicing the virtues. John wrote,

A man is truly dispassionate – and is known to be such – when he has cleansed his flesh of all corruption; when he has lifted his mind above everything created, and has made it master of all the senses; when he keeps his soul continually in the presence of the Lord and reaches out beyond the borderline of strength to Him. And there are some who would claim that dispassion is resurrection of the soul prior to that of the body, while others would insist that it is a perfect knowledge of God, a knowledge second only to that of the angels. … The man deemed worthy to be of this sort during his lifetime has God always within him, to guide him in all he has to say or do or think. The will of the Lord becomes for him a sort of inner voice through illumination.[90]

There are thirty steps to the *Ladder*, one for each year of the life of Jesus before he began his public career, which are concerned with the monks' break with the world, the practice of the virtues, the struggle against passions, the higher virtues, and union with God. The twenty-seventh step is stillness, and, "He who has achieved stillness has arrived at the very center of the mysteries."[91] The thirtieth and final step is that of faith, hope and love, which brings the monk face to face with God: "Love grants prophecy, miracles. It is an abyss of illumination, a fountain of fire, bubbling up to inflame the thirsty soul. It is the condition of angels, and the progress of eternity."[92] At the end of his work, John exhorted his readers, "Ascend, my brothers, ascend eagerly. Let your hearts' resolve be to climb."[93]

Following in the tradition of the Desert Fathers, John was practical, cautioning against excessive weight being given to paranormal experiences, for the gift of prophecy given in one's dreams can come from the devil. However, "To a monk is to know ecstasy without end"[94] and rapture, or ecstasy, is "the way of the mind mysteriously and marvelously carried into the light of Christ,"[95] and rapture in the Lord is the highest form of prayer.[96] John frequently related the experiences of others while in rapture and even provided a rare first-hand account of his own experience:

A light came to me as I was thirsting and I asked there what the Lord was before He took visible form. The angel could not tell me because he was not permitted to do so. So I asked him: "In what state is He now?" and the answer was that He was in the state appropriate to Him, though not us. "What is the nature of the standing or sitting at the right hand of the Father?" I asked. "Such mysteries cannot be taken in by the human ear," he replied. Then I pleaded with him right then to bring me where my heart was longing to go, but he said that the time was not yet ripe, since the fire of incorruption was not yet mighty enough within me. And whether during all this, I was in the body or out of it, I cannot rightly say.[97]

Sometime in the years around 500, a writer, perhaps a monk in Syria, using the name of Dionysius the Areopagite (an Athenian converted to Christianity by St. Paul, mentioned in Acts 17.34) wrote a number of works which were regarded as quasi-apostolic and gained stature and authority very close to that of the Bible. Among the works of this author, now called Pseudo-Dionysius, was the very short tract *Mystical Theology*, presenting an essentially Platonic description of mysticism. To see "the mysterious things," one must pass beyond the intellect and reason and leave behind

> everything perceived and understood, everything perceptible and understandable, all that is not and all that is, and, with your understanding laid aside, to strive upward as much as you can toward union with him who is beyond all being and knowledge.[98]

One must

> plunge into the truly mysterious darkness of unknowing. Here, renouncing all that the mind can conceive, wrapped entirely in the intangible and the invisible, he belongs completely to him who is beyond everything. Here, being neither oneself nor someone else, one is supremely united by a completely unknowing inactivity of all knowledge, and knows beyond the mind by knowing nothing.[99]

God, the author argued, was beyond all description, having "neither shape nor form, quality, quantity, or weight" and can "neither be seen nor be touched. It is neither perceived nor is it perceptible."[100] One ascends to God, who "cannot be grasped by understanding," who "is beyond assertion and denial."[101] The farther upward one flies, the more "our words are confined to the ideas we are capable of forming; so that now as we plunge into that darkness which is beyond intellect, we shall find ourselves not simply running short of words but actually speechless and unknowing."[102]

For Pseudo-Dionysius, one could reach God only by entering into a darkness of unknowing, for God transcends all human language and concepts. In this and in other extant works bearing his name, the author stresses the superiority of the *apophatic* method of describing God (that is, the way of negation, of stating what God is not) over the *cataphatic* (the way of affirming what God is), because the way of negation

> seems to me much more appropriate, for, as the secret and sacred tradition has instructed, God is in no way like the things that have being and we have no knowledge at all of his incomprehensible and ineffable transcendence and invisibility.[103]

The works of Pseudo-Dionysius, especially the *Mystical Theology*, with their presumed apostolic authorship, were extremely influential in the Byzantine church and in the Western Middle Ages, providing their readers with a strongly Platonic conceptual framework and language for mysticism. They became part of the basic library of mysticism that was drawn upon for centuries afterwards. One of the most important of these promoters of Pseudo-Dionysian thought is Maximus the Confessor (580–662), ascetic monk and champion of orthodoxy. He was born to a noble family in Constantinople and received a thorough education. After a brief career as secretary in the court of the emperor, perhaps even heading the imperial chancellery, he abandoned his secular career and became a monk in a monastery near Constantinople. However, the monastery was too entrenched in the affairs of the world for Maximus, who desired a life of constant prayer, and around 625 he moved to a monastery more distant from the capital. But shortly thereafter an invading Persian army swept over Asia Minor, forcing Maximus and the other monks of his house to flee. By 630 he is known to have been in North Africa, where he soon acquired a great reputation for his understanding of theology.

Very naturally he became mired in the great theological dispute of that time, Monotheletism, promoted by Emperor Heraclius (610–41), which taught that Christ had two natures, the divine and the human, but a single divine will. This imperial theological policy was continued under the son and successor of Heraclius, Emperor Constans II (641–68), but it encountered the stiff opposition of Pope Martin I (649–55) as well as Maximus, who was then in Rome. Resistance to an emperor was always dangerous for one's career as well as one's health and in 653 the emperor had Pope Martin arrested, brought to the capital of Constantinople and tried for treason. Martin was condemned to death but the sentence was commuted to exile in the Crimean region, where he died.

Maximus then took up the leadership of Western opposition to Monotheletism and was likewise brought to Constantinople for trial and condemned to exile, in Thrace on the modern Turkish-Bulgarian border. However Maximus stood firm in his opposition to Monotheletism and was retried and again condemned. His right hand and his tongue were cut off, thus earning him his name of Confessor, and he was exiled to the province of Lazica, in modern Georgia on the Black Sea, where he died in 662.

Maximus was a champion of orthodoxy but his great reputation also rests on his writings. Many of them defend Trinitarianism against Monotheletism, by which Maximus gained his sobriquet of "the Theologian," but most of his works were concerned with the asceticism of monks, exhorting them to cultivate the virtues and overcome the bodily passions, whereby the monk could attain perfection. Of course the goal of the monk was mystical, as it always had been, aiming at union with God which would thereby deify the monk, making him God, and his writings form a monk's handbook deserving study by subsequent generations of monastics on the path to deification. Maximus described this experience:

> When in the full ardor of its love for God the mind goes out of itself, then it has no perception at all either of itself or of any creatures. For once illumined by the divine and infinite light, it remains insensible to anything that is made by him, just as the physical eye has no sensation of the stars when the sun has risen. … [A]t the very onset of prayer the mind is taken hold of by the divine and infinite light and is conscious neither of itself nor of any other being whatever except of him who through love brings about such brightness in it.[104]

Maximus subscribed to the Neoplatonic teachings of Pseudo-Dionysius and made frequent references to the language and imagery found in his works. Thus Maximus's own writings were a popular and powerful vehicle for a constant affirmation of the apophatic, negative theology of mysticism:

> The one who speaks of God in positive affirmations is making the Word flesh. Making use only of what can be seen and felt he knows God as their cause. But the one who speaks of God negatively through negations is making the Word spirit, as in the beginning he was God and with God. Using absolutely nothing which can be known he knows in a better way the utterly Unknowable.[105]

Maximus also gave priority to the experience of the word of God in mysticism over the reading of the word of God in Scriptures:

> Thus it is necessary that the one who seeks after God in a religious way never hold fast to the letter [of the Scripture] lest he mistakenly understand things said about God for God himself. In this case we unwisely are satisfied with the words of Scripture in place of the Word, and the Word slips out of the mind while we thought by holding on to his garments we could possess the incorporeal Word. ... The meaning of Holy Writ reveals itself gradually to the more discerning mind in loftier senses when it has put off the complex whole of the words formed in it bodily, as in the sound of a gentle breeze.[106]

By the tenth century, monasticism in the Eastern Church had developed into a staid institution lacking the fire and zeal of the first several centuries. Although theology had become an intellectual pursuit somewhat separated from the mystical experiences of individual Christians, mysticism retained its theoretical and theological positions in the Eastern Church even though largely subsumed under an emphasis on asceticism for its own sake. By the latter tenth century, a monk appeared determined to reinvigorate monasticism with the all-consuming enthusiasm for contemplation and union with God that had characterized fourth-century monasticism and the church of the New Testament.

Symeon the New Theologian (ca. 949–1022), "perhaps the most remarkable and influential mystic to appear in the history of the medieval Byzantine Church,"[107] was born into a wealthy family in the Byzantine province of Paphlagonia, in modern north central Turkey. The family had contacts with the imperial capital of Constantinople and young Symeon was taken to the court for his secondary education. While there he fell under the influence of the holy Symeon the Pious, a monk of the famous Studion monastery in Constantinople. Under the direction of the latter, the younger Symeon was led into prayer and had his first mystical vision, in which he saw God as light:

> suddenly a flood of divine radiance appeared from above and filled all the room. As this happened the young man [the young Symeon himself] lost all awareness of his surroundings and forgot that he was in a house or that he was under a roof. He saw nothing but light all around him ... he was wholly in the presence

of immaterial light and seemed to himself to have turned into light. Oblivious of all the world he was filled with tears and with ineffable joy and gladness. His mind then ascended to heaven and beheld another light, which was clearer than that which was close at hand.[108]

In a second vision, the young Symeon fell to the ground and

a great light was immaterially shining on me and seized hold of my whole mind and soul, so that I was struck with amazement at the unexpected marvel and I was, as it were, in ecstasy. Moreover I forgot the place where I stood, who I was, and where, and could only cry out, "Lord, have mercy."[109]

Symeon did not enter the monastic life at Studion until he was twenty-seven and was already zealous to lead the monks "back to their prophetic, charismatic role within the Church … calling monks back to a state of constant brokenness, austere asceticism, purity of heart and constant prayer."[110] He knew that in the here and now one "can truly experience God mystically, directly, and intensely, habitually living in the consciousness of God's immanent indwelling."[111] The new monk's zeal to reform the life of the monastery was not welcomed by either the abbot or the monks of Studion and the elder Symeon transferred him to the nearby monastery of Saint Mamas. In only three years he was the abbot of the house and from this position he worked for twenty years to make St. Mamas a model of ascetic, penitential and mystical monasticism. This was no easy task, for he faced an armed uprising against him by the monks and suffered the powerful opposition of Archbishop Stephen of Nicomedia, who disliked Symeon's mystical theology, his lack of respect for the hierarchy of the church and especially his teaching that monks, even though not ordained as priests, could hear confessions and grant absolution of sins. In 1009 the archbishop succeeded in having Symeon exiled across the Bosphorus, where he built a small monastery and continued his life of mystical union with God until his death in 1022.

Much of the intense opposition to his mystical emphasis rested on the belief that the charismatic age of mysticism was a thing of the past, belonging to the age of the Fathers, and was no longer a living phenomenon:

But of the men of whom I speak and whom I call heretics are those who say there is no one in our times and in our midst who is able to keep the Gospel commandments and become like the holy fathers … Now those who say this is impossible have not fallen into one particular heresy, but rather into all of them.[112]

Thus in his writings, most notably his *Discourses* and his hymns, Symeon took the unusual step of describing in vivid detail his own visionary ecstasies:

As I ascended I was given other ascents, at the end of the ascents I was given light, and by the light an even clearer light. In the midst thereof a sun shone brightly and from it a ray shone forth that filled all things. The object of my thought remained beyond understanding, and in this state I remained while I wept most sweetly and marveled at the ineffable. The divine mind conversed with my own mind and taught me. ... suddenly a flood of divine radiance appeared from above and filled all the room. As this happened, the young man [Symeon himself] lost all awareness (of his surroundings) ... he was wholly in the presence of immaterial light and seemed to himself to have turned into light. Oblivious of all the world he was filled with tears and with ineffable joy and gladness. His mind then ascended to heaven and beheld yet another light, which was clearer than that which was close at hand.[113]

Symeon went even farther, however, in his promotion of the reality of the experience of the indwelling of the Holy Spirit, which was known by the senses, for God "is both seen and heard, is sweet to the taste and perfume to the sense of smell; He is felt and so made known."[114] Further antagonizing his opponents, Symeon held that only one thus illuminated could properly be called a Christian and only through that means could one know God. Those who presumed to teach, preach or theologize on any basis other than knowledge gained from the direct experience of God were only proferring "empty and specious arguments."[115] On the other hand, those who had God within them had "passed through the holy Scripture" and no longer needed to read those books, for such a person "himself becomes a divinely inspired book for others."[116]

In his hymns, Symeon adopted classical metrical forms to express his mysticism and his call for asceticism and repentance in beautifully lyrical poetry:

> But, O what intoxication of light, O what movements of fire!
> Oh, what swirlings of the flame in me, miserable one that I am,
> coming from You and Your glory! ...
> I remained seated in the middle of the darkness, I know,
> but while I was there surrounded by darkness
> You appeared as light, illuminating me completely from Your total light.
> And I became light in the dark, I who was found in the midst of darkness.[117]

In his *Dialogues* Symeon had stressed that in mystical union Christ "unites Himself to our souls" and that "He Himself comes down from heaven and enters into our body as into a tomb."[118] But in one of his hymns, he made this complete identification with Christ even more graphic and more challenging for the Christian:

> I receive in Communion
> the Body divinized as being that of God.
> I too become god
> in this inexpressible union.[119]

But Symeon went even farther in his vision of the completeness of human identity with Christ brought about in mystical union:

We become members of Christ – and Christ becomes our members,
Christ becomes my hand, Christ, my miserable foot;
and I, unhappy one, am Christ's hand, Christ's foot!
I move my hand, and my hand is the whole Christ …
I move my foot, and behold, it shines like That – one! …
and all which is dishonorable in us He will make honorable
by adorning it with His divine beauty and His divine glory,
since living with God at the same time, we shall become gods,
no longer seeing the shamefullness of our body at all,
each member of our body will be the whole Christ; …
Now, well you recognize Christ in my finger,
and in [my penis] – did you not shudder or blush?
But God was not ashamed to become like you
and you, you are ashamed to be like Him?[120]

Symeon preferred to stress the unknowability of God, who is "without beginning, without end, unapproachable, unsearchable, invisible, ineffable, intangible, untouchable, dispassionate, inexpressible,"[121] and his constant image of God was that of light, "God is light, a light infinite and incomprehensible, … Everything to do with God is light."[122] Nonetheless he recognized the worth of developing positive statements about God, including the maternal, nurturing aspect of the divine, as when Christ comes to those who are infants spiritually and "appears as a breast of light, placed in the mouth of their intellect to suckle them."[123]

In the end, Symeon triumphed over Archbishop Stephen and his other opponents. The patriarch of Constantinople revoked Symeon's exile and was prepared to make him a bishop, an honor that Symeon refused. He remained in his solitude, practicing his severe monastic life, providing spiritual guidance to others, and completing his magnificent hymns.

Symeon's expression of "light mysticism" was continued by the Eastern mystics who followed him, especially by the hesychasts of the fourteenth century. *Hesychia* (quietness) had always been a goal of the Eastern Christian mystics and by the fourteenth century it was combined with light mysticism, the constant repetition of the Jesus Prayer (now standardized into the short formulation "Lord Jesus Christ, Son of God, have mercy on me"), while entailing specific breathing postures, such as sitting with the chin down against the chest with the eyes of the monk fixed "on his breast or on his navel, as a point of concentration."[124] Those who practiced these techniques believed that, with God's help, they thus were united in mind as well as in body with divine light, which was the same as that seen by Jesus's disciples on Mount Tabor at the Transfiguration,[125] and was considered to be nothing less than the light of the Godhead.

These claims were not without their critics, especially by those who preferred to understand God through philosophy and theology rather than by experience. One can turn apophatic theology against the mystics by arguing that because God truly is unknowable, he can be known only indirectly and not in direct experiences.

Moreover, to those who believed that the body and the soul are opposed to each other, that the body is a detriment to spiritual growth, the notion that the physical body, that is, the eyes, are involved in encountering God was repugnant.

The fiercest of these critics was Barlaam, a Greek monk from Calabria, in southern Italy, who had come to Constantinople to study Aristotle. While there he also discovered the hesychasts and denounced their practices while denying the validity of their mystical experience of God. He argued that God is transcendent and thus unknowable in any experiential sense and derided the hesychasts as "people with souls in their navels." In addition, he accused them of the heresy of Messalianism,[126] that is, neglecting the sacraments in order to devote themselves exclusively to prayer, which would produce a vision of the very essence of God perceivable with their physical eyes.

The strongest and most able defender of hesychasm was Gregory Palamas (1296–1359), a member of a noble family with close connections to the imperial court in Constantinople. At age twenty he entered the famous collection of monasteries on Mount Athos, on the Acte peninsula of northeast Greece (see plate 2), where he was ordained a priest and lived as a hermit practicing hesychasm. Around 1337 Gregory began his correspondence with Barlaam in defense of both the practices and the theology of the hesychasts (thus hesychasm is sometimes known as Palamism). Gregory's most famous work is his three-part treatise *On the Acquisition of Wisdom, On Prayer,* and *On the Light of Knowledge,* with each part written in three sections for which the works are known collectively as the *Triads.*

The *Triads* argue the distinction between the transcendent essence of God and the energy of God in the form of the divine, uncreated light of Christ, thus exonerating the hesychasts of the charge of Messalianism. In the course of his defense of hesychasm, Gregory discussed in great detail the experience of this divine light and thus provides a rare nuanced description of the hesychasts' union with that light. The hesychast did not see by sense perception, but by clear vision, seeing "by going out of himself, for through the mysterious sweetness of his vision he is ravished beyond all objects and all objective thought, and even beyond himself."[127] The hesychast saw "hypostatic light" which "is an illumination immaterial and divine, a grace invisibly seen and ignorantly known. *What* it is, they do not pretend to know."[128] This light could "speak" with "ineffable words, to him who contemplates it."[129] Other visions, "mystical and supernatural," came to "the purified and illuminated mind, when clearly participating in the grace of God"[130] and these were visions shared by "prophets and patriarchs, … especially the most divine ones."[131]

The dispute caught the attention of the emperor, who called two councils in Constantinople to decide the matter in 1341. The victory was for Gregory Palamas, and hesychasm was recognized as the official teaching of the Eastern Church. Barlaam returned to the West and converted to the Western Church, becoming a bishop in his native Calabria, but with an anathema pronounced on him by the Eastern Church. Gregory Palamas became archbishop of Thessalonica in 1347, and in 1368, only nine years after his death, he was proclaimed a saint of the Eastern Church.

The victory of hesychasm bolstered the mysticism of the monastery. While few would argue against the path to deification practiced by the ascetics of the Eastern

Church for more than a millennium, it was one that excluded most Christians who, occupied with the details of their daily lives in the world, were unable to make the requisite abandonment of that world. Nicholas Cabasilas (ca. 1322 to after 1391) was a strong supporter of hesychasm, for he was from Thessalonica where his uncle succeeded Gregory Palamas as bishop of the city and he himself wrote a tract in support of Palamas. However, in contrast with hesychasm, he developed a vision of a union with God that was open to everyone to supplement the traditional ascetic and monastic path.

There is much unknown about the life of Cabasilas, but from Thessalonica he went to Constantinople and entered imperial service, becoming a confidant and friend of the emperor John VI Cantacuzenus, who had given such strong support to hesychasm. However, this was a period in which the Ottomon Turks completed their conquest of Byzantine Asia Minor and crossed over into Europe, at Gallipoli, to continue their advance against an enfeebled Byzantine Empire. An understandable panic ran through Constantinople and in 1354 John VI was forced to abdicate, entering a monastery under the name Joasaph. Cabasilas, closely attached to John VI, withdrew from public life and turned to scholarship and religion. He, too, became a monk and was probably ordained a priest.

Cabasilas was one of the last great theological writers in the twilight of the Byzantine Empire. One of his most famous works is his *Commentary on the Divine Liturgy*, explaining the elaborate symbolism of the liturgy of the Eastern Church, and which is "the classic Orthodox work on this subject."[132] Cabasilas's other great religious book is *The Life in Christ*, an exposition of the mystical life that is open for all, not just monks and ascetics. For him, the life of the Christian is centered on the sacraments, especially the Eucharist, and it is especially through the Eucharist that humans become divinized.

Central for him was meditation on the Law of the Spirit, or the Law of Love, to which people can devote themselves anywhere:

> There is no toil involved in applying ourselves to this law [of the Spirit], neither is it necessary to suffer hardship or to spend money, nor is there dishonour or shame, nor shall we be worse off in any other respect. It makes it no less possible to exercise our skills and it places no obstacle in the way of any occupation. … One need not betake oneself to a remote spot, nor eat unaccustomed food, nor even dress differently, nor ruin one's health nor venture on any reckless act. It is possible for one who stays at home and loses none of his possessions constantly to be engaged in the law of the Spirit.[133]

The essential divine command to follow was to "pray without ceasing,"[134] which Cabasilas interpreted as a path to meditation which could also be achieved in ordinary life outside of a monastery:

> There is no need whatever of special formalities for prayers nor need those who call upon Him have any special places or a loud voice. There is no place in

which He is not present; it is impossible for Him not to be near us. For those who seek Him He is actually closer than their very heart.[135]

The ordinary person need not worry about the supernatural powers so often associated with the great monastic mystics of the past,

As for miraculous powers, no one who had understanding ever found out how to acquire them. More than that, those saints who did not have them neither desired them nor sought for them. If we have them we may not even rejoice in them. ... Not even if a man enjoys visions and obtains revelations and knows all mysteries, will we pay attention to him or admire him. While such occasionally accompany those who live in Christ, they neither constitute nor effect that life, so that if one look to them alone it will not further him in virtue.[136]

Cabasilas emphasized Christ's promise to his disciples not only to be present with them but also to abide with them, and this abiding meant union, becoming one spirit, with Christ. Those who wanted to be united to Christ "must therefore share with Him in His flesh, partake of deification, and share in His death and resurrection."[137] It is especially in the Eucharist that this happens, "For in it we obtain God himself and God is united with us in a most perfect union, for what attachment can be more complete than to become one spirit with God?"[138] Therefore one should not "unnecessarily abstain from the holy table and thus greatly weaken our souls on the pretext that we are not worthy of the Mysteries."[139] Baptism likewise provides "some experience of God," in which one receives the glory of God, "an immediate perception of God ... What fairer knowledge could there be, and purer from error, than to know God himself, when He Himself opens the eye of the soul and turns it to Himself."[140]

Thus Cabasilas centers mysticism in the sacraments and makes it not only attainable by all but also incumbent on all who would be true Christians. He held out a vision of light to those who would truly live in Christ:

What a sight – to see a countless multitude of luminaries above the clouds, an incomparable company of men exalted as a people of gods surrounding God! ... Christ descends from heaven like lightning to earth, while the earth hands back other suns to the Sun of righteousness, and all is filled with light.[141]

By the beginning of the fifteenth century, the frontiers of the Byzantine Empire were rapidly contracting as the Ottoman Turks swept into Europe. In 1453 the Ottoman Sultan Mehmet II "the Conqueror" drew up his massive cannons before Constantinople and swiftly breached the ancient walls of the city. Almost anticlimactically the city fell to him, signaling the end of the empire that had stood for more than 1100 years. To the far north, the princes of Moscow soon proclaimed themselves as the heir of Byzantium and Moscow as the "Third Rome."

THE RUSSIAN CHURCH

The Russian Church was a true daughter of the Byzantine Church. When Prince Vladimir of Kiev converted to Christianity, traditionally dated to 988, he gave his religious adherence to Constantinople, not Rome, and Greek missionaries were sent north to organize the church and to evangelize the people. By the mid-eleventh century the primate of that church was the metropolitan of Kiev, an appointee of the Patriarch of Constantinople, and the Greek influence was so pronounced that, by the time of the invasion of the Mongols of 1238–40 that ended the Kievan period of Russian history, seventeen of the twenty-three metropolitans of Kiev had been Greek.

Similarly, in the mid-eleventh century, Russian monasticism was founded on Greek models, especially when the rule for monks of the Constantinopolitan monastery of Studion became the standard for Russian monasteries. Symeon the New Theologian lived into the eleventh century, but, as has been seen,[142] the typical Byzantine monasticism of his time had lost the mystical element of the Eastern tradition and his mysticism had been rejected by the Studion monastery that shaped Russian monasticism. "The revival of mystic life in Constantinople of the tenth and eleventh centuries, thanks to Simeon the 'New Theologian', seems to have remained unnoticed in Kiev,"[143] and there is no evidence that Symeon's works were known in Russia before the fourteenth century. Russian monasticism continued the pattern of its Byzantine prototype, concentrating on perfecting the ascetical life of the monks to the virtual exclusion of mysticism. "If there were a mystical or even purely contemplative life somewhere in Kiev, it found no author to reveal it."[144]

The invasion of the Mongols and the establishment of their Khanate of the Golden Horde was disastrous for Russian cenobitic monasticism,[145] so closely associated with the cities that received the brunt of the Mongol attacks. The surviving monasteries suffered "the disappearance of the ideal of personal sanctity,"[146] which forced those determined to follow the tradition of the Desert Fathers to leave the monasteries for testing. "Russia did not have any 'desert' in the literal sense, but monks could still escape both men and civilization: the vast Northern *forest* thus became the 'desert' of the Russian monks."[147] Henceforth, the image of the Russian saint would be dominated by the solitary figure of the forest hermit facing hunger, the cold and the beasts, and the temptations of the devil in the wild, virgin forests of the North.

The most renowned of the early forest saints of Russia was Sergius of Radonezh (1314–92), born with the name Bartholomew to a noble family of Rostov, one of the three great Russian cities not under Mongol domination. However, about the time that Sergius was born, Rostov was falling under the control of the princes of Moscow and the family moved to Radonezh, about forty miles northwest of Moscow, to lands provided by their new Muscovite overlord. Sergius left no direct accounts of his mystical life but it can be inferred from the *vita* written twenty-five years after his death by one of his disciples.

Bartholomew was able to follow his dream of becoming a monk after his parents themselves retired to monastic communities. Along with his brother Stephen he set out to a desert place, following "the voice of God" deep into the forest, where nowhere around was "any village, nor house, nor people; neither was there road or pathway, but everywhere on all sides was forest and waste land."[148] The isolation was too much for Stephen, who departed for a monastery in Moscow, while Bartholomew stayed in the wilderness and was given a monk's tonsure, along with the name Sergius, by his spiritual guide. Sergius was left "alone to silence and the wilderness" where he lived an ascetic life in solitude and in secret meditation. Over time a dozen monks gathered around him and, when Sergius's spiritual director died, the monks insisted that he be their abbot. His humility led him to resist their demands but his obedience required him to obey the decision of the metropolitan of Moscow that he accept the abbotship. In only two days he was ordained subdeacon, deacon and priest and then became abbot of the small collection of hermits.

Sergius's reputation as a holy man continued to attract others seeking the ascetic life until, with the advice of Greeks from Constantinople and at the direction of the metropolitan of Moscow, he organized the monks into a monastery. Sergius was a kindly abbot, never turning away any desiring to become monks and offering hospitality to all visitors. As the number of monks rose, dissensions appeared, with grumbling against Sergius's asceticism and authority. The abbot simply walked away and took up residence at another monastery until his monks begged the metropolitan for Sergius's return.

The *vita* of Sergius indicates that all of the characteristics of a mystical life were abundant in the holy man. The *vita* opens with a portrayal of Sergius as one taught by God. Unlike his two brothers, the young Bartholomew had difficulty learning to read or write but he prayed to God that "he might receive knowledge from God and not from men."[149] He encountered a monk in the forest who gave him a piece of bread similar to the Sacrament and soon, without further instruction, he began reading with ease, whereupon the monk vanished. At his monastic tonsure "he partook of the Holy Sacrament and received grace and the gift of the Holy Spirit" and as a solitary hermit he practiced "secret meditations."[150] In one of the most famous scenes from his life, reminiscent of St. Francis and the birds,[151] Sergius's residence in the forest placed him in the midst of wild animals but the holy man was able to feed by hand a bear that would come to him (see plate 4), and at times he would give the bear the only bread that he had, "being unwilling to disappoint [the bear] of his food."[152]

Sergius was also a miracle-worker, finding a pool of rain water and turning it into a flowing spring for the monks, healing the sick and possessed, and even raising a boy from the dead. A demoniac was cured when he saw a great flame coming out of Sergius, an image that was continued when one of Sergius's disciples observed the abbot saying Mass. He saw "a flame pass along the altar, illuminating it and surrounding the holy table; as the saint was about to partake of the Blessed Sacrament the glorious flame coiled itself and entered the sacred chalice; and the saint thus received Communion."[153]

Sergius himself was granted wondrous visions, the first recorded for a Russian saint. In one, "A great radiance shone in the heavens, the night sky was illumined by its brilliance, exceeding the light of day," and he was shown "a multitude of beautiful birds, flying, not only on to the monastery, but all around," and a voice assured him that the number of his disciples would not decrease after his death.[154] On another occasion, while in prayer he was favored by a visit from the Virgin Mary and the apostles Peter and John, as "a dazzling radiance shone upon [Sergius], brighter than the sun." The Virgin again warranted the continued flourishing of his monastery after his death. As the vision ended, Sergius, "in ecstasy, stood in trembling awe and wonder" and he was in such ecstasy that his face glowed. "All night long the saint remained in meditation on this ineffable vision."[155] In addition, a monk once observed Sergius taking part in the saying of Mass with two other priests and saw "a fourth person serving at the altar … of a bright, shining appearance, and in dazzling apparel." Upon being pressed for an explanation, Sergius admitted that, "He whom you beheld was an angel of the Lord, and not only this time but every time I, unworthy as I am, serve with the messenger of the Lord."[156]

Sergius's fame in Russian history is not just as one of the first forest hermits, for he is intimately associated with the rise of the power of Moscow against the Mongols. In 1380 Prince Dimitri of Moscow was ready to take the field against the invading Mongols and sought the advice and blessing of Abbot Sergius. Despite his earlier opposition to the prospect of a bloody war, Sergius assured the prince that he would be victorious and, in a clairvoyant vision, he saw the Muscovite victory at the battle of Kulikovo. "Within an hour of the final defeat of the ungodly, the saint, who was a seer, announced to the brotherhood what had happened."[157] Sergius, the patron saint of Russia, left behind a powerful reputation for preserving Russia in times of crisis. He was repeatedly besought in times of troubles in Russian history, and "an icon representing the appearance of the Virgin to Saint Sergius always accompanied the Russian armies."[158] During the "Time of Troubles" (1605–13), the monastery of Holy Trinity-St. Sergius withstood a sixteenth-month siege by an invading Polish army and was credited with saving the country, reinforcing the popular feeling that the fate of St. Sergius and that of Russia were inextricably intertwined. Moreover, his ascetic tradition played an important role in the revival of monasticism in the fourteenth and fifteenth centuries as his disciples established almost thirty monasteries in Russia.

With Sergius of Radonezh the ascetic ideals of the Desert Fathers had been reestablished in Russia and monasticism prospered to such an extent that monasteries received donations of vast estates from the faithful, eager to gain celestial blessings. The Russian monks divided over the issue of whether to be "possessors" or "non-possessors" of estates, a conflict similar to that faced by the Western Franciscans in the thirteenth and fourteenth centuries.[159] In the middle of the storm stood "the first great Russian mystic,"[160] Nilus of Sora (Sorsky), a spiritual heir of Sergius who almost by his own efforts reconnected Russia with its monastic and ascetic origins in the Byzantine Church. There is no extant contemporary *vita* of Nilus (1433–1508) and thus whether he was of noble or peasant origins is unclear, but it is most likely that his family, the Maikovs, were of the highest nobility in Moscow. He professed as a monk at the Kirillo-Belozersky monastery at White Lake in the far northern forests, founded by Cyril, who passed on to Nilus the teachings of Sergius that he himself had learned in Moscow from Sergius's nephew.

Nilus left Russia to visit the monasteries of Greece and arrived at Mount Athos to discover the hesychastic teaching that had triumphed in Byzantium under Gregory

Palamas as well as the use of the Jesus Prayer that was integral to that spirituality. Nilus spent more than a decade learning hesychasm and reading the great ascetical and hesychastic works of the Greeks before returning to Cyril's monastery on White Lake. However, Nilus did not rejoin the cenobitic life but rather established a *skete* a few miles from the monastery. A *skete* was a middle way of monasticism between life in a cenobium and life as a hermit, that is, essentially a Greek laura,[161] with a few monks living near each other in individual cells and coming together only for church services.

For the benefit of those interested in following sketic life, "in our sterile times" when finding proper spiritual direction was almost impossible,[162] Nilus wrote his *Rule*, "the first Russian summary of the ascetic doctrine of the ancient Fathers."[163] There is nothing original to Nilus's *Rule*, for it is a pastiche of quotations, with commentary, from his spiritual mentors, including John Climacus, Symeon the New Theologian and Gregory of Sinai. In this treatise Nilus led his readers through the techniques of hesychastic prayer and the Jesus Prayer, with a tantalizing description of the mystical experience which they produced. He informed his readers of how, in this high state, this "awe and vision of prayer," the mind "dwells on things ineffable and knows not where it is," as the mind is "lifted above utterance." According to the Fathers, the mind "is in ecstasy," the "soul is drawn to what is divine, and through this ineffable union becomes like God, being illumined in its movements by the light from on high." During this prayer, suddenly "the soul is infused with joy, and this incomparable feast paralyzes the tongue. The heart overflows with sweetness, and while this delight endures a man is drawn unwittingly from all sensible things." The consciousness of this sweetness convinces the hesychast that "this indeed is the kingdom of heaven and can be nothing else."[164] Nilus was too steeped in the Greek traditions to provide any trace of his own experiences, but he could quote freely from his sources, particularly the graphic description of Symeon the New Theologian:

> Within my own being I gaze upon the Creator of the world, and I converse with Him and love Him and feed on Him, am nourished only by this vision of God, and I unite myself with Him. And I rise above heaven: this I know surely and for certain.[165]

Nilus's little treatise passed on the Fathers' praise for the life of solitude and silence:

> Retire from the sight of the world and cut off conversations; do not let friends enter your cell, even under the pretext of a well-meaning visit, unless they have the same spirit and intention as yourself and are likewise practising mystical prayer.[166]

Nilus also followed his sources in expressing the traditional paradox of the gifts of the Spirit. On the one hand the ascetic receives "secret visitations of God's mercy" and the humble ascetics "are elevated by an infusion of power from God, in the name of which they can do all things, even to the working of miracles."[167] On the other hand, "When we are conscious of the infusion of grace, we should not grow careless or become too easily elated," and he warned, "pay no attention whatever to the dreams and images which may present themselves, lest you be seduced."[168] Nilus also dedicated one of his eleven chapters to the gift of tears, one of the most important of the graces of the Holy Spirit. He quoted Pope Gregory I, who wrote that no matter what other gifts an ascetic might have received, if he "has not received the gift of tears, he should pray to obtain it either through the fear of judgment or through the love of the kingdom of heaven."[169] Nilus commented that the grace of God manifested itself, "kindling the heart and diffusing its glow throughout our being, comforting the soul, inflaming us with an ineffable love of God and men, delighting the mind and producing joy and interior sweetness – then tears flow freely and without our effort."[170]

By the time that Nilus returned to Russia, Abbot Cyril's policy of refusing to accept estates had been abandoned by the monastery, creating division and factionalism in the monastery. Nilus was dedicated to following the path of complete renunciation of wealth and joined the "Non-Possessors," prompting the abbot to bar his readmission to the monastery. The issue of the possession of monastic estates was finally settled at a church council in Moscow in 1503, where Nilus spoke for the Non-Possessors while the leader of the Possessors was Abbot Joseph of Volokolamsk. Abbot Joseph was not a lax monk but rather a severe ascetic who imposed the same discipline on his monks, ignoring the contemplative life. Just as in the case of the Franciscans, the victory went to the Possessors, the "Josephites," and Nilus returned to his *skete* for the remaining five years of his life.

Also similar to the aftermath of the Franciscan dispute over possessions, the Non-Possessors were persecuted in the Russian Church, not only for their opposition to monastic estates but also because they followed Nilus in opposing the penalty of burning at the stake for the sect of the Judaizers,[171] which left them open to the charge of laxity towards heresy. Nilus's opinion was sought on the matter and he stood against the use of coercive force against heretics, believing that "a monk should seek not to correct them, but to pray to God who alone can enlighten minds to see the truth."[172] A number of the supporters of Nilus, called the Transvolgans because they were concentrated in the northern forests beyond the Volga, were imprisoned or fled Russia to avoid captivity. Contemplative, mystical monasticism was in full retreat in the sixteenth century in the face of the dominant Josephite party, which was marked by its devotion to asceticism, missionary endeavors to convert the pagans that were falling under Moscow's expansionist rule and devotion to the rituals and liturgy of the church.

The Josephites enjoyed their triumph for a century and a half before church councils in 1666–7 approved the proposal of the tsar and the patriarch of Moscow to modernize corrupt spellings in the Russian liturgical texts and to bring certain rituals into conformity with Greek usages, such as making the sign of the cross with three fingers rather than two. The arch-conservative Josephites rejected the changes and brought schism to the church. The non-conforming conservatives, the "Old Believers," suffered a savage persecution while thousands burned themselves alive rather than submit.

At the same time, the landed estates of the monasteries which the Josephites had fought to retain were coming under state attack. One third of Russian territory belonged to the church and most of that to monasteries. Already in the latter sixteenth century, Tsar Ivan IV "the Terrible" (1533–84) forbade the endowing of monasteries with estates and limited the number of monks. The Westernization program of Peter I the Great (1682–1725) continued the restrictions on the role of the church in Russian life by discouraging monasticism and abolishing the patriarchate of Moscow and replacing it with the Holy Synod, composed of clerics whom he nominated. His plan to abolish the monasteries and to confiscate their estates was thwarted only by his death but the attack on monasticism continued under Catherine II the Great (1762–96), who closed over half of Russia's monasteries and secularized church lands.

In this atmosphere of secularization, Westernization, modernization and admiration for Rationalism, the Enlightenment and "Voltairism" among the Russian upper classes, it was still possible for genuine spirituality and an ascetical life to thrive among Russian monastics closely associated with the Crown. The bishop St. Tikhon of Zadonsk (1724–83) was one such monk. Born Timothy Sokolovsky, he was only a small child when his father, the sexton of a village in the diocese of Novgorod, died and the family was thrown into destitution. In spite of crushing poverty, Timothy's mother kept the family together and, with the financial backing of his older brother, he was able to attend school in Novgorod before seminary in the same city on a scholarship. His education was decidedly Western, for Novgorod was a member of the Hanseatic League and thus enjoyed close contact with the Baltic and North Sea cities of the West. Moreover, Russian seminaries were modeled on those of Kiev, which followed the Jesuit pattern of instruction and even conducted the classes in Latin. "For nearly 150 years all Russian bishops and priests were trained in the Latin language in the same manner as Catholic priests."[173] Timothy was obviously an extremely bright and promising student, remaining at the seminary to teach Greek and poetry after completing his studies.

He might have found a career in teaching but he felt that divine providence directed him to pursue the solitary life after an incident while he was visiting a monastery. He ascended the bell tower and, without testing the soundness of the railings, he leaned on them. They gave way but "an invisible hand seemed to push me back, so that I fell at the foot of the bell, half fainting."[174] His inclination to become a monk was then reinforced by a vision. His habit, even as a seminary teacher, was to spend the night in meditation. On one such occasion he went out of his room to his porch while meditating on eternal bliss. "Suddenly the skies opened and were filled with a glow and a dazzling light … This lasted but a moment, and then the skies regained their ordinary appearance." The effect of the vision led him "to conceive an ardent desire to lead a life of solitude."[175]

Timothy professed as a monk with the name of Tikhon in 1758 but he did not find a life of solitude. He was ordained deacon and then priest, was named to head the Zhelitkov and Otroch monasteries and became rector of the seminary at Tver. In 1761, only three years after his monastic profession, at the age of thirty-seven, he was appointed suffragan bishop of Novgorod. As bishop he now had sufficient income to support his sister, a widow who had been working scrubbing the floors of the wealthy.

Observing her brother's high state she wept in joy, remembering their childhood poverty and how often they had gone hungry. For the next two years Tikhon actually administered the prestigious diocese of Novgorod while the metropolitan was away in Moscow as a member of the Holy Synod. During the months around the coronation of Empress Catherine the Great, at which the higher clergy participated, Tikhon headed the affairs of the Holy Synod. The next year, in 1763, the empress herself picked Tikhon to be bishop of Voronezh, a sprawling diocese equidistant between Moscow and the Black Sea.

Tikhon's diocese was no plum appointment. It was unruly and dominated by the Don Cossacks, who distrusted him as a representative of Northern domination. He arrived in his capital to find the cathedral in ashes, a dilapidated episcopal residence, no seminary, poorly-trained and apathetic clergy, monks lacking in discipline and morality and a great number of hostile Old Believers. For more than four years Tikhon threw himself into repairing all of these problems and enjoyed a fair measure of success until his health began to fail. Still possessing the favor of the Holy Synod and Catherine II, he successfully petitioned to be allowed to retire to the solitude of a monastery.

Tikhon eventually settled in the nearby monastery of Zadonsk and at last found the solitude for which he had been longing. His manner of life was extremely simple, especially for a former bishop. He had no bed in his bare cell and wore only the simplest of clothing. "His thoughts constantly reached out towards solitude and life in the wilderness"[176] and he devoted his time to meditation. "When he was absorbed in meditation, particularly if this occurred in the morning, nobody dared go near his cell, not even his attendants,"[177] wrote one of those attendants, who also reported that Tikhon was given to visions and ecstasies in his meditations, as he heard the singing of angels and engaged in conversations with the Virgin Mary and the apostles Peter and Paul. Tikhon's meditation has a very Western feel to it, for in Jesuit fashion but unusual for a Russian, he meditated on the sufferings and Passion of Jesus. On one occasion he went "quite outside himself. Then he beheld Christ descending from Golgotha, having left that very cross, walking toward him, his tortured body covered with wounds and blood."[178]

In addition, he had the gift of clairvoyance, seeing in his meditation the great flood of St. Petersburg in 1777. Tikhon was also especially favored with tears. Another of his attendants remembered that "he rarely sang without tears. It may truly be said that he had a special gift of tears granted by God. Two springs ever flowed from his eyes."[179] At times during the saying of Mass he would weep and sob audibly even though many were in attendance.

The retired bishop did more than meditate, for he was sought out as a *staretz* (pl. *startzi*), a Slavonic word for "elder," one gifted with spiritual insight and especially qualified to serve as a spiritual director. He received many visitors and was frequently invited out of the monastery to people's homes. He often refused such invitations, saying "He who leaves his solitude, even though it be for a salutary deed, does not return home the same as he was before. … Solitude collects spiritual treasures, a journey disperses them."[180] And he also wrote prolifically, producing works that fill five volumes, making him "one of the very few Russian saints who left abundant writings which are regarded as standard works on moral and ascetico-mystical theology."[181]

Tikhon died in 1783 with a great reputation for sanctity. Pilgrims frequented his monastery and posthumous miracles were credited to his intervention. He was canonized a saint of the Russian Church in 1861 and Dostoevsky used him as a model for the character of Elder Zosima in *The Brothers Karamazov*, for he "found in the simple Russian saint his initial idea of perfection."[182]

As great as was the fame of Bishop Tikhon, the nineteenth-century Golden Age of Russian mysticism was not due to him but rather to a monk forced to go outside Russia because of the restrictions imposed on the Russian Church in the eighteenth century. Paisius Velichkovsky (1722–94) was born in the Ukrainian city of Poltava, some 200 miles southeast of Kiev, where his father was dean of the cathedral, and was given the baptismal name Peter. He was only four years old when his father died and his brother John succeeded their father as dean. Only eight years later John died and the position was reserved for Peter, then a common practice, and he was sent to school in Kiev. Although he had a prestigious position awaiting him at the cathedral, Peter's education brought him in contact with the ascetical works of the Church Fathers and he was determined to follow them in a life of severe monasticism.

Peter had several false starts initiating his monastic life before leaving Russian territory for the Romanian districts of Walachia and Moldavia, then under the nominal rule of the Turks. He eventually settled at the *skete* of the famed ascetic Onuphrius where he was instructed in the life of solitude and asceticism, which he mastered so proficiently that the twenty-four year old was called the young *staretz*. After three years he desired to study directly the source of the teachings of Onuphrius and he set out for Mount Athos, where he lived as a hermit for three years before he professed as a monk under the name of Paisius. His mastery of the ascetic life attracted so many pupils that he was repeatedly forced to find larger residences to accommodate their numbers and he even became the spiritual director of a retired patriarch of Constantinople. While on Athos Paisius continued to study the Fathers of the Church and discovered that the translations of many of their works into Slavonic, the common language of the Church among Slavic peoples, were often faulty. He learned Greek and set about making fresh translations for himself and his pupils, a task that occupied him for the rest of his life. Among the most important of the texts that he came across in his close contact with Athos was an anthology of the Fathers concerning the contemplative life, the *Philokalia* of two Greek monks on Athos, Macarios of Corinth (1731–1805) and Nicodemus of the Holy Mountain (1749–1809). Nicodemus described the *Philokalia* as a "treasury of watchfulness, the keeper of the mind, the mystical school of the prayer of the heart."[183] At the center of the spirituality of the compilation are selections on hesychastic prayer by such figures as Symeon the New Theologian, Gregory of Sinai and Gregory Palamas, as well as advocacy of the Jesus Prayer.

The great number of Paisius's followers, coupled with the outbreak of war between Russia and Turkey, led Paisius and sixty-four of his pupils to leave Athos and return to Romania, for the restrictions on monasticism under Catherine II made it impossible for him to establish a new community in Russia. The prince of the region gave Paisius the monastery of Neamets and another monastery also came under his authority. In a short time he had 500 monks under his direction. Paisius's rule was strict, marked by silence, daily confession of thoughts to one's superior and interior, hesychastic prayer and the Jesus Prayer. Hesychasm was new to Romania and came under attack, prompting Paisius to defend it in a treatise, *The Scroll.* In this work he cited many of the authorities in the *Philokalia* to establish that "this Divine Work of sacred mental prayer was the unceasing occupation of our God-bearing Fathers of antiquity, and in many desert places as well as in cenobitic monasteries it shone forth like the sun among monks."[184] This method, he wrote, leads up the mind "to the above-mentioned spiritual visions, revealing to it according to the degree of purification the unutterable Divine mysteries to which the mind cannot attain. And it is this that in truth is called true spiritual vision."[185] In his final chapter of the work, Paisius quoted Symeon the New Theologian on the effects on the mind of this method: "immediately it sees what it has never seen before; it sees air in the midst of its heart, and itself entirely bright and filled with discernment."[186] Paisius practiced this method and gained a reputation for his holiness. He was seen to be transformed by his attendant who happened on him:

> I looked at him and saw that his faced looked as if it were flaming, while usually it was white and pale. I repeated myself in a louder voice. The starets did not respond again. It became clear to me that the starets was engrossed in prayer, which explained why his face was aflame.[187]

In addition to his transfigured appearance, he was recorded as having been given dreams that accurately foretold future events.

Paisius's fame attracted a thousand monks, mostly Russian, to his Romanian houses, where they learned his asceticism and spirituality based on hesychasm and the Jesus Prayer. Within a few years of the death of Paisius in 1794, a new religious atmosphere settled over Russia. Tsar Alexander I (1801–25) favored monks and mysticism and relaxed the restrictions on monastic estates while his successors began to look upon the Church as a bulwark against revolutionary Western ideas. Over 300 new monasteries were founded in the nineteenth century and Paisius's disciples could now return to Russia and spread his teachings throughout Russian monastic life. They have been traced to over 100 monasteries in thirty-five dioceses of Russia[188] where they continued the propagation of hesychasm and the Jesus Prayer. Where hesychasm went, mysticism followed. It has been claimed that "all the Russian mystics after Paisius may be regarded as his disciples in one way or another."[189]

The second axis of Paisius's enduring influence on Russian mysticism was through his Slavonic translation of the *Philokalia.* The metropolitan of St. Petersburg-Novgorod learned of the translation and prevailed upon Paisius to send him a copy, which was published in 1793 under its Slavonic title *Dobrotolyubie,* a literal translation of *Philokalia,* "love of beauty."[190] The influence of Paisius's translations, and especially of the *Philokalia,* cannot be overestimated: "All the Russian contemplatives and mystics of the nineteenth and twentieth centuries were brought up either on the Paisius Slavonic *Dobrotolyubie* or on its Russian version."[191]

Nevertheless, "the most popular saint of the nineteenth century,"[192] St. Seraphim of Sarov (1759–1833), a younger contemporary of Paisius, was not one of those direct or indirect pupils although he shared the same devotion to hesychasm and the Jesus Prayer. Seraphim was already a monk before the publication of Paisius's translation of the *Philokalia* and thus was "spiritually formed before this, having read numerous other patristic books that taught the same spiritual doctrine."[193] He was born Prokhor Moshnin into a merchant family in Kursk, a city in the southern steppes some 300 miles southeast of Moscow. His father was a successful building contractor who was engaged in the building of the cathedral of the Mother of God in Kursk when he died, leaving the task to be completed by his widow. Prokhor resisted his mother's efforts to have him take up the life of a merchant and instead, when he was nineteen, he entered the monastery of Sarov, located in a wilderness 200 miles to the northeast of Kursk. During this time of restrictions on monasticism under Catherine II, permission from the Holy Synod was required before any monk could be professed, and Prokhor had to wait eight years before the approval was granted. He was professed under the name of Seraphim in 1786, by which time he had become well-read in the Scriptures and the writings of the church Fathers and was living a severely ascetical life. His reputation for learning and holiness led him to be ordained deacon in the same year of his tonsuring and the next year he was ordained a priest.

Seraphim desired to lead a life of solitude and gained permission to withdraw into the forest to a small hut a few miles from the monastery. Many other monks came to live near him but none could persist in the severity of life that he followed, including spending a thousand days and nights kneeling and praying on a large stone. Like St. Sergius, he also lived in harmony with the wild animals of the forest and also fed a bear by hand. However, in 1804 he was set upon by robbers but he refused to offer resistance and was very nearly beaten to death. In this dire state he was granted a four-hour visitation by the Virgin Mary, along with the apostles Peter and John, and she repeated a message that she had given him in a previous illness, "He is one of ours."[194] His attackers were later captured but Seraphim had them pardoned. After five months' convalescence Seraphim was able to return to his solitude, but as a consequence of his injuries he was severely stooped at the waist for the rest of his life. He was now determined to live in total silence, for he believed that "absolute silence is a cross upon which a man must crucify himself with all the passions and desires."[195] After three years his physical difficulties forced him to return to the monastery of Sarov, where he shut himself in his cell and maintained complete silence for another five years. His silent reclusion brought him visions of the celestial life:

> If you knew what sweetness awaits the souls of the just in heaven, you would be resolved to endure all the sorrows, persecutions and insults in this passing life with gratitude. ... I cannot tell you of the heavenly joy and sweetness which I experienced there.[196]

This phase of his life was brought to an end by another visitation of the Virgin Mary and Seraphim's public life as an elder, a *staretz*, began. He was given the spiritual direction of the nuns at the nearby Diveyevo convent and great crowds clamored to see him. His spiritual gifts were many, for he could read the thoughts of those who came to see him, even knowing their names and life stories before they spoke with him, he could discern the nature of his visitors' spiritual illnesses and what could cure them, he could heal physical illnesses and he had clairvoyant powers. Moreover, nuns and others observed him levitating, "walking through the air above ground."[197]

The young nobleman Nicholas Motovilov was among those whom he healed, whose association with the *staretz* produced a remarkable record of Seraphim's teaching as well as of his own transfiguration. Motovilov wrote the *Conversation*, a record of one particular meeting he had with Seraphim in the forest on a snowy day in 1831. The *staretz* read the thoughts of Motovilov, who had long been burdened with a great desire to know the aim of Christian life and had been unable to find a satisfactory answer from the clerics to whom he had posed the question. Seraphim told him plainly, "The true aim of our Christian life consists in the acquisition of the HOLY SPIRIT OF GOD." Laudable external acts such as fasts, vigils, almsgiving and prayer "are only the means for acquiring the Holy Spirit of God."[198] The monk then cited the many examples in Scripture of humans conversing with God, from Adam and Moses to the apostles in the New Testament, and he deplored the contemporary opinion that such events no longer occurred:

> This failure to understand has come about because we have departed from the simplicity of the original Christian knowledge. Under the pretext of education, we have reached such a darkness of ignorance that what the ancients understood so clearly seems to us almost inconceivable.[199]

Seraphim held out to Motovilov the same experience of the Holy Spirit as that of the apostles, assuring him "The word of God does not say in vain: *The Kingdom of God is within you.*"[200]

The *staretz* had told his inquirer that he should always ask himself, "Am I in the Spirit of God or not?," but Motovilov asked Fr. Seraphim how he could be certain that he was in the grace of the Holy Spirit. The monk gave his friend a demonstration. He took Motovilov by the shoulders and said, "We are both in the Spirit of God now," and he ordered the man to look at him. Motovilov saw lightning flashing from his eyes and exclaimed, "Your face has become brighter than the sun, and my eyes ache with pain."[201]

> After these words I glanced at his face and there came over me an even greater reverent awe. Imagine in the center of the sun, in the dazzling light of its midday rays, the face of a man talking to you. You see the movement of his lips and the changing expression of his eyes, you hear his voice, you feel someone holding your shoulder; yet you do not see his hands, you do not even see yourself or his figure, but only a blinding light spreading far around for several yards and

illuminating with its glaring sheen both the snow blanket which covered the forest glade and the snowflakes which besprinkled me and the great Elder.[202]

Along with the transfigured appearance of Fr. Seraphim, Motovilov was aware of sensations that accompanied the presence of the Holy Spirit – the fragrance of the Holy Spirit "beyond the sweetest earthly fragrance," along with extraordinary sweetness, joy and warmth even though the snow on them had not melted, for "the warmth is not in the air but in us."[203] Seraphim assured Motovilov that all this had happened because the "Kingdom of God is now within us … It fills the surrounding air with many fragrant odors, sweetens our senses with heavenly delight and floods our hearts with unutterable joy."[204] Moreover, the Holy Spirit would come to monk and layperson alike as the reward for faith, for, as God had said, "I am not a God far off, but a God near at hand."[205]

Seraphim left a letter containing prophecy of Russian history that assumed greater significance after 1917, for it was "about the fall and resurrection of Russia … a prophecy concerning those horrors and misfortunes which would befall Russia … about the pardon and salvation of Russia." One who read the prophecy could not remember exactly when the salvation and deliverance of Russia would come, but it would be "in any case, in the last years of the 20th century."[206]

An indication of the role that Fr. Seraphim played in the lives of those who came to him for spiritual counsel can be gathered from the life of the recluse Athanasia, born Anastasia Logacheva (1809–75), the daughter of peasants in the diocese of Nizhegorod, in the region of Gorky, east of Moscow. When she was very young her father was called up for military service and his wife accompanied him along with one of their daughters, but Anastasia was left behind with relatives. She grew up lonely, disliking the normal amusements of girls her own age but finding solace in her prayers and in church services. By the time she was twelve she began her life of solitude by digging a cave for herself where she would stay for a week or more fasting and praying.

The fame of Fr. Seraphim's ascetical life reached her and when she was seventeen she went to the elder. Having never seen her before, he knew her desire to live as a recluse and said, "What you are thinking about, what you desire, the Queen of Heaven blesses, but the time has not come yet."[207] A few years later she returned to Seraphim, who told her to go to Kiev to venerate the holy relics there. She complied and while on the pilgrimage she learned to read and write amazingly quickly. At age twenty-three she went again to Fr. Seraphim, who now blessed her intention to live a solitary life, telling her to settle where there was the fragrance of burning incense and giving her permission to wear chains for the mortification of the flesh.

Anastasia went back to the spot in the forest where she had first dug her cave, nine miles distant from her home village, where there was indeed the odor of burning incense, and she took up the solitary life. To avoid attention, she visited relatives in her village only at night, returning to her cave after only a few hours. In the forest she practiced her feats of asceticism. In the manner of Seraphim, she fasted for forty days while remaining unmoving on a rock, and she was seen standing on an anthill, covered with ants and mosquitoes, with blood pouring from her body. She also had to endure demonic temptations and torments of "visions and frightful spectacles,"[208] as she saw animals threatening to eat her, her cabin engulfed in flames, people coming to tear apart her poor building. However, also like Seraphim, she actually lived comfortably with the wild animals of the forest and even ordered bears away from her garden.

Despite her efforts to remain inconspicuous, her renown spread and great numbers of visitors came to her as an eldress for spiritual counsel and advice on how to pray. Others attempted to live with her in the forest but usually they found the life too severe. One man who was thinking of taking up the solitary life asked her about it. She answered, "It is just as difficult to live in solitude as it is to sit peacefully naked on an anthill,"[209] which ended his ambitions. During this time her intense prayer was observed by those around her, as tears would stream down her face and she would be so deeply absorbed in her prayers that she was oblivious to those around her. Later in her life, shining rays were seen radiating from her face as she prayed. Anastasia was also gifted with foreknowledge of events and would even have fresh berries waiting for guests intending to make surprise visits to her.

The number of women who wanted to join her compelled her to go to the authorities for permission to establish a women's community in the forest. Disastrously, the authorities not only refused her permission because "she is often not in her right mind"[210] but they also ordered her to leave her cells, which they then demolished. She was officially attached to the nearby Ardatov Protection Convent but she returned to her home village and dug another cell in which she placed a coffin so that she could, in the monastic tradition, contemplate death constantly. To avoid being disturbed, she announced to all that she was going on a pilgrimage and then closed her window, locked her door from the inside and stayed in the cell "as though in the desert."[211]

Anastasia went on a pilgrimage to Jerusalem and when she returned after nine months, again the authorities intervened, destroying her cell and ordering her to the Ardatov Convent, a hardship for a recluse accustomed to living alone. Her cellmate was a difficult novice who obstructed her prayers, leading Anastasia to pray for deliverance from the girl. An angry Archangel Michael appeared to her, fiery sword in hand, demanding, "Is this the way people pray to the God of love and peace?"[212] Anastasia repented and continued to enjoy the favor of heaven, and the Virgin Mary again appeared to her, "standing in the air in a prayerful stance, with Her arms outstretched."[213]

In 1863 Anastasia's fortunes changed again when she was named to be the superior of the newly established convent of St. Nicholas in the Siberian diocese of Tomsk with the bishop himself tonsuring her under her new name of Athanasia. She remained there for the remaining eleven years of her life, living simply and providing counsel for her nuns, who would leave her presence flying away "as on wings, so light it would be on the soul."[214] After her death in 1875, her grave became a pilgrimage site as many were healed of illnesses by drinking the earth from her grave mixed with water.

In the latter nineteenth century, the *Philokalia* became available in the Russian language, making it more accessible to the general population. The person most responsible for this wider dissemination of the patristic sources of mysticism was Bishop Theophan the Recluse (1815–94), perhaps the most scholarly and certainly the most cosmopolitan of the Russian mystics. Before becoming a monk he was known as George Govorev, the son of a priest in the province of Orel. From the beginning he was an apt pupil, distinguishing himself in clerical school and graduating from the seminary in Orel at the head of the class. In 1841 he professed as a monk with the name Theophan and in the same year he was named to head the Kiev Clerical School, followed by appointments to the leading seminaries and ecclesiastical academies in Russia. In 1857 Theophan was a member of a committee that traveled to the Holy Land, where he came into contact with various branches of the Orthodox Church as well as with Roman Catholic and Protestant missionaries from the West. During this time he learned French, Greek, Hebrew and Arabic and traveled to Italy and Germany.

In 1859 Theophan was named bishop of Tambov and four years later was transferred to the see of Vladimir. He was a great admirer of Tikhon of Zadonsk and imitated him in instituting reforms in his dioceses, believing that asceticism was not just for monastics but was for all Christians. While the nineteenth century was glorious for monasticism, it was not so in the complacent State church at large and Theophan's reforms were resented by many of those whose comfortable lives were being threatened. In 1866 his opponents attacked him when a female relative paid a visit to him in his episcopal residence. While she was waiting for him in his private quarters she apparently fainted on his bed. Rumors of impropriety were soon flying about and the exasperated bishop suddenly submitted his resignation and, like Tikhon of Zadonsk, retired to a monastery. Six years later Theophan earned his sobriquet of the Recluse by going into complete isolation. He had a private chapel in which he celebrated Mass daily and saw only his confessor and one monastic official.

In his life of reclusion Theophan carried on active correspondence and wrote five volumes of literature on the spiritual life. His most important work was *The Path to Salvation*, in which he affirmed that the goal of the Christian life is "a living unity with God"[215] and instructed his readers in the ascetic life that would lead to such union. One of the principal means to this end was ceaseless prayer, and "the easiest means for ascending to ceaseless prayer is the habit of doing the Jesus Prayer and rooting it in yourself."[216] Moreover, a consciousness of the presence of God was vital, "for He is near," and it could be achieved by "mental silence or being taken up to God. This may come and go, but it should be made a permanent state, for it is the goal."[217] Those who gain the indwelling of God "are God's mystics, and their state is the same as that of the Apostles," for they "hear a certain inner voice … they mystically learn His words from Him."[218] When one comes into contact with God, the soul becomes enraptured, although the nature of the rapture varies: "Many of the saints were in a state of unceasing exultation to God, and upon others the Spirit fell temporarily but often."[219] Remarkably for a writer on the spiritual life, Theophan provided a first-hand account of the coming of God into the soul, as a "spiritual flame" appeared in the heart: "When this little flame appears or when a continuous warmth is formed in heart, then the whirling of thoughts stops. … In this state prayer becomes more or less unceasing. The prayer of Jesus serves as an intermediary."[220]

While much of Theophan's fame rests on his translations of spiritual works into Russian, he was not devoted to making literal translations. To a friend who was translating Francis de Sales' *Introduction to the Devout Life*,[221] he advised, "There is no need to be a slave to the letter. You should translate in such a way that it comes forth as words of your own from your own heart,"[222] a method which he himself employed in translating the *Philokalia*, which has been described as "rather an adaptation than a translation."[223] Even in this essential text of modern Eastern monasticism, Theophan rearranged chapters and added new material. Theophan's fame pursued him even in retirement. He continued to receive honors and was even offered the metropolitanate of Kiev, but he could not be tempted out of his reclusion. Unlike so many mystics, Theophan enjoyed robust health for almost all of his life and died just short of his eightieth birthday in 1894.

The flowering of the seeds cast by the disciples of Paisius Velichkovsky produced the great nineteenth-century golden age of mysticism and no monastery of this period shone with as much splendor as Optina in the diocese of Kaluga, 100 miles southwest of Moscow. Optina's fame rests on its three great *startzi*, Leonid, Macarius and Ambrose, whose successive elderships covered the years 1829–91. Optina was a small and obscure monastery that had been closed briefly under Peter the Great and when it reopened it was limited to only seven monks. By the beginning of the nineteenth century it was still languishing and the bishop of Kaluga urged Moses, one of the hermits of the Roslavl forest in his diocese, to establish a *skete* at Optina. Moses knew many of the circle of Paisius Velichkovsky and he, among others, urged the first of the great elders to come to Optina so that the eldership system might be instituted there. The importance of these *startzi* in reinvigorating the spiritual life of the Russian Orthodox Church in nineteenth and twentieth centuries was proclaimed by the glorification (canonization as saints) of the Assembly of the Elders of Optina, including the three elders discussed here, in 1990 by the Russian Orthodox Church Abroad and 1996 by the Moscow Patriarchate.

Elder Leonid (1768–1841) was born Leo Nagolkin, the son of a merchant family in Karachev, in the province of Orlov. At first he worked in business and traveled extensively in Russia, gaining wide experience in human relations that would benefit him later as a spiritual director. However, at age twenty-one he abandoned the world for the monastery, going first to Optina, which was fortunate enough to possess a copy of Paisius's Slavonic translation of the *Philokalia*. But after two years he left for the monastery of White Bluff (Beloberezhsky), where he advanced rapidly. In 1801 he was professed a monk with the name Leonid and in three years he had been ordained deacon and priest and had been appointed abbot of the monastery. By this time he had also made a brief stay at the nearby Cholnsk monastery where he became a disciple of the renowned monk Elder Theodore of Svir, a disciple of Paisius who had been sent back to Russia when Tsar Alexander I relaxed the restrictions on monasticism. When Leonid became abbot of White Bluff, Theodore joined him. However, they both sought greater solitude and Leonid resigned his abbotship and set out with Theodore on a perambulating journey to several *sketes* and monasteries, often igniting controversy by instituting Paisian monasticism featuring the elder to whom the monks made a daily confession of all of their thoughts, seemingly bypassing the authority of the abbot.

After Theodore's death, Leonid finally accepted the invitation of Moses, now Abbot of Optina, to come to his *skete* (see plate 3) and immediately he was made the *staretz* of all of the monks there while also directing nuns at a number of convents. As an elder, Leonid made enemies among the monks for his new methods and complaints were lodged with the bishop concerning the great crowds of the laity who came to speak to the *staretz*. The bishop ordered Leonid to receive no more visitors but he then himself sent petitioners to the elder. Leonid chose to interpret the bishop's action as giving him freedom to receive all who came to him, being unwilling to receive some but not all. He defied arrest for his disobedience:

> So what? You can exile me to Siberia, you can build a bonfire, you can burn me at the stake, but I will still be the same Leonid. I don't beckon anyone, but when a person comes of his own accord I cannot chase him away.[224]

Finally the metropolitan of Kiev came to investigate matters and lifted the restrictions on Leonid.

"The inner life of Fr. Leonid was especially difficult to capture; ... it remained a mystery even for the closest observers and his most devout disciples,"[225] but the stories told about him provide a sufficient picture of his method to know that he was a thorough hesychast, "saturated with the reading of the patristic writings on monastic life."[226] He was a formidable confessor, for he was a big bear of a man, tall and bulky, and possessed extraordinary strength. In addition, he was a clairvoyant who displayed knowledge of the lives of people whom he had never before met, while possessing prophetic abilities and a knowledge of the sins forgotten or omitted by those under his direction. His disciples learned that "he read, as it were, the souls of each of them – that even their hidden thoughts could not be kept from his piercing gaze."[227] There was one gentleman who was coming to see the elder for the first time, having boasted that he would see right through the monk as soon as he laid his eyes on him. As the man approached, Leonid stated, "Eh, the blockhead is coming! He's come to look straight through sinful Leonid. But he, the rascal, hasn't been to confession and Holy Communion for seventeen years."[228] It was all true, and the man broke down in tears and repented. Father Leonid expected that those who sought his advice then follow his instructions before returning. He had another gentleman thrown out of his presence, explaining that the man had fallen into the passion of being addicted to tobacco: "I told him to stop using tobacco and gave him a commandment never to use it again and not to come to see me until he quits. But without fulfilling the first commandment, he came for another."[229]

There was also a touch of the Zen Master in Elder Leonid. He had little patience with monks who wanted to practice extreme asceticism while lacking the essential monastic quality of humility. One monk made repeated pleas for permission to wear chains. Finally Leonid went to the smith and told him that when that monk should come to him for chains, he should give him a good slap. Leonid then gave his permission to the monk, who promptly sought out the smith, who did as the elder had instructed him. When the monk burst into anger at being struck, Leonid asked, "How can you dare to wear chains when you are unable to endure a mere slap on the face?"[230]

Father Leonid also had healing powers, effective for both physical ailments and demonic possession. He disguised his power by anointing the ill with oil taken from a lamp that stood before an ikon of the Virgin Mary in his cell. Moreover he scandalized his disciples by anointing women with the sign of the cross "not only on the forehead, lips and cheeks, but sometimes also made the cross on their throat and breast."[231] One of his disciples asked him how he had gained his spiritual gifts. His response was simple, "Live as simply as possible; God will not abandon you."[232]

Great crowds came to seek words of direction and inspiration from Leonid. One of the monks remembered the scene:

> Almost the entire cell was filled with individuals from various walks of life: land-owners, merchants and simple folk. All were standing on their knees in fear and trembling, as if before a fearsome judge; and each one was waiting for his replies and instruction. I fell on my knees behind everyone else. The Elder was sitting on his bed and braiding a belt. This was his handiwork, braiding belts, and he gave them as a blessing to his visitors.[233]

Leonid was unselfish in his position as elder at Optina and shared his authority with the monk Macarius, who had been at the Ploschansk monastery under the direction of one of the disciples of Paisius Velichkovsky. After his *staretz* died, Macarius came to know Leonid during his brief stay there before moving on to Optina and in 1834 Macarius followed his new mentor to Optina. Leonid called on Macarius to assist him in his spiritual direction and had his correspondence sent out in both their names. In the last five years of his life, he permitted those under his direction also to seek guidance from Macarius, whom he regarded as a saint. Thus when Leonid died in October 1841 the Optina eldership passed smoothly to Macarius.

When Macarius (1788–1860) arrived at Optina, he was already a seasoned and respected monk. His name in the world had been Michael Ivanov, a son of a devout noble family in the district of Orel. His mother died when he was eight and he and his brothers and sister went to live with relatives. By age fourteen Michael was employed as a bookkeeper in the District Treasury of Lgov and then as head of the Treasury Department at Kursk. Michael inherited the family estate when he was only eighteen but he was a failure as an estate manager, for he would not punish the peasants when they misbehaved but instead applied reason and quotations from the Scriptures to correct them.

His heart was not in being a prosperous landowner but rather in being a monk. In 1810 he visited the Ploschansk monastery and never returned, abandoning the estate to his brothers. Michael was immediately embraced by the monastery. He was quickly enrolled as a novice, given his initial tonsure with the name Melchizidek and put to work as the monastery's secretary. Five years later he was given his second tonsure and named Macarius, followed by ordination as deacon and priest. He rose to the position of dean of Ploschansk and confessor to the monks and even served as treasurer and steward of the Holy Synod in St. Petersburg.

However, Macarius felt "bogged down by committees"[234] and yearned to pursue in earnest the Paisian spirituality that he had been following since 1815. In that year Elder Athanasius, a disciple of Paisius, arrived at Ploschansk and Macarius became his devoted disciple and assistant. Athanasius possessed copies of Paisius's Slavonic translations of the writings of the great Church Fathers and his translations of patristic sources, which permitted Macarius, just like Leonid, to become "saturated" with the writings of the Fathers whose works were the basis of the *Philokalia*. The close association of Macarius and Athanasius continued until the death of the latter in 1825, leaving Macarius adrift. In 1828 Elder Leonid arrived at Ploschansk, providing Macarius with a new spiritual director of far greater discernment and ability than Athanasius. Leonid left for Optina within a few months but Macarius maintained contact with his new elder by correspondence until, in 1834, twenty-three years after his entry into Ploschansk, he transferred to Fr. Leonid's *skete* at Optina. At once Leonid associated him in the eldership and Abbot Moses appointed him confessor of the monastery and superior of the *skete*.

For the next seven years Macarius collaborated with Leonid in the eldership of Optina while also learning more deeply of hesychasm and the Jesus Prayer. When Leonid died in 1841 Macarius continued Leonid's style of eldership, including daily confession of thoughts, and he exhibited the same spiritual gifts as his mentor. His clairvoyance made him an intimidating confessor, as did his piercing eyes that seemed to look right into one's heart. He was gifted with the power to heal physical and emotional illnesses and he also anointed with oil as a physical sign of the healing. At times he was seen falling into ecstasy and, as was so common among Russian mystics, his face "shone with an unearthly beauty" and "was white and bright like an angel of God."[235]

As a spiritual director, Macarius had the monks occupy themselves with the reading of the Fathers of the church, noting that "monks nowadays neglect reading the Fathers. That is why they are so weak."[236] His lasting contribution to Russian spiritual life was making the writings of the Fathers more accessible to monastics and the laity alike. In 1845 he published a life of Paisius, whose success led to his editing the writings of Paisius for publication in 1847. By the time of his death in 1860, the elder had supervised the publication of sixteen volumes of Paisius's translations of Church Fathers as well as the writings of Russian spiritual guides. To make the volumes available for the spiritual education of Russia's future ecclesiastical leaders, Optina sent copies of the editions to all of Russia's bishops, monasteries, seminaries and academies as well as to many of the monasteries on Mount Athos. Macarius wrote of his joy in the publications, for those marvelous patristic writings "will not be given over to final oblivion, and zealots may the more easily acquire them."[237]

Father Macarius had other interests as well. He was very fond of nature and especially of flowers. Upon his arrival at the *skete* he put in a small flower garden under the window of his cell. His zeal found imitators and in time there were flower gardens under the windows of every cell in the *skete* and all the paths of the *skete*'s garden were lined with flowers. Macarius also loved animals and was especially concerned that the birds should have enough food in winter. Thus he would put out seed on the shelf of his window making sure that the jays did not take the entire amount.

Just as Leonid's disciple and assistant Macarius succeeded to the Optina eldership, it was Macarius's disciple and assistant Ambrose who succeeded to that position. Upon his arrival at Optina in 1839, Ambrose caught the attention of Fr. Leonid, who handed him over directly to Macarius saying, "He will be of help to you."[238] Ambrose (1812–91) was born Alexander Grenkov, son of a poor village sexton in the province of Tambov. His family lived with his paternal grandfather, who was the priest and chancellor of the village, and Alexander was taught to read and write Slavonic before he entered the Tambov Church School. He was a very bright student, graduating first of 148 students, and he went on to the Tambov Theological Seminary.

Alexander was not thinking of a monastic life, although others seemed to believe that it was in his destiny, until he fell seriously ill and there seemed to be no hope for his life. He made a promise to God that he would enter a monastery if he were cured. After a surprising recovery he delayed fulfilling his vow out of concern that he was not mature enough to become a monk. However, he organized his life so that he would be free to make such a move when he thought the time was right. After he finished his education, he tutored the children of a prosperous landowner and then taught at a theological school. His destiny seemed to catch up with him when, as was his custom, he was walking in the nearby woods and came to a waterfall. In the gurgling of the water he began to hear quite distinct words, "Praise God, hold on to God!"[239] Still uneasy about taking such a step without more specific guidance, he went to a holy recluse, who told him, "Go to Optina … you are needed in Optina!"[240]

Alexander's decision appears to have been determined by an overwhelming experience, which he recorded and kept with him at Optina. He wrote that he was enjoying a walk in the forest when he "went deeply into the spiritual apprehension of the Creator." The reality in which he had been seemed to disappear and he found himself in another world where all around him was bright, transcendent light. "The whole of the heavenly firmament has transformed itself before me into one general bright light. … I also am white and bright as they are. … I am all peace and rapture." Around him he found "nothing else in the world except for the white, bright light and these equally radiant numberless beings. … Amidst them I feel myself incredibly peaceful." Alexander and the other beings there found that "all of our questions are solved with one glance, which sees everything and everyone." Despite their moving in different directions, "one peace reigns in all the images of entities. One light is endless for all. Oneness of light is comprehensible to all." Ambrose found the experience to be enrapturing in an eternal rest: "I was at peace and joyful and desired nothing better for myself." This was a timelessness that "lasted without end, without measure, without expectation, without sleep." He no longer remembered life before this experience: "I only felt that the present life is *mine*, and that *I* was not a stranger in it." However, suddenly the experience ended and he was back in the forest lamenting the loss of that rapture. He was now certain that the soul is distinct from the body and that the spiritual world is indeed special, but he still did not know the meaning of life. "And in order to penetrate into this mystery, I left this world into which I was born and embraced the monastic life."[241]

His decision came to him suddenly and he immediately left for Optina without bothering to inform his school superiors. Alexander became a monk under the name Ambrose and subsequently was ordained deacon and priest. As has been seen, he caught the attention of Elder Leonid, who predicted that he would be a great man and handed him over to Macarius. He became the cell attendant to Macarius, assisting him in his heavy correspondence and participating in the publication of the patristic writings. Macarius began to associate Ambrose with him in his eldership duties, giving his blessing to monks who wished to speak to the younger monk. One of the monks remembered Ambrose during that period, living "in complete silence. I went to him nearly every day to reveal my thoughts, and I always found him reading patristic texts. … It seemed to me that Elder Ambrose always walked in the presence of God."[242] Large numbers came to speak to Ambrose, prompting Macarius to joke, "Look at that! Ambrose is stealing my bread and butter."[243]

Like Leonid and Macarius, Ambrose achieved great fame as a spiritual director, drawing large crowds from all classes of Russian society. They sought spiritual advice to be sure, but suppliants also asked for direction on agricultural or trading matters, what kind of irrigation system to install in an orchard, or even what kind of shower to build in a home. Ambrose continued the eldership tradition of Leonid and Macarius and loved to quote the words of his mentors or those of the Church Fathers. He was assisted in his eldership by the same spiritual gifts enjoyed by his predecessors. Others were impressed by "his characteristic clairvoyance"[244] and ability to know the future and he had a special gift of discernment, allowing him to know the spiritual condition of those who came to him, including sins they were avoiding or forgetting to confess. He also disguised his healing powers so as not to draw attention to himself. One monk was suffering a severe toothache and Ambrose hit him in the teeth, presumably not too strongly, and the pain went away. However, this technique was noticed and those with headaches would cry out, "Batiushka [Father] Abrosim, hit me; my head hurts."[245]

Also like Leonid and Macarius, "during prayer he was immersed in contemplation of unspeakable heavenly glory, and his entire face was transfigured. … It was somehow especially illuminated, and everything in his cell had taken on a solemn appearance."[246] On one occasion his secretary came to him and was amazed to find Ambrose glowing. After the blessing, the glow ebbed and the monk asked, "'Batiushka, have you seen some kind of vision?!' The Elder did not answer a word and tapped him lightly on the head. This was a sign of the Elder's special favor."[247]

The last years of Ambrose were cloaked in controversy and, in the eyes of those hostile to him, scandal. Like Leonid and Macarius, Ambrose directed a number of convents, including the new foundation of Shamordino a short distance from Optina. Ambrose began spending his summers there in 1888 to assist in the direction of the workmen who were putting up the new buildings of the convent, but as he prepared to leave in July of 1890, the monk, now living in his seventy-eighth year, fell so ill that he was unable to return to his monastery. He lived out the last two years of his life in the company of the nuns while continuing to see streams of monks coming over from

Optina to make their daily confession of thought to him. Reports that Ambrose had abandoned his monastery to live with the women reached the bishop, who threatened, "I myself will go to Shamordino, seat the Elder on the coach, and take him to Optina!"[248] However, Ambrose never regained his health and died at the convent in October 1891. The nuns fought to inter the holy man at their convent while the monks of Optina were equally determined to possess the body of their elder. The Holy Synod was forced to intervene and by its order Ambrose was buried alongside Leonid and Macarius in Optina.

Russian mysticism is overwhelmingly monastic but the spiritual classic *The Way of a Pilgrim*, whose Russian title is *Sincere Tales of a Pilgrim to His Spiritual Father*, provides precious insight into the awareness of hesychasm and the Jesus Prayer among the Russian laity of the last half of the nineteenth century. It presents the account of the spiritual and physical journey of its unidentified author as he traveled around Russia. The odyssey began when he heard a reading of the Apostle Paul's advice, "pray constantly" (1 Thessalonians 5.17) and he became determined to discover how one could possibly fulfill such a command. Desiring an explanation, he searched for famous preachers who could tell him how this could be done.

One of the principal themes of the book is the failure of almost everyone he asked to provide an adequate answer to his question. One preacher gave a sermon on spiritual prayer but failed to discuss a method to achieve it. A devout gentleman in a village asserted that "ceaseless interior prayer is a continual yearning of the human heart toward God. ... Pray more, and pray more fervently. It is prayer itself which will reveal to you how it can be achieved unceasingly." When pressed on the method itself, the man could only say, "it is very difficult."[249] A pompous government official opined that interior prayer was "the mysterious sighing of creation, the innate aspiration of every soul toward God, ... it is innate in every one of us." As to the method of achieving it, he could only say, "I don't know whether there is anything on the subject in theological books."[250]

The pilgrim was put on the right course when he found a *staretz* in a monastery who was unsurprised that he had not found a ready answer to his question. The monk stated that most of those who write on the subject base their thoughts on "speculation and the working of natural wisdom, and not upon active experience" and apply "the human standard to the divine," incorrectly taking "the fruits and the results of prayer for the means of attaining it." What is required is "mystical knowledge, not simply the learning of the schools," for it can be gained "neither by the wisdom of this world, nor by the mere outward desire for knowledge," but rather "it is found in poverty of spirit and in active experience in simplicity of heart."[251] The monk explained that prayer without ceasing was "the constant uninterrupted calling upon the divine name of Jesus with the lips, in the spirit, in the heart," that is, the Jesus Prayer. The *staretz* introduced the pilgrim to the *Philokalia*, which contained full information on the "science of constant prayer, ... It contains clear explanations of what the Bible holds in secret and which cannot be easily grasped by our shortsighted understanding."[252] The monk instructed the pilgrim to repeat the Jesus Prayer, "Lord Jesus Christ, have mercy on me," three thousand times each day, and then six thousand times each day, and finally twelve thousand times each day. To his amazement, the pilgrim found that he did it easily and he spent the summer repeating the Jesus Prayer ceaselessly.

At the end of the summer the *staretz* died and the pilgrim resumed his wanderings. He soon purchased a copy of the *Philokalia* and throughout the remainder of *The Way of a Pilgrim* two themes dominate, the pilgrim's teaching of the Jesus Prayer and his recommendation of the *Philokalia* to all with whom he came in contact. The pilgrim was confirmed in this by a dream in which his deceased *staretz* appeared and quoted the *Philokalia*: "we are bound to reveal [the Jesus Prayer] and teach it to others, to everyone in general, religious and secular, learned and simple, men, women, and children, and to inspire them all with zeal for prayer without ceasing."[253] The pilgrim discovered that the Prayer bore fruit in three ways. In spirit were "the sweetness of the love of God, inward peace, gladness of mind, purity of thought, and the sweet remembrance of God." In feelings were "pleasant warmth of the heart, fullness of delight in all one's limbs, the joyous 'bubbling' in the heart, lightness and courage, the joy of living, power not to feel sickness and sorrow." The third way, revelations, produced "light given to the mind, understanding of holy Scripture, knowledge of the speech of created things ... certainty of the nearness of God and of His love for us."[254]

The phenomenon the pilgrim reported most frequently was a warmth, delightful and gracious, that spread throughout his chest. Moreover, "sometimes I felt as light as though I had no body and were floating happily through the air instead of walking."[255] Interior prayer is available to all, the pilgrim argued, and the one who practices it "feels at once the inward light, everything becomes understandable to him, he even catches sight of this light of some of the mysteries of the kingdom of God." The obstacle, he felt, is that "we live far from ourselves and have but little wish to get any nearer to ourselves. Indeed we are running away all the time to avoid coming face to face with our real selves, and we barter the truth for trifles."[256]

He also found that everything around him was transformed, all of nature "seemed delightful and marvelous. The trees, the grass, the birds, the earth, the air, the light ... proved the love of God for man, that all things prayed to God and sang his praise." Connected to this harmony of God and of all nature and reminiscent of the ability of the forest hermits to live peacefully and closely with wild beasts was the pilgrim's gaining of "the knowledge of the speech of all creatures ... the means by which converse could be held with God's creatures."[257] He came to look upon all creatures, people, trees, plants, animals, as his own kin, and he found that on his travels "everybody was kind to me; it was as though everyone loved me."[258] However, at the same time the pilgrim felt a great need for solitude for his prayers and for reading the *Philokalia*. When reprimanded for his need to withdraw, the pilgrim retorted, "Everyone has his own gift from God. ... Everyone does what he can, as he sees his own path, with the thought that God Himself shows him the way of his salvation."[259]

The pilgrim found the *Philokalia* to be "a secret treasury of the hidden judgments of God" and "a key to the mysteries of holy Scripture," and through it he found kindled in his heart a "desire for union with God by means of interior prayer."[260] Most of those to whom he recommended the *Philokalia* felt that, however marvelous it was, it was not for ordinary laypeople. However, another postmortem dream-appearance of the pilgrim's *staretz* taught him that only theologians should read the chapters of the *Philokalia* in order. "Simple folk" should read specific chapters of certain writers in a specified sequence. The pilgrim read those chapters in the proper order to a blind fellow-pilgrim and within five days the man began to feel warmth, began to see light, and "sometimes, when he made the entrance into his heart, it seemed to him as though a flame as of a lighted candle, blazed up strongly and happily in his heart, and rushing outward through his throat flooded him with light."[261] The blind man even became a clairvoyant, seeing details of a fire in a village many miles distant.

Thus *The Way of a Pilgrim* is charmingly written advocacy for the Jesus Prayer, the *Philokalia*, and mysticism for all, not just for monastics. It can be read simply as a piece of spiritual literature, but at Optina it was believed that the author was indeed an actual wandering pilgrim. Elder Ambrose reported that he heard from Fr. Macarius that "there came to him a layman who had attained such a level of spiritual prayer that Fr. Makary [Macarius] did not know what to do when the layman told him the various conditions of prayer of the heart." All he could think to say to the man was "'keep your humility.' And afterwards he spoke with amazement about this." After Ambrose read the manuscript of *The Way of a Pilgrim*, he stated, "I now think it was perhaps that layman."[262] He approved of the text, "In it there is nothing wrong. The pilgrim lived as a pilgrim and lived the life of a wanderer, not tied down by any cares or duties, freely exerting himself in prayer as he desired."[263]

The Way of a Pilgrim was published in 1884, just a few months after a story appeared in the St. Petersburg newspaper *Novoye Vremia* (*New Time*), carrying testimonials of people cured by a priest of the cathedral of Kronstadt, Father John Sergiev (1829–1908), who thereby became a national celebrity. The sick and possessed all over Russia came to him for healing and he was even summoned to the Crimea to attend to the dying tsar Alexander III. When Father John of Kronstadt died in 1908, 60,000 people attended his funeral, which was conducted by the metropolitan of the capital. The funeral cortege was routed to pass in front of the Winter Palace in St. Petersburg, where the imperial family appeared on the balcony to honor the nationally revered cleric. In 1964 and 1990 the Russian Orthodox Church (first by the church abroad and subsequently by the Moscow patriarchate) proclaimed him a saint, a rare designation for a married parish priest.

This renown was eloquent homage to the life of a man who performed miracles – "a sea, an ocean of miracles!"[264] – and unexpected for the son of a poor village cleric in the Arctic province of Archangel. Father John's emphasis as a priest was on prayer, "it is absolutely necessary to pray in order to support the life of the soul," he wrote in his most famous work, *My Life in Christ*,[265] and from childhood he discovered the dramatic power of prayer. His parents worked to educate him but by the time he went to parochial school in Archangel at the age of ten, he still had great trouble in reading and writing and ranked last in his school. Alone and without help, he fell on his knees and began to pray intensely for understanding. "I remember how, suddenly, it was as if a veil were lifted from my mind, and I began to comprehend studies well."[266] John went on to finish school at the top of his class and was given a full scholarship to the St. Petersburg Theological Academy, which he completed in 1855. For a time he hoped to become a missionary but he realized that there were many Christians in Russia in desperate need of a priest. He accepted a position as assistant priest in the cathedral of Kronstadt after he agreed to marry Elizabeth, the daughter of the retiring archpriest of the cathedral. She was startled to be told by her new husband that he intended to remain in a state of virginity and that they should live together chastely, but she eventually accepted the arrangement and came to call him "Brother John."

Fr. John found that Kronstadt was perfect for displaying Christian charity. It was most important as a naval fortress protecting the approach to St. Petersburg but it was also a site to which the government banished beggars and criminals. They lived with their families in appalling poverty, misery and widespread alcoholism and were often hostile to religion. John began drawing the families to church by concentrating first on the children, which led to invitations into their homes where he treated the families with kindness and love. He would even give away the shoes on his feet to those in need. However, he also dreamed of providing more than handouts to the needy by putting those willing to work into productive jobs. After years of fundraising efforts, he founded the House of Industry in Kronstadt with workshops producing bags and hats, in which over 7000 workers were employed. The Home also had dormitories, refectories, libraries and an orphanage, while providing free elementary education for children and free medical care, along with newspapers, Sunday Schools and lecture series.

John's wider fame, however, resulted from his healing work. From the beginning of his priesthood he was asked to pray for the recovery of the ill but he resisted, believing that "Nowadays only a few miracles are performed by God's saints, nor is it necessary for us, in our times, to perform miracles!"[267] Constant requests by his parishioners wore down his resistance and he began praying with his characteristic intensity: "I began to appeal to God to heal the sick and debilitated of soul and body. The Lord heard my prayers, though unworthy, and answered them: the sick and infirm were healed. This encouraged and strengthened me."[268]

John's work, *My Life in Christ*, is in large part a manual on prayer in which he instructed his readers that prayer is a form of union with God, "the uplifting of the mind and heart to God, the contemplation of God … by cleaving to God during prayer, I become one spirit with him, and unite with myself by faith and love, those for whom I pray."[269] In prayer, this union with God, one becomes "one spirit with him."[270] In prayer, there is great intimacy with God, who "often and sensibly touches my invisible soul … the chief thing in prayer is the nearness of the heart to God, as proved by the sweetness of God's presence in the soul."[271] There are other sensations that come from this prayerful union with God, apart from sweetness, as "our soul immediately becomes vivified, warm, and fruitful. What sudden tranquillity, what lightness, what emotion, what inward holy fire, … what an abundant stream of living water is diffused in the heart."[272] Sometimes the feeling was like that of electricity as "the Spirit of God suddenly visits the chamber of our soul, the body, and the light shines in it."[273] This union with God in prayer is the essential concern of Christianity, for "the object of our life is union with God."[274] Thus Father John taught that one should pray constantly, advising "Learn to pray, force yourself to pray."[275] When this is done, God cannot refuse to grant prayers: "ask of Jesus Christ in the Holy Spirit whatever you desire, and you will obtain it. ... We may therefore ask God for everything, trustfully, in the name of Jesus Christ, every blessing or gift we can think of." However, there were limits to prayer, for God, the creator of nature, also had respect for nature and "usually accomplishes his will through nature and her laws ... Therefore do not request miracles of him without extreme necessity."[276]

At the heart of John's spirituality were the Eucharist and the other sacraments of the church. In contrast with the contemporary custom of taking Communion only once a year, he insisted on frequent Communion for all who came to him and thus "set in motion the Eucharistic and liturgical revival in the Russian Church."[277] Of course it was necessary first to confess before receiving the Eucharist and the great crowds who sought him out drove him to the radical expedient of mass, public confession of sins, sometimes with several thousands participating at the same time, an innovation in the Russian Church that did not survive him.

While John was not himself a frequent recipient of visions, he did possess gifts of the Holy Spirit. As with the monastic mystics, his face was transfigured when he prayed. He was a renowned clairvoyant who could address strangers by their names and he knew the thoughts of those who came to him. In addition, there were many reports of his appearing in distant places to those who had written to him for his prayers, either before their eyes or in their dreams. However, great mobs of people sought out Father John in person wherever he went, sometimes leading to miracles on the run. One man had to run up to John's moving carriage, crying out "Father, pray for me, I am a stammerer!" As the carriage rolled, the priest struck him on the cheek and repeated, "Speak clearly, speak clearly," and the cure was effected.[278] Father John's celebrity had its price. "Father John himself was regularly knocked down, pulled in all directions, and even bitten by devotees who wished to have his 'living' relics."[279] Moreover, to his horror, one group of his admirers, named the "Ioannites" ("Johnites") by their opponents in the hierarchy of the Russian Orthodox Church, awaited the fast approaching end of the world and proclaimed Father John to be the incarnation of Jesus Christ. Undeterred by his death in 1908, they then expected his imminent return.

Among those who sought out Father John was Thaisia, the abbess of the convent of Leushino. In 1891 she discovered that the famous priest was in the same town as she and forced herself through the crowd surrounding him, insisting that he come to her convent so that her nuns could meet him. Fr. John complied and he became quite attached to the convent as well as to Abbess Thaisia, making it his practice to visit Leushino every summer. The abbess was able to witness John's intense prayer, observing that during his secret prayer, "it seemed that he would see God before his eyes and converse with Him as with someone close to him. It seemed that he was asking questions of God and receiving communications from Him."[280] She also was the recipient of his ability to receive divine revelations. She had confided to John her concern over her mother's post-mortem state. He then sat motionless, staring off into the distance for a quarter of an hour, whereupon he announced, "She obtained God's mercy." The abbess was surprised, saying "you speak as though you received a revelation from above." He replied, "How else? Don't you know that one cannot speak without a revelation? One can't joke about it."[281] For the last sixteen years of John's life, Abbess Thaisia enjoyed his full support and inspiration.

Abbess Thaisia (1840–1915) became the most famous nun of Russia at the turn of the twentieth century, for she was "the most profound woman mystic in Russia."[282] She was renowned because of her writings, especially her remarkable *Autobiography*, the manuscript of which John of Kronstadt read and approved, "Wonderful, most divine! Print it for the general edification!"[283] In addition, her *Letters to a Beginning Nun* was distributed by the Holy Synod to all Russian monasteries, making it "a main guidebook for female monastic aspirants."[284] Like so many nuns of the Western Middle Ages, she wrote her autobiography at the urging of her male spiritual advisors so that all could benefit from the "spiritual phenomena and visions"[285] given to her by God.

Thaisia was the daughter of nobles in the province of Novgorod, being named Maria as the answer to prayers to the Virgin Mary after two previous children had died shortly after birth. Her social class ensured that she would receive a good education and at the age of ten she was enrolled in the Pavlovsky Institute for Young Noble Women in St. Petersburg. She must have impressed her fellow students with her religious nature for the kinder of her nicknames at school were "Nun" and "Abbess." The first experiences with the divine recorded in her memoirs came to her at the age of twelve when she awoke on the night before Easter and heard the rustling of wings as "a sunlit, winged being, flying beneath the ceiling" repeated "Christ is risen! Christ is risen!" The effect of the vision on her was transformative, giving her a sweet feeling in her soul that never left. "It was as if that feeling was a beginning of something new, something mysterious, which was unclear to me at that time."[286] Later that year she had an even more striking vision in a dream, as were most of her visions. She saw herself kneeling in a meadow praying when she began rising higher and higher until she was in heaven. Matthew the Evangelist came to her and, knowing that she wanted to see Jesus, told her, "The Lord is here, all around us. He is always with us and at your side!" Then, in a state of rapture, she saw Jesus, who touched the crown of her head and said, "It is not yet time!" When she awoke: "My head still seemed to feel the divine touch … My pillow and chest were wet with tears that I must have shed during the vision."[287] She confided the vision to her priest, who told her, "That is your calling. Keep your secret, and the Lord Himself will complete His work."[288] Maria felt that her decision to become a nun had already been made and she began living a more withdrawn life, avoiding dances, and preferring to fast, pray and read spiritual literature.

Many years were to pass before she was able to enter a convent. Her mother was deeply attached to her and adamantly withheld her permission for Maria to become a nun. After her graduation from the Institute, Maria tutored children in the city of Borovichi, also in the province of Novgorod, attended church frequently and sought spiritual advice from priests in a nearby monastery. Finally, in 1864, she was permitted to enter monastic life when her mother received a vision in which the Virgin Mary scolded her for her refusal to allow her daughter to enter a convent. Maria entered her novitiate at the Convent of the Entry of the Mother of God into the Temple at

Tikhvin in the province of Novgorod. The noble nun had difficulty with the physical labor required of novices but continuing dream visions of Christ and of the Virgin Mary comforted her with assurances of favor, which stiffened her resolve to remain in the house. Moreover, she had realized the depth of prayer possible for nuns when she happened upon one of the sisters praying in her cell. Oblivious to her surroundings, the nun was on her knees with arms uplifted, moving her lips and weeping streams of tears for more than an hour.

Maria's autobiography records her struggle with the other sisters in the convent, portraying herself as the innocent victim of lies and calumnies. However, the storms passed and in 1870 she was tonsured as a nun with the name of Arcadia. This was a time when her spiritual state was one of paradise on earth and she "experienced the force of Christ's words, 'The Kingdom of God is within you,'"[289] and she also experienced the same sort of rapturous prayer that she had previously observed in the nun. A more severe crisis came after she had spent six years in the convent and was transferred to a dark and moldy cell that injured her health so severely that she was forced to spend several months convalescing in Novgorod. In 1872, she transferred to the Zverin-Protection of the Mother of God convent in that city. Arcadia had escaped from her damp cell but she was appalled by the lack of discipline in her new monastery and again found herself to be the object of envy on the part of other nuns. Her despair was relieved by a vision that caused her to rejoice that never had "the Lord left me without making me listen to reason and giving me comfort."[290] However, she could also receive reprimands in her visions. She had slipped into a habit of not making a full confession before taking the Eucharist but, in a dream, she was holding the Christ child in her arms and to her disgust she saw that her hands, arms and cassock were dirty and sooty. The vision taught her to make "a thorough preparation for receiving the Holy Mysteries."[291]

Arcadia was then moved to the Zvansky Convent of the Sign of the Mother of God to serve as treasurer of the house and as assistant director of the diocesan college for girls. After one year she received the higher monastic tonsure and the new name of Thaisia. Again personality difficulties followed her as, in her opinion, her abbess abused her with "caustic and biting insults."[292] No doubt Thaisia's revealing her dream that she was walking in a grain field as a voice announced, "You are the one who will have to harvest this whole field," followed by an abbess's staff dropping down to her from above,[293] did little to endear her to her own abbess. However, the prophetic dream was soon realized when, in 1881, the metropolitan of St. Petersburg appointed her to be superior of the recently established Leushino community of women.

The Leushino community was foundering and the metropolitan was threatening to close it if order could not be established. The mercantile family that donated the land for the community was attempting to direct its every move, monastic discipline was poor, finances were abysmal, and Thaisia was the fourth head in four years. Thaisia was herself soon wishing to abandon the community but she was halted by a vision of the Virgin Mary, who was accompanied by the head of John the Baptist lying at her feet. They promised her that "We are always guarding our community! Do not fear anything! Have faith!"[294] Her determination was fortified and she set out to remedy the problems. It was a daunting task and she had to contend with open hostility on all fronts, a secession of a substantial group of nuns and constant complaints against her being forwarded to the metropolitan. At one point she suffered an onset of paralysis and was unable to move her arms or legs. Gradually she regained movement of her arms but her full recovery did not come until she had a vision of the Archangel Michael, who entered a room carrying an ikon of himself. He kissed her three times and repeated, "Go with God to your convent; the Archangel will be with you."[295] When the vision ended, Thaisia stood up for the first time in two months.

For Thaisia, her illness and healing were a turning point for her as head of the Leushino community. The complaints faded away and the community progressed to such an extent that in 1885 it was raised to the status of a full convent, Thaisia became an abbess and the house could now have professed nuns. At the first tonsurings, the new abbess looked up and saw what seemed to be Jesus surrounded by angels: "Something was happening, but what it was I am unable to tell, although I saw and heard everything. It was not of this world. From the beginning of the vision, I seemed to fall into an ecstatic rapture."[296] For over thirty years Thaisia supervised Leushino and put it on a sound basis as she built a great stone church for the convent and established a school that became a girls' ecclesiastical college, "which in turn made the Leushino Convent a seedbed for spiritual education and enlightenment in the northern regions of the Novgorod diocese."[297] It has been stated that during her thirty-year abbacy, "there was literally not one newly founded convent organized without Abbess Thaisia's active participation."[298]

Thaisia's determination to meet John of Kronstadt is an indication of his importance in Russian spiritual life, which is also found in the life of the monk Silouan (1866–1938). He was ready to depart for Mount Athos to commence his monastic life but wished first to go to Kronstadt to obtain Fr. John's prayers and blessing. He had previously observed the transfigured appearance of the priest, "who by nature was an ordinary-looking man, until grace gave his face the beauty of an angel and made one want to gaze on him."[299] Unable to find the priest at home, he left a written message, "Batioushka, I want to become a monk. Pray that the world may not hold me back." The very next day the future monk Silouan began to feel "the flames of hell roaring" around him and they remained with him all the way to Athos and for a long time afterwards.[300] This aid he credited to the power of John's prayers.

Silouan was born Simeon Antonov, a peasant from the province of Tambov who received very little formal education, having attended his village school for only two winters. Simeon grew up to be a very large and powerfully-built man who, when confronted by a village bully, very nearly killed the man by giving him a powerful blow to the chest. At an early age Simeon was drawn to the monastic life but he followed his father's advice and first completed his military service. While in the army, he demonstrated his skills as a future *staretz* on Mount Athos. One of his friends was disturbed because his wife had given birth to a child while he was away and he was so worried at what he might do to her that he was refusing to return home. Simeon reminded the man of how many times he had gone to a brothel and urged him, "Go home, accept the child as your own and, you'll see, everything will be all right."[301] His friend followed Simeon's counsel and later wrote a letter of thanks to him.

In 1892 Simeon entered the Russian monastery of St. Panteleimon on Mount Athos, making his profession as the monk Silouan four years later. Upon beginning his novitiate, he was of course instructed in hesychastic prayer and especially in the Jesus Prayer. After only three weeks' practice of the Jesus Prayer, while standing before an ikon of the Virgin Mary, "the prayer entered into his heart, to continue there, day and night, of its own accord." At the time the simple young novice did not realize what a "sublime and rare gift he had received from the Mother of God."[302] Even with this gift, Silouan faced the common temptation of beginning monks, his ardor began to cool and he began to lose heart. This came to an end when he was granted a vision of Christ, as a Divine Light shone on him and, with "his whole being filled with the fire of the grace of the Holy Spirit … he was taken out of this world and transported in spirit to heaven where he heard ineffable words … [and] he saw God in the Holy Spirit."[303] He explained the experience simply, "By the Holy Spirit my soul came to know the Lord."[304] Once again, he did not at first understand how exceptional was the gift that he had received, but his experience did give him a profound and sure knowledge of God. He wrote, "There is a wide difference between the simplest man who has come to know the Lord by the Holy Spirit and even a very great man ignorant of the grace of the Holy Spirit." For him, this knowledge went far beyond "merely believing that God exists, in seeing Him in nature or in the Scriptures," for it was "knowing the Lord by the Holy Spirit."[305] In the tradition of the Desert Fathers, Silouan was reluctant to discuss his experiences, but he did state, "The spiritual man soars like an eagle in the heights, and with his soul feels God, and beholds the whole world, though his prayer be in the darkness of the night."[306] Henceforth he addressed God personally, talking "face to face with God."[307] The effect of this vision was to give him the "light of knowledge"[308] and he began to understand the Scriptures and the writings of the church Fathers. On the basis of this and other experiences Silouan was sought out as a *staretz*. His fellow monk wrote of the authoritative nature of Silouan's spiritual advice that "he spoke out of an experience granted from on high, and I looked upon his words to a certain extent as the Christian world looks upon the holy Scriptures which impart truths as acknowledged and certain facts."[309]

At the heart of Silouan's spirituality was a compassionate love for all the human family, including one's enemies. He could not understand one hermit's satisfaction at the thought of atheists being burned in the everlasting fires of hell and he asked him how he could possibly feel happy with that specter, reminding him, "we must pray for all."[310] He believed that if contemplation left one with "a profound indifference to the fate of the world and the destinies of man, it was certainly fallacious."[311] The true spiritual path could be distinguished from false ones when, filled with the love of God, the soul feels "compassion for all and prays for the whole world. … The Holy Spirit teaches us to love God and our neighbour."[312] This extended to one's enemies, for "the *Staretz* regarded presence of love for enemies as the criterion of true faith, of true communion with God and a sign of the real action of grace. … He would say that for Christ there are no enemies."[313]

73

A quarter century after Silouan arrived at Athos, Russia was rocked by the Bolshevik Revolution, whose success led to repression of the Russian Orthodox Church, so closely identified with the tsarist regime. Churches and monasteries were closed and thousands of clerics and monks were killed, creating conditions that "do not generally favor the growth and development of monasteries, the natural cradles of mystics."[314] The revival of the Russian Church after the fall of the Soviet government may well permit the reflorescence of Russian mysticism, which has repeatedly withered only to flower again over the course of its millennium of existence.

CHAPTER III

THE WESTERN CHURCH IN THE MIDDLE AGES

—— •◦• ——

THE EARLIER MIDDLE AGES

Mystics abounded during the European Middle Ages; they were a natural product of the flourishing monastic life of the period. The two usual preconditions for mysticism, an ascetic life that allows one to overcome the pull of the body's delight in things physical and a life devoted to prayer, meditation and contemplation that open one to the "still, small voice," are more easily attained by nuns, monks, anchoresses and hermits than by lay people whose lives are dominated by the affairs of daily life and the needs of the body – food, drink, shelter, children. As in the East, monasticism was generally regarded as the highest form of Christian life precisely because only it allowed one to concentrate on God.

From its beginnings in the West and for almost 800 years, mysticism was strongly monastic and drew heavily from the asceticism of the Desert Fathers. The first of the three great founders of Western mysticism, all of whom were monks, was John Cassian (ca. 365 to ca. 435), probably a native of Scythia (modern Romania). Cassian first lived among the Desert Fathers in Egypt and after his ordination as a priest, he traveled to the West, where he established a house for monks and another for nuns at Marseille in Gaul (France). In his two great works, *Institutes* and *Conferences*, he propounded the ascetic ideals of the Egyptian Fathers along with his own spiritual teaching. Following his mentors, Cassian argued for a God who transcended all images and sensations:

> [The pure prayer of the faithful] centers on no contemplation of some image or other. It is masked by no attendant sounds or words. It is a fiery outbreak, an indescribable exaltation, an insatiable thrust of the soul. Free of what is sensed and seen, ineffable in its groans and sighs, the soul pours itself out to God.[1]

The goal of the ascetic was union with God, "to have the soul so removed from all dalliance with the body that it rises each day to the things of the spirit until all its living and all its wishing become one unending prayer."[2] The primary good for the Christian was contemplation, in which "someone still on the upward road comes at last to that which is unique, namely the sight of God Himself, which comes with God's help."[3]

Cassian's influence extended long after his death. When Benedict of Nursia wrote his famous Rule, he specifically commended Cassian's *Institutes* and *Conferences* as worthy reading for monks, as "tools of virtue for right-living and obedient monks."[4] This recommendation assured that Cassian's promotion of the ascetic life of mysticism would be received by virtually every monastic and spiritual leader of the Middle Ages.

Slightly younger than Cassian, Augustine (354–430), bishop of Hippo in North Africa, is often viewed as the first great Latin theologian, but he was also a promoter of monasticism and mysticism. Scholarly disagreement over the definition of mysticism[5] has led some to deny that Augustine was a mystic,[6] but Dom Cuthbert Butler, one of the first scholars of Christian mysticism, wrote:

> Augustine is for me the Prince of Mystics, uniting in himself, in a manner I do not find in any other, the two elements of mystical experience, viz. the most penetrating intellectual vision into things divine, and a love of God that was a consuming passion.[7]

Augustine's career indicates that he was a charismatic figure of impressive intellect. He was born to a well-to-do though not aristocratic provincial family in Roman North Africa, in what is now Algeria, and he excelled in the traditional education in rhetoric available to him. He became a teacher of rhetoric first in North Africa and then in Italy, in Rome and Milan. However, Augustine was also a religious seeker. He embraced philosophy, which he left for Manicheanism, which had strong similarities to Judaism and Christianity, which he then abandoned for Neoplatonism. Eventually, under the powerful influence of Bishop Ambrose of Milan, he converted to Christianity and returned to North Africa, where he established a monastery so that he might pursue a life of ascetical solitude. However, Augustine's monastic career was short-lived. While passing through the nearby city of Hippo, its bishop coerced him into becoming a priest and co-bishop of the city, and he succeeded as sole bishop shortly afterwards. Augustine's life as a bishop was extremely active as he became the dominant figure in the North African Church, combating the heresies of Donatism and Pelagianism, preaching sermons to his congregation and guiding his diocese while also writing over a hundred theological works.

However, Augustine was at heart a monastic, an ascetic and a mystic. He wrote no work specifically on mysticism but his writings propound his mystical themes. For example, he wrote often of the inexpressibility of God and that one cannot know God but only what God is not:

> So what are we to say, brothers, about God? For if you have fully grasped what you want to say, it isn't God. If you have been able to comprehend it, you have comprehended something else instead of God. If you think you have been able to comprehend, your thoughts have deceived you.[8]

In his apophaticism[9] he urged that all corporeal images concerning the Trinity should be rejected, "for it is no slight approach to the thought of God if, before we are able to know what He is, we begin to know what He is not."[10] One should not speak of God, "who is better known by unknowing,"[11] and, Augustine added, "There is no knowledge of God in the soul, only to know how to unknow him."[12] Even to say that God is unspeakable is an error, for "to say even this is to speak of Him. … And this opposition of words is rather to be avoided by silence than to be explained away by speech."[13]

His study of the "Platonic books"[14] provided him with both an intellectual framework and a sophisticated vocabulary with which to express his mystical views.[15] Augustine's mystical experiences are not portrayed as visions but rather as "intelligible intuitions – flashes of spiritual light."[16] One of the most famous experiences that he reported expresses the eternal mystical view of God as the very center of human beings. In his *Confessions*, one of the most influential spiritual works of the Middle Ages, he wrote of an experience he had with his mother Monica. As they were standing by a window overlooking the garden of their house in the Roman port city of Ostia, they began discussing spiritual matters. They agreed that the greatest bodily delights could not match the joys of eternal life and then:

> Our minds were lifted up by an ardent affection towards eternal being itself. Step by step we climbed beyond all corporeal objects and the heaven itself, where sun, moon, and stars shed light on the earth. We ascended even further by internal reflection and dialogue and wonder at your works, and we entered into our own minds. We moved up beyond them so as to attain to the region of inexhaustible abundance where you feed Israel eternally with truth for food.[17]

Other passages in the *Confessions* describe Augustine's further mystical experiences, presenting the great mystical paradox of a God who is both immanent and transcendent, whom one reaches by descending within: "But you were more inward than my most inward part and higher than the highest element within me."[18] In one of his more expressive passages Augustine wrote:

> With you as my guide I entered into my innermost citadel, and was given power to do so because you had become my helper. I entered and with my soul's eye, such as it was, saw above that same eye of my soul the immutable light higher than my mind – not the light of very day, obvious to anyone, nor a larger version of the same kind which would, as it were, have given out a much brighter light and filled everything with its magnitude. It was not that light, but a different thing, utterly different from all our kinds of light. It transcended my mind, not in the way that oil floats on water, nor as heaven is above earth. … And you cried from far away: "Now, I am who I am." I heard in the way one hears within the heart, and all doubt left me. I would have found it easier to doubt whether I was myself alive than there was no truth "understood from the things that are made."[19]

One of Augustine's most celebrated sayings, "Love and do what you will *(dilige et quidvis fac)* … let love be rooted in you, and from this root nothing but good can grow,"[20] is strongly suggestive of a mystical insight, emphasizing love as the basis of all human actions. Moreover, even Augustine's doctrines of predestination and grace have perhaps a foundation in mysticism. Mystics are aware that the experience of God is a divine gift and not a product of their effort or goodness, for its granting is a mystery, given for reasons known only to God without merit on the part of the mystic.[21] Moreover, surprising in a man who has been seen as grim and joyless, Augustine could write of the indescribable sweetness of his spiritual experiences: "And sometimes you cause me to enter into an extraordinary depth of feeling marked by a strange sweetness. If it were brought to perfection in me, it would be an experience quite beyond anything in this life."[22] In addition to sweetness, there was fire, one of the most frequent mystical expressions: "By your gift we are set on fire and carried upwards: we grow red hot and ascend. ... Lit by your fire, your good fire, we grow red hot and ascend."[23] Apparently speaking from his experiences, Augustine stated that God visits "the minds of the wise, when emancipated from the body, with an intelligible and ineffable presence, though this be only occasional, and as it were a swift flash of light athwart the darkness."[24] The brevity of these visitations and their likeness to flashes of light were Augustine's repeated themes while mysticism was an integral part of his view of the relationship between God and his creation. Augustine's esteem as the first Latin theologian ensured that his writings, with their strongly mystical coloring, would be read by virtually all scholars over the following centuries.

The third founder of Western Christian mysticism was Pope Gregory I, "the Great," bishop of Rome from 590 to 604 during a tumultuous time in Italian history. In 568 the Lombards invaded Italy from the North and quickly captured half of the peninsula. By the time of Gregory's pontificate, they were attacking Rome itself and Gregory was forced to organize the defenses of the duchy of Rome. Gregory was a Roman aristocrat who had been a papal ambassador to the imperial court in Constantinople but he was also a monastic, the first monk to become bishop of Rome, and he used his own resources to establish seven monasteries around Rome. In his own lifetime, Gregory was not a commanding figure nor was he known as "the Great," but he did work ceaselessly but futilely to gain the assistance of the Roman emperor in Constantinople against the Lombards and equally without result to heal the schism in the church in Italy.[25] He sent missionaries to convert the pagan Anglo-Saxons to Christianity, supported the recent conversion of the Visigoths in Spain from heretical Arianism to orthodox Christianity, opposed Donatism in Africa, managed the papal estates in southern Italy and Sicily and wrote letters to most of the rulers in the West. His writings were among the most influential and widely read works of the Middle Ages, with the *Pastoral Rule* serving as a basic guidebook for bishops. His *Dialogues* recorded the holy deeds of Italian saints and his biblical commentaries and sermons were in great demand in his own time and for centuries to come.

Like Augustine, Gregory wrote no tract specifically dealing with mysticism but the subject permeated his works. For example, in his commentary on Job 33.16, Gregory quoted Psalm 31.22 and added:

> For after beholding that inward light, which flashed within his mind with bright rays through the grace of contemplation, he returned to himself; and

discerned, by the knowledge he had gained, either the blessings which were there, of which he was deprived, or the evils with which he was here surrounded.[26]

As a monk, Gregory was devoted to asceticism and contemplation, the purpose of which was to attain the vision of God, which had been enjoyed by Adam but was lost in the Fall. This vision was possible for all Christians but obviously much more difficult for those not living a life of contemplation.

Gregory left no direct account of his own visions, but he did write "perhaps the most famous non-biblical vision of the early Middle Ages."[27] The second book of Gregory's *Dialogues* is devoted to the miracles of his hero, St. Benedict of Nursia, the author of the Benedictine Rule. There he described a vision given to Benedict, who was standing in prayer before his window:

> In the dead of night he suddenly beheld a flood of light shining down from above more brilliant than the sun, and with it every trace of darkness cleared away. Another remarkable sight followed. According to his own description, the whole world was gathered up before his eyes in what appeared to be a single ray of light.[28]

Gregory added that Benedict then saw the soul of Bishop Germanus of Capua being carried up to heaven in a ball of light and then added a commentary on the mystical vision:

> All creation is bound to appear small to a soul that sees the Creator. Once it beholds a little of His light, it finds all creatures small indeed. The light of holy contemplation enlarges and expands the mind in God until it stands above the world. In fact, the soul that sees Him rises even above itself, and as it is drawn upward in His light all its inner powers unfold. Then, when it looks down from above, it sees how small everything is that was beyond its grasp before.[29]

Moreover, Gregory alluded to his experiences before his episcopal duties threw him headlong into the busy affairs of the world:

> I recall those earlier days in the monastery where all the fleeting things of time were in a world below me, and I could rise far above the vanities of life. Heavenly thoughts would fill my mind, and while still held within the body I passed beyond its narrow confines in contemplation. Even death, which nearly everyone regards as evil, I cherished as the entrance into life and the reward for labor. … At times I find myself reflecting with even greater regret on the life that others lead who have totally abandoned the present world.[30]

Drawn from his own experiences, Gregory's mysticism is filled with the imagery of sweetness and light as well as of joyfulness and the inexpressible nature of the experience.

Gregory's influence on medieval mysticism is of tremendous importance. The mysticism and accounts of mystical experiences scattered throughout his writings promoted mysticism as the goal of every Christian while he also advocated monasticism as the form of Christian life best suited to attain the vision of God. In addition, he fostered the reputation of St. Benedict through his *Dialogues* and hailed the Rule of St. Benedict as being "remarkable for its discretion and its clarity of language,"[31] while Benedict's Rule encouraged the reading of Cassian's *Institutes* and *Conferences*.

Cassian, Augustine and Gregory provided a solid foundation of respected and authoritative works that promoted monasticism, asceticism, contemplation and mysticism. Following the Desert Fathers, they assumed that mysticism was the ultimate aim of Christians in this earthly life and a foretaste of the vision of God that would come in heaven. In the centuries following Gregory I, Benedictine monasticism came to dominate Western Europe to the virtual exclusion of all other forms. While the Benedictine form of monasticism could produce mystics, it was not renowned for its asceticism. Benedictine monks were allowed generous rations of food and drink and their dedication to the demanding schedule of recited, collective daily prayers left little time for private contemplation. By the eleventh century, medieval Europe was growing increasingly populous and wealthy, giving rise to new movements within monasticism that stressed an ideal far more reminiscent of the Desert Fathers. The reformers advocated lives of stricter asceticism, forsaking all worldly goods and comforts and escaping to deserted places where they could devote themselves to contemplation. At the end of the eleventh century there were a number of these new ascetical movements, the most successful of which was the Cistercian order of monks. The most famous and influential of all Cistercians was one of the archmystics of the European Middle Ages, Bernard of Clairvaux (1090–1153).

Bernard is an unlikely mystic to many who know him only as the unrelenting opponent of the errant philosopher Peter Abelard, which makes him appear to be an intolerant bigot, an image unmitigated by his role as the preacher of the Second Crusade. This is hardly the territory expected of a mystic. However, while Bernard was preaching the Second Crusade, the monk Radulfus was engaged in his own preaching campaign, informing Christians in France and Germany that they did not have to travel all the way to the Holy Land to begin killing God's enemies, for Jews were nearer at hand, resulting in riots that swept the Rhineland, destroying synagogues and killing many Jews. Bernard denounced Radulfus, urging Christians to refrain from persecutions.[32] In the end, Bernard tracked down Radulfus and convinced him to return to his own monastery.[33]

While it is true that Bernard found Peter Abelard's insistence on the primacy of reason and the intellect to be directly opposite his own mystical approach to understanding Christianity, he did not initiate the condemnation of Abelard. Rather Bernard spoke privately with him and gained Abelard's empty promise to moderate his published views. Bernard originally had no intention of attending the council at which Abelard was condemned and did so only when some charged that he was afraid of the brilliant Abelard, who, it was claimed, was bringing a large number of his own supporters to the council.

Bernard was a monk but he was no sheltered recluse. In addition to his activities regarding the Second Crusade and the Abelard affair, he was abbot of the monastery of Clairvaux in the French region of Burgundy and by the time of his death he had established over 150 daughter houses. Bernard campaigned for church reform, acted to end the papal schism that began in 1130 and preached against heretics in southern France. Once his public career was launched, he was away from his monastery one third of his time. Moreover, Bernard wrote in all about 3500 pages, seemingly without end.

There is no doubt that he also was a mystic. The later Middle Ages saw him as the archmystic and in Dante's *Paradiso*, Bernard replaced Beatrice as the poet's guide (canto 31) so that by contemplation he might be led to his ultimate goal, the vision of God (canto 33). While the tradition of the Desert Fathers was not to discuss one's own mystical experiences,[34] Bernard is one of the first examples of the "new mysticism" of the later Middle Ages[35] in his emphasis on experiences. "Today we read the book of experience," he wrote, adding, "if anyone once receives the spiritual kiss of Christ's mouth[36] he seeks eagerly to have it again and again."[37] Bernard did not hesitate to encourage his readers to mysticism by providing an account of his own mystical experience:

> I tell you that the Word has come even to me ... and that he has come more than once. Yet however often he has come, I have never been aware of the moment of his coming. I have known he was there; I have remembered his presence afterward; sometimes I had an inkling that he was coming. But I never felt it, nor his leaving me. And where he comes from when he enters my soul, or where he goes when he leaves it, and how he enters and leaves, I frankly do not know.

It was not through sensory organs that God came into him:

> He did not enter by the eyes, for he has no color; nor by the ears, for he made no sound; nor by the nostrils, for he is not mingled with the air, but the mind. ... Or perhaps he did not enter at all, because he did not come from outside? ... Yet he does not come from within me, for he is good, and I know that there is not good in me. I have climbed up to the highest that is in me, and see! The Word is far, far above. A curious explorer, I plumbed my own depths, and he was far deeper than that. If I looked outward, I saw him far beyond. If I looked inward, he was further in still.

The only sign of the coming of Christ was sensation of warmth:

> You ask then how I knew he was present. ... when the Bridegroom, the Word, came to me he never made any sign that he was coming; there was no sound of his voice, no glimpse of his face, no footfall. There was no movement of his by which I could know his coming; none of my senses showed me that he had flooded the depths of my being. Only by the warmth of my heart, as I said before, did I know that he was there. ... But when the Word has left me, and all

these things become dim and weak and cold, as though you had taken the fire from under a boiling pot, I know that he has gone. Then my soul cannot help being sorrowful until he returns, and my heart grows warm within me, and I know he is there.[38]

Like Augustine and Gregory the Great, Bernard's immense talent led the contemplative monk into a life of action in the world. Also like his mystical predecessors, he composed no single work on mysticism, but it dominated his works, especially his eighty-five sermons on the Song of Songs. He wrote as a monk for a monastic audience whose life reflected his own, for they rejected the world, lived lives of asceticism, were devoted to prayer and desired lives of contemplation. To them he wrote:

To you, brothers, I shall say what I should not say to those who are in the world, or at least I shall say it in a different way. The preacher who follows the Apostle Paul's method of teaching will give them milk to drink, not solid food. Before those who are spiritually minded more solid food must be set ... And so be ready to eat not milk but bread.[39]

Bernard's mysticism was essentially monastic, for while anyone can attain the mystical vision of God, the necessary preparation of humility, asceticism, contemplation and complete devotion to God are more likely to be found among monastics than ordinary laypeople.

Contemporary with Bernard was Abbess Hildegard of Bingen (1098–1179), truly a multimedia mystic who wrote dramatic accounts of her mystical visions, dictated stunning artistic representations of those visions (see plate 5) and recorded notations of the music that she heard during the visions. In her lifetime she was considered to be a great prophet and healer, both by means of herbal medicine as well as by miraculous healing using exorcism, touch and prayer.[40] She convinced the pope of her authenticity and authority and gained permission to conduct preaching missions throughout the Rhineland, a unique accomplishment for a woman in the Middle Ages. She carried on correspondence with the great men of her day, including popes, kings, emperors and Bernard of Clairvaux. Moreover, she was one of the first great women writers of the Middle Ages. Her best-known work is the *Scivias* (a shortened form of *Scito vias Domini*, "know the ways of the Lord"), a long explication of twenty-six visions on the relationship between God and humans, written at heavenly command ("Say and write what you see and hear ... Cry out therefore, and write thus!"[41]). Her visions also served as the source of the *Book of Life's Merits* and the *Book of Divine Works*. Her scientific works include the *Book of Simple Medicine*, a summary of natural science, and the *Book of Composite Medicine* (*Causae et Curae*), on the causes of illnesses and their natural remedies. Thus, like Augustine, Gregory and Bernard, she was a contemplative who was fully-engaged in an active life in the world all the way to the end of her life. When she was eighty, only six months before her death, she defied an order from the clergy of Mainz to disinter a man from the convent's cemetery because he had been excommunicated. The penalty of interdict was imposed, prohibiting divine services in the convent, but Hildegard stood her ground and convinced the archbishop of Mainz to lift the interdict.

Hildegard was a daughter of the German aristocracy and was given to the Benedictine convent at Disiboden at the age of eight. Before she was forty, she rose to be the abbess of the convent and later, acting on a divine revelation, she overcame tremendous opposition from her male superiors to establish her own convent near Bingen, on the Rhine. According to Hildegard, her mystical life began with visions when she was three: "I saw such a light that my soul trembled, but because I was just an infant, I could say nothing of these things." When she was fifteen, "I saw many things and spoke about several of them frankly. Those who heard about them were moved to wonder whence and from whom these things came." Because only she saw and heard the visions and voices, Hildegard kept her experiences secret and her public career as preacher and prophet did not commence until she was an abbess:

> When I was forty-two years and seven months old, Heaven was opened and a fiery light of exceeding brilliance came and permeated my whole brain, and inflamed my whole heart and my whole breast, not like a burning but like a warming flame, as the sun warms everything its rays touch. And immediately I knew the meaning of the exposition of the Scriptures ... though I did not have the interpretation of the words of their texts or the division of the syllables or the knowledge of cases or tenses. But I had sensed in myself wonderfully the power and mystery of secret and admirable visions from my childhood – that is, from the age of five – up to that time, as I do now.[42]

Thus when Hildegard spoke she did so with the authority of God: "These words come not from me nor from any other mortal: but I present them as I received them in a vision from above."[43] At the age of seventy-seven, Hildegard described her visions to her secretary:

> But I do not hear these things with my outer ears, nor do I perceive them with the rational parts of my mind, nor with any combination of my five senses: but only in my soul, with my outer eyes open, so that I never suffer in them any unconsciousness induced by ecstasy, but I see them when I am awake, by day and by night.

Her vision was one of light "far, far brighter than a cloud which carries the sun; nor can I gauge its height or length or breadth, and it is known to me by the name of the 'reflection of the living light.'"[44] Moreover, the visions brought her understanding, especially of the Scriptures:

> Whatever I see or learn in this vision, I hold in my memory for a long time; so that when I recall what I have seen and heard, I simultaneously see and hear and understand and, as it were, learn in this moment, what I understand. But what I do not see, I do not understand, because I am unlearned. And what I write in

the vision, I see and hear; nor do I put down words other than those I hear in the vision, and I present them in Latin, unpolished, just as I hear them in the vision. For I am not taught in this vision to write as the philosophers write; and the words in this vision are not like those which sound from the mouth of man, but like a trembling flame, or like a cloud stirred by the clear air.[45]

Like Gregory and Bernard, Hildegard could not withdraw from the world to enjoy her interior life of contemplation. She was an active monastic with a mission, "to unlock the mysteries of Scripture, to proclaim the way of salvation, to admonish priests and prelates, to instruct the people of God."[46] Her writings are practical, dealing with the relationship between God and creation, with natural history and diseases and their cures.

Another presager of the new mysticism was the English hermit Christina Markyate (ca. 1096 to ca. 1160), whose life reads as much like a series of cliffhanger adventures as it does a saintly biography. She was born near the end of the eleventh century to an Anglo-Saxon noble family. Her *vita*[47] informs us that from an early age she was given to self-mortification and a firm desire to dedicate her virginity to God by entering a monastic house. However, when she escaped an attempted sexual assault by the bishop of Durham, the frustrated prelate encouraged her parents to have her married and she was coerced into a betrothal to a young nobleman. Christina's determination to guard her virginity and not to proceed with the marriage enraged her parents, who used threats, bribery, punishments and efforts to get her drunk in vain attempts to arrange the loss of her virginity, and they resorted to love potions and charms to gain her consent to the marriage. Nonetheless, constantly comforted and confirmed in her resolve by frequent visions of the Virgin Mary, Christina resisted and escaped to a group of nearby hermits.

She found a protector in Roger, the leader of the hermits and "their holy affection grew day by day,"[48] to such an extent that she actually lived in Roger's cell in a tiny space covered over with planks to conceal her presence. In this irregular arrangement Roger was a good mentor in her mystical life, for he "taught her things about heavenly secrets which are hardly credible, and acted as if he were on earth only in body, whilst his mind was fixed on heaven."[49] In her prayers she was rapt "above the clouds to heaven" and she "saw in one flash the whole wide world. But above all else she turned her eyes towards Roger's cell and chapel … and she said: 'I wish to have that place to dwell in.'"[50]

Acting on her behalf, Roger sought the assistance of the archbishop of York, who supported Christina by annulling her marriage and confirming her vow of virginity. She remained with Roger until his death around 1122. The archbishop then provided her with another priest as a spiritual director, an arrangement quickly complicated when they were seized by a strong romantic passion for each other. The cleric's ardor was cooled when St. John the Evangelist, St. Benedict and Mary Magdalen appeared and reproached him for his feelings, while Christina remained enamored with him until Christ appeared to her, coming as a small child and remaining with her for an entire day. Christina held him "to her virginal breast" and felt his presence within her and at last "the fire of lust" left her, never to return.[51]

Christina received a number of mystic gifts, for she acted as a healer, had the gift of prophecy and knew others' thoughts. Her fame as a holy woman spread and she was visited by dignitaries, while King Henry II contributed money for her support. The archbishop attempted to make her abbess of one of his own foundations for women or of other famous convents in France, but she refused these offers and made her nun's profession at St. Albans around 1131. Abbot Geoffrey of St. Albans was initially hostile to her but he soon became her unswerving supporter and relied upon her word "as if it were a divine oracle,"[52] scarcely making any important move without first consulting her. The abbot allowed her to take the Eucharist whenever he said Mass, during which she would become "so rapt, that, unaware of earthly things, she gave herself to the contemplation of the countenance of her Creator."[53] Even while speaking she could fall into ecstasies, in which she "saw things that the Holy Spirit showed her. At such times she felt and knew nothing of what went on about her or what was spoken."[54]

THE NEW MYSTICISM

By the eleventh century, Western Europe was in the early stages of an astonishing three-century-long period of economic expansion. New agricultural techniques and a warmer climate combined to produce much higher crop yields, creating harvest surpluses that both fueled an increase in the wealth of Europe and supported an unprecedented population growth. Linked to these stimuli were a marked increase in trade and an unprecedented urban revival. Throughout Europe cities and towns were founded or expanded, bringing into existence a large lay mercantile class, literate for the most part, which began to thrust urban lay concerns into the forefront of medieval society, including the church. The laity began to sponsor vernacular translations of the Scriptures which they read without the benefit of theological training, resulting in widespread heretical movements for the first time in medieval history. At the same time, the new wealth of the urban laity presented a challenge to the theology of the church, which stressed renunciation, detachment and the model of apostolic poverty.

One product of these changes was the "new mysticism"[55] that emerged in the twelfth century. For the first time, mystical works were produced outside of monasteries and were far more expressive of individual mystical experiences, especially of the laity and in particular of women. While the older mysticism never disappeared, the new mysticism developed independently of the framework of monastic mysticism that looked to the Desert Fathers as its model. St. Francis of Assisi (1182–1226), the founder of the Franciscan order of friars, was one of the manifestations of the new mysticism, for he was never ordained a priest and the Franciscans were not cloistered in monasteries.

Born into a merchant family in central Italy, Francis participated in the incessant warfare of the cities of Umbria. While on his way to Rome to fight in the papal armies, he had a transforming vision that sent him back to Assisi as a different person. He withdrew from his former life and sought isolation, while exchanging his fine clothes for the rags of a poor man, praying incessantly and receiving visions of Jesus. In one of the most celebrated events of his life, Francis was meditating in the fields and entered the dilapidated church of St. Damian, whereupon he heard a voice coming from the church's crucifix, "Francis, go and repair my house which, as you see, is falling completely into ruin,"[56] which sent him into a state of ecstasy. To fulfill this divine request, Francis sold all that he had (see plate 6) as well as some of his family's property, prompting his father to disown him. Francis survived by begging for alms and preferred to live with lepers, whose sores he healed by kissing them. Francis soon took literally the command of Jesus that his disciples should own nothing and gave away his few remaining possessions, contenting himself with only a tunic and a belt. From that time on he was devoted to Lady Poverty and called upon others to join him in his apostolic life. As unlikely as it seems, Francis gained a core of followers, which forced him to write a "simple rule" for them, thus creating the Franciscan Order, officially known as the Friars Minor ("Little Brothers").

Francis was a mystic but he was neither simply a nature mystic nor the prototype of the Flower Child of his modern popular image. Like John the Baptist he was a fiery preacher of repentance and penance, for it was said of him that "he did not know how to touch the faults of others gingerly but only how to lance them."[57] In the manner of a desert ascetic he called the body Brother Ass and urged his followers to hate their bodies, while, like Plato, drawing on the image of the soul as a charioteer attempting to bring the body under control.[58] Moreover, Francis counseled his friars to avoid contact with women as much as possible. He was no impractical, otherworld, starry-eyed dreamer, for he founded his Order despite initial papal hesitation to authorize it, wrote its rule and oversaw its amazing growth (by the time of his death there were 5000 Franciscan friars). He established the Poor Clares, the "second order" of Franciscans for women, and carried on an active preaching life, even preaching to the sultan of Egypt as he accompanied the Fifth Crusade (1217–21). He had hoped to gain a holy martyrdom but only succeeded in impressing his Muslim audience with his holiness.

Francis left no personal account of his experiences, but his biographer described the coming of the Holy Spirit in Francis:

> He was accustomed not to pass over negligently any visitation of the Spirit. When it was granted, he followed it and as long as the Lord allowed, he enjoyed the sweetness offered him. When he was on a journey and felt the breathing of the divine Spirit, letting his companions go on ahead, he would stand still and render this new inspiration fruitful, not receiving the grace in vain. Many times he was lifted up in ecstatic contemplation so that, rapt out of himself and experiencing what is beyond human understanding, he was unaware of what went on about him.[59]

Francis was gifted with the power to heal, exorcize, and prophesy and the ability to bilocate (to be "where he was absent"[60]).

His appreciation of nature came from his recognition that God was in all creatures. Thus he spoke of the birds as sisters and brothers[61] and wanted to preach to them and to all creatures so that they might praise their creator. His biography is filled with accounts of his unique charisma with animals, so that even wild beasts would easily approach him, reminiscent of the animal encounters of the Russian mystics.[62] Francis's sense of the oneness of human kind with nature was expressed passionately in his *Canticle of Brother Sun*, where he thanked God for Brother Sun, Sister Moon, Brother Wind and Sister Water, Brother Fire and Mother Earth, even for "our sister Bodily Death."[63] Even as he was undergoing a cauterization, he prayed, "My brother fire … Be kind to me in this hour, be courteous! I beseech the great Lord who created you to temper your heat for me so that you will burn gently and I can endure it."[64] Fittingly, in 1980 Pope John Paul II declared Francis to be the Patron of Ecology.

Because Francis devoted his life to imitating the life that he believed Jesus and his disciples had led, those around him saw it as appropriate that, towards the end of his life, he miraculously received on his hands, feet and side the wounds of Jesus – the best known instance of the Stigmata. Not only did bleeding wounds appear, but somehow his tissues formed what looked like nails in the wounds. Francis died in 1226 and was proclaimed a saint only two years later.

One of those who followed Francis in a life devoted to poverty and penance was the laywoman Angela (ca. 1248–1309), from the town of Foligno, only seven miles from Assisi. Of her external life in the world we know very little and all of that principally from a single source, her own *Book*. However, that work provides an extremely detailed account of her mystical life and teachings. The first part of the *Book*, the *Memorial*, was written by her confessor, a Franciscan priest thought to be named Arnaldo, who transcribed her vivid descriptions of her visions. The second part, the *Instructions*, presents her spiritual teachings derived from those same visions.

Angela had been a married woman and a mother, obviously well-to-do, for she was literate and could afford expensive luxuries. In 1285, when she was about thirty-seven years old, Angela became obsessed with an unnamed unconfessed sin and with fear of damnation in hell. In despair, she turned to St. Francis and asked him to provide her with a confessor. That very night she had a vision of an elderly friar who told her, "Sister, if you had asked me sooner, I would have complied with your request sooner. Nonetheless, your request is granted."[65] Soon afterwards she entered the cathedral of Foligno, where her kinsman Brother Arnaldo was preaching. She decided that he should be her confessor.

For the next five years she struggled with her conversion to the penitential life while progressing in an ever-deepening spiritual life, especially in the path of poverty, fortified by illuminations and visions. She was shown that "if I wanted to go to the cross, I would need to strip myself in order to be lighter and go naked to it."[66] During this time her husband, sons and mother all died, which did not bereave her, for indeed she had prayed for their deaths. With astonishing honesty she confessed, "I felt a great consolation when it happened."[67]

Angela became increasingly devoted to poverty and gave away most of her possessions even though Brother Arnaldo and other Franciscans tried to restrain her. She also became a Franciscan tertiary, that is, she entered the Third Order of St. Francis. (Tertiaries like Angela were lay people attached to monastic orders after having taken certain semi-monastic vows, but they were not cloistered.) Then, while standing at the portals of the church of St. Francis in Assisi, Angela suddenly began screaming, shrieking and shouting. Brother Arnaldo witnessed the scene and, fearing that she was acting under the influence of evil, forbade her ever to return to Assisi. When he later inquired of her the cause of the outburst, her response was so amazing that Brother Arnaldo began writing down what she had been experiencing over the past five years. At first he brought two or three sheets of paper for the purpose but she suggested that he would need a large copybook for the task.

Angela told him that the screams were due to an experience as she was returning from a pilgrimage to Rome. The Holy Spirit came to her, calling her "my daughter and my sweet spouse" and affirming "I love you so much more than any other woman in the valley of Spoleto."[68] She told Brother Arnaldo of the great joy she felt "when I heard God tell me: 'I am the Holy Spirit who enters into your deepest self.'"[69] God promised not to leave her until she entered the church of St. Francis. She said that she turned her gaze on God,

> I saw something full of such immense majesty that I do not know how to describe it, but it seemed to me that it was the All Good. Moreover, he spoke many words of endearment as he withdrew from me. And he withdrew, so very gently and so very gradually. After he had withdrawn, I began to cry out without any shame: "Love still unknown, why did you leave me?"[70]

Arnaldo spent the next four years recording in Latin what Angela told him in her native Umbrian dialect of Italian, being careful to write only what she said, querying her for further information or explanation at some points and reading back what he had written to verify its accuracy. Eventually his Franciscan superiors became so concerned over the time that he was spending with her that he was forced to use a young boy as an intermediary between the two of them. Arnaldo's journal of her experiences ends around the year 1296 and we know little about the rest of her life other than the date of her death, 4 January 1309.

From Arnaldo's text we learn of the great depth and detail of Angela's mystical and spiritual life. In typical Franciscan style, Angela emphasized a life of penance and recognition of one's own sinfulness and nothingness, "how she herself was nothing and created out of vile substance; how [God] found nothing good in her, and yet he loved her and she herself could love him."[71] As Angela's mystical life developed, she went from visions of Christ or St. Francis to deeper experiences of the Trinity itself and she became overwhelmed by the knowledge of the transcendence and omnipresence of God, seeing in her visions "the whole world and all things in it as if they were almost nothing, and yet filled with the overflowing presence of God."[72] God himself told her, "'It is true that the whole world is full of me.' And then I saw that every creature was indeed full of his presence."[73]

God spoke to her directly in her heart and

in a vision I beheld the fullness of God in which I beheld and comprehended the whole of creation, that is, what is on this side and what is beyond the sea, the abyss, the sea itself, and everything else. And in everything that I saw, I could perceive nothing except the presence of the power of God, and in a manner totally indescribable. And my soul in an excess of wonder cried out: "This world is pregnant with God!" Wherefore I understood how small is the whole of creation – that is, what is on this side and what is beyond the sea, the abyss, the sea itself, and everything else – but the power of God fills it all to overflowing.[74]

God also showed Angela that, in an absolute manner,

God is present in every creature and in everything that has being, in a devil and a good angel, in heaven and hell, in good deeds and adultery or homicide, in all things … I also understand that he is no less present in a devil than a good angel.[75]

In her later and deeper experiences, Angela felt complete union with God, so that God could say to her, "You are I and I am you."[76]

Brother Arnaldo asked Angela for fuller descriptions of what form God had in her visions. She denied that God had a bodily form, saying, "I saw a plenitude, a beauty wherein I saw the All Good … I saw a fullness, a brightness with which I felt myself so filled that words fail me, nor can I find anything to compare it with."[77] However, she did provide a moving description of the coming of God into the soul, reminiscent of the account of Bernard of Clairvaux:[78]

Sometimes God comes into the soul without being summoned, and when he does, he instills in the soul both fire and love, and sometimes a sweet feeling of his presence. But the soul believes that this experience comes from God and delights in it. But it is still unaware that he himself is in the soul, that is, it does not perceive that he is in the soul, but is aware of the presence of his grace from which it takes delight. … The soul also experiences God's coming into it when it hears him speaking very sweetly to it, … And then the soul sees him taking shape within itself and it sees him more clearly than a person can see another person, for the eyes of the soul, in this experience, see a fullness of God of which I am not able to speak. … This vision is not tangible or imaginable, but something ineffable.[79]

Her constant teaching was of the ineffability of her mystical experiences and she feared that even what she was saying to Brother Arnaldo was so far from expressing the reality that she had experienced that it was blasphemy.

In her mystical encounters with God, Angela's soul was

often elevated into the secrets of God and sees the divine secrets; I am able to understand how the Scriptures were written … Thus when I return to myself after perceiving these divine secrets, I can say some words with security about them.[80]

Thus like so many mystics, Angela felt the conflict between what she knew from her experiences to be absolutely certain and what was preached in church. She was especially critical of preachers, for God showed her that nothing of mystical delights was being preached: "Preachers cannot preach it; they do not understand what they preach."[81] She went on to compare the incomprehensible mysteries of the Scriptures with those of mystical experience. No one, not even those with learning and spirit, can fully understand Scripture, yet "they babble something about it. But of these ineffable workings which are produced in the soul when God disclosed himself to it, nothing at all can be said or babbled."[82]

Angela sometimes saw Christ in the host, where he was "so beautiful and so magnificently adorned. He looked like a child of twelve."[83] At another time Christ called her to place her mouth to the wound on her side, from which she drank the blood flowing out.[84] In perhaps the most graphic and sensual experience that she related, in a state of ecstasy Angela

> found herself in the sepulcher with Christ. She said she had first of all kissed Christ's breast – and saw that he lay dead, with his eyes closed – then she kissed his mouth, from which, she added, a delightful fragrance emanated, one impossible to describe. This moment lasted only a short while. Afterward, she placed her cheek on Christ's own and he, in turn, placed his hand on her other cheek, pressing her closely to him.[85]

Angela also had mystical encounters with the Virgin Mary, whom she saw as a representative of womankind: "I had delight in seeing a woman placed in such a position of nobility, glory, and dignity as was the Blessed Virgin, and in seeing her placed in the position of interceding for the human race."[86] However, as she progressed in her mystical ascent, in keeping with the formlessness of God that she knew, her experiences were increasingly of the Trinity. God told her, "in you rests the entire Trinity; indeed the complete truth rests in you, so that you hold me and I hold you" and Angela added, "suddenly my soul is elevated by God and I hold dominion over and comprehend the whole world. It seems to me, then, as if I am no longer on earth but in heaven, in God."[87]

Angela repeatedly condemned those who were in the "spirit of freedom," those who claimed that their mystical experiences made them incapable of sin, similar to the distinctive teachings of those of the "Free Spirit" movement in the next century.[88] However, she also showed many of the characteristics of the Spirit of Freedom[89] and even said that when God was within her soul, "it cannot commit any offense."[90] Fine is the line between heresy and orthodoxy in mysticism.

The Italian district of Umbria produced not only Francis and Angela but also the mystical poet Jacopone da Todi (ca. 1236–1306), born Jacopo dei Benedetti to a family of the lower nobility. After receiving a legal education, perhaps at the great law school at Bologna, he became a notary (one who draws up legal documents), married and lived only for the moment in the enjoyment of the pleasures of the world. However, Jacopo's life took a dramatic turn, probably in 1268, when he abandoned his life in that world, became a Franciscan tertiary and wandered the countryside as a hermit, leading many to believe that he had lost his mind. After about ten years as an itinerant ascetic experiencing mystical encounters with God, Jacopo, now generally called Jacopone ("Big Jim"), became a full member of the Franciscan Order in Todi, probably in 1278.

Jacopone craved a life of solitude[91] but he picked a very bad time to become a Franciscan. By the closing years of the thirteenth century the Franciscan Order was rent into two hostile factions. One, the Conventuals, accepted the Order's acquisition of property and wealth but regarded the possessions as owned not by individuals but by either the Order collectively or the papacy on behalf of the Order. Thus St. Francis's intention that his friars own nothing was technically respected. The other faction, purists known as the Spirituals, including Jacopone, strongly opposed any relaxation of the Order's dedication to absolute poverty. By the end of the century the dispute had reached the pope.

Pope Boniface VIII (1294–1303) decided against the Spirituals and they reciprocated with bitter opposition to him. The pope had a reputation for corruption and immorality and had played a significant role in the shocking resignation from the papacy of his predecessor, Celestine V, a holy man and a hermit but clearly incompetent as pope. Jacopone found it difficult to bear the new pope and regarded him with utter contempt. He joined with other Spirituals and Boniface's Italian political opponents to denounce him and to declare that he was no true pope. In the resulting warfare Boniface defeated his enemies and captured Jacopone, whom he then imprisoned in solitary confinement. Although Jacopone repeatedly begged the pope to release him, he languished in prison until the death of Boniface VIII in 1303. The final three years of his life were spent at a Franciscan house a few miles away from Todi.

Jacopone's vernacular poems, the *Lauds*, were his chief means of self-expression, employed to denounce Boniface VIII as well as to let his heart sing of mystical union with God. He chastised those who, unmindful of the certain death that awaited each person, sought worldly pleasures and satisfied their bodily appetites. He urged the ascetical life and the cultivation of the virtues, particularly poverty. Typical of Spiritual Franciscans as well as of mystics, Jacopone was scornful of the intellect, especially regarding its inability to know the unknowable: "Acquired knowledge, however long its meditation/ Cannot engender properly ordered love./ Infused knowledge, as soon as it touches you, fills you/ With burning love, makes peace between you and God."[92] Jacopone's mysticism was decidedly apophatic: "Led by grace, the created will becomes one with infinity,/ Drawn upward in a steep ascent,/ Like iron to a magnet. The will rejoices,/ In the sky of unknowing, in the beloved Unseen."[93]

Jacopone of course taught that the path to union lies through detachment from all things and in the annihilation of understanding and of the self. Union with God was described as a radical reorientation of truth: "Once united with God it knows/ That what you think is day is night,/ What you think is light is darkness./ Until you reach this point, and the self is annihilated,/ Everything that you think is true is really false."[94] Moreover, his poetry captured the rapture of the soul caught up in union with God:

> Love, Love, You have wounded me,
> Your name only can I invoke;
> Love, Love, I am one with You,
> Let me embrace You alone.
> Love, Love, You have swept me up violently,
> My heart is beside itself with love;
> I want to faint, Love; may I always be close to You:
> Love, I beseech You, let me die of love. …
> Love, Love, I have contempt for life;
> Love, Love, may my soul be one with You!
> Love, You are my life – my soul cannot live without You;
> Why do You make it faint, clasping it so tightly, Love?[95]

The most enduring image that Jacopone left was that of himself as a madman, a fool for God, renouncing the world and its enticements for eternal rewards and union with God: "It is right and fitting, I believe,/ To go mad over the fair Messiah. … The man who enrolls in this school/ Will discover a new discipline;/ Only those who have experienced this madness/ Have an inkling of what it is."[96] This divine madness is only an imitation of the sacrifice of Christ for insignificant humanity: "Who would ever be mad enough/ To turn himself into an ant/ So as to serve an army of ants,/ An undeserving, ungrateful army of ants?"[97]

The same late twelfth-century urban environment that produced Francis and his order of friars also led to the very similar order of friars, the Order of Preachers, or the Dominicans, founded by the Spaniard Dominic Guzman (ca. 1170–1221). Dominic was a Castilian priest of the cathedral of Osma who, while traveling with his bishop through southern France in 1203, was appalled to discover thriving there the heresy of the Cathars, or Albigensians.[98] The local clergy of the region were held in low esteem because of their lax morality and were no competition for the Cathar leadership, the "Perfected Ones," who lived lives of extreme asceticism. Concerned popes had dispatched to the region Cistercian missionaries, known for their asceticism but lacking the education and preaching skills to refute Cathar teachings. Dominic felt he knew the remedy for the problem, for he was fired with zeal to put into action the spirit of apostolic life consisting of evangelism and voluntary poverty, which, he hoped, would bring the Cathars back into orthodoxy. He settled in Toulouse and soon a small community of preachers and teachers grew around him and in 1216 Pope Honorius III gave confirmation to the brotherhood as a new monastic order. Unlike so many of his contemporary monastic leaders, Dominic was solicitous of the spiritual welfare of women, welcoming them into his order, and Pope Honorius gave him the responsibility of reforming the nuns of Rome. One of those nuns left a loving physical description of him:

Dominic was of middling height and slender build. His face was beautiful and slightly ruddy, and his hair and beard were reddish. He had beautiful eyes. A kind of radiance shone from his forehead and between his eyebrows, which drew everyone to venerate and love him.[99]

Dominic might not have seen supervision of women as an onerous task, for at the end of his life he told his brothers that he had remained a virgin "but I confess that I have not escaped from the imperfection of being more excited by the conversation of young women than by being talked to by old women."[100] Dominic died in August 1221 and was canonized only thirteen years later by Pope Gregory IX.

Only a few letters of Dominic survive, limiting our knowledge of his interior life, but the memory that he left behind was that of a mystic "seeing God by contemplation."[101] Dominic's mission to preach the word of God was confirmed by a powerful vision he received while he was praying in St. Peter's in Rome. The apostles Peter and Paul appeared to him and charged him, "Go and preach, because you have been chosen for this ministry by God."[102] He was remembered as a contemplative and "sometimes it seemed from the very way that he looked that he had penetrated heaven in his mind, and then he would suddenly appear radiant with joy, wiping away the abundant tears running down his face."[103] Many of his close associates recalled the tears that he shed while praying, being unable to "stop himself from bursting out loudly, so that even at a distance people could hear him roaring and crying."[104] Dominic was often "caught up above himself to speak with God and the angels"[105] and his own custom was always "to speak about God or with God," a phrase he had inserted into the constitution of his new order.[106] While praying in church Dominic was observed to levitate "some eight or nine inches above the ground, not touching it at all,"[107] and, due to his intimacy with the Holy Spirit, he was given knowledge of "hidden things."[108]

From the beginning, Dominic wanted his friars to be learned, an essential ingredient for a successful preacher, and soon this learning became especially associated with the scholasticism of the new universities in Europe. The Dominican Order produced some of the great minds of the later Middle Ages and perhaps the most celebrated intellectual of this period is St. Thomas Aquinas (1224/6–74), who could well be the ikon of the intellectualization of Christianity and the antithesis of mysticism.

Thomas was born to a family of the minor nobility in southern Italy and at the age of five he entered the famed monastery of St. Benedict at Monte Cassino, whose abbot his family hoped someday he would become. However, Thomas discovered the new and growing Dominican Order, which, very much against his family's wishes, he joined. To thwart his intentions, his family kidnapped him and held him in loose captivity for about two years, even sending an attractive young woman into his room in the futile hope that somehow she would tempt him away from his religious zeal. Once released by his family, Thomas continued as a Dominican and studied in Paris as well as Cologne. He progressed to teach theology in Paris, Rome, Viterbo, Bologna and Naples, during which time he also wrote a large number of works on Scripture, philosophy and theology, including his great compendia of Christian theology, the *Summa Contra Gentiles* and *Summa Theologiae*.

Thomas's goal was to clear away sloppy philosophical reasoning and to make Christian theology more coherent. Although he had a great reputation for chastity, he was certainly no desert ascetic, for he was known for his girth.[109] For most of his life he also was no mystic. In his writings, he displaced mysticism from the height of Christianity. For Thomas, who was a teacher and preacher, the highest Christian life was that of teachers and preachers. He wrote that God loves contemplatives less than those who live the active life and he was prepared to argue that teaching was part of the contemplative life.[110] Prayer was not the constant fixing of the mind and soul on God, as it was for mystics, but rather was ordinary petitions directed to God.[111] Moreover, he minimized supernatural events and, while admitting that mystical raptures could occur, he believed that there had been only two known instances – those of Moses and of St. Paul.[112]

However, towards the close of his brief life, Thomas appears to have had a mystical encounter that overwhelmed his intellectual side. In December 1273, while celebrating Mass, something happened to him. He seemed in a daze and refused to resume work on his *Summa Theologiae*. He stated, "All that I have written seems to me like straw compared with what has now been revealed to me."[113] He began a commentary on that supreme mystical scripture, the Song of Songs,[114] but died shortly afterwards, on 7 March 1274.

THE BEGUINES

The greater expression of mysticism by women that was one important feature of the new mysticism was most clearly represented by the Beguines. Compelled by the same drive to lead the apostolic life that gave birth to the Cistercians and the Franciscans, the Beguines were women who were not professed nuns but nevertheless devoted themselves to God, especially in the Low Countries, the Rhineland and France beginning in the latter twelfth century. Occasionally the Beguines were individual hermits but more commonly they associated themselves into small sisterhoods of four or five individuals or even large associations of hundreds of women. They supported themselves by their own labor while also engaging in charitable work and they were free to leave the group if they desired, for example to marry or to enter a true convent.

The Beguines were especially devoted to contemplation, the precursor of mysticism, and a distinctive style of mysticism developed among the Beguines, Bridal Mysticism. While other mystics, notably the Cistercians, had written of the soul's union with God in the allegorical language of mystical marriage, the Beguines frequently drew upon the contemporary poetic style of Courtly Love to describe being ravished by God or by Jesus, whom they often portrayed as a dashing and handsome young man.

Our knowledge of the early Beguines is dependent on biographies written by their priests and confessors who were attracted by their sanctity and wished to perpetuate the memory of their subjects' manner of life and the miracles they performed. The question will always be open as to the accuracy of the biographies and to what degree the biographers have structured the lives of their subjects to conform with the expectations of hagiography and to promote their own theological interests. One of those biographers was Jacques de Vitry (ca. 1170–1240), who was born into a noble family in France and studied theology at Paris. He was ordained a priest and became one of the most famed preachers of his day. Later he was named bishop of Acre in the Holy Land and was named to be a member of the College of Cardinals. While he was a student in Paris he heard of one of the first Beguines, Marie (1177/8–1213), a remarkable woman living at Oignies, in the Belgian diocese of Liège. He interrupted his studies to see Marie for himself and she had a remarkable effect on him, as she fired him with apostolic zeal while serving as his spiritual mentor.

In his life of Marie of Oignies, Jacques was so concerned to perpetuate the memory of her holy life that little of her own personality is evident. He also recast the events of Marie's life to present it as an example of the stages of the mystical life described by Richard of St. Victor in his book *The Twelve Patriarchs*,[115] making it difficult to reconstruct a chronology of Marie's life. However, in Jacques' account, she was born in Nivelles, near Liège, to a family perhaps of the lower nobility. When she was fourteen her parents arranged for her to marry but she was already in love with the ascetic life and persuaded her good-natured husband to consent to living a chaste life together.[116] De Vitry recorded that the married but chaste Marie was also devoted to a life imitating the poverty of Christ, owning nothing while begging door-to-door.[117] She was given to abundant tears that flowed down in streams, covering the ground of the church in her muddy footprints, and her weeping became so loud that a priest had to ask her to control herself.[118] Marie was also frequently in ecstasy, out of her body in mystical rapture. Jacques stated:

> Sometimes she would gently rest with the Lord in a sweet and blessed silence for thirty-five days and she never ate any corporeal food and could utter no word except this alone: "I want the Body of our Lord Jesus Christ." When she had received it, she would remain with the Lord in silence for whole days at a time. On those days she had the feeling that her spirit was separated, as it were, from her body. ... Sometimes when she was in her cell, she heard the most sweet voice of the Lord saying, "Here is my beloved daughter in whom I take great delight." When she was rapt outside of herself, it seemed to her that her head was lying upon the knees of the glorified Christ.[119]

As would become typical for Beguines, Marie had visions of Jesus as a baby or as a handsome boy:

> Frequently when the priest was raising the host she saw between the hands of the priest the outward appearance of a beautiful boy and an army of the heavenly spirits descending with a great light. ... When the Lord appeared to her in the likeness of a boy tasting of honey and smelling like spices, she would

often gladly admit him into the pure and richly decorated chamber of her heart. … She was tormented, she cried out and begged that [God] remain and it seemed that she embraced him within her arms lest he leave and tearfully prayed that he show himself more clearly to her. Sometimes it seemed to her that she held him more tightly between her breasts like a clinging baby for three or more days and she would hide him there lest he be seen by others and at other times she kissed him as if he were an infant.[120]

Her biographer reported that she also experienced the mystical "fire of love," with her body radiating discernible heat while her clothing gave off the odor of incense.[121] In addition, she was given even more spiritual gifts – clairvoyancy, prophecy and healing by laying her hands on those afflicted by illness.[122] Even after her death, Marie continued to come to the assistance of her loved ones, providing them with instructions and warning them of dangers, removing "from their hearts all doubt by certain and secret signs."[123]

One of those graced by a posthumous appearance by Marie was the nun Lutgard of Aywières (1200–64). Her *Life* was written by Thomas of Cantimpré (ca. 1200 to ca. 1270), also a native of the region of Liège. As a young man he was moved by the preaching of Jacques de Vitry and entered the monastery of Augustinian Canons at Cantimpré outside Cambrai, where he came to know Lutgard, abbess of the Cistercian convent at nearby Aywières. In time Lutgard became Thomas's spiritual mentor just as Marie of Oignies had been with Jacques de Vitry. Thomas eventually left Cantimpré to join the Dominican order of friars and studied theology at Paris and probably also Cologne before returning to his native region for a career as a preacher. Thomas was greatly impressed by the holy women of his home region and wrote lives of Lutgard, Christina Mirabilis, Margaret of Ypres and a supplement to Jacques de Vitry's life of Marie of Oignies. In the life of Lutgard, however, like Jacques's life of Marie, "her real person remains shrouded behind the elaborate mystical structure imposed on her *vita*."[124]

Thomas's *vita* relates that Lutgard was born in Tongres, near Liège, to a noble mother and a father of the burgher class. God intervened to frustrate her father's marriage plans for her and at the age of twelve she entered the Benedictine convent of St. Catherine, next to the town of St. Trond. Soon she began manifesting the phenomena of a mystical life. She was observed levitating in the air during the chants for Pentecost, a brilliant light appeared over her head during her vigils, lasting through the night, and she experienced such heat that sweat poured from her.[125] Thomas also recorded an experience that came over her while she was standing before an image of Christ, expressing a fascination with the wounds of Christ that characterized much of Beguine spirituality:

Then her eyes would close and her limbs would sink to the ground and, fainting and no longer able to stand on her feet, she would be rapt in spirit. Then she would see Christ with the bloody wound in his side and, pressing the mouth of her heart against it, she would suck such sweetness that nothing at all could distress her.[126]

There was also unusual sound associated with her visions of Christ. While she was chanting:

> Christ, with outward appearance of a lamb, positioning himself on her breast so that one foot was on her right shoulder and the other on her left. He would place His mouth on her mouth and by thus sucking, would draw out from her breast a melody of wondrous mellowness.[127]

Lutgard was chosen prioress of the convent but at the age of twenty-four she moved to the house of Cistercian nuns at Aywières, in the duchy of Brabant, where she spent the remaining forty years of her life, eventually rising to the position of abbess. At Aywières her mystical experiences continued. When asked how the face of Christ appeared to her in contemplation, she answered:

> An indescribable brilliance appears to me in an instant as I see the ineffable beauty of His glorified Being as if it were a resplendence. Were this vision not to pass quickly from the gaze of my contemplation, I would not be able to endure it nor continue to live. After this resplendence disappears, there still remains an intellectual brilliance and "when I seek him" in that brilliance, "I cannot find him."[128]

As with Marie of Oignies, Lutgard was given the gift of prophecy and she also wept tears in such abundance that they amazed even her biographer: "I myself once saw such floods of tears that one could scarcely bear it without weeping oneself."[129]

Another contemporary with Lutgard and Marie of Oignies was Christina of St. Trond (1150–1224), called Mirabilis ("the Astonishing"), who was a frequent visitor to St. Catherine's and knew Lutgard. Thomas of Cantimpré was also her hagiographer, composing her *vita* within eight years of her death. Thomas related that God had given Christina "the grace of an inward sweetness and very often visited her with heavenly secrets."[130] However, "she grew sick in body by virtue of the exercise of inward contemplation and she died."[131] But then, as the Requiem mass was being said for her, she returned to life. In what must be the most extreme case of levitation among mystics, her body then ascended to the rafters, causing most of the would-be mourners to run from the church. Once brought down to earth, Christina described her near-death-experience, how "ministers of light" took her past purgatory and on to paradise, where Jesus gave her the choice of staying with him there or returning to her body to suffer great torments which, however, would free from purgatory those whom she had seen and pitied there. Without hesitation she returned to her body.[132] Christina came back to life with an unusual insight, for she had seen a place near hell, which was not purgatory but held the souls of those who had committed great sins which they had not confessed but had been repented. That place differed from hell in that its residents had hope of mercy.[133]

Christina then indeed suffered torments. She fled the company of people, arousing suspicion that she was possessed by demons, and she was put in chains. However, she was miraculously freed of the chains and she fled to remote places where she dwelt in the top of trees. She would crawl into fiery ovens and boiling cauldrons of water and escape unharmed while also living under the freezing waters of the river Meuse for almost a week and emerging alive. Maddeningly for her, people sought her out and clustered around her, driving her back into the wildernesses and to the tree-tops.

She also visited Catherine's convent at St. Trond and spoke with the nuns there. Christina must have astonished them as well, for,

> she would speak of Christ and suddenly and unexpectedly she would be ravished in the spirit and her body would roll and whirl like a hoop. She whirled around with such extreme violence that the individual limbs of her body could not be distinguished. When she had whirled around for a long time in this manner, it seemed as if she became weakened by the violence of the rolling and all her limbs grew quiet. Then a wondrous harmony sounded between her throat and breast which no mortal man could understand nor could it be imitated by any artificial instrument.[134]

Thomas reported a melodious miracle at St. Catherine's for Christina:

> she would utter such sweet songs that they seemed to be the songs of angels and not of human origin. This song was so marvelous to hear that it surpassed the music of all instruments and the voices of all mortals. Nevertheless this song was less sweet and much unequal to the sweet song of harmony which sounded incomparably from between her throat and breast and which surpassed human understanding.[135]

Christina had a gift for prophecy and was credited with predicting the fall of Jerusalem to the Muslims in 1187 as well as "many other wondrous things which have now been fulfilled and which we believe will be fulfilled in the future."[136] It was at St. Catherine's that Christina died a second time, forty-two years after her first experience. This time she was fetched back to life by the fervent prayers of one of the nuns. An irritated Christina came back to life demanding to know why she had been disturbed, for "Just now I was being led to the face of Christ!"[137] She then died a third and final time.

Christina was incomparable but another of the early Beguines, Margaret of Ypres (1216–37), gained a high reputation for her asceticism and mysticism in the three short years of her devotion to a life of poverty and mortification of the flesh. She died at the age of twenty-one, perhaps as a result of her severe fasting, for she ate no more than a small child would.[138] In her *vita*, also written by Thomas of Cantimpré, she was described as being born to a good burgher family in Ypres and having been educated at a nearby convent. However, at age eighteen, she fell under the influence of a

Dominican preacher and adopted the life of a Beguine while continuing to live at home. For all her sanctity, she must have been a difficult child. She practiced silence to such a degree that her spiritual father, acting at her mother's request, ordered her to speak for a short, strictly defined period each day. Margaret preferred to spend her time on her balcony where "she rested in prayer and meditation during the middle of the day." She said, "I must unite myself with Christ in meditation on my balcony upstairs, I am affected with so much inner joy that I cannot stand on my feet at that time."[139]

Margaret received many divine revelations which she revealed only to her spiritual father. However, Thomas was able to give some brief glimpses into her visions:

> Once when she entered the church, she was suddenly filled with a wonderful joy. Afterwards she said that never had she conceived such joy except when her spirit went outside itself in contemplation … she raised her eyes to heaven and at once it appeared that she was seen to be drawn heavenward and to be suddenly rapt in ecstasy. What she saw there, we can only guess but cannot say.[141]

Margaret was visited with tears, once spending three days and nights in continuous grief for her sins. Her body also became so warm that she wore a single tunic even in extreme cold and Thomas of Cantimpré said that she burned in the fire of love for Christ.[142] As her brief life drew to an end, she suffered a severe hemorrhage and became paralyzed, but she reveled in her suffering. She told her mother she was willing to remain in that state until the Day of Judgment: "I consider that to be in hell with the approval of Christ is the highest good and, in this case, I consider that I am doing something worthy of Christ."[143]

These biographies present images of lives of such extremes of asceticism and absolute devotion to God, all of them amazing in different ways, that they have appalled many who have studied them. But it has been noted that the *vitae* "no doubt provoked equal revulsion among fourteenth-century readers, and in all likelihood they were intended to have just that impact."[144] The purpose of the biographies was not to serve as achievable models of the Christian life for the masses but rather to inspire ordinary people to devote more effort into living up to the common standards of morality.

Mechthild of Magdeburg (ca. 1210 to ca. 1282) is a mystical Beguine who told her own story. She is an example of a Beguine who gave up that life to become a cloistered nun, arriving at the north German Benedictine convent of St Mary's at Helfta at about the age of sixty after having already lived a life of mystical revelations and dialogues. She was the first mystic to write in a vernacular language, in her case Middle Low German, and she provides all that is known of her life in *The Flowing Light of the Godhead*. She related that her mystical life began when she was twelve, when she:

> was greeted so overwhelmingly by the Holy Spirit … while I was alone, with such an outpouring that I could never, after that endure letting myself be led into a clear venial sin. This precious greeting occurred every day and lovingly

spoiled me for all worldly sweetness, and it is still increasing day by day. This happened over thirty-one years.[145]

A few years later she became a Beguine at Magdeburg and continued receiving visions for the next twenty years. Around 1270, she entered the cloister at Helfta and there she wrote the seventh and final book of *The Flowing Light of the Godhead*.

Mechthild wrote one of the fullest expressions of the Bridal Mysticism that typified the Beguines, as she wrote the words of Christ, the divine bridegroom, "Look at me, my bride. See how beautiful are my eyes, how comely is my mouth, how on fire is my heart, how agile are my hands, and how swift are my feet. So, follow me!"[146] In dialogue form she portrayed the union between the soul and God quite sexually:

> "Stay, Lady Soul."
> "What do you bid me, Lord?"
> "Take off your clothes."
> "Lord, what will happen to me then?"
> "Lady Soul, you are so utterly formed to my nature
> That not the slightest thing can be between you and me. ... "
> "Lord, now I am a naked soul
> And you in yourself are a well-adorned God.
> Our shared lot is eternal life
> Without death."
> Then a blessed stillness
> That both desire comes over them.
> He surrenders himself to her,
> And she surrenders herself to him.[147]

Even before Mechthild arrived at Helfta, that house had produced a remarkable pair of mystics. Gertrude the Great (1256–1302) entered the convent at the age of four and had her first vision when she was twenty-five, which she recorded in her Latin work, *The Herald of Divine Love*:

> I was standing in the middle of the dormitory ... I looked up and saw before me a youth of about sixteen years of age, handsome and gracious. Young as I then was, the beauty of his form was all that I could have desired, entirely pleasing to the outward eye. Courteously and in a gentle voice, he said to me: "Soon will come your salvation ... " While he was speaking ... it seemed to me that I was in the Choir, in the corner where I usually say my tepid prayers; and it was there that I heard these words: "I will save you. I will deliver you. Do not fear." With this, I saw his hand, tender and fine, holding mine, as though to plight a troth.[148]

Those who knew her understood that "she was constantly favored with the divine presence."[149] She not only saw Jesus and had conversations with him but she also received understanding of Scriptures and religious truths, which allowed the other nuns at Helfta to pose questions to Jesus through her. In answer to her prayer that she might always keep before her the wounds of Jesus, she was given a special favor: "I knew in my spirit that I had received the stigmata of your adorable and venerable wounds interiorly in my heart, just as though they had been made on the natural places of the body."[150]

Gertrude's fellow nun and friend at Helfta was Mechthild of Hackeborn (ca. 1241–99), who was also a renowned mystic who had dramatic visions. Like Gertrude, Mechthild was a mediator between Jesus and her community as well as to the world outside of the convent as many brought their petitions to God to her:

> She gave teaching with such abundance that such a one has never been seen in the monastery and we fear, alas, will never be seen again. The sisters gathered around her as around a preacher to hear the word of God. She was the refuge and consoler of all and by a singular gift had the ability to make others open to her in trust the secrets of their hearts; how many not only in the monastery but also from outside, religious and secular, came from afar and were rescued by her from their troubles; and they said that they had discovered such consolation nowhere except with her.[151]

THE AGE OF REPRESSION AND THE MYSTICS OF THE RHINELAND AND THE LOW COUNTRIES

By the latter twelfth century, about the time that Mechthild was entering Helfta, the great period of European expansion was drawing to a close, putting all of society, including the church, under stress. The three-century-long period of economic growth began to flag in the latter thirteenth century. Lands put to the plow during the years of expansion now saw decreased productivity and shrinking harvests, which led to food shortages. These disasters were exacerbated by a long-term cooling trend in the European climate that shortened the growing season and further reduced the harvests. A series of disastrous crop failures left the people of western Europe in misery in the first two decades of the fourteenth century, followed by the arrival of the Black Death in the 1340s, which dramatically reduced the problem of overpopulation by carrying off one third to one half of the population in the space of only three years.

Moreover, the growth of the monarchies of Europe, especially those of England and France, featured those kings striving to consolidate both the territories which they claimed and their positions over the entire state – over aristocracy, church, law and government. Kings of England set about conquering Wales and Scotland while kings of France worked to bring the south under their control and to expand to the west and the northwest. In contrast, the German monarchy collapsed in the latter thirteenth century, leaving Germany a patchwork of virtually independent duchies, counties, bishoprics and cities.

Moreover, heresies seemed to be everywhere. In southern France the Cathar movement had been unaffected by all orthodox efforts at conversion by persuasion, even those of Dominic and his friars. The Albigensian Crusade preached against the Cathars in 1208 resulted in a twenty-year war that concluded in the military conquest of that region by royal armies, mostly from the north. However, despite all this, the Cathars survived. The problem was to discover those who were Cathars and either lead them to orthodoxy or remove them from society. The solution was the Inquisition, created by the papacy in the 1230s specifically for the Cathar heresy but it was useful as a powerful weapon against actual or presumed heretics of all varieties as well as those who were simply unpopular.

The creation of the Inquisition was only one sign that the church, along with the states, was becoming increasingly centralized, institutionalized and regulated. "As the church became increasingly institutionalised so it was less able to tolerate any disruptive force in its midst."[152] There was more religious enthusiasm than the church could fathom, while official religious orders proliferated and unofficial movements of laypeople, such as the Beguines and Beghards (the male counterparts of the Beguines), seemed to be everywhere. In particular, the Beguines and Beghards were associated with the heresy of the Free Spirit, which was not an organized sect but rather was a set of tenets believed to have been held by individual mystics. The authorities understood these teachings to include antinomianism, the belief that the adherents could become so perfected in this life that their souls were at liberty and no longer capable of sin, thus they no longer needed divine grace or the church and its sacraments. In the decree *Ad Nostrum* in 1312, a council at Vienne condemned these views as well as the Beguines.[153] The real targets of the council were itinerant women for it condoned "truly pious women" who lived penitently in communal houses. Nevertheless, authorities tended to regard with suspicion even the "good" Beguines who lived in communities and numbers of their houses were closed in the following years.

The repressive measures of the thirteenth and fourteenth centuries also condemned as heretics the ascetical Waldensians and the mystical Amalricians[154] while the Spiritual Franciscans were condemned by Pope John XXII (1316–34)[155] and some of them were burnt at the stake. Even Thomas Aquinas was not immune from attack and several aspects of his teachings were condemned as heretical by masters at Paris and Oxford after his death.[156]

Into this age of intolerance and repression appeared the astonishing mystical teaching of Meister Eckhart (ca. 1260–1327/8), who has attracted great modern scholarly interest, for he was the most philosophical and theological medieval writer on mysticism and is thus often more attractive to modern scholars than visionary mystics. He left no personal account of mystical experiences and with Eckhart the modern researcher does not have to deal with embarrassments like visions or miracles. However, the large corpus of his writings reveals the depth of his mystical thinking and it is difficult to believe that he devoted such effort to a subject whose interest for him was merely theoretical.

Johannes Eckhart was born in Thuringia, in Germany, and became a Dominican friar when he was fifteen. He studied both at Cologne and Paris, where he also taught theology as a master, the source of his title "Meister." He was active in the administration of the Dominican order in Germany and supervised women's convents as well. In his pastoral life Eckhart was an active preacher and spiritual director, writing tracts and sermons in both German and Latin.

Eckhart's mystical ideas go far beyond simply expounding traditional Christian mysticism, for they have long been seen to have much in common with Eastern thought, especially Vedantic Hinduism and Zen Buddhism.[157] It is intriguing to read his statements that all suffering comes from attachment, that there is nothing but God, that God is in everything and that there is only the eternal now[158] while marveling at their similarity to Eastern concepts.

His central idea of the possible union between humans and God is firmly planted in almost all of his writings and his description of the means for this union and the proper way of understanding God are very similar to those found in Plato, Plotinus and Pseudo-Dionysius. Complete union with God is expressed in Platonic concepts, being possible because the spark of the soul is itself divine and this union can occur through self-renunciation and detachment from false images of God. One must abandon all images, names and concepts of God, even that of God, for "God's being is transcendent, he is beyond all knowledge."[159] In a teaching that would shock any Christian of an ordinary religious education, Eckhart argued that there was a God higher than the God of the Christian Trinity:

> God is nameless, for no one can speak of him or know him. ... Accordingly, if I say that "God is good," this is not true. ... If I say again that "God is wise," then this too is not true. ... Or if I say that "God exists," this also is not true. He is being beyond being, he is a nothingness beyond being. Therefore St Augustine says: "The finest thing that we can say of God is to be silent concerning him from the wisdom of inner riches." Be silent therefore, and do not chatter about God, for by chattering about him, you tell lies and commit a sin. ... If you wish to be perfect and without sin, then do not prattle about God. Also you should not wish to understand anything about God, for God is beyond all understanding. A master [Augustine, sermon 117] says: If I had a God that I could understand, I would not regard him as God.[160]

Eckhart wrote that whatever is called God cannot be God, for "God is above names and nature."[161] Because the God of the Trinity can be named and has attributes, it cannot be the ultimate God, which he styled the Godhead, therefore "God and Godhead are as far apart from each other as heaven and earth." Thus he stated the paradox

> that we should forsake God is altogether what God intends, for as long as the soul has God, knows God and is aware of God, she is far from God. This then is God's desire – that God should reduce himself to nothing in the soul so that the soul may lose herself.[162]

Eckhart went even farther, writing, "Therefore I ask God to make me free of 'God,' for my most essential being is above 'God' in so far as we conceive of God as the origin of creatures."[163] Like Pseudo-Dionysius, for Meister Eckhart, one could know God only by an unknowing:

> If you wish to know God in a divine manner, then your knowing must become a pure unknowing, a forgetting of yourself and of all creatures. … You are never better placed than when you are in complete darkness and unknowing. [164]

In perhaps his boldest statement of complete unity with God, Eckhart described this union as "becoming God." He wrote that, for those who dwell in God, "between that person and God there is no distinction and they are one. … Between such a person and God, however, not only is there no distinction, but there is no multiplicity, since there is only One."[165] Eckhart added, "Such a person is established in God's knowledge and in God's love and is nothing other than what God is"[166] and he quoted St. Augustine: "through love we become what we love. Now should we say that if we love God, we become God?" Asking rhetorically if that statement sounded like paganism, Eckhart answered, "It may sound strange to say that we can become God in such a way in love, and yet this is true in the eternal truth. Our Lord Jesus Christ proves it."[167]

Such concepts might not have been shocking to Byzantine hesychasts but they were certainly unfamiliar to Westerners and some of his statements were condemned as erroneous or heretical in a papal bull in 1329 shortly after his death. However, this was a very limited condemnation, for it concerned only twenty-eight articles of Eckhart's writings. Moreover it resulted from a personal vendetta against Eckhart by the archbishop of Cologne, who prevailed on Pope John XXII, who owed him political debts, to issue the bull. It was published only in Cologne even though Eckhart had lived and preached in Erfurt and Strasbourg. However, the condemnations did have a chilling effect on open citation of Eckhart's works. His followers in the Rhineland did not abandon his ideas but they were careful to phrase them in more traditional and conservative language. As a result, Eckhart's works were largely ignored until the nineteenth century.

Among those who continued to propagate Eckhart's teachings was John Tauler (ca. 1300–61), who did not know Eckhart personally but rather studied the master's teachings and became solidly Eckhartian. Tauler was the son of a prosperous burgher family in Strasbourg, then a German city in the Holy Roman Empire, and he became a Dominican by 1314. He received the usual Dominican rigorous theological training and became a preacher while also providing spiritual direction to Dominican nuns in Strasbourg.

By means of his sermons delivered in the vernacular Middle High German to the nuns under his supervision, Tauler ensured the survival of the essence of Meister Eckhart's apophatic mystical theology in his advice to his spiritual daughters. The core of his message was the same as that of all of the ascetical Desert Fathers and monastic writers of the Eastern Church, that Christians should shun vices and cultivate the virtues, detach themselves from transitory worldly pleasures and abandon their self-will and themselves to God, stripping away from themselves all that is not God. This movement to God would result in God's movement to them, producing the birth of God in the ground of the soul, concluding with union with God so complete that the soul would become one spirit with God. Detachment, abandonment and union were Tauler's repetitive themes.

Some have doubted that Tauler himself ever experienced union with God,[168] for he never made claims about himself, but what we know of Tauler's thoughts comes from his sermons, which are didactic and not autobiographical, to the nuns under his direction. His primary aim was to encourage the nuns to live the true Christian life that leads to union with God: "we must renounce our own will, desire, and worldly activity, so that we can orient ourselves singlemindedly toward God, and meet Him only in complete abandonment of self. What should remain is a pure cleaving to God alone."[169] He was a tireless preacher of unitive mysticism and he vividly and movingly expressed the coming of the Holy Spirit into the soul:

> He causes a burning love, a flaming love which sets the soul on fire. The heat flashes off sparks and this engenders a thirst for God and a loving desire. … As soon as the Holy Spirit can come with His presence and freely flood the depth of the soul with His wondrous radiance and divine light, then He, who is rightly called the Comforter, is able to exercise His sweet comfort there – oh, what a blissful rapture is now to occur![170]

Tauler warned his nuns that the path to union was not easy, for progress came in stages and union was unlikely to occur before one's fortieth year, while another ten years would be required before the Holy Spirit would be one's own.[171] He repeatedly extolled the inward life over outward observances. Contrasting unfavorably those who merely study the Scriptures with those who live them, he stated that it was better "to experience the working of the Trinity" than to talk about it, and he recommended "true prayer," which is "an ascent of the mind to God," over mechanical prayers, which are mere babbling.[172] The Dominican sisters under his direction received constant encouragement and exhortation, couched in Eckhartian phraseology and imagery, to follow the demanding path that led to mystical union with God.

Another vehicle for the transmission of Eckhart's mystical theology and the elaboration of the arduous journey to God was Tauler's associate Henry Suso, or Seuss, another Dominican friar charged with the spiritual instruction of women in his Order and whose life in many ways paralleled that of Tauler. Suso (1295–1366) was born to a noble family in Constance, in Switzerland. His original name was Henry von Berg but later, to honor his beloved mother, he adopted her family name of Sus, or Süss, Latinized into Suso. We know far more about Suso than we do of Tauler because, in a reversal of the usual pattern of male clerics writing the spiritual lives of female mystics, Elsbeth Stagel, a nun under his direction at the Dominican convent at Töss, in the Swiss canton of Zurich, quizzed him about his life and surreptitiously recorded his responses. Her stealthy work forms the core of his "autobiography," the *Life of the Servant*. When Suso learned of what she had done, he demanded that she hand over the manuscript, which he began burning until "a celestial message from God"[173] ordered him to stop. He then edited and amended the text and added three of his spiritual treatises to form what is today known as *The Exemplar*. One of those treatises was *The Little Book of Eternal Wisdom*, an examination in German of his important theme of detachment. He also wrote a Latin version of the book, the *Horologium Sapientiae* ("The Clock of Wisdom"), which became one of the most widely read books of the Middle Ages, being copied repeatedly and widely disseminated.

Suso entered the Dominican house at Constance at the age of thirteen, two years earlier than customary, and received a thorough theological education very much like that of Tauler. For his higher studies, he was sent to Cologne, where he encountered Meister Eckhart and embraced his teachings. Around 1326 Suso returned to his Dominican house at Cologne and became lector, directing the education of the novices. He might have imbibed a bit too deeply of Eckhart's theology for it appears that he faced a charge of heresy. He was cleared of the accusation but he lost his post. He was humbled but his career was not seriously harmed and soon afterwards he became the prior (the superior) of his house and also undertook the supervision of Dominican women.

In contrast to Tauler, only a few of Suso's sermons survive and they provide no glimpse into his interior life. However, thanks to the clandestine biographical work of Elsbeth Stagel, we have a precious record of his spiritual life of growth and progression. He regarded the first five years of his monastic life as unremarkable but then he experienced a sudden conversion to a more rigorous life and was led along the same path that Tauler preached – detachment, abandonment, inwardness, single-mindedness.[174] By that conversion, God drew "him in a hidden but illuminating manner" and he was called to "a painful rejection of everything that could be an obstacle for him."[175] Even as a beginner on the path to God, Suso began experiencing vivid visions. As he was standing alone in the choir,

> he saw and heard what all tongues cannot express. It was without form or definite manner of being, yet it contained within itself the joyous, delightful wealth of all forms and manners. His heart was full of desire, yet sated. His mind was cheerful and pleased. He had no further wishes and his desires faded away. He did nothing but stare into the bright refulgence, which made him forget himself and all else. Was it day or night? He did not know. It was a bursting forth of the delight of eternal life, present to his awareness, notionless, calm. Then he said, "If this is not heaven, I do not know what heaven is. Enduring all the suffering that one can put into words is not rightly enough to justify one's possessing this eternally." This overpowering transport lasted perhaps an hour, perhaps only a half hour. Whether the soul remained in the body or had been separated from the body, he did not know.[176]

The experiences were a frequent occurrence to him, as

> flashes from heaven came time and again deep within him and it seemed to him

somehow he was floating in the air. The powers of his soul were filled with the sweet tastes of heaven … [and] this heavenly fragrance stayed with him long afterward and gave him a heavenly longing for God.[177]

For ten years, Suso had similar experiences twice a day, during which

he sank so completely in God into eternal Wisdom that he was unable to speak of it. Sometimes he held an intimate conversation with God, sighed in lament, wept with longing, or sometimes smiled quietly. He often felt as though he were floating in the air and swimming in the deep flow of God's boundless marvels between time and eternity.[178]

Suso also devoted himself to strict ascetic and penitential practices, for which, unfortunately, he is often best known today. He observed virtual total silence for thirty years, ate only one meal a day and abstained from meat, fish and eggs, and practiced poverty so completely that he would not even touch the smallest coin. He tortured his body with every device that the medieval monastic mind could devise. He slept on an old door wearing gloves covered with tacks which, should he try to relieve the itching of his hairshirt or vermin bites, would rip into his skin. In addition to his hairshirt, he wore iron chains to chafe his skin, had straps of nails next to his skin, and on his back he carried a wooden cross with iron nails and needles sticking out of it. He carved into his own skin, above his heart, the name of Jesus in the form of the IHS.

However, Suso described these self-tortures in such detail for the purpose of emphasizing their futility. By elaborating on his extreme penitential life, he established his credentials – no one could be more penitential than Henry Suso and yet it was not enough. After years of these practices, he had a vision in which "a heavenly gathering … announced to him that God no longer wanted this of him. He put an end to it and threw everything into the river."[179] He came to understand that all he had done was "nothing more than a good beginning."[180] What God wanted was detachment and complete forgetfulness of self, that is, abandonment. In his spiritual advice to Elsbeth Stagel he counseled against exaggerated severity, stating that "austerity practiced in moderation is better than immoderate practices."[181] Suso specified that it was in his fortieth year[182] that he abandoned his great severity and set out to follow a different path, an "advanced school" which was "complete and perfect detachment from oneself, so that a person becomes so utterly nothing … that he strives continually to be in a state of going away from his 'self,' … and he aims alone at God's praise and honor."[183]

Suso criticized those who merely made a show of religious practices without making an interior change and truly following Christ through detachment and abandonment. Tauler had agreed, branding as Pharisees those whose religious acts are actually forms of seeking themselves instead of abandoning themselves to God, even though they might spend more time on external pious exercises than those who were "God's friends."[184] Tauler stated simply, "God does not demand a lot of external devotions. … The more inward a devotion is, the better it is."[185]

The phrase "friend of God" is an important theme in the writings of both Tauler and Suso as indeed it had been for Eckhart, and it was not a pious cliché. The two Dominican preachers were part of a wider movement in the fourteenth century encompassing laity and clergy, women and men, who believed that the institutional church of the later Middle Ages had accommodated itself all too cozily to the religiously lukewarm. It seemed to emphasize the fulfillment of external acts and practices to the neglect of genuine interior transformation and obliged Christians to confess their sins and take the Eucharist only once each year. Moreover, corruption ran through the church establishment. Ubiquitous priests of low moral character became stock characters in works of literature such as Boccaccio's *Decameron* or Chaucer's *Canterbury Tales.* They were merely office-holders drawing an income, failing to call the faithful to sacrifice or awaken them to the rigorous life of attempting to imitate the life of Christ. Indeed, the problem ran right to the top, to the papal court itself, which acquired a reputation for avarice that scandalized the more serious-minded Christians of Europe.

Christians like Tauler and Suso were dissatisfied with a religion of external devotions and desired to live up to the highest ideals of the church in a life of apostolic poverty and asceticism. In the Rhineland in the fourteenth century many of these more rigorous Christians formed a loose association of acquaintances dedicated to the principles preached by Tauler and Suso – detachment, abandonment, inwardness, single-minded devotion to God – principles that were the essential preparation for mysticism. This small "church within the church" provided mutual support and encouragement in pursuing an intensely interior spiritual life and recruited others of similar inclinations into their association. The term they used for themselves was Friends of God.[186]

One glimpse into the organization of the Friends of God is provided by one of their number, Henry of Nördlingen, a priest in southwestern Germany who traveled throughout the region as a spiritual advisor to Cistercian and Dominican convents and monasteries. In this role he visited the Dominican women's house of Maria Medingen in the Swabian region of southwestern Bavaria, northwest of Augsburg, in 1332. One of the nuns directed to him for counseling was Margaret Ebner. Their encounter sparkled with the energy of the meeting of two kindred souls. She found Henry to be a gift from God while Henry discovered that she was a profound mystic whose spiritual growth he could nurture. He provided her with mystical works, such as those by Mechthild of Magdeburg and Henry Suso, introduced her to other Friends of God, such as Tauler and Suso, and, most importantly, urged her to record her past mystical experiences as well as her new ones. Despite her initial reluctance, she eventually threw herself into the task and became convinced that she was writing at the command of God. The result was her first-hand account, *Revelations.*

Margaret (ca. 1291–1350) was from a rich and influential Swabian family in Donauwörth. When she was fifteen she followed a family tradition and entered the convent of Maria Medingen. Of her first twenty years there, Margaret had little to say, but her mystical experiences seem to have begun as a result of her intense prayers for the "Poor Souls." These were souls in purgatory, many of whom were deceased sisters of her community, who began appearing to her to express their thanks for her prayers. In time Margaret also had visionary encounters with Jesus, the Virgin Mary and her favorite apostle, St. John the Evangelist. She was also given revelations of truth of hidden things: "It illumined me in the light of true Christian faith, so that for me all things were comprehensible which are with God or flow from God."[187] The experiences were so profound that she feared losing her human senses, but she was repeatedly reassured by God, "I am not a robber of the senses, I am an enlightener of the senses."[188] Indeed, Margaret reported strong sensory perceptions associated with her experiences, especially sweetness and a strong, wonderful fragrance. Along with so many mystics of her age, Margaret wanted to share in the sufferings of Jesus. She prayed to receive the Stigmata as St. Francis had and, like so many Beguines, she desired to drink from the wounds of Jesus on the cross. She experienced raptures that left her feeling lightness of her body, even to the point of no longer touching the ground.[189] In the end, she could only exclaim, "Can heaven be better than this?"[190]

There were also trials for her to suffer. She had a chronic illness that left her debilitated and requiring the help of another sister for her needs. But she also had uncontrollable responses to her experiences, "binding silences" in which she was unable to utter a word, as well as "speakings" in which she repeated "Jesus Christus" until she was hoarse and exhausted. However, the speakings might also be "inner," audible only to her. At times she would burst out into fits of laughter or produce loud "outcries," in which she screamed out such phrases as "Oh, no! Oh, no! My beloved Lord, Jesus Christ"[191] so loudly that she had to absent herself from Mass to avoid disrupting the service. At times these manifestations followed each other in rapid succession.

In an example of "mother mysticism,"[192] which could also be experienced by men, the Christ child was the special object of Margaret's devotion, for she desired to nurture, hold and nurse the baby Jesus. She reported that in her room she had a statue, or doll, of the child Jesus which spoke to her, "If you do not suckle me, then I will draw away from you and you will take no delight in me." She took up the statue, placed it against her naked breast and the child suckled. She "perceived then the most powerful grace in the presence of God that I began to wonder how our dear Lady could have endured the continuous presence of God."[193] Margaret used the opportunities of her intimacies with the child Jesus to ask him questions that were not answered in the Gospels – was it cold when he was born (it was), what happened to the rich gifts of the Magi (they were given away so that Jesus always lived in poverty), and did his circumcision hurt (it did, greatly).

Margaret and Henry were actually together on only eight occasions over the almost twenty years of their acquaintance, but they had an active correspondence. Their separation was necessary because of the bitter dispute between the Holy Roman Emperor Louis IV of Bavaria (1314–47) and Pope John XXII. In the last of the great medieval clashes between emperor and pope, in 1327 John XXII refused to accept Louis as emperor and Louis declared John XXII deposed as pope. The pope placed Germany under interdict, which prohibited the performance of any church service, including the celebration of the Mass, and the emperor responded by threatening punishment to those clergy in his lands who respected the interdict, forcing clerics to choose between pope and emperor. Henry of Nördlingen sided with John XXII and prudently moved out of Germany to Basle, where he continued to organize Friends of God. Tauler and Suso followed the allegiance of their Order and obeyed the pope, necessitating their absence from their native cities for several years. Margaret, however, was an adamant supporter of the emperor, a fellow Bavarian with close connections to her native city of Donauwörth. She prayed for him constantly and was assured by God that she had helped prolong his life. After his death, it was revealed to her that Louis IV was in purgatory but she was assured that he would soon be in heaven. God told her that opposition to Louis, presumably including that of the pope, came about because "human judgment is often mistaken."[194] Margaret and her sisters clearly were no blind respecters of all ecclesiastical authority, for they continued to have Mass celebrated in defiance of the interdict and Christ reassured her in this disobedience: "Whoever desires me in true love, I will never renounce here or hereafter."[195] Margaret also recorded that her convent allowed a laywoman to be buried at their house in spite of the bishop's prohibition, but, discretely, it was done in secret.[196]

Perhaps the true leader of the Friends of God was the layman Rulman Merswin (1307–82), who was also associated with Henry of Nördlingen, Margaret Ebner and John Tauler, who was his confessor. Merswin was a wealthy banker of Strasbourg but in 1347 he gave up his business and, along with his wife Gertrude, renounced the world, taking an oath of chastity and devoting his life to being a "serious Christian." Merswin died in 1382 and soon afterwards one hears no more of the Friends of God. Their movement was obviously a very small one, confined to the close circle of associates.

Merswin wrote an account of the early years of his conversion in the short book *The Four Beginning Years*. In it he described an experience just after his retirement to the simple life, as he was walking in his garden:

> it came to pass that a clear light quickly surrounded me, and I was taken up and swept up from the earth and carried in all directions back and forth throughout the garden. And as I was being carried in this way I felt as if extremely sweet words were being spoken to me. What this light was and this leading power and the sweet words, I do not know; God certainly knows, but it was all beyond my comprehension. When this happy hour was over and I came to myself once again, I found myself standing alone in the garden. And I looked around and saw no one nor anything else, but felt only a copious stream of tears flowing from my eyes, which I was unable to stop.[197]

Merswin reported that he had frequent experiences of this nature, which made him want to shout out in exultation at "a foretaste of the eternal happiness."[198] He also had revelations "that would seem strange and meaningless to the average Christian, and that many men would regard as incredible."[199] Merswin was not content merely to bask in mystical visionary bliss, for he wanted to encourage serious Christianity and he had the money to finance his plans. He bought a dilapidated abbey on Green Isle, in the Ill river near Strasbourg, which he repaired and opened as a retreat center for Friends of God.

Merswin also wrote a number of tracts setting forth the essential teaching of the Friends of God. *The Book of Nine Rocks* exposes the lamentable state of Christendom. All classes and persons were equally culpable, being unwilling to live the Christian life as God intended it to be. Merswin described a vision that came to him, an allegory of a mountain with nine rocks, or stages, in the Christian ascent to God, "the origin." The struggles and dangers are exquisitely detailed, along with the basic argument of the Friends of God that people must surrender themselves in obedience to God and forsake transient things. God provides his luminous grace to those on the eighth rock almost always in the form of visions. However, God, the origin, cannot be seen in a vision because "no words or images can express it."[200] Those at the highest stage of the ascent

> desire nothing but to follow the vision of Christ simply in faith. They do not wish any comfort, nor do they desire it; they have been so converted into the faith that they have no desire for knowledge. They are completely humble, and they think themselves unworthy of all divine solace and do not desire it. … They have no desire, except how the glory of God may be perfected. They have completely surrendered to God; they are pleased with whatever God does with them. … They live in unknowing and desire not to know.[201]

In his vision, Merswin also saw a man on the ninth rock, shining like an angel, who descended into the mist at the lowest level. It was explained that this person, very much like a Buddhist bodhisattva,[202] had been enlightened and "the origin of all created things" was revealed to him. He then "conceived so much compassion for his fellow men that he ran down under the mist to see whether, with God's help, he could convert some poor sinner and help him to escape the mist."[203]

As discussed above, in the new age of increasing intolerance of those who inhabited the fringes of a steadily narrowing definition of orthodoxy, the Beguines were also the target of repressive ecclesiastical legislation, for the popular mind associated them closely with the heresy of the Free Spirit.[204] This coalescence of intolerance towards dissent, mistrust of the Beguines and watchfulness to suppress the heresy of the Free Spirit led to the condemnation of one of the best known victims of the Inquisition, Marguerite Porete, burned at the stake in Paris in 1310 for her stubborn refusal to abandon her alleged Free Spirit teachings set forth in her book, *The Mirror of Simple Souls*. Little is known of Marguerite's life, but she was from Hainault, on the modern French-Belgian border, was well-educated and thus probably of aristocratic origins. It is doubtful that she was of the merchant class, which she labeled "crude."[205] She was acquainted with orthodox mystical literature and was considered to have been a Beguine, probably of the type who did not live in a community. Between 1296 and 1308 the bishop of Cambrai burned her book and warned her against any further communication of her ideas.

Certainly her book contained much that would have sparked opposition from the church establishment. The book was addressed to women and to "little ones of the church"[206] and its prologue declared: "You who would read this book,/ If you indeed wish to grasp it,/ ... Theologians and other clerks,/ You will not have the intellect for it,/ No matter how brilliant your abilities,/ If you do not proceed humbly."[207] Near the end of her work, Marguerite listed those whom she doubted would understand her work, a list which included many who in fact led lives of poverty and asceticism: "Beguines say I err,/ priests, clerics and Preachers,/ Augustinians, Carmelites,/ and the Friars Minor,/ Because I wrote about the being/ of the one purified by Love."[208] Equally unwelcome would have been her contrasting of Holy Church the Great, governed by Love (the souls annihilated in the Love of God) with Holy Church the Little, governed by Reason.[209] This latter church, the established church, was also styled "Holy-Church-Below-This-Church," while the higher church was identical to Holy Church the Great (the church of the mystics), which is "properly called Holy Church, for they sustain and teach and feed the whole Holy Church."[210] *The Mirror* affirmed that Holy Church the Little, whose authorities were now judging Marguerite, was drawing to a close.[211]

Marguerite wrote that the soul in the state of perfection "no longer takes Holy Church as exemplar in her life ... Holy Church does not know how to understand her."[212] Such a soul has little use for the institutions of the church, for it "neither desires nor despises poverty nor tribulation, neither mass nor sermon, neither fast nor prayer,"[213] and it "no longer seeks God through penitence, nor through any sacrament of Holy Church."[214] All of this reeked of the heresy of the Free Spirit.

The book itself is written in the lyrical style of courtly literature as a dialogue among Love, Reason, the Soul and other personifications, providing an exposition of seven stages of progression, or states of grace. In the fifth stage the soul completely surrenders its will to God and thus in the sixth stage becomes liberated, perfected, annihilated and "such a Soul is nothing, for she sees her nothingness by means of the abundance of divine Understanding, which makes her nothing and places her in nothingness."[215] The soul "sees neither God nor herself ... God shows to her that there is nothing except Him."[216] The culmination in the seventh stage is glorification, union of the soul with God. However, Marguerite refused to describe this stage, for we can have no understanding of it until the soul leaves the body and of it, "none know how to speak."[217]

Marguerite's actions indicated her supreme assurance in what she wrote. Although prohibited from the further dissemination of *The Mirror*, she persisted, even sending it to a Franciscan, a Cistercian and a Parisian theologian, who all granted it their approval. However, between 1306 and 1308 a new bishop of Cambrai sent Marguerite to Paris, where she was interrogated by the inquisitor William Humbert. She refused all cooperation with the proceedings, even refraining from answering questions. After more than three years of stalemate, the inquisitor excerpted from *The Mirror* a number of statements which a panel of theologians of the University of Paris judged to be heretical. Marguerite was resolute and was committed to the flames on 1 June 1310.

The Mirror, however, could not be destroyed, for it was very popular and was translated into Latin, Italian and Middle English and widely disseminated. However, it was unwise to possess a banned book written by a condemned heretic and *The Mirror of Simple Souls* circulated either anonymously or under the name of safer mystics. It was not until 1946 that Marguerite's authorship of *The Mirror* was established.[218] Modern scholars are just as divided on the question of Marguerite's heresy as her contemporaries were. However, there may have been more to her condemnation than clear theological issues. The inquisitor who handled Marguerite's case was the confessor of the king of France, Philip IV, and was also managing that king's effort to destroy the soldier-monks of the Order of the Temple. Just a few years earlier Philip IV quarreled with Pope Boniface VIII and sent his military forces into Italy to capture the pontiff. Perhaps tossing to the flames a Beguine, a term that was often a synonym for heretic, would provide an appropriate demonstration of royal orthodoxy and placate other monastic orders, few of which had much sympathy for Beguines, especially the itinerant variety.[219]

One of those who probably would have agreed that Marguerite indeed was a heretic was Jan van Ruusbroec, or Ruysbroeck (1293–1381), who was strident in his denunciation of the wrong kind of mysticism, a man whose "hatred of heresy was probably the most intense of all the fourteenth-century mystics."[220] In his most famous work, *The Spiritual Espousals*, he excoriated those who, like Marguerite, "stand in a pure passivity," being "void of all virtue and so empty that they wish neither to thank nor to praise God."[221] He was bitterly opposed to the Free Spirit movement and was determined to exterminate it, arguing that "they should rightly be burned at the stake, for in God's eyes they are damned and belong in the pit of hell, far beneath the devils."[222]

Ruusbroec, however, was no enemy of mysticism, only of the wrong sort of mysticism. He decried the corruption in the church and lamented its lack of proper instruction to combat the Free Spirit. In his view the essential problem of the church was that ecclesiastical authorities lacked a personal experience of God whereby they might refute the Free Spirit or even exhort ordinary Christians to nurture and develop their interior lives. He equally criticized the laity who were "lazy and slow to serve God, but hasty and quick to please the devil and their own flesh," and monastics who looked only to their own interests, ignored the prescribed prayers, and traveled freely outside their monasteries. He stormed at "popes and bishops, princes and prelates," who bowed down to wealth, at money-hungry clerics, rotten priests ("if the priesthood had lived as offensively at the inception of the Holy Church as it does today, the Christian faith would never have spread so far and wide"), and abbots concerned solely with earthly affairs.[223] His denunciations were so vitriolic that later copyists of his works expurgated some of the acerbic passages.

Ruusbroec's task was to serve as a propagandist for mysticism. In all of his many writings he presented union with God as the natural purpose of the Christian life, a union for which Christ prayed, "and this is the union that is without intermediary, for the love of God is not only out-flowing but it is also drawing-in into unity. And those who feel and experience this become interior, enlightened men."[224] In his lifetime he gained renown as a mystic and visitors from all over the Rhineland, perhaps including

John Tauler, sought him out in his not very secluded refuge from the world a few miles from Brussels.

Little is known of Ruusbroec's life before he moved to his retreat. At the age of eleven he went to Brussels to live with his uncle, a priest, and was educated. He must have been an outstanding student for he was ordained a priest at the age of twenty-four, a year before the required age. For the next quarter of a century he served as a priest at the same church in Brussels at which his uncle was a priest, combated the Free Spirit and began writing his books on the spiritual life, including *The Spiritual Espousals*. In 1343, Ruusbroec, his uncle and a third priest abandoned life in the world to take up residence at a former hermitage at Groenendaal, where they could deepen their spiritual lives in greater isolation. They adopted the rule of St. Augustine and Ruusbroec became the prior of the small community. For almost forty years Ruusbroec lived at Groenendaal, received his visitors, provided spiritual instruction and wrote books. Ruusbroec's biographer, who knew him in his later years, recorded that Ruusbroec would go off into the woods and write down on a wax tablet the words given him by the Holy Spirit, with Ruusbroec once affirming, "I put down not a word in my books except by the inspiration of the Holy Spirit."[225]

Ruusbroec's writings taught his readers the fundamentals of achieving union with God, in a contemplation of God:

> in a modelessness and in a darkness in which all contemplatives wander around in enjoyment and can no longer find themselves in a creaturely mode. In the abyss of this darkness in which the loving spirit has died to itself, there begin the revelation of God and eternal life.[226]

Because there was no tradition of mysticism, at least in his home region in the duchy of Brabant, Ruusbroec also found it necessary to give those under his direction graphic descriptions of physical phenomena that they might experience as part of their union with God, using the familiar concept of spiritual inebriation but dressing it in a more graphic expression than is usually found, one more in keeping with the convulsions at St. Médard or in the Appalachian revivals.[227] He wrote of the "strange behavior" that might be manifested as one lost control of oneself, including singing out, weeping, clapping hands, crying out in a loud voice, lifting one's head up to heaven, leaping, running, kneeling and "making a fuss in many ways." In addition,

> Sometimes it seems to him that the whole world feels what he feels. At certain times, it seems to him that no one tastes that [state] into which he has come. It often seems to him that he neither can, nor ever shall, lose this well-being. Sometimes he is amazed that all people do not become divine. Sometimes it seems to him that God belongs entirely to him alone, and to no one so much as him.[228]

These people, he wrote, "have passed away into God in a dark luminosity."[229]

Ruusbroec also cautioned that the unitive life was not all continual bliss, for, quite unexpectedly, "God will hide himself and withdraw his hand, placing between himself and you a darkness which you will not be able to see through. You will then lament, moan, and groan like a poor abandoned exile." Nonetheless, even in this state, "If God has hidden himself from your sight, you are nevertheless not hidden from him, for he lives within you and has left the gift of his mirror and image, namely, his Son Jesus Christ, your Bridegroom."[230]

Ironically, Ruusbroec, the scourge of heretical mystics, was himself suspected of dangerous mystical teachings. He was usually quite explicit that in union with God there still remained a distinction between God and the creature, when "we are one spirit and one life with him, but we always remain creatures, … for the creature does not become God nor God creature, … our created being does not become God, nor does God's image become a creature."[231] However, in the third part of *The Spiritual Espousals*, he wrote: "For to comprehend and to understand God, above all similitudes, as He is in Himself means to be God with God, without intermediary or any otherness which can create a hindrance or a mediation."[232] When Jean Gerson, chancellor of the University of Paris and one of the most renowned theologians of the late fourteenth and early fifteenth centuries, read this and similar passages in that work, he found them contaminated with heresy. The first two parts of the book contained "much material that is beneficial and profound," with no teaching that "cannot be maintained according to good faith and purity of morals."[233] But the third part "is to be wholly rejected and removed,"[234] for it seemed to teach that in mystical union with God, the soul "is converted or transformed and absorbed into the divine being," a teaching specifically condemned by the Council of Vienne in 1312.[235] Gerson's judgment was a blow to Ruusbroec's posthumous reputation in France, but in the Rhineland and the Low Countries Ruusbroec's influence remained high in the century after his death.

Gerson was no more anti-mystical in denouncing Ruusbroec's work than Ruusbroec had been in attacking the Free Spirit, for he spent much of his career as chancellor at Paris engaged in the same activity as Ruusbroec, calling on Christians of all ranks and status to advance as far in contemplation as possible, reaching for the ultimate goal of mystical union. He composed some works on this subject in French for lay readers, especially women, and others in Latin for clerics and scholars. However, he was extremely cautious in his discussion of mysticism, holding firmly to the conceptions and phraseology of the revered past masters who were his guides in contemplation, Cassian, Pseudo-Dionysius the Areopagite, Augustine, Gregory the Great, Bernard of Clairvaux, Richard and Hugh of St. Victor, and Bonaventure. As chancellor at Paris, heading the most respected theological faculty in Christendom, he was the guardian of the gate of Orthodoxy. The theologian's task was, he wrote, "to distinguish between true and false religion."[236] All religion must conform to the Scriptures to be genuine, for it was through that means that "God once and for all spoke to us. This revelation he will not repeat."[237] In matters of mysticism, Gerson believed there was much that was counterfeit, namely the Beghards and Beguines, the Free Spirit, antinomians such as Marguerite Porete and the suspect passages in Ruusbroec.

Jean le Charlier de Gerson (1363–1429) was a "Wunderkind,"[238] the first of twelve children of a family of farmers of middling means who nonetheless were able to send him to Paris for his higher education. After receiving his Bachelor of Arts degree he went on to study theology and in 1395, only a year after receiving his doctorate, he was named chancellor of the University of Paris at the age of thirty-two. Perhaps all times are trying, but Gerson's chancellorship coincided with one of the most severe crises of the medieval church, the scandal of the Great Schism of the papacy. It began in 1378 with the election of two different popes, one residing at Rome and the other at Avignon, dividing Europe into two camps, each recognizing a different pope. By the beginning of the fifteenth century after a quarter of a century of schism, no resolution was in sight. Secular powers turned to the theologians of the University of Paris to find a means of restoring unity to the church. Gerson played an important role in the church councils at Pisa (1409) and then at Constance (1414–17), the latter of which brought an end to the schism with the election of a single pope, Martin V.

During the same time there was political turmoil in France. King Charles VI (1380–1422) fell into long periodic bouts of insanity, prompting a scramble for power among the nobles of the kingdom with faction opposing faction. In 1407 the duke of Orléans was assassinated in a plot arranged by Gerson's own patron, the duke of Burgundy, and Gerson's unremitting condemnation of that murder eventually led his erstwhile benefactor to withdraw offices that he had given the chancellor. A few years later, during a civil uprising in Paris, armed insurgents invaded Gerson's own quarters and he fled for refuge to the crypts of the cathedral of Notre-Dame. To make matters worse, in 1413 King Henry V of England, in alliance with the duke of Burgundy, renewed the Hundred Years' War. Following Henry's victory at Agincourt in 1415, the Anglo-Burgundian forces conquered all of northern France, including Paris. Gerson, now detested by the duke of Burgundy, could not return to Paris after the Council of Constance but instead found refuge in Austria and Bavaria before taking up residence in Lyon. There he lived out the last ten years of his life, writing, teaching and catechizing young students.

There is no indication that Gerson himself had a mystical experience, which perhaps explains why he was far more comfortable with mystical theologians than with actual mystics. But even if Gerson were only a writer on mysticism, his works were extremely influential, inspiring the deep spirituality of the Brethren of Common Life, as well as Ignatius of Loyola and Francis de Sales.[239] Gerson's most important work is *The Mountain of Contemplation*, written to his own sisters living together at home under religious discipline but without taking formal vows, very much like the Beguines whom he so disliked. The purpose of the work was to guide them as well as his spiritual sisters on the path of contemplation, which was not just for the learned, who were prone to arrogance and conceit, but also for the simple and unlettered. Gerson assured his sisters that the contemplative life "is better acquired through good and humble simplicity than through academic learning."[240] Using the classical image of the spiritual ascent as a ladder or staircase, Gerson wrote that it had three parts. The first is humility and penance that brings the body under control, as one no longer desires the pleasures of the world. Then one should find "secrecy of place and silence" for contemplation, preferably within one's own soul, but even there one is not truly hidden, for "the devout soul is not alone when it is in contemplation, for it is never less alone than when it is alone."[241] The third step is perseverance through the temptations, tribulations and vacillations that would follow, for "it is because of this lack of perseverance that so few people come to perfect contemplation."[242]

Gerson, the careful guide to mysticism, reminded his sisters of the incomprehensibility of God:

> Every time that, in your contemplation, you think of God and you know what you are looking at, and it looks somewhat similar to the things here below, then know for sure that you are not seeing God through clear vision. The same is true of angels, for God is not great in size, nor is he white, nor red, nor clear, nor colored, and neither are the angels.

Gerson the theologian quickly added to this description, "I do not say that one cannot conceive what God is in his human nature, for he has body and is formed like any other man, but I speak of God in his divine essence."[243] He went on to inform his readers that those who contemplate do have various "consolations and spiritual joys," such as sweetness, certainty, "an expansion of the heart or of the intelligence and will contain in itself more than all the world," and "something like a spiritual intoxication, which will move it into making, in a sober manner, spiritual praises, with holy and devout sighs."[244]

Gerson usually urged caution concerning unusual mystical experiences. He warned a new hermit to suspect all "unusual visions," which should be explained away "either by an injury to the head or else by your bad deeds and sins." He added, "it is impossible for a person who is pleased with himself in such experiences to be completely pleasing to God."[245] However, he tried to keep an open mind on the subject, for indeed there were genuine revelations. The task was to discern the true from the false, which prompted him to write *On Distinguishing True From False Revelations*. A sure indication of a false revelation was when someone was "eager to have unusual revelations, if he thinks himself worthy of them and delights in boastful telling of such matters."[246] Gerson concluded favorably on the general topic:

> For I believe in all warnings that are given, all the strong instincts, every revelation, every miracle, every experience of ecstatic love, all contemplation, rapture, and finally every interior and exterior operation, so long as humility precedes, accompanies, and follows them, if nothing harmful is mixed in with them. If these conditions are met, you will not be deceived about their having the mark of being from God or his good angel.[247]

It was as a theological expert on discerning false from genuine revelations that Gerson became involved in the matter of Joan of Arc. Joan (ca. 1412–31) was the daughter of poor farmers in Domremy, a village in the far northeast of France on the border with the duchy of Lorraine. Even as a child she had encounters with angels, especially St. Michael, and with saints, in particular St. Catherine and St. Margaret. At about the age of thirteen she began hearing "the voice," which she understood to be from God and which was almost always accompanied by a "great light." The constant message that she received over several years was that it was God's will that she go to the king of France, Charles VII, have him crowned and consecrated king at Reims, and help him liberate the kingdom from the English. "The first time that I heard the voice, I promised to keep my virginity for as long as it should please God, and that was at the age of thirteen or thereabouts."[248] Those who knew the young Joan affirmed that she was of the highest morals and always to be found in church. In 1429 Joan, at the direction of the voice, left Domremy on her mission from God. Incredibly, the girl of only about sixteen years convinced the local military commander to take her to the king at Chinon where she met privately with Charles VII. She presented the king with a secret sign that only God could know and he emerged from the meeting fully convinced of Joan's divine credentials. However, he took the precaution of having Joan examined by the theologians of the University of Poitiers. They sought assistance on this delicate matter from Chancellor Gerson, who wrote a short treatise on the question, *De quadam puellam*, perhaps his last work, in which he reported discovering no reason to believe that Joan was false or an agent of the devil. The Poitevin theologians agreed with his guidance and found in her "no evil, but only good, humility, virginity, devotion, honesty, simplicity."[249]

The king followed Joan's direction to send a force to Orléans, under siege by the English. Joan, now wearing men's clothing and equipped with armor and a body of soldiers provided by the king, accompanied the force. On this and subsequent campaigns, Joan harshly reprimanded the soldiers for swearing, constantly urged them to confess and go to Mass, and did her best to rid the army of the corps of prostitutes following the troops. During the battle to break the English siege, Joan astounded the French commanders with her military skill. They reported that she "behaved as if she had been the shrewedest captain in the world and had all her life been learning war," and were astonished that in warfare, especially in the deployment of artillery, she comported herself "as might a captain of twenty or thirty years experience have done."[250] In addition, with an extremely valuable ability in military affairs, she displayed gifts of foreknowledge of the course of events in the fighting.

After successfully relieving Orléans, Joan insisted that Charles VII go to Reims, deep in enemy territory, for his coronation and consecration as king, which was accomplished in July 1429. In the warfare that followed, the forces of Charles VII overran more and more territory, as Joan, in the thick of the fighting, was wounded several times. Through it all, she was constantly guided by the voices and visits from her saints and angels. Interestingly, when Joan met another woman who claimed to receive visions and revelations, she regarded the matter as "folly and nullity," urged the woman to go back to her husband and children and did her best to expose what she judged to be a fraud.[251]

In May 1430, only a bit more than a year after her sudden appearance, Joan was captured by Burgundians and sold to the English, who put her on trial in a court of the Inquisition at Rouen. The Anglo-Burgundian side recognized Joan's importance in their military defeats and thus Joan was a political prisoner whose fate was determined before the trial began. There were blatant breaches of the rules of procedure for such a trial and Joan was interrogated ruthlessly by the inquisitors and the theologians of Paris. The uneducated girl defended herself quite ably in the face of her formidable opponents, constantly proclaiming "All that I have done I have done at the Lord's commandment ... I am come from God ... But for the grace of God I could do nothing. ... I have done nothing but by God's commandment."[252] In the end she was duly found guilty of "being a schismatic, an apostate, a liar, a soothsayer, suspect of heresy; of erring in the faith, and being a blasphemer of God and the saints."[253] She may well have been tricked into signing a document in which she abjured her errors, including the wearing of men's clothing. Her captors then provided her with nothing but men's clothing to wear and when she put them on she was declared a relapsed heretic and immediately burnt at the stake, 30 May 1431.

Rouen was taken by Charles VII in 1449 and then, with the capture of the official papers of her trial, Joan's rehabilitation began. In 1456 her trial was judged to have been "tainted with fraud, calumny, iniquity, contradiction and manifest errors of fact and of law"[254] and her condemnation was annulled. While Joan was no longer a condemned heretic, her rehabilitation was not finally concluded until 1920 when she was proclaimed a saint of the church.

ENGLISH MYSTICS OF THE FOURTEENTH AND FIFTEENTH CENTURIES

As the brilliant series of Rhineland mystics was flourishing, a comparable collection of mystics and mystical writers appeared in England. Mysticism was not complicated by fear of contamination of the Free Spirit in England, but rather by official concern over a native-bred heresy, that of the Lollards, followers of the teachings of the priest John Wyclif, who preached predestination and the authority of the Scriptures while attacking the corruption of the clergy and the sacramental system of the church.

The first of the fourteenth-century English mystics was Richard Rolle, the Hermit of Hampole, who not only provides us with lovely alliteration but also was widely-acclaimed for his mystical experiences and holiness in his own lifetime and for years following his death. He was popularly acclaimed as a saint, but Henry VIII's attack on monasticism[255] ended his cult. Rolle was born ca. 1290–1300 to a Yorkshire family of middling economic means, yet he was able to take up studies at the University of Oxford. However, in the course of those studies, when he was nineteen, he had a life-changing experience and refused to return to his formal studies. Taking tunics begged from his sister, he fashioned them into a hermit's habit and for the rest of his life he devoted himself to the life of a solitary. From his cell in Hampole, in the south of Yorkshire, he acted as a spiritual advisor and counselor while also writing works extolling the solitary life as the surest means of experiencing God. He died 29 September 1349 as the Black Death was ravaging England, making it tempting to suppose that he was its victim.

Like many of the mystics on the Continent during this time, Rolle was a layperson.

He composed his works in Latin as well as the vernacular, being one of the first writers in English and one of the major figures in the development of written English. It is with only a bit of exaggeration that he is sometimes called the Father of English Prose. Rolle's writings are remarkable for providing extraordinary detail about his experiences, especially in his most famous work, *The Fire of Love.* There he described his initial experience as an adolescent longing for God, as "[God] lifted and transferred my soul from the depths up to the heights," which led him to embrace and to preach the solitary life. Almost four years later, as he was sitting in a chapel in prayer and meditation, "suddenly I felt within myself an unusually pleasant heat. At first I wondered where it came from, but it was not long before I realized that it was from none of his creatures but from the creator himself." Nine months later "a conscious and incredibly sweet warmth kindled me, and I knew the infusion and understanding of heavenly, spiritual sounds, sounds which pertain to the song of eternal praise, and to the sweetness of unheard melody." Moreover, he also heard "above my head it seemed, the joyful ring of psalmody, or perhaps I should say, the singing," prompting him to wonder at such gifts given him by God, "the like of which I did not know I could ask for, and such that I thought that not even the most holy could have received in this life." In the course of the next four years, "I was able to reach the heights of loving Christ. ... And now, my brothers, I have told you how I came to the fire of love."[256] Rolle is most insistent on the physical sensation of heat that he felt:

> It was real warmth too, not imaginary, and it felt as if it were actually on fire. I was astonished at the way the heat surged up, and how this new sensation brought great and unexpected comfort. I had to keep feeling my breast to make sure there was no physical reason for it! But once I realized that it came entirely from within, that this fire of love had no cause, material or sinful, but was the gift of my Maker, I was absolutely delighted, and wanted my love to be even greater. ... If we put our finger near a fire we feel the heat; in much the same way a soul on fire with love feels, I say, a genuine warmth.[257]

As seen, Rolle's experiences involved other sensations and he affirmed, "I have found that to love Christ above all else will involve three things: warmth and song and sweetness. And these three, as I know from personal experience, cannot exist for long without there being great quiet."[258] Like Symeon the New Theologian,[259] Rolle provided such graphic descriptions in order to convince his readers that such experiences were not confined to Biblical figures but were possible here and now. He wished to encourage others to pursue the life of contemplation as a solitary so that they too could be united with God. He wrote to a female recluse, "The condition of life in which you live, in other words, solitude, is the most suitable of all for the revelation of the Holy Spirit."[260]

When Rolle left Oxford he also abandoned forever the attempt to know God through the human mind and reason. He now wrote not for the attention "of the philosophers and sages of this world, not of great theologians bogged down in their interminable questionings," but rather for "the simple and unlearned, who are seeking rather to love God than to amass knowledge. For he is not known by argument, but by what we do and how we love."[261] He added, "Nowadays too many are consumed with a desire for knowledge rather than for love … An old woman can be more expert in the love of God – and less worldly too – than your theologian with his useless studying."[262]

Rolle was a strong critic of the clergy as well as of ecclesiastical officials and had a general reputation as a curmudgeon. Moreover, he has also long been considered a misogynist. He did indeed give out strong warnings about avoiding women,[263] but his intent was to provide advice on living the solitary life and he seems to have had a particular fondness for women. He relates that once he commented to a woman on her rather large breasts and that on another occasion he was going to touch a woman, but both women gave him well deserved sharp rebukes.[264] It is known that he served as a spiritual counselor to women and that women were active in his cult after his death and thus his strictures concerning the dangers of women probably revealed his own weaknesses, for women were a strong temptation to him.

Rolle was remembered through his posthumous cult and his writings were very popular in the fourteenth and fifteenth centuries. He was so effective in using his own experiences as a medium of promoting the mystical, solitary life that many others in the surrounding region imitated Rolle's way of life and also experienced fire, sound and sweetness. In response to this enthusiasm for Rolle's sensory mysticism, an unknown Carthusian monk deplored Rolle's influence, which had "destroyed as many men as it saved," had "made men judges of themselves" and had taught them the "superstition" of the "material fire of love."[265] Rolle's defender was the hermit Thomas Basset, who derided those lacking spiritual gifts who refused to believe that such gifts could be given to people simpler but more virtuous than themselves. He argued, "Whoever feels the spirit of God within himself, without fiction or presumption, humbly and true, is aware that he possesses the spirit of God."[266] Some modern scholars have viewed Rolle not much more favorably than did the Carthusian. For example, Dom David Knowles consigned Rolle to "a relatively elementary stage of the spiritual life"[267] because of the sensory perceptions associated with his mystical experiences. However, others have defended Rolle, noting that he is not alone in reporting sensations of mystical heat, for they are also found in the writings of mystics in the Eastern Church.[268]

A vociferous near-contemporary critic of Rolle and especially of his teaching on the sensory perceptions associated with mysticism was Walter Hilton (died 1396), whose major work is *The Scale* (or *Ladder*) *of Perfection*, composed in English only a few years before his death. There were many reasons for Hilton to oppose Rolle's teachings and influence. The Lollards were attracted to some of Rolle's works and recopied them with their own interpolations, dragging Rolle into an unwitting association with heresy. Criticism of the clergy and prelates like that of Rolle was now connected with heresy and would not have been welcome to Hilton, himself a priest. However, it is also clear that Hilton simply disliked Rolle's view of mysticism and of the life of the solitary as the one best suited for the experience of God.

Hilton was trained as a lawyer at Cambridge before being ordained for the priesthood. Following his initial desire for the solitary quest for God, he took up the life of a hermit as Rolle had done. However, solitude was not for Hilton and he abandoned it to become a canon at the Augustinian priory at Thurgarton, near Nottingham. The Rule of St. Augustine suited Hilton far better. It "breathes ... the spirit of mildness and discretion"[269] and was known for its emphasis on moderation, permitting Augustinian canons more generous food portions than even the Benedictine Rule, and "study and intellectual pursuits were commended in place of manual labour."[270]

In his many works, written in both English and Latin, Hilton acted as a spiritual advisor to those dedicated to or considering adopting the religious life. *The Scale of Perfection* was addressed to an anchoress, that is a woman who took semi-monastic vows and enclosed herself in a cell, and in the work Hilton wrote as a theologian, covering all of the spiritual life, extolling the need for absolute love of God and for re-forming the image of Jesus within the Christian, showing "what is required in preparation for the life of union with God in contemplation."[271] To be sure, Hilton made the traditional division between the active and contemplative lives and argued that the latter is higher.[272] However, Hilton's is a different kind of mysticism. Gone are the usual exhortations to abandon the world, seek the desert and wilderness and overcome the passions. Instead, the anchoress is urged to eat and sleep as the body requires, so long as these needs are not enjoyed for their own sake.[273] Because the goal of the Christian is complete love of God, any Christian may have this, rich or poor, male or female, vowed religious or layperson. Hilton lauded those who chose lives as enclosed anchoresses, but he was always quick to give equal praise to those who entered any religious order approved by the church,[274] of course including the Augustinian Order. While Hilton was somewhat familiar with the mystical theology of Pseudo-Dionysius, he abandoned the approach of knowing God by unknowing, of abandoning reason in order to know God. On the contrary, for him mysticism was a divinely illuminated reason which leads to knowledge of God:

> That is, you are reformed, not in bodily feeling or in imagination, but in the higher part of your reason ... That is, your reason, which is properly the image of God through grace of the Holy Spirit, shall be clothed in a new light of truth, holiness and righteousness, and then it is reformed in feeling. ... As he illumines the reason through the touch and shining of his blessed light, he opens the inner eyes of the soul, to see him and know him ... this knowledge is the glory and the end of a soul. ... For in a pure soul knowledge rises above all this, to gaze upon the blessed nature of Jesus himself.[275]

Hilton reinterpreted the coming of the Holy Spirit to the apostles on the day of Pentecost so that it was no longer an ecstatic event but rather an intellectual one:

> [the Holy Spirit] was felt invisibly in the powers of their souls, for he enlightened their reason and kindled their affection through his blessed presence so clearly and ardently that they suddenly had the spiritual knowledge of truth and the perfection of love, as our Lord promised them ... That is: The Holy Spirit

shall teach you all truth, … so it is in other souls that are visited and illumined inwardly by the Holy Spirit.[276]

Hilton was especially opposed to those followers of Rolle who welcomed visions or sensations as signs of mysticism: "these are not truly contemplation. They are only simple and secondary."[277] Grappling directly with Rolle's famous phrase of "the fire of love," Hilton wrote:

> Not all those who speak of the fire of love really know what it is, for what it is I cannot tell you, except this. It can be felt in prayer or devotion by a soul who exists in a body, but he does not feel it by any bodily sense.[278]

While Hilton disclaimed knowledge of the fire of love he also felt competent to pronounce on it. Repeatedly through *The Scale of Perfection*, Hilton proclaimed that he had no personal experience of the contemplative life and when he attempted to describe true contemplation, he employed "a whole series of standard expressions derived from others" in a very "bookish" description of the categories of contemplation.[279]

Thus Hilton was unwilling to concede the high ground of contemplation, which was generally agreed to be the ultimate goal of the Christian life, to the likes of Richard Rolle and his followers, those who followed a way of life that he himself had abandoned, warning that the devil especially tempted those in the solitary life by appearing to them either bodily or in visions.[280] Therefore the true mystic was someone like Hilton himself, one given to moderation and discretion, someone who obeyed the laws and ordinances of the church unquestioningly. Hilton did open up the possibility that Christian perfection was attainable by all, not just ascetics, a "more and more democratic notion,"[281] but he did so by taking traditional concepts of contemplation and investing them with altered meanings.

Hilton was not alone in his attack on the "fire of love" mystical movement initiated by Richard Rolle. A contemporary of Hilton's, probably a Cistercian priest whose name has been lost to history, also wrote several works concerned with mysticism, most importantly *The Cloud of Unknowing* and *The Epistle of Privy Counsel*. In *The Cloud*, the author used harsh words against those who claimed to feel physical sensations in contemplation, denouncing the "spurious warmth" that they imagine "to be the fire of love, lighted and fanned by the grace and goodness of the Holy Ghost." The author affirmed that "the devil has his contemplatives as God has his … often the devil will deceive their ears with quaint sounds, their eyes with quaint lights and shinings, their noses with wonderful smells – and they are all false!"[282] Like Hilton, the writer was alarmed at the spread of heresy in late fourteenth-century England and he emphasized that Christians should live in obedience to the Holy Church.

However, the two writers shared little more in their approaches to mysticism. The author of *Cloud* was devoted to the apophatic approach of Pseudo-Dionysius and made an English translation of the *Mystical Theology*.[283] Like Rolle, the *Cloud* author denied that God could be found through reason and the intellect. Instead, the "cloud of unknowing" that surrounds God can be penetrated by love alone. The author stated his theme succinctly: "So if you are to stand and not fall, never give up your firm intention: beat away at this cloud of unknowing between you and God with that sharp dart of longing love."[284] In fact, very much like Rolle, the author described his own mystical experience, when God sends out

> a shaft of spiritual light, which pierces this cloud of unknowing between you, and shows you some of his secrets, of which it is not permissible or possible to speak. Then will you feel your affection flame with the fire of his love, far more than I can possibly say now. For I dare not take upon myself with my blundering, earthly tongue to speak of what belongs solely to God.[285]

The author never tired of denigrating the usefulness of reason in knowing God, stating pithily, "[God] may well be loved, but not thought. By love he can be caught and held, but by thinking never. ... Why, love may reach up to God himself even in this life – but not knowledge."[286] "Seek experience rather than knowledge," he implored, for "knowledge can often lead one astray through pride, whereas humble, loving experience does not lie."[287] The author asked the question, "can anyone achieve [union with God] by intellectual means only? The answer is quite simple, 'Never.'"[288] The author was just as firm that study, even of *The Cloud of Unknowing*, was not the path to God: "But don't study these words, for you will never achieve your object so, or come to contemplation; it is never attained by study, but only by grace."[289]

The *Cloud* author shared other elements with Rolle. He, too, felt that he had to persuade his contemporaries that mysticism was a living fact, not a phenomenon that ended centuries before. He defended the contemplative life against attacks of those in the active life and he added, "Let our Lord cry to those actives ... don't interfere with my contemplatives."[290] As Rolle had urged his readers most strongly to fix their minds firmly on the name of Jesus and "meditate on it in your heart night and day,"[291] the *Cloud* author urged his reader to find a single word, preferably a short one of one syllable, such as "God" or "love," and to "fix this word fast to your heart so that it is always there come what may. ... With this word you will suppress all thoughts under the cloud of forgetting."[292]

Among all of the English mystics of the fourteenth and fifteenth centuries, the one who today is the most widely read but who lived out her own life in relative obscurity is Julian of Norwich (1342 to after 1416). Her actual name is unknown (she is called Julian because of her connection to the church of St. Julian in Norwich) or the year of her death or very much about her outside of the information she provides in her work *Showings* (or *Revelations*) *of Divine Love*. There is no indication that this work was widely read until the mid-seventeenth century but today she is prominent in virtually every anthology and discussion of medieval mysticism.

For all we know, Julian may have had only a single mystical experience, part of a near-death-experience that she describes in her *Showings*. When she was thirty she was struck by a severe bodily sickness that may have paralyzed her for a time, leaving her unable even to speak, and everything became dark around her. Everyone assumed that she would die but suddenly the illness broke. During this time she was given sixteen divine revelations.

This experience profoundly changed her life, leading her to become an anchoress,[293] and she moved to a single-room cell attached to the church of St. Julian in Norwich (see plate 7). One window allowed her to witness the divine services in the church and another permitted communication with the outside world. In her cell she was sought out as a spiritual advisor,[294] which gave her many opportunities to reflect on the meaning and interpretation of her revelations while being aided by divine understanding. Julian produced two written versions of her revelations and their interpretation, the *Showings*, whose Short Text came not long after her experience. After twenty years of reflection on her revelations, she amplified the work in the Long Text, three times longer than the original.

Julian's interpretation of her revelations has drawn intense modern interest, for she presents a view of God that is personal and unique, brimming with optimism and couched in simple and direct language. Her ideas are as stunning as those of Meister Eckhart in their presentation of religious concepts that are unusual in the European Middle Ages. In one of her most famous images, she said that God showed her all that was made and it was so little, no bigger than a hazelnut in the palm of her hand, "so little that it could suddenly fall into nothing."[295] Julian was shown that God is in all things, including humankind,[296] and, in the phrase of Augustine, "God is closer to us than our own soul."[297] "When wretchedness is separated from us," she wrote, "God and the soul are wholly at unity and God and man are wholly one."[298]

This God cannot be angry, for he has no wrath,[299] and indeed, there is no reason for God's wrath because Julian knew that sin was nothing – she had been shown all that was and had seen no sin.[300] Julian found constant consolation in the reassurance given her in her revelations by Jesus, "all will be well, and all will be well, and every kind of thing will be well,"[301] and "I will make all things well, I shall make all things well, I may make all things well and I can make all things well."[302] She understood this promise absolutely literally, that all of creation would be well, meaning that all humans would be saved, which she stated explicitly: "our good Lord said: Every kind of thing will be well … you will see for yourself that every kind of thing will be well." Jesus himself interpreted this to mean "I shall preserve my word in everything, and I shall make everything well" because "What is impossible to you is not impossible to me."[303] Moreover, God had shown her all that was and she saw only those to be saved; she saw no hell or purgatory nor did she see anything of Jews being condemned.

One of the most interesting images of God that Julian taught was that of mother, emphasizing the divine procreative and nurturing nature, for "God almighty is our loving Father, and God all wisdom is our loving Mother."[304] Christ, the second person of the Trinity, "who is our Mother, substantially the same beloved person, has now become our mother sensually."[305] Jesus Christ "is our true Mother. We have our being from him, where the foundation of motherhood begins, with all the sweet protection of love which endlessly follows."[306] Reflection on this maternal aspect of the divine nature did not begin with Julian, for it had a long history in Christianity, going back to St. Paul and the Hebrew Bible and continuing on in medieval and English sources that might have been an inspiration for her.[307] But Julian perhaps emphasized it more frequently than previously and did so in language that is clear and compelling. For modern readers, it is often Julian who provides their introduction to what is often seen as a modern conception, the Motherhood of God.

Obviously many of her revelations clashed with the teachings of the Church, but Julian was far more circumspect in her language than Marguerite Porete had been, for during her lifetime the dissenting Lollards were being persecuted in England. Parliament legislated the burning of heretics in an act of 1401 and before the ink was dry on the act Lollards were being committed to the flames. Thus Julian was always quick to add to the exposition of her revelations, "still I was not drawn by [the revelation] away from any article of the faith which Holy Church teaches me to believe."[308] Nonetheless, it is obvious that she never doubted the truth of her revelations and she was confident that somehow the infinite love and power of God would be able to make all things well.

The last of the remarkable mystics of late medieval England, Margery Kempe (ca. 1373 to after 1436), is as controversial as Richard Rolle, as a result of her "autobiography," which reveals more about her inner and outer life than we have for virtually any other medieval figure. Her self-revelation, called simply *The Book of Margery Kempe*, is the first autobiographical work written in English and its contents have led some to discount her as a mystic. David Knowles, who discounted Rolle as a mystic, likewise dismissed her as simply an hysterical woman.[309] For more than 400 years after her death Margery had little influence on the study of mysticism because her *Book* was lost not long after its composition and was known only through fragmentary extracts published in 1501. Margery was believed to have been an anchoress, like Julian, in Bishop's Lynn, now King's Lynn, not far from Norwich, and Evelyn Underhill assigned her to the latter thirteenth century.[310] But in 1934 a full manuscript of Margery's *Book* was discovered and the truth about Margery was learned. She had been no thirteenth-century recluse but lived a century later and was a businesswoman, a wife, a mother of fourteen children and was fully-involved in the world.

Even ignoring Margery's spiritual life, she was a remarkable woman. Her father was five times mayor of Bishop's Lynn and represented the borough in Parliament while she ran a brewery although without much success. Margery's book often reads like a travelogue as she constantly moved about England from Bristol to London to York and gained interviews with the archbishops of Canterbury and York, the bishops of Norwich, Lincoln and Worcester, and she even paid a visit to Julian of Norwich.[311] Margery wrote that Julian listened to the story of her spiritual journey, encouraged her to remain steadfast in the face of opposition and always obey God's will.[312] She also went on distant pilgrimages unaccompanied by her husband, to Rome, Jerusalem and Santiago de Compostela, while other travels took her to Norway, Germany and Danzig. In the course of her adventures she was frequently abandoned by her traveling companions, arrested by local authorities and tried for the Lollard heresy.

Margery is surprisingly self-revealing in her book. She had not been particularly religious but was given to vanity and wearing the latest fashions. Her first pregnancy was a difficult one and she was constantly ill, becoming obsessed with an unconfessed sin. After giving birth, Margery became demented. "I went out of my mind. For half a year, eight weeks, and a few odd days I was terribly disturbed and plagued by evil spirits. … I was tied and forcibly restrained by day and night." But then came a divine intervention:

> I was lying alone without anyone minding me; our merciful Lord Jesus Christ … appeared to me although I had deserted him. He was in human form, yet most pleasingly beautiful, truly he was the loveliest sight that human eyes could ever gaze upon. Wearing a mantle of purple silk, he sat upon my bed; he looked at me with such a joyful face that I felt a sudden inner response as if strengthened in my soul. Then he spoke the following words to me: "My daughter, why have you left me, when I never for one moment went away from you?"[313]

Margery was instantly cured of her madness and resumed her normal life in the household, but she was a changed woman. She had learned that although people think that Christ "is far away from them … in truth he is very near indeed with his merciful grace."[314] Other mystical experiences followed, filled with sensory perceptions, as she heard "a sound of music so sweet and delightful that I thought I must be in Paradise. As soon as I heard it I got out of bed, saying: 'Alas that I did ever sin, for it is so merry in heaven.'"[315] She also heard "the kind of noise a pair of bellows makes that seemed to blow directly into my ear," which she understood as the sound of the Holy Spirit. Jesus changed this sound "into the sound of the cooing of a dove; and later he turned it into the song of a robin redbreast, who would often sing very merrily in my right ear."[316] Frequently she would hear "tunes and melodies that were so loud and real to me that I would be unable to hear what people were saying unless they raised their voices to me."[317] Reminiscent of Richard Rolle, Margery felt the fire of love within her: "And often I would feel a flame just like fire in my breast, yet even as it enfolded me, it was utterly pleasureable."[318] This warmth was given as a sign so that "you will know that the Holy Spirit is in you."[319] Margery saw God everywhere, "my mind and my every thought were so fixed upon God that I never forgot him; he was constantly on my mind, and I would see him in all his creatures."[320] In the manner of the Beguines, Margery also experienced a mystical marriage, in which "the Father spoke to my soul saying, 'I take you, Margery, for my wedded wife, for fairer, for fouler, for richer, for poorer, so that you will always be ready and compliant to all that I bid you.'"[321]

Margery lived surrounded by the divine, enjoying constant conversation with Christ. He was always with her, answering her every question and appeal, encouraging her devotions and, very importantly, ever supporting her throughout the numerous hardships that she suffered on his behalf. Margery's *Book* is filled with her extended conversations with Jesus or sometimes God. Also in the style of Richard Rolle, Margery gave priority and authority to her conversations with Christ, who himself assured her, "There is not a scholar in all this world, daughter, who can teach you better than I can."[322]

Margery was determined to devote her life entirely to Christ. After many years' struggle and the birth of thirteen more children, she convinced her husband to agree to abstain from sexual relations and, on divine instructions, she began wearing the white clothing of nuns, symbolizing virginity. This not only drew the scorn of those who knew her but it also smacked of heresy.[323] However, there was much more that attracted almost instant hostility towards her. She was very outspoken, quick to scold and reprimand those whom she detected sinning, especially the swearing of crude oaths. Weeping in compunction for one's sins or in recalling the wounds suffered by Jesus on behalf of all humanity was a common phenomenon among mystics, but Margery took weeping to new decibel levels. By her own account she did not merely weep, for she cried, bellowed and roared. She admitted, "I cried out with an amazing great roar that could be heard a long way off. I simply could not prevent myself from doing so."[324] It could strike anywhere, but a church service would almost certainly prompt such a manifestation. Her disruptive noise led one Franciscan preacher in Lynn to ban her from his sermons while the entire town turned against her and insisted that she take up residence somewhere else. Margery, well-acquainted with the mystical literature of her day, defended herself by pointing to loud crying by Marie d'Oignies, Bonaventure and Richard Rolle,[325] while Catherine of Siena could be added as well.[326]

Margery was fortunate to have survived in the religious atmosphere of early fifteenth-century England when Lollards were savagely persecuted. Margery was no Lollard but even in a world well-acquainted with anchoresses and hermits her behavior was certainly aberrant, irritating and lacking in subtlety. Thus charges of heresy and Lollardy were frequently flung at her but she always satisfied the authorities regarding the orthodoxy of her beliefs. Alongside the harsh opposition that she provoked, Margery was also able to convince many of the genuineness of her revelations and the holiness of her life. Some priests urged her to have her story committed to writing but she was reluctant to do so, in part because of the ineffability of her experiences, saying "my body would be sometimes so enfeebled by the experience of such grace that I always failed to put into words exactly what I felt within my soul."[327]

MYSTICS IN ITALY IN THE FOURTEENTH AND FIFTEENTH CENTURIES

Along with Hildegard of Bingen, Catherine of Siena (1347–80) was one of the mystics of the medieval church who had the greatest influence at the highest levels of her contemporary society. While Hildegard lived for over eighty years, Catherine was a brief shooting star streaking across the sky, dying at the age of thirty-three. In the short span of her life she gathered renown as a mystic and an extreme ascetic, a prophet and a healer, an ambassador for the pope and a tireless worker for church reform and for the return of the papacy from Avignon to Rome.[328] At the outbreak of the Great Schism she rallied support around the Roman pope. In recognition of her sanctity she was canonized in 1461 and in 1970 she was given the title of Doctor (Teacher) of the Church, a distinction shared by only one other woman, Teresa of Ávila.[329]

Catherine was the daughter of Giacomo Benincasa, a Sienese maker of textile dyes, and his wife Lapa, an astoundingly fertile woman who had given birth to twenty-two children before Catherine and her twin sister were born. As presented in her *Life*, written by her last confessor, the Dominican friar Raymond of Capua, the signs of Catherine's future saintly and mystical life emerged very early. At about the age of six, she and her brother were returning from visiting a sister and she looked up:

> and there, hanging in the air in front of her over the roof of the church of the Friars Preachers, she saw a most beautiful bridal chamber decked out in regal splendour, in which, on the imperial throne, dressed in pontifical attire and with the tiara on His head (that is to say, the monarchical papal mitre), sat the Lord Jesus Christ, the Saviour of the world. ... Then, gazing straight at her with eyes full of majesty, and smiling most lovingly, He raised His right hand over her, made the sign of the cross of salvation like a priest, and graciously gave her His eternal benediction. The grace of this gift was so immediately effective upon the little girl that she was taken right out of herself.[330]

This vision had a profound effect upon the little girl. Wanting to imitate the lives of the Desert Fathers, she sought out hidden places where she could scourge herself. At the age of seven she dedicated her virginity to Jesus and begged the Virgin Mary to give her son as a husband to Catherine. By the time she reached the age of twelve, that secret vow collided with her parents' wish to arrange a fitting marriage for her. Following the advice of a helpful Dominican friar, she cut off her hair to make herself less desirable and she further disturbed her parents by the extremes of her ascetical life, such as eating very little, sleeping only a quarter of an hour a day, drinking only water, and winding a chain around herself so tightly that her skin was chafed away.

In the end, Catherine's determination broke down her parents' opposition. She had long venerated Dominican friars and had been given a dream in which St. Dominic himself brought her the habit of the Sisters of Penance of St. Dominic, an association of lay women tertiaries[331] of the Dominican Order popularly known as the *Mantellate*. The Sisters of Penance, typically "respectable widows of mature age,"[332] were initially reluctant to admit the eighteen-year-old virgin to their number but, after divine pressure was applied, they consented. Catherine now drove herself into an even more ascetical life. Her mystical ecstasies became more frequent, sometimes coming over her by the simple act of saying the Our Father, as well as more profound. She would become rigid and paralyzed, with her hands clenched, eyes shut tightly, with her neck so stiff that it could not be moved. During her ecstasies she was prone to levitating, for "it was quite evident that a great power was attracting her spirit."[333] Her biographer related that she was almost always in contemplation, spending "most of her time in a region beyond sense."[334]

When she was twenty-one, Catherine experienced the fulfillment of her devotion to Christ in her mystical marriage. While she was praying, Jesus appeared to her, along with the Virgin Mary, John the Evangelist, St. Paul, St. Dominic and King David. Jesus placed on her finger a gold ring, with pearls and a diamond, saying "There! I marry you to me in faith, to me, your Creator and Saviour."[335] The vision faded but the ring on her finger was always apparent to Catherine although to no one else. In another vision, Christ came to her, opened up the left side of her body, and removed her heart. The vision was later completed when she came out of an ecstasy and again Christ appeared to her, holding his own heart. He opened her left side and placed in it his own heart, telling her, "as I took your heart away from you the other day, now, you see, I am giving you mine, so that you can go on living with it forever."[336] Her biographer was assured by her companions that there was a scar on Catherine's body at the site of the exchange of hearts.

Like almost all the female mystics of the thirteenth and fourteenth centuries, Catherine was especially devoted to the Eucharist and, in contrast with common practice, she received it frequently. During the elevation of the bread, Catherine had frequent visions, seeing between the hands of the priest Jesus as a baby or as an older boy. Almost always after receiving Communion Catherine went into ecstasy for three or four hours, with her entire body becoming so rigid that she was immovable although she might levitate while in this state. However, before receiving the Eucharist she often fell into profuse weeping so loud that it drove her confessor to order her to stay far away from the altar in order not to disturb the other priests who were saying Mass. She did so but she also prayed that he would realize that some movements of the Holy Spirit could not be repressed. Indeed, such a divine revelation came to her confessor, who learned that "such spiritual favors cannot be inwardly restrained."[337]

The final sign of her mystical life came in a vision in 1375. She had prayed for eternal life and Christ had promised it to her, but she now desired a sign. Jesus asked for her hand and when she extended it he pressed a nail into the palm with such force that it seemed to her that it had been struck by a hammer. She now had a wound, a stigma, which she could feel, but it was as invisible to others as the ring of her mystical marriage.[338]

Catherine was transformed from a reclusive Dominican tertiary into a public figure by her "mystical death" in 1368. While in ecstasy she experienced Christ's passion and his love for all humans. She related to her confessor that the experience of this love was so forceful that she died and her soul left her body for four hours. During that time, as she said, "my soul saw and understood everything in the other world that to us is invisible … my soul contemplated the Divine Essence," and she saw the souls in hell and purgatory. Catherine then received a divine command to return to life to make sinners understand their sins, but she was also warned that her life would change, that she would carry this message to people of all ranks and conditions, even to popes. However, Christ reassured her, "I shall be with you always." She did return to her body but she wept for three days because of the loss of that "sublime degree of glory."[339]

Catherine left her cell and soon gained a group of disciples, her "family," comprising men and women, lay people and clerics, who referred to her as "Mother." Catherine soon attained great fame as a result of her teachings, ecstasies, prophecies and healing the sick merely by the touch of her hand. She also began writing letters, of which 382 survive, to all whom she thought would benefit, constantly urging her readers to take the Christian life seriously, reminding them that no one knew when death might come – a timely warning in a society struck by recurring waves of the Black Death.

Soon she was drawn into the turbulent world of Italian politics and attempted to mediate the incessant disputes among the independent city-states of her native Tuscany. She was even sent as an ambassador from Florence to Pope Gregory XI in Avignon, where a series of French popes had been residing since 1309.[340] There she was struck by the corruption that had resulted from the great wealth and power of the papal court. Never shy, she spoke directly to the pope and "bewailed the fact that at the Roman Court, which should have been paradise of heavenly virtues, there was a stench of all the vices of hell." The congenial pope expressed his amazement that in only a few days at his court she had gotten to know its state so well.[341] Catherine was devoted to the cause of reforming the abuses in the church and urged Gregory to use his papal powers to this end. She reminded him that God had given him his papal authority which, having accepted, he should be using. She added sharply, "If you don't intend to use it, it would be better and more to God's honor and the good of your soul to resign."[342]

Catherine profoundly impressed Gregory XI and he employed her as his envoy to Florence, where a popular uprising nearly took her life. She was also influential in convincing the pope to leave Avignon and return to Rome. However, at the death of Gregory XI in Rome in 1378, the cardinals elected a new pope, the stern Italian Urban VI, whose acerbity and harshness caused them to regret their decision almost immediately. They declared him deposed and elected in his place another French pope, Clement VII, who returned to Avignon with the cardinals. Now the Western Christian Church was divided in loyalty to the two popes, creating the Great Schism, which dragged on for forty years.[343] Catherine worked with all the strength that her frail and ailing body possessed to convince the Christian world to end its division and support Urban VI.

In this period Catherine, in ecstasy, dictated her book, the *Dialogue*, while also continuing her vast output of letters. But she had little time remaining in her life. As her health failed, she could neither eat nor swallow water and became paralyzed. She died in Rome on 29 April 1380.

Raymond of Capua was careful to name the sources of his information and the accounts of Catherine's mystical experiences – her first vision, her mystical marriage, her exchange of hearts with Jesus, her reception of stigmata, her mystical death – came directly from her and thus are probably relatively close to Catherine's own words. Her letters are perhaps somewhat closer to her own spoken words, for she dictated them while in ecstasy and her scribes then turned them into proper prose. In one of her letters she reported a vision that she received in 1376:

> God disclosed his secrets more than usual. He showed his marvels in such a way that my soul seemed to be outside my body and was so overwhelmed with joy that I can't really describe it in words. ... The fire of holy desire was growing within me as I gazed. ... And there were such mysteries as words can never

describe, nor heart imagine, nor eye see. Now what words could ever describe the wonderful things of God?[344]

Her biographer reported that during her raptures, Catherine would mutter "wonderful phrases and the most profound sayings," and on one occasion he heard her say "Vidi arcana Dei" ("I saw the hidden things of God").[345] Her revelations made her impatient with those who dealt only with the literal meaning of the Scriptures and she railed against corrupt priests who understood nothing but "the outer crust, the letter, of Scripture," whose understanding was darkness.[346] As a result, she taught that the soul possessed free will and could be bound by sin only if it consented to it. For her, the demons were God's ministers, tormenting those in hell and testing the virtues of souls on earth, and, for that matter, even the devil was weak and could do only what God permitted.[347] She also saw the feminine aspect of God, who spoke of the poor: "I hold them to my breast and give them the milk of great consolation."[348]

Catherine was insistent on the union of the soul with God in ecstasy, with God stating that such a soul "is another me,"[349] and she developed her own metaphor for the union of the soul and God: "Just as the fish is in the sea and the sea in the fish, so am I in the soul and the soul in me, the sea of peace."[350] Raymond quoted Catherine as saying "Through this vision of love, increasing from day to day, the soul is so transformed into God that it cannot think or understand or love or remember anything but God and the things of God."[351]

Catherine's fame as a holy woman was widespread and the report of her death spread throughout Rome despite efforts of her intimates to keep it quiet, resulting in a "great rush of people to the church. It was a general scramble, with everyone wanting to touch the dead person's clothes and feet." Finally her body had to be placed behind iron railings to control the crowds.[352]

Catherine was not the only vocal female mystic in Italy attempting to bring the popes back to Rome from Avignon and to reform the church. Not long after Catherine's birth, the Swedish noble lady Birgitta, or Bridget, arrived at the papal court to gain approval for the order of nuns that she had founded in Sweden while also admonishing the pope to return to Rome from Avignon. Birgitta (1303–73) was the daughter of the governor of the Swedish province of Uppland, a pious man who had undertaken several long pilgrimages, and she was cousin to the Swedish king Magnus Eriksson. According to Birgitta's biography, written by two of her confessors who gained the information directly from her, her mystical life began when she was six years old. She saw a lady in shining clothes sitting above the altar where she was standing. The lady held a precious crown and asked Birgitta if she wanted it. She nodded her affirmation and the lady "put the crown on her head so that Birgitta then felt, as it were, the circle of the crown touching her head. But when she returned to bed, the vision disappeared; and yet she could never forget it."[353] In the next years she had a number of other visions and was given to devout prayers, but many more years would pass before she could devote herself to the religious life. Her father betrothed her to the nobleman Ulf of Ulvåsa and they married when she was thirteen. However, her intense prayer and mystical experiences continued as she fasted and followed other ascetical practices and received visions of Christ, the Virgin Mary and many saints. She and her husband went on distant pilgrimages, including Santiago de Compostela, and she was given prophecies of her future pilgrimages to Rome and Jerusalem.

After eight children were born, she and Ulf agreed to live chastely and to enter the monastic life. In 1344 a more intensely mystical life began for Birgitta. God came to her in the form of a bright light, assuring her, "you shall be my bride and my channel, and you shall hear and see spiritual things, and my Spirit shall remain with you even to your death."[354] Authorities granted Birgitta the rare dispensation to retire to a Cistercian monastery for men, where her revelations intensified. She was given knowledge of the souls of the dead, whether they were in purgatory, what was the nature of their punishments and in what way prayers and alms on earth could free them from their suffering. She also gained renown as a great prophet of matters past, present and future, while she could also clarify difficult points of Scripture.

Birgitta described her experiences as one of being "inebriated with the sweetness of love ... suspended in an ecstasy of mental contemplation,"[355] and "it seemed to her as if her heart were on fire with divine charity and entirely full of spiritual joy so that her body itself seemed to fail in its strength."[356] On another occasion, she said that, as "she was suspended in an ecstasy of contemplation, she saw herself caught up in a spirit to that place that was of incomprehensible size and indescribable beauty" where she saw Christ and his saints.[357] The fifth book of her Revelations (*The Book of Questions*) was given to her as "she was caught up in the spirit and went, as it were, outside herself, alienated from the senses of her body and suspended in an ecstasy of mental contemplation."[358] In addition, in a divine revelation she received the rule of a new order of nuns, the Order of the Most Holy Savior, now usually called the Bridgettines. Her confessors, anxious to assert the authenticity of the written texts of her revelations, affirmed that she dictated or wrote down her revelations in Swedish which they then translated into Latin. She would then review their translations to ensure that not one word was in error. Thus while her writings have been mediated through her confessors, the texts stand in the form that she approved.

In 1346, Birgitta began a more public career. God told her to go to the court of her cousin King Magnus where, like Moses, her mouth would be filled with what she was to say to him, which was a warning against the heavy taxes he was imposing on his subjects. Despite this interference, King Magnus supported Birgitta's plans for a new order of nuns and donated a royal estate at Vadstena for the convent. Her revelations then commanded her to go to Rome personally to seek the pope's approval for her order. But she was also to command Pope Clement VI in the name of Christ to make peace between King Edward III of England and King John II of France, this being in the midst of the Hundred Years' War, and to reform his own behavior or face divine disfavor: "Just as I caused you to ascend through all the [clerical] grades [to the papal throne], so you will descend through other grades, which you will experience truly in body and soul unless you obey my words."[359]

Perhaps a little diplomacy while serving as an ambassadress, even for God, might have been advisable, for the chastised pope refused to approve Birgitta's new order, suggesting instead that she adopt the existing Rule of St. Augustine. Clement's successor Urban V adhered to this position even though God again spoke through Birgitta, demanding that the pope confirm her order of nuns: "I have dictated it and endowed it with spiritual endowment. ... You must approve publicly, in front of men, that which has been sanctified in the presence of My heavenly assembly."[360] Birgitta even attempted to enlist the Holy Roman Emperor Charles IV in her cause, speaking for Christ, "Read [the Rule] and do your utmost to see that what comes from Me may be approved by the Supreme Pontiff."[361] Her primary mission was a failure but she resided in Rome until her death and even established a hostel for Scandinavian pilgrims. Under the guidance of her revelations she made a pilgrimage to Jerusalem and Bethlehem, where the Virgin Mary allowed her, "as if suspended in an ecstasy of contemplation, inebriated with divine sweetness,"[362] to witness the birth of Jesus and the coming of the Magi. She went to Assisi, where St. Francis appeared to her, and she was frequently in the kingdom of Naples, fruitlessly attempting to correct the notorious immorality of the court of Queen Joanna.

Discouraged by her failures, Birgitta reached the end of her life in Rome at the age of seventy. However, five days before her death, Christ appeared to her and assured her that she would "be counted not only as my bride, but also as a nun and a mother in Vadstena."[363] Birgitta's daughter Catherine took her body back to Sweden, to her convent at Vadstena. Five years later, in 1378, Pope Urban VI at last approved her Rule and the Bridgettine Order spread quickly to Italy, Norway, Germany, Poland, England, Spain, and from Spain on to the New World.

Birgitta left a vibrant memory in Rome. Thirty-five years after her death, the English pilgrim and mystic Margery Kempe[364] was in Rome and visited the room in which Birgitta died. She knelt at the very spot where Christ appeared to her five days before her death and spoke to a woman who had been Birgitta's maidservant, whom Margaret asked what kind of person her mistress had been. The servant replied, "Saint Bridget had been kind and behaved gently toward everyone. She said she always had a laughing face." Another man there remembered her not "as a saint or holy woman, since she was always homely [unpretentious] and kind with everyone who approached her."[365]

While most mystics emphasized the necessity of blending the contemplative life with the active life, few of them achieved that goal as effectively as Catherine of Genoa (1447–1510), who was born to an aristocratic Genoese family that claimed popes, cardinals and bishops among its members. When she was thirteen Catherine attempted to enter a convent but she was refused owing to her youth. Her father then died and her brother married Catherine to Giuliano Adorno, the son of another aristocratic Genoese family. The marriage was not a great success. Her husband was dissolute, unfaithful and unreliable, while Catherine was lonely and depressed and distracted herself with a busy social life. However, Catherine's life changed during her Lenten confession in 1473, as

A ray of God's love wounded her heart, making her soul experience a flaming love arising from the divine fount. At that instant, she was outside of herself, beyond intellect, tongue or feeling. Fixed in that pure and divine love, henceforth she never ceased to dwell on it.

She was given an understanding of her sins, which led her to cry out in despair, "O Lord, no more world, no more sins!" At this point "the ray of God so united her to Him that from this time no force or passion could separate them from one another."[366] Catherine was especially struck by a strong feeling of guilt for her sins and realized her need for contrition and penance.

Her life was so transformed by her experience that she was extolled as the model of such mystical transformation in Baron Friedrich von Hügel's 1909 pioneering work on mysticism, *The Mystical Element of Religion as Studied in Saint Catherine of Genoa and Her Friends.*[367] A year later she began to move out into the world, visiting Genoa's slums and attempting to care for the poor. Her husband suffered bankruptcy but was also converted to the religious life and the couple agreed to live without sexual relations. He became a Franciscan tertiary but Catherine never became attached to a religious order. In 1479 they moved into a small house near the great Pammatone hospital of Genoa even though they had sufficient income to afford much better and they began working with the poor and sick of that district. At first Catherine was a nurse at the hospital but later she became its director (1490–96), a task that must have been overwhelming during the great plague outbreak of 1493 that claimed the lives of four out of five residents who remained in the city. During all of this time Catherine had frequent ecstasies and even seemed to levitate. However, most refreshing in an age of extreme fasting among women mystics, she had an almost insatiable appetite and commonly needed food immediately after Communion.

Catherine's husband died in 1497 and she came under the spiritual direction of the priest Cattaneo Marabotto, to whom she confided the account of her mystical experiences and the teachings that she had been given. The written *vita* of Catherine and the two spiritual works that carry her name, the *Treatise on Purgatory* and the *Spiritual Dialogues*, were actually composed by Marabotto and one of her "spiritual sons," Ettore Vernazza, who himself founded several charitable institutions. For the rest of her life Catherine worked at the Pammatone hospital along with other high-born women who formed the Ladies of Mercy. Just before she died on 15 September 1510, "she saw herself without body and without soul, as she had always wished to be; that is, with her spirit completely in God, and having lost sight of heaven and earth, as if she no longer existed."[368]

While Catherine seemed obsessed with guilt and penance, especially that experience in purgatory, in the earlier stages of her spiritual development following her conversion, it was not a morbid fixation. It was joined with joy because through penance one was joined with God:

> While still in the flesh this blessed soul [Catherine] experienced the fiery love of God, a love that consumed her, cleansing and purifying all, so that once quitted this life she could appear forthwith in God's presence. As she dwelt on this love, the condition of the souls of the faithful in purgatory, where they are cleansed of

135

the remaining rust and stain of sin, became clear to her. She rejoiced in her union with God in this loving purgatory, and so did the souls in purgatory.[369]

Catherine affirmed that the souls in purgatory suffered most from the knowledge that they had displeased God and that they willingly undertook their suffering in order to come closer to God.[370] Her view of hell was likewise optimistic, for to her heaven and hell were not places but rather states of the soul. The souls in hell were there because of their desire to rebel against God and were they to be granted even a drop of union with God, they would be deprived of their rebellion: "For Hell is everywhere where there is such rebellion; and Life Eternal, wheresoever there is such union."[371]

Catherine's experiences led her, like St. Francis, to feelings of sharing the same existence with animals:

> Catherine's soul, like the seraphim, had penetrated into essential fire, because of which she would cry out many times. She would often turn tenderly to animals and say, "Aren't you, too, creatures of God?" – and all this she did because of the fire in her heart.[372]

She could not bear even to see a tree cut down and would address plants and trees, "Are you not creatures created by my God? Are not you obedient to him?"[373]

Those around Catherine observed that her union with God was consuming her with divine fire, noting that her skin turned saffron yellow from the fires that she felt burning inside of her, "a sign that the inner fire was consuming her humanity."[374] The fires caused her great pain and, in the final months of her life, "it seemed that her body was on fire like that of a saint, for it thrashed about in all directions." On the next day, she was visited by God and drawn to him. When she returned from the ecstasy, "she was asked what she had seen. She answered that God had shown her a spark of the joys of eternal life and that had made her laugh out of sheer joy."[375]

Perhaps the most fitting mystic with which to end the medieval period was the Genoese Franciscan tertiary whose career is often seen as signifying the end of the Middle Ages. Christopher Columbus (1451–1506), the discoverer of the New World for Europeans, has been regarded in many lights. Until the twentieth century he was often viewed as a brilliant navigator, the herald of a new age, an upholder of science and learning in the face of "medieval" superstition and ignorance. More recent opinion has been less kind to him, regarding him as the advance guard for the plundering of the western hemisphere and the enslavement of its peoples. Between two extremes, certain traits of Columbus have always been prominent. His zeal to sail West to the Indies was a fanatical drive which he never abandoned despite years of frustration and failure while remaining supremely self-confident that his enterprise would be successful. After he found the New World, he obstinately refused to admit that he had discovered an entirely new continent that was in fact thousands of miles to the East of the Indies. In one of his less savory interests, he seemed greedily obsessed with finding gold in the lands that he had discovered.

Recent scholarship has discovered the religious life of Christopher Columbus. He was a devout tertiary of the Franciscan Order and even wore a Franciscan habit in public. He associated with the apocalyptic, mystical branch of the Franciscans, the Spirituals, and was widely read in the body of apocalyptic and prophetic literature that circulated among them. Through his reading of the Bible he became convinced that the world was in its end times, having only about 150 years remaining before the return of Christ. However, a number of events would precede the Second Coming – the discovery of the Indies, the conversion of all peoples to Christianity and the retaking and rebuilding of the Holy Temple in Jerusalem.

Columbus was convinced that he was a divinely chosen agent to make all of this possible. God had revealed to him that the Indies could be reached by sailing West, which was in fact secondary to the main objective. The legendary gold mines of King Solomon were said to lie on the eastern fringe of Asia and to hold enough gold to finance a great crusade led by the Spanish monarchs for the purpose of retaking Jerusalem from the Muslims and rebuilding the Holy Temple. Thus the way for the imminent return of Jesus would be cleared. Columbus was a man on a mission from God. His obsession with gold derived from his absolute assurance that he was participating in the unfolding of prophesied events heralding the Second Coming, especially in financing the crusade to retake the Temple. Likewise the inhabitants of the lands he discovered were to be converted to Christianity, another fulfillment of prophecy.[376]

While in Spain in 1501–02, Columbus wrote the Book of Prophecies, *El libro de las profecías*, consisting of a string of biblical prophecies that served as proof of his apocalyptic view that the discovery of islands and peoples off the coast of Asia presaged Christ's return. In that book he also explained to King Ferdinand and Queen Isabella that it was God who told him to find the Indies by sailing West:

> With a hand that could be felt, the Lord opened my mind to the fact that it would be possible to sail from here to the Indies, and he opened my will to desire to accomplish the project. This was the fire that burned within me when I came to visit Your Highnesses. … Who can doubt that this fire was not merely mine, but also of the Holy Spirit who encouraged me with a radiance of marvelous illumination from his sacred Holy Scriptures … urging me to press forward?[377]

Columbus also claimed two divine visions. In his youth, the Holy Spirit had spoken to him assuring him that "his name would be proclaimed throughout the world." In another vision, in 1503 his ship was being buffeted by a severe storm while he was surrounded by hostile Indians. In exhaustion he fell asleep and a voice came to him, upbraiding him for his lack of faith and urging him to confess his sins. He wrote, "I heard all of this as if in a trance."[378]

Oddly, for a man who got all of his geography wrong and twisted his calculations to argue that Japan was located about where the Bahamas turned out to be, Columbus was amazingly correct. He found islands lying off a continental mainland about where he said they would be, there indeed were inhabitants there who were won over, willingly or not, to Christianity and vast quantities of gold and silver[379] were found there which indeed could have financed a crusade to retake Jerusalem if the

Spanish rulers had chosen to use the wealth for that purpose. Columbus erred only in identifying the geography with the Indies. One may well ponder how much of his enterprise to the Indies came from the revelations and how much was his own interpretation of them.

The discoveries of Columbus initiated the Age of Exploration, but the beginning of the sixteenth century also was a time of tremendous religious upheaval in Europe, the Reformation Era. As will be seen, the new religious atmosphere made it much more difficult for mysticism to thrive, but mystics continued to appear even in the greatly altered religious landscape.

CHAPTER IV

MYSTICS IN
EARLY MODERN EUROPE

THE REFORMATION, THE EFFLORESCENCE OF MYSTICISM IN SPAIN AND FRANCE

— •◆• —

The Reformation deposed mysticism from its ancient position as the highest form of Christianity as the Reformers emphasized Scripture, considered to be God's chosen means of self-revelation, as the sole source of authority while tending to suspicion of private revelations as a means of communication with the divine. In general they rejected religious institutions and practices which seemed to them to lack a scriptural basis, such as the papacy, relics, the cult of the saints and pilgrimages. They easily rejected mystical visions, voices and ecstasies as medieval excesses, along with fasts and severe methods for bringing under control the body and its appetites. The mysticism of the early church was often viewed as a special divine dispensation peculiar to that time and place whose purpose was to illustrate God's power and assist the foundation of the church. The canon of Christian scriptures was seen as a sufficient and complete divine revelation.

Moreover, monasticism, which for more than a thousand years had been the nursery of mysticism, was rejected as a medieval non-scriptural accretion. The Reformers emphasized the role of the laity in the church yet the life of the ordinary lay person did not embrace the ascetical practices that had been seen as the necessary preparation for mysticism. In addition, the works of Pseudo-Dionysius were now recognized not to have been written by a companion of St. Paul but rather by a much later author and thus were rejected as non-authoritative forgeries. With the repudiation of the preceding millennium of Christian history as "Roman Catholic" and "Papist," it was unlikely that the writings of the great medieval mystics would be read by many Protestants, for they not only lacked authority but were also filled with the now rejected visions and ecstasies, miracles and mysticism.

Thus Protestantism has tended to view mysticism with suspicion, regarding it as weird, egocentric and likely to divide the church. There is the maxim that, as far as Protestants are concerned, mysticism begins in a mist, ends in schism and has "I" in the middle. But occasionally Protestants could find themselves having a direct experience of the divine, although some manifestations of Protestant mysticism only stiffened the Protestant mistrust of such phenomena.

ANABAPTISTS AND LUTHERANS

Protestant antipathy towards mysticism crystallized in the early Reformation with the rise of the Anabaptist movement in the mid-1520s in Switzerland and Germany. "Anabaptist" refers to a style of religion rather than to an organized movement, for more than forty separate Anabaptist groups swiftly appeared. They had no common theology, but in general, like Luther, they rejected the authority of the papacy, which they supplanted with a literal interpretation of the Scriptures as they attempted to recreate the church of the New Testament. They especially opposed infant baptism and insisted on rebaptizing adult believers, a practice that gave rise to their collective name ("Anabaptist" means "re-baptizer"). In common with Luther and Calvin, they also tended to be awaiting the imminent end of the world but they often assigned a precise, relatively proximate date for this event.

For Anabaptists, the Bible should be interpreted through the individual's direct inspiration by the Holy Spirit, as is found in the New Testament Church. Anabaptist reverence of the Scriptures led many to assert that only inspirations consistent with the New Testament were to be considered valid, but for others, direct communication with God was more reliable and more authoritative than Scripture and some consigned their New Testaments to the fire. Soon it seemed as if Anabaptist mystics were everywhere. In the first years of the movement, prophets proliferated, some proclaiming that the Last Day was at hand and the way had to be prepared by eliminating from the earth all rulers and all who were not of the elect. Some claimed divinity for themselves and demanded absolute obedience from their disciples. Visions and extreme ecstasies were commonplace, with Anabaptists falling down as if dead for hours or writhing about on the ground. As with the movement of the Free Spirit,[1] antinomian licentiousness appeared and complete sexual freedom was proclaimed for the elect.

The immediate forerunner of the Anabaptists was Thomas Müntzer (1488/89–1525). He was born to a prosperous family in Saxony and attended universities in Leipzig and Frankfurt an der Oder, received his Master's degree and was then ordained a priest. He was trained in theology, philosophy and the Scriptures and learned Hebrew and Greek. For a time he was an itinerant priest before becoming one of the first converts to Martin Luther, on whose recommendation he was appointed priest in Zwickau.

One of the most important influences that took Müntzer down the path of revolution was his reading of John Tauler.

> [Tauler's] central emphasis on the *experience* of conversion through the power of the Holy Spirit, the argument that this was the only way to enable a person to live a "successful" Christian life, that such a person was a "friend of God" in contrast to the traditional and learned scribes and Pharisees, that one was enable to plumb the depths of God's wisdom immediately through the indwelling Holy Spirit, and that all of this took place in the abyss of the human soul without the "written Word," were all to impress Müntzer in profound ways.[2]

In a sense, Müntzer was a sixteenth-century Friend of God,[3] but with a difference. Through his study of church history Müntzer became convinced that the church of the New Testament had been filled with and led by the Holy Spirit. However, "after the deaths of the pupils of the apostles the immaculate and virginal church of Christ was contaminated, prostituted and exposed to hag-like adultery by the activities of perfidious priestlings"[4] who did not possess the Holy Spirit. Müntzer's own mystical life began by 1519 and thereafter he constantly claimed that he possessed the Holy Spirit. Soon he argued that all must experience the Holy Spirit, "For anyone who does not feel the spirit of Christ within him, or is not quite sure of having it, is not a member of Christ, but of the devil,"[5] and he urged the church "not to worship a mute God, but a living and speaking one."[6] He progressed from lamenting the loss of the Holy Spirit in the church to becoming obsessed with restoring the first-century church by re-establishing a Spirit-filled church. This could be done only by expelling those who did not have the Spirit and filling the church with those who, like Müntzer, were striving to lead Christians to the experience of God. Müntzer taught that there would be a final struggle between good and evil followed by extermination of the godless, he thus becoming one of those rare creatures, a violent mystic, the result of blending apocalypticalism with mysticism.

Once at Zwickau, Müntzer came into contact with the Zwickau Prophets, who taught that in the current last days of the world, God was communicating directly with his chosen people and that the Turks would conquer the world, which would be ruled by the Antichrist. The second coming of Christ would be announced by God's chosen ones rising up to annihilate the unrighteous. Müntzer joined with the Prophets but Luther refused to be associated with them and he and Müntzer were irretrievably estranged. Müntzer was eventually expelled from Zwickau and resumed his itinerancy as he continued to preach his apocalyptic mysticism.

In 1523 Müntzer, now married, was called to be pastor at Allstedt, in Thuringia, where he created a new liturgy in the German language and, as a prophet inspired by God, began publishing his teachings in fiery tracts. In particular he defended the validity of visions and dreams and denounced those who denied that God still inspired individuals as he had done in the days of the Apostles. Müntzer's fame spread among the discontented peasantry in the countryside and he organized the League of the Elect to prepare the way for the Second Coming. Then, in 1524, the Peasants' War broke out in southern Germany. There had been many previous peasants' rebellions and Germany had seen a recent outbreak, the *Bundshuh*, suppressed only in 1517. But this Peasants' War combined all of the older elements of discontent with a desire to spread the Reformation and Lutheranism.

The outbreak of war seemed to Müntzer to be the beginning of the final conflagration that he had been prophesying and he joined the rebels and became their spiritual leader in Thuringia. Filled with confidence in God's assurances that he would triumph, he led 300 of his followers out to ally with a force of several thousand revolutionaries at nearby Frankenhausen. However, the authorities and the lords, the intended victims of the peasants, had by now raised their own forces. The peasants advanced singing spiritual songs while the lords advanced with cannon. The peasants were utterly routed and were cut down in their thousands. Müntzer fled but was later captured, tortured and beheaded while throughout Germany the peasants were crushed and massacred in their tens of thousands.

Ironically it was the peasants who became associated with violence, as did their religious emphasis on apocalypticism and their mysticism of the necessity for God's direct communication with the soul of the believer – tenets that were prominent with the Anabaptists who appeared in the aftermath of the Peasants' War. The Anabaptist reputation for peasant revolution and violence was confirmed by their reverence of Müntzer's memory (which was also revived by German Marxists in the nineteenth and twentieth centuries).

Not all Anabaptists were apocalyptic nor indeed did they all seek for or gain raptures and visions, but almost from the beginning, the militant form of Anabaptism in Müntzer's tradition emerged and burst into similar socio-religious movements of violence in the 1530s. This was a period significant in apocalyptic thought because of the fifteenth centenary of the death, resurrection and heavenly ascension of Jesus, presumed to be the year 1533. The German city of Münster was one of their first centers as prophetic preachers abounded and their followers experienced visions and ecstasies. In 1534 Lutherans began to flee the city and the Dutch Anabaptist revolutionary leader Jan Matthys arrived and swiftly established a despotic theocracy, expelling all non-Anabaptists and abolishing private property. Matthys died but his disciple Jon Bockelson succeeded him and tightened the theocracy as fresh revelations from God reinforced his authority. He instituted a polygamous society in Münster, proclaimed himself king of New Jerusalem and began executing those who sinned. The bishop of Münster besieged the city and in June of 1535 his army forced an entry and slaughtered virtually all of the inhabitants, including those who had surrendered and been promised safe conduct.

The Münster incident solidified the image of Anabaptists as being violent revolutionaries claiming the sanction of mystical inspiration received directly from the Holy Spirit. Anabaptists were persecuted severely but in the end the peaceful wing of the Anabaptists, such as the Mennonites and Hutterites, survived. However, mysticism and divine inspiration were now thoroughly contaminated in the eyes of most Protestants, including Lutherans. Moreover, as the Reformation progressed, Lutheranism became increasingly defined by the documents setting forth its faith, the Augsburg Confession and the Apology for the Augsburg Confession, both in 1530, and the Schmalkald Articles of 1538. For the next forty years, however, Lutherans waged internecine polemical wars over the interpretation of these definitions, concluding in the Formula of Concord of 1580. By that time a form of Lutheran Scholasticism had emerged, demanding acceptance of tightly-argued expositions of the faith in order to be accepted as an orthodox Lutheran. To the Lutheran pastor Johann Arndt (1555–1621), his church had become a set of finely nuanced articles of faith rather than a faith living within each Christian. In his most famous work, *True Christianity*, he denounced disputation and "the many useless and unnecessary books." He wrote that renewal in Christ was "the end of all theology and the whole of Christianity. This is the union with God, the marriage with our heavenly Bridegroom, Jesus Christ, the living faith, the new birth, Christ's dwelling in us."[7] True Christianity, he wrote, "consists, not in words or in external show, but in living faith, from which arise righteous fruits, and all manner of Christian virtues, as from Christ himself."[8]

Arndt was himself the son of a pastor in Ballenstedt, in the modern German state of Halle. For a time he studied medicine but a health crisis led him to take up theology. He married and served as a pastor in a number of towns in Saxony where he was constantly engaged in controversy, especially because he clung to many aspects of medieval Christianity that had been rejected by his fellow Lutherans as being Popish. In particular he read and recommended medieval mystical books, especially those of Bernard of Clairvaux, Angela of Foligno and John Tauler. Arndt was a throwback, for in his soul he was a Friend of God along with Tauler, dedicated to practicing and preaching a life of Christian virtue. He revered those in the past "who practiced the noble and holy life of Christ in simplicity, purity of heart and pure love [as being] among the most enlightened" and he cherished the emphasis on repentance and the renewal of the inner person that he found in the old mystical texts, "old, short books that lead to a holy life."[9] He excoriated those who "think that theology is a mere science, or rhetoric, whereas it is a living experience and practice. Everyone now endeavors to be eminent and distinguished in the world, but no one is willing to learn to be pious."[10] To him, true knowledge of God was not the preserve of the Scholastics, for it "does not consist in words or in mere learning but in a living, loving, gracious, powerful consolation in which through grace one tastes the sweetness, joyousness, loveliness, and graciousness of God in his heart."[11]

For Arndt, the path to God was essentially the same as that laid out by his favorite models:

> a man must deny himself; that is, break his own self-will, give himself completely to God's will; not love himself but hold himself as the most unworthy, miserable man; deny all that he has; that is, reject the world and his honor and glory; consider his own wisdom and power as nothing; not depend on himself or on any creature but only and simply on God; hate his own life, that is, the fleshly lusts and desires such as pride, covetousness, lust, wrath, and envy; have no pleasure in himself, and consider all his acts as nothing; … die to the world, that is, the lust of the eyes, the lust of the flesh, and the pride of life; be crucified to the world.[12]

The denial of the self, true repentance and mortification of the flesh, by which Arndt meant dying to the world, would lead to the Christian's feeling wretched, which was to be desired: "The more miserable you are in your heart, the dearer you are to God."[13] With a person thus emptied, Christ alone could dwell within, that is, union with Christ is achieved. For this "God gives himself to our soul to taste and touch"[14] and

> no creature can know how great a joy it has from this and how it feels in its heart, how fervent it is internally, how it rejoices and shouts for joy because of love, … No one, I say, can know this except the person who has experienced it.

143

To feel and to experience this is possible for a man but to express it is impossible, for it is a spiritual mystery and divine matter concerning which man dare not speak so that he carry no fault against the Bridegroom who loves to dwell in the mystery and in the stillness of the heart.[15]

To Arndt, the Lutheran insistence on the authority of the Scriptures confirmed that the end and goal of a Christian was union with Christ, for he argued that God did not give the Scriptures to remain a dead letter on paper, for they were a witness to "what must occur in faith in all men. ... What the Scripture teaches I must experience for my own comfort and faith."[16]

True Christianity, first published in 1605, achieved immediate popularity, appearing in twenty editions by the time of Arndt's death in 1621. Its theme of truly living the Christian life was taken up by the later Pietists of Germany and led to Arndt's being called the Father of German Pietism. Predictably, Lutheran theologians, the "learned doctors" so opposed by Arndt, condemned him as a heretic, horrified both by his teachings themselves as well as their appeal to those considered heretical by orthodox Lutherans. Moreover, about the same time that Arndt died, the mystical works of Jacob Boehme were creating a sensation in the far eastern regions of the German-speaking world, which solidified Lutheran hostility to mysticism.

Boehme (1575–1624) was the son of a prosperous farmer in the Margravate of Upper Lusatia, which today is on the eastern frontier between Germany and Poland. Very little is known of his life before 1600. His family provided him with at least a basic education and at age fourteen he was apprenticed to a shoemaker. At about the age of twenty he moved to the nearby provincial capital of Görlitz, establishing himself as a shoemaker and marrying a well-dowered wife. At that point he had perhaps his first mystical experience. His disciple and hagiographer Abraham von Franckenberg records that it happened when Boehme's glance at a pewter dish "introduced [him] into the innermost ground or center of the ... hidden treasure."[17] In Boehme's own description of the experience that transformed his life he wrote that "the Spirit shot through me like a bolt of lightning"[18] and understanding came to him:

the gate was opened unto me, that in one-quarter of an hour I saw and knew more than if I had been many years together at a University ... For I saw and knew the Being of all Beings, the Byss and the Abyss ... the descent, and original of this world, and of all creatures ... I knew and saw in myself all three worlds; namely the divine, angelical, and paradisical world and then the dark world; ... And then thirdly, the external and visible world; and I saw, and knew the whole Being in the evil and in the good; and the mutual original, and existence of each of them.[19]

He also wrote of this experience, "I am not climbed up into the Deity ... but the Deity is climbed up into me, and from *its* love are these things revealed to me," and he entered "into the innermost birth or geniture of the Deity ... In this light my spirit suddenly saw through all, and *in* and *by* all the creatures, even in herbs and grass it knew God."[20] This was only the beginning of many more such experiences over the next twelve years. "I was as it were pregnant with all, and found a powerful driving and instigation within me … whatsoever I could apprehend, and bring into the eternal principle of my mind the same I wrote down."[21] Indeed he wrote, for his collected writings fill eleven volumes. All that he wrote came from his own experiences, "I wrote only my own mind as I understood it in the Deep."[22]

Boehme's general mystical path is consistent with that of other Christian mystics. The Christian first gains self-knowledge, patiently endures persecution, demonstrates love for neighbors and love for God, detaches from false images and all creaturely things, and then mystical union would follow. However, for Boehme it was not just union with God or with the Holy Spirit, but rather with the virgin Sophia, the wisdom of God. At first he wrote only for himself, not intending his writings to be read by others, a wise precaution because Boehme gained revelations that were very dangerous in an age devoid of religious toleration.

The wars of religion were still raging with ferocity in Germany and the Holy Roman Empire as local authorities were given the right to impose their own faith on all who dwelt in their regions. Görlitz and Upper Lusatia were Lutheran, as was Boehme, but he was no ordinary Lutheran. He was part of a movement that rejected religious dogmatism and creedal intolerance. He despaired that:

> the whole of titular Christendom is turned into mere sects and orders, where one sect despises and brands another as unrighteous. And thus they have made of Christendom a mere murdering den, full of blasphemies about Christ's person; and have bound the spirit of Christ … to the forms and orders of disputation. … In the stone-houses of the churches, cathedrals, and cloisters … they do counterfeit somewhat of Christ … spend their time with disputing, confuting, and contending about sects (and different mental idols and opinions), in so much that one party is brought wholly to condemn the other … whence nothing but wars and disdainful provocations do arise, to the desolation of countries and cities.[23]

He argued forcefully for freedom from definitions of theology and formulas of faith in order to follow the guidance of the Spirit:

> Now, faith is not an historical knowledge, that man should frame articles to himself and depend on them alone, and force his mind into the works of his reason; but faith is one spirit with God, for the Holy Spirit moves in the spirit of faith.[24]

Boehme did not limit himself to attacking the dogmatism of the denominations. He saw God as a deity present in all things, giving his favor to all people, even "Jews, Turks, heathens." However, throughout all of his life Boehme remained a faithful, church-going Lutheran, especially attached to the sacraments of Baptism and the Eucharist.

The difficulty for the modern reader, as indeed it was for his contemporaries, is the language in which he described his experiences and illuminations. In many ways Boehme writes as a para-Christian, almost as a Theist. During this period Görlitz received virtually every current strand of Kabbalistic, occult, esoteric and alchemical thought, all of which deeply affected Boehme. While his writings evolved over the dozen years of his literary career, most of it is obscured in deep layers of alchemy, numerology, allegory and symbolism so dense as to make his treatises "virtually unreadable."[25] Boehme wandered in and out of the signs of the Zodiac, the seven planets, the four humors and four elements, and the three constituents of sulphur, mercury and salt as he described all of nature as an expression of God. God was hidden in nature and, in the language of alchemy and the other esoteric sciences, he could express the way that God was written into all of nature. However, in Boehme's lifetime and for more than two centuries to follow, he was as controversial as he was influential. His own pastor in Görlitz carried on a virtual vendetta against him yet he had crowds of admirers seek him out and he was courted by aristocrats and authorities. He inspired spiritual seekers like William Law and William Blake[26] as well as generations of German Romantics and philosophers.

By the end of the seventeenth century, Lutheranism produced another mystic reminiscent of Boehme, the Swede Emanuel Swedenborg. When Lutherans do become mystics, they seem to do so with a flourish, for, like Boehme, Swedenborg (1688–1772) produced a mysticism that was only just on the banks of the mainstream of the Christian tradition. Also like Boehme, he profoundly influenced writers, poets and philosophers all over Europe for centuries after his death. However, unlike Boehme, Swedenborg was born into privilege and power. His mother, who died when Emanuel was eight years old, was a wealthy heiress of a mining family in Sweden, while his father, Jesper Swedberg, was descended from farmers and miners able to send him to university theological studies. Jesper's first position was as chaplain to the Royal Life Guards, where his bold preaching won the admiration of King Charles XI, who named him successively court chaplain, professor of theology at Upsala University, and rector and dean of the cathedral of Upsala. In 1702 King Charles XII elevated him to the position of bishop of Skara, a city fifteen miles from the shores of Lake Vänern in southwestern Sweden. In 1719, Bishop Swedberg's children were ennobled, a common reward for bishops, under the new surname of Swedenborg.

The young Emanuel grew up in this atmosphere of religion, wealth and prominence under his brilliant and domineering father and a loving stepmother. His university studies at Upsala concentrated on science and mathematics rather than theology. After completing university studies in 1709, he journeyed abroad for five years, studying in England, Holland, France and Italy. He came back to Sweden more widely-educated in mathematics as well as in mining techniques, possessing a list of inventions he had developed on the basis of his ideas in mechanics, including a ship which "with its one-man crew, could go under the sea, in any desired direction, and could inflict much injury on enemy ships" and a "flying carriage, or the possibility of staying in the air and of being carried through it."[27] At this time he also founded Sweden's first scientific journal, *Daedalus Hyperboreus*. In 1716 the king appointed the twenty-eight year old Emanuel to the post of Extraordinary Assessor in the Royal College of Mines, a position previously held by one of his grandfathers. For the next thirty years Swedenborg carried out his official duties, concerned himself in national affairs as he faithfully attended meetings of the House of Nobles in the Swedish Riksdag, continued his travels around Europe and widened his studies to include anatomy, biology and psychology. He was especially determined to discover the location of the seat of the soul in the human body and produced conclusions far ahead of contemporary science, anticipating the lungs' oxygenation of the blood, the existence of the cerebrospinal fluid and brain cells.

While on one of his journeys abroad, in 1743–44, Swedenborg recorded in his *Journal of Dreams*[28] the struggles of his great religious crisis. He experienced vivid, detailed, and symbolic dreams accompanied by tremblings throughout his body and "temptations" (inner conflicts). The experiences reached a crescendo on the night of April 6–7, 1744, the day following Easter. After having extreme shuddering, "I found that something holy was upon me."[29] He then fell asleep, only to awaken in the night around 2 o'clock with

a strong shuddering from head to foot, with a thundering noise as if many winds beat together; which shook me; it was indescribable and prostrated me on my face. Then, at the time I was prostrated, at that very moment I was wide awake, and I saw that I was cast down. ... And I spoke as if I were awake; but found nevertheless that the words were put into my mouth. "And oh! Almighty Jesus Christ, that thou, of thy so great mercy, deignest to come to so great a sinner. Make me worthy of they grace." I held together my hands, and prayed, and then came forth a hand, which squeezed my hands hard. ... At that moment I sat in his bosom, and saw him face to face; it was a face of holy mien, and in all it was indescribable, and he smiled so that I believe that his face had indeed been like this when he lived on earth. ... So I found that it was God's own son, who came down with this thunder, and prostrated me to the ground, from himself, and made the prayer, and so, said I, it was Jesus himself. ... Afterwards, about daybreak I fell again into sleep, and then it was chiefly in my thoughts how Christ unites himself to mankind.[30]

In the days that followed, Swedenborg struggled to comprehend what had happened to him, sweating heavily and frequently bursting into tears. He also had more experiences of the divine: "The movement and the power of the spirit came to me, and I felt that I would rather go mad."[31] He compared himself to a "peasant [who] is raised to power as a chief or king and can command all that his heart desired; but who yet had something in him that caused him to wish to learn that of which he himself knew nothing."[32] He was struck by the intensity of his struggle that was entirely internal, for throughout this period, "I was in society as usual and no one could in the least [observe in me any change]."[33] About a year later, while in London, God came to Swedenborg, declaring that "He had chosen me to declare to men the spiritual contents of Scripture; and that He Himself would declare to me what I should write on the subject."[34]

For the rest of his life, Swedenborg was in almost constant communication with angels (highly evolved spirits), spirits associated with the planets and spirits of the dead as he functioned as a medium or channeler. He knew that some would not believe him, holding that "no one can possibly speak with spirits and angels as long as he lives in the body; ... [but] I have seen, I have heard, I have felt."[35] He felt called to promulgate a new divine revelation and in the last twenty-seven years of his life he abandoned his former scientific work and recorded in prolific detail over thirty volumes of his revelations. His detailed and intricate system is far too complex to summarize briefly, but it indeed was a new revelation. It taught the complete correspondence of the heavenly world with the earthly world and indeed the human body and affirmed the unity of God and denied the traditional teaching of the Trinity. Moreover, it also denied the doctrine of the Atonement, the eventual resurrection of the body, the existence of the Devil and evil as being anything other than wrongdoing.

He was no proselytizer for his teachings, for he wrote his works in Latin and his early treatises were anonymous, but soon he gained renown as a clairvoyant and seer. In 1759, while dining with friends in the city of Göteborg, he saw, accurately as it turned out, that a fire had broken out in Stockholm, some 300 miles away, and he noted with relief that his own house had narrowly escaped the flames. News of his feat spread quickly to the provincial governor, who summoned Swedenborg to provide a personal account of his vision.

Swedenborg's authorship of the books of revelations from the spirit world became known and he was sought out for assistance. The widow of the Dutch ambassador to Sweden was able to find a missing receipt when Swedenborg spoke with her deceased husband. In 1761 he met with the queen of Sweden, the Prussian Lovisa Ulrika. Having heard of his reputation for conversing with the dead, she asked him to ask for a message from her brother who had died three years earlier. At his next meeting with the queen, he passed on a private message, whereupon she turned pale and exclaimed, "That is something which no one else could have told, except my brother!"[36]

The Lutheran pastors in Sweden also heard reports of his exploits and the rural clergy were not favorably inclined to his new theology. One of them accused Swedenborg of heresy, charging that his teaching was "corrupting, heretical, injurious, and, in the highest degree, objectionable."[37] After a long set of hearings, in 1770 the royal council that was charged with the case "totally condemned, rejected and forbade the theological doctrines in Swedenborg's writings."[38] The case was appealed and the theologians at the University of Upsala were asked to rule on the matter but they declined to become involved. However, by that time Swedenborg had died, in London, 29 March 1772, on the very day that he had predicted. His teachings have had a long and deep influence, inspiring writers such as Blake, Balzac, Baudelaire, Emerson, Yeats and Strindberg, and produced the "Swedenborgian church," the Church of the New Jerusalem.

SPANISH MYSTICS OF THE GOLDEN AGE

Spain remained staunchly Catholic and monastic and mysticism flourished as sixteenth-century Spain swarmed with mystics of every variety, from the most sublime mystics who sought the union of the soul in Spiritual Marriage to those given to receiving visions, voices and prophecies. The mystical literature that was produced in such profusion in the sixteenth century was to a great degree the foundation of the Golden Age of Spanish Literature, but at the same time the widespread mystical movements attracted the unwelcome attention of the newly-established Spanish Inquisition, keen to sniff out all aberrations from orthodox Christianity.

Many factors contributed to this efflorescence of mysticism. One of the most important was the printing press, cranking out relatively inexpensive copies of the great mystical literature of previous centuries as well as of the newer works produced in Spain and the rest of Europe. One of the first to take advantage of the press to disseminate mystical literature was the towering figure of Cardinal Francisco Jiménez de Cisneros, a Franciscan monk given to asceticism and attracted to the distinctive Franciscan spirituality that emphasized mysticism and prophecy. His sanctity led to his appointment as confessor to Queen Isabella of Castile and then as archbishop of Toledo (the primate of the Spanish Church), regent of the kingdom of Castile, a member of the College of Cardinals and Inquisitor General. Under his aegis Spanish translations of the works and lives of such mystical figures as John Climacus, Angela of Foligno, Catherine of Siena and Pseudo-Dionysius were made and published, but equally important, he not only tolerated mysticism and prophecies, he positively encouraged them. He saw to the publication of the spiritual tracts from previous centuries while carefully expurgating from the texts any warnings against placing too much faith in ecstasies and visions. In particular, Jiménez was inclined to place great confidence in the authenticity of the mystical experiences of the many *beatas* in Spain, women living either cloistered or alone, under a simple vow of chastity, wearing habits, and observing religious rules. "During the primacy of Cardinal Cisneros the *beatas* and the visionaries were not the objects of local piety alone. ... they were supported by the court and the nobility and had the approval of at least part of the ecclesiastical hierarchy."[39] During this tidal wave of mysticism some went so far as to argue that mysticism was for all, not just a spiritual élite who could adopt a life of asceticism and contemplation, but was in fact an easy shortcut to God, open even to the unlearned.

Another important element in the development of mysticism in Spain came from the Order of Carmel, a mystical monastic order. It had been established in the mid-twelfth century in the Crusader Kingdom of Jerusalem as a loose collection of hermits gathered on Mount Carmel living a life of seclusion, silence, prayer and severe asceticism in imitation of the Hebrew prophet and mystic Elijah. With the fall of the Crusader Kingdom in the thirteenth century, the Carmelites transferred to Europe and adapted to the new circumstances. They relaxed their rule, began living in monasteries and generally modeled themselves after the Dominicans and the Franciscans. Even though the Carmelites now aspired to a more active life of teaching and preaching in

149

the world, they never abandoned their emphasis on prayer and meditation and their goal remained to encounter God.

By the 1520s, after Cardinal Jiménez had died, mysticism in the form of the Alumbrados collided with the Inquisition. Alumbrado means "illuminated" and it was used as a term of derision by opponents of mysticism. The first Alumbrados were a loosely-associated group of mystics in the area of Toledo who stressed the interior life and Detachment as the way to God – simple submission to God and a determination not to sin. They flourished in the last years of Cardinal Jiménez, but they opposed the flamboyant mystical manifestations of voices, visions and prophecies that he encouraged. This led to conflicts with many *beatas* but at the same time their low esteem for outward acts of piety gave them more in common with the growing Protestant movement in Europe than the Inquisition was willing to tolerate. Moreover, internal disputes within the group provoked vengeful denunciations of some of the leaders of the Inquisition, some of whom received harsh but non-lethal penalties while others were allowed simply to disavow heretical statements that they were alleged to have made.

In the 1570s there was another round of attacks on mystics, this time principally in southwestern Spain and fueled in part by scandals involving supposed mystics who admitted to having received visions from the devil or to having faked levitations and the stigmata. Others had slipped into that common mystical heresy of antinomianism and its related excess, libertinism. Unlike those scrutinized in the 1520s, they tended to the more enthusiastic manifestations of mysticism but they were considered Alumbrados by the Inquisition, for by the end of the sixteenth century that term was used for all who were believed to be guilty of false, hypocritical or ostentatious religiosity or those given to trances and ecstasies. In the early seventeenth century, another group of mystics in Seville, also attracted to charismatic, ecstatic leaders and making claims of inability to sin, were tried and punished by the Inquisition and again charged with the vague accusation of being Alumbrados.

Thus in sixteenth-century Spain there was widespread interest in mysticism, including extreme enthusiasts, charlatans, and heretics, while simultaneously there was strong opposition to mysticism by those who could easily utilize the Inquisition to harass their opponents. The first great writer to emerge out of this churning pool of mysticism was Francisco de Osuna (ca. 1492 to ca. 1540), whose works were highly esteemed by his contemporaries and repeatedly reprinted. It is Osuna's misfortune that his reputation has been overshadowed by the other great mystics of sixteenth-century Spain. Unfortunately, his life is largely unknown and even the dates of his birth and death are conjectured. He was from the town of Osuna, in the region of Seville in southern Spain. He became a priest, entered the Franciscan Order, engaged in university studies, and wrote over 500 works. Among them were six Spiritual Alphabets, collections of his maxims on the spiritual life arranged in alphabetical order and accompanied by lengthy commentaries so they would not be misunderstood – an important precaution in the inquisitorial climate of sixteenth-century Spain. The most important of these is the *Third Spiritual Alphabet*, which put Teresa of Ávila on the path of mysticism.[40]

The *Third Spiritual Alphabet* is a defense of the mystical technique of Recollection rather than the Detachment that was advocated by the original group of "Alumbrados." Recollection was an emphasis on an active focusing of the mind and reformation of the vices, while Detachment was more passive in nature, waiting for God to come to the quieted soul. The end of Recollection was union with God, where one "is made one spirit with him by an interchange of wills whereby he wants only what God wants … they almost cease to be themselves and become totally conformed into a third being."[41]

The alphabetical arrangement of the maxims lacks a clear organization, but the text is replete with sound, practical advice for the would-be mystic, especially in urging moderation in ascetical practices. Its essential message is typical of manuals on mysticism, urging renunciation of sin, exercise of the virtues, detachment from material objects, and performing acts of genuine love. Osuna's mysticism urged the way of negation, citing previous writers who wrote that God cannot be known through the intellect or through the senses, for God "is more truly and completely explained when we deny rather than affirm what he is."[42] Moreover, he wrote that silent, mental prayers reach God more quickly than do verbal prayers, "The greater your silence in asking, the more [God] clearly hears you … vocal prayer is of little use and is greatly harmful for the proficient because it can obstruct much greater perfection." Citing St. Augustine, he added, "Once devotion is attained, words should cease."[43]

Osuna took often awkward stands on both sides of the current debates concerning mysticism. Union with God was certainly not obtainable by short cuts, for the road to such union was a very long one, demanding years of effort, and he had no patience for beginners who wanted to become "hermits in a matter of days."[44] He cautioned that Recollection was not for everyone while also promising that it was as available to his reader as to anyone else, for what was required was "that we single-mindedly set out for God."[45] He enticed "lords, gentlemen, and rich men" and even merchants (people "who seem most opposed and contrary to spirituality") and all good Christians to make time in their lives for Recollection. In fact, "any faithful person – even a little woman or simpleton"[46] can follow the path of Recollection.

On "consolations," that is, visions, voices, sensations, Osuna was cautionary, moderate and not entirely consistent. He counseled that external signs ought to be avoided – provided that true devotion was not stifled – yet genuine grace that comes into the soul always leaves a trace and the ascent to God can produce feelings of an intense, sweet fire. Sometimes God teaches humans through a voice, but voices are most susceptible to suspicion while dreams are extremely uncertain. Osuna knew that some who engaged in contemplation wept profusely or groaned loudly, even falling down to the ground as if dead and trembling, but these manifestations were generally caused by their own imaginations and they should be squelched immediately. He related the account of a woman who seemed to have raptures, converse with saints, and receive prophecies, but in the end came to realize that these were false experiences. On the other hand, profuse tears are the most excellent devotion to God and should never be abandoned.

While Osuna related mystical experiences of people whom he knew, he never presented any as being his own. However, he was most adamant that no one should teach on mysticism who had not experienced it and that those who had ascended to the heights of contemplation must not forget those still down below, but rather teach them "how to soar" as St. Paul had done. Very significantly, he also counseled that when experienced persons revealed the consolations they had received from God, they should describe them as having happened to someone else. Therefore we are left to speculate that the experiences that Osuna attributed to unnamed other people – the man who received a different kind of grace from God each day for a year; the monk who fell into such a rapture while asleep that he appeared to be dead and others began shrouding him for burial before he returned to normal consciousness; or the man who "felt his entire being moved and opened to love God most sweetly" – might in fact be his own.[47]

In great contrast to the meager scraps of biographical information available for Francisco de Osuna, there are rich details of the life of his exact contemporary, Ignatius of Loyola (ca. 1491–1556). Ignatius is best known as the founder of the Society of Jesus – the Jesuits, the shock troops of papacy in the Counter-Reformation – and no doubt he would have been satisfied with that reputation. However, at the same time he was a profound mystic who was given almost daily experiences for long periods of his life. It is not as a mystic that Ignatius wanted to be known, for he tried to destroy his daily record of his experiences, the *Spiritual Diary*. The surviving fragment covers only about a year, February 1544–February 1545, and, astonishingly, it was not published in its entirety until 1934. The second great record of his mystical experiences comes from the so-called *Autobiography*, which is actually a record of his responses to questions about his life put to him by his disciples in 1552 when they feared he was about to die. It is likewise incomplete, covering the years 1521–38 and also like the *Spiritual Diary* it languished in relative obscurity for several centuries. A Latin translation was first published in 1731 but the original Spanish and Italian text was published only in 1904. Thus the non-mystical Ignatius became firmly fixed in historical consciousness long before scholars began to be fully aware of his mystical side.

Ignatius was a nobleman from the Basque region of Spain, whose ancestral castle of Loyola lay northwest of Pamplona in Navarre, in the Pyrenees. He was born Iñigo (Ignatius) López, the last of thirteen children. He received the education typical for a boy of the aristocratic class, preparing him for a life of dissolution and glory-seeking. He described himself as having grown up to be "a man given to the vanities of the world; and what he enjoyed most was warlike sport, with a great and foolish desire to win fame."[48]

However, in 1521 he was fighting in the defense of Pamplona against a French invasion when a cannon ball ripped into him, shattering one leg, badly injuring the other and setting him on a new course in his life. A lengthy, painful and dangerous period of recuperation awaited him. His more badly-damaged leg had to be rebroken, a procedure he labeled "butchery," and when the bones knit, the leg was shorter than the other, with a bone protruding in an ugly manner. He had the bone cut away and the leg stretched to lengthen it. During his long convalescence he read books, including the lives of Christ and saints. They affected him deeply during his ordeal and he became especially attracted to St. Dominic and St. Francis and desired to imitate their lives. His conversion to a new life was confirmed by a vision of the Virgin Mary and the infant Jesus and he now loathed his former life: "Thus from that hour until August '53 when this was written, he never gave the slightest consent to the things of the flesh."[49]

After his convalescence, Ignatius took to wearing sackcloth as he received additional visions. On one occasion he saw the Trinity in the form of three musical keys, on another "something white, from which rays were coming and God made light from this," and on another, as the host was being elevated at Mass, "he saw with interior eyes something like white rays" coming from it. His most famous experience from this period was one he had while sitting beside the river Cordoner:

> While he was seated there, the eyes of his understanding began to be opened; not that he saw any vision, but he understood and learnt many things, both spiritual matters and matters of faith and of scholarship, and this with so great an enlightenment that everything seemed new to him. The details that he understood then, though there were many, cannot be stated, but only that he experienced a great clarity in his understanding. This was such that in the whole course of his life, after completing sixty-two years, even if he gathered up all the various helps that he may have had from God and all the various things he has known, even adding them all together, he does not think that he had got as much as at that one time.[50]

Ignatius made a pilgrimage to Jerusalem during which "it seemed to him that he saw Christ over him continually."[51] Once back in Spain, he took up studies at Barcelona and then Alcalà, where he taught Christian doctrine and attracted crowds of followers, including a large number of women, the younger of whom seemed prone to falling into fits and ecstasies. However, at this time the Inquisition was investigating the first Alumbrados in Toledo and Ignatius came under scrutiny. He and his companions were wearing distinctive identical long gray habits and gray hoods even though they were not members of any religious order and thus were accused of being Alumbrados. After several months' imprisonment they were released but were ordered to abandon their habits while Ignatius was forbidden to preach for three years. Showing a legalistic mind that would soon become characteristic of the Jesuits, Ignatius and companions moved to Salamanca, a different jurisdiction, and continued on as before. Here he fell into the clutches of hostile Dominicans and was again imprisoned. He endured another grilling and his preaching was again restricted. It was time for another change of jurisdiction, "So he decided to go to Paris to study."[52]

Ignatius needed theological credentials if he hoped to be allowed to preach and teach freely and the study of theology required learning Latin. Thus at the age of thirty-seven he began his study of the language, sitting in a class of young boys. He advanced rapidly and in 1533 he received his Licentiate in Arts and in 1535 his Master of Arts degree, which allowed him to teach anywhere in the world. Ignatius recalled that he had very few spiritual visions while engaged in his theological studies in Paris but he continued giving spiritual instruction, once again drawing the attention of the Inquisition. Again he cleared himself and he and his companions left Paris determined to live in strict poverty and to "spend their lives for the good of souls."[53]

They were ordained as priests and set out for Rome to place themselves at the service of the pope. "On this journey he was visited very especially by God," and while he was praying at the church of La Storta near Rome he "experienced such a change in his soul and saw so clearly that God the Father placed him with Christ his Son that he would not dare doubt it."[54] In 1539 Ignatius and his nine companions organized themselves into a new religious order, the Society of Jesus, with Ignatius as the first superior general. The order grew very rapidly and by the time of his death in 1556 there were about 1000 Jesuits organized into twelve provinces in Europe as well as in India and Brazil. However, the Jesuits also emphasized education and by 1556 Ignatius had established thirty-three colleges.

Throughout this hectic period of organization and development, Ignatius received almost constant mystical experiences, if the events in the surviving section of his *Spiritual Diary* of 1544–5 are typical. He recorded daily visitations of tears, tangible feelings of warmth, interior voices and visions, insights and understandings. He had visions of the Virgin Mary, of Jesus, of the Father, of "the Divine Being" and of heaven. On 9 February 1544, he wrote, "I felt in myself a motion toward the Father or that I was being lifted up before him."[55] Two days later he wrote that, while speaking with the Holy Spirit, "I seemed to see him or perceive him in dense brightness or in the color of a flame of fire burning in an unusual way."[56] On 21 February, "Once or several times I was unable to speak, experiencing spiritual insights to such an extent that I seemed to understand that there was, so to speak, nothing more to be known about this matter of the Holy Trinity."[57] These experiences could come to him anywhere, even when walking down the street, when "Jesus represented himself to me and I experienced strong motions and tears."[58] He said of himself that he found God at any hour that he wished, "And even now he often had visions, especially those mentioned above when he saw Christ as the sun. This often happened while he was engaged in important matters."[59]

Ignatius's mysticism extended even into his most famous work, the *Spiritual Exercises*, his program of spiritual training now used as a retreat manual by all Jesuits and by many others as well. The *Spiritual Exercises* are organized as a month-long series of meditations or contemplations for the purpose of discerning God's will for oneself. The pattern of the meditations corresponds to the stages of mystical union with God, the illuminative way, the purgative way and then the unitive way. The retreatants are "to ask for an interior knowledge of our Lord" with the goal of obtaining an experience wherein "the Creator and Lord himself should communicate himself to the devout soul."[60] In this direct communication with God, the retreatants can experience a religious conversion and can have God's will revealed directly to them, as Ignatius had throughout his life. However, the *Spiritual Exercises* were attacked by many in the older religious orders, especially the Dominicans, for they bore traces of Alumbradism, being written in the vernacular and having perfection as their purpose while ignoring the element of preaching. Throughout his life Ignatius continued to be hounded by direct or oblique charges of Alumbradism by opponents who could with considerable justification point out his many brushes with the Inquisition, sneering that "the pilgrim [Ignatius] and his companions were fugitives from Spain, from Paris, and from Venice."[61]

Equal to Ignatius as one of the greatest of the Spanish mystics but gaining great contemporary renown for her mystical life was Teresa of Ávila (1515–82), who was of mixed Jewish-Christian and noble-mercantile origins. When she was twelve her mother died, at sixteen she entered a boarding school run by Augustinian nuns and at twenty-one, much against her father's wishes, she joined the Carmelite convent of the Incarnation in Ávila with the monastic name Teresa of Jesus.

The regimen of the convent damaged her health and she was forced to return home for a year to recuperate, during which time she read Francisco de Osuna's *Third Spiritual Alphabet*. Previously she had not known how to pray or to practice Recollection, although as she related in her autobiography, she did possess the gift of tears. "I now began to spend time in solitude, to confess frequently, and to start on the way of prayer, with this book as my guide."[62] Within nine months she had a brief experience of union that "left such an effect behind that, although I was not then twenty, I seemed to feel the world far below me, and I remember pitying those who followed its ways even on their lawful pursuits."[63]

She found spiritual progress to be "laborious and painful"[64] and for the first twenty years of her monastic life Teresa had only fleeting mystical experiences. But then, in 1555, her mystical life intensified. She began experiencing more intense visions, fell into deep raptures and ecstasies (plate 8), had frequent conversations with Jesus and was given an understanding of spiritual mysteries. Within three years, Teresa felt directed to begin a reform of the Carmelites, to return the order to its original ascetic way of life in apostolic poverty and strict seclusion. Despite bitter opposition from Carmelites not ready for such severity, from her ecclesiastical superiors and from the citizens of Ávila, Teresa spent the rest of her life establishing the Discalced ("unshod") Carmelites.

Teresa wrote extensively of her mystical experiences and of her understanding of prayer, contemplation and mysticism. In the wake of the trials of the Alumbrados and the pseudo-mystical scandals of mid-century and after having read Francisco de Osuna, she was well aware that hearing mystical voices and seeing mystical visions could be the product of one's own imagination, but she felt it possible to discern between false and genuine voices, for "once [one] has heard some genuine message, he will see clearly what this voice is, for … false locution is like something that we cannot clearly make out; it is as if we were asleep."[65] She was also quick to argue that such locutions could not be merely one's own imagination, for "if all locutions came from the intellect, I think we could hear them whenever we liked, and every time we prayed we might think we heard them. But this is not the case with divine locutions."[66] She was especially expressive of her sense of being in the presence of God: "there would come to me unexpectedly such a feeling of the presence of God as made it impossible for me to doubt that he was within me, or that I was totally engulfed in Him. This was no kind of vision."[67] She affirmed that she experienced rapture so complete that she levitated above the ground: "my soul has been carried away, and usually my head as well, without my being able to prevent it; and sometimes it has affected my whole body, which has been lifted from the ground."[68] Sometimes these feelings came in raptures that seemed "to leave my body as light as if it had lost all its weight, and sometimes so light that I hardly knew whether my feet were touching the ground." However, during the rapture, "the body is very often like a corpse, unable to do anything of itself. ... The subject rarely loses consciousness; I have occasionally lost it entirely, but not very often and only for a short time." The rapture was generally a brief one, but, "While it lasts, however, none of the senses perceives or knows what is taking place."[69]

These experiences changed Teresa profoundly, making her aware of her sinfulness, and she concluded that the devil would not use a method "to take away my vices and give me virtues and strength instead. For I clearly saw that these visions had made me a different person."[70] They also gave Teresa an understanding of the lack of reality of this world in comparison with the world of her experiences: "Everything seems to me like a dream. That which I see with eyes of the body is a mockery, and that which I have seen with the eyes of the soul is what the soul desires."[71] She also came to realize that God is present in all things, for once as she was praying, "I saw for a brief moment, without distinctness of form but with complete clarity, how all things are seen in God and how He contains all things within Him." Teresa was merely describing her own experiences which were not intended to become a standard for mysticism, for she readily admitted that others may have quite different experiences: "God leads souls along many roads and paths, as He has led mine. It is of mine that I wish to speak here – I will not meddle with the souls of others."[72]

Teresa's autobiography provides the fullest expression of her mystical experiences but she also expounded her mystical teaching in *The Interior Castle*, a description of the soul's mystical progress to God through stages of prayer that came to her as a revelation. In that work she discussed God's dwelling within the most interior part of the soul and how one reaches "this dwelling of His, which is the center of the soul itself."[73] Her other major work is *The Way of Perfection*, a practical guide to prayer and contemplation for her nuns. Teresa died in 1582, was canonized as a saint in 1622 and in 1970 she was proclaimed a Doctor of the church.

Teresa's partner both in reforming the Carmelite Order and in producing some of the finest mystical literature in the Christian tradition is John of the Cross (1542–91), a Castilian whose name at birth was Juan de Ypes. His father Gonzalo was the son of a wealthy family of silk merchants. Gonzalo married Catalina Alvarez, the daughter of a poor family of weavers suspected of being of Moorish descent. Consequently Gonzalo's family disowned and disinherited him for making such a bad match. When John was only two, his father died, leaving Catalina and their three sons utterly destitute. Spurned by Gonzalo's family, she moved to Medina del Campo to support herself by working as a weaver. After attending a school for poor children, John was able to enroll at a newly-established Jesuit college, which thoroughly grounded his education in the tradition of Ignatius of Loyola.

John had opportunities to become a parish priest or a Jesuit but he entered the

Carmelite Order in 1563 under the name of John of St. Matthias. He undertook university studies in theology and philosophy at Salamanca and was ordained a priest in 1567. Upon meeting Teresa of Ávila, he was immediately enlisted in the cause of expanding Carmelite reform to include the brothers as well as the sisters. The two giants of Spanish mysticism forged a close friendship and partnership. In 1568 John was a member of the first group of Reformed Carmelite friars and changed his name to John of the Cross.

However, the path to reform was not to be an easy one. John faced the hostility of those opposed to reform and was caught up in Carmelite politics. Twice he was arrested by leaders of his own order and was even imprisoned in solitary confinement in a tiny cell. After enduring floggings and a meager diet for nine months (a hardship on his slight frame, for he was not quite five feet tall), he engineered a daring escape from his imprisonment, taking with him one of the finest pieces of prison literature ever composed, his *Spiritual Canticle*. If asceticism, Recollection, Detachment and Abandonment are essential for mystical experiences, John's harsh confinement was a perfect formula for attaining union with God. The stanzas of this poem, John wrote, "were composed in love flowing from abundant mystical understanding"[74] and he used his experiences to write his commentary on the poem, also called *The Spiritual Canticle*. Despite this incarceration, persecutions and efforts to expel him from the Order, John held many high positions, serving as novice master, spiritual director to Teresa and her nuns at the convent of the Incarnation in Ávila, rector of the Carmelite college in Baeza, prior of the monastery in Granada (where he designed and built a new aqueduct and building), and councillor of the Order. He died in 1591 of a severe leg infection. John's vindication came in 1726 when he was canonized as a saint and in 1926 when he was declared a Doctor of the Church.

John's most celebrated work is the two-part *The Ascent of Mount Carmel* and *The Dark Night*, together forming 350 pages of commentary and explanation of his poem *The Dark Night*. The works were not intended for all, but rather their purpose was to "describe the way that leads to the summit of the mount – that high state of perfection we here call union of a soul with God" for monastics of his own order who were "already detached to a great extent from the temporal things of this world."[75] As he guided his readers through the progression of the soul through the three stages of mysticism, he provided no explicit accounts of his own experiences for mystical models.

John was appalled by the climate of spiritual enthusiasm in later sixteenth-century Spain, complaining,

> If any soul whatever after a few pennies worth of reflection experiences one of these locutions in some reflection, it will immediately baptize all as coming from God and, supposing this, say "God told me," "God answered me."[76]

He was concerned that those who pursued the mystical path would become so distracted by phenomena such as voices, visions, prophecies and sensory perceptions that they would never progress beyond them to achieve union with God: "Illusions and deceptions so multiply in some, and they become so inveterate in them, that it is very doubtful whether they will return to the pure road of virtue and authentic spirituality."[77] Therefore John was unswerving in his denunciation of such experiences. They were very frequently the work of the devil but even when they came from God they should be entirely disregarded, and "this rejection is no affront to [God]."[78] Nonetheless, John indeed did experience these phenomena that he attributed to the early stages of mysticism. It was a voice and visions that revealed to him the escape plan that led him out of his imprisonment and it was in a vision that he received the image that he then drew with his own hand – the crucified Christ hanging forward on the cross, as seen from above and to the right side by the Father – a depiction that differs radically from all previous crucifixion scenes in Christian art (see plate 9), although afterwards serving as inspiration for Salvador Dali.

John's mysticism was decidedly apophatic,[79] for "to reach union with the wisdom of God a person must advance by unknowing rather than by knowing,"[80] and

> God's being cannot be grasped by the intellect, appetite, imagination, or any other sense; nor can it be known in this life. The most that can be felt and tasted of God in this life is infinitely distant from God and the pure possession of him.[81]

His major contribution to mystical teaching is his detailed explanation of the "Dark Night" of the soul, whose very length makes one suspect that again he is writing of his own experiences. The Dark Night is a time of purgation when one moves into the stage of the proficients, when God moves from illuminating the senses to illuminating the soul. To those thrown into this state, it is a terrible time in which all of the means by which one previously experienced God become completely useless and the contemplatives "believe that there will be no more spiritual blessings for them and that God has abandoned them."[82] However, the contemplatives must remain patient for the effect is of great spiritual benefit, raising them from their beginner's status "to liberate them from the lowly exercise of the senses and of discursive meditation"[83] so that they can enter the pure contemplation of mystical wisdom which "occasionally so engulfs the soul in its secret abyss that they have the keen awareness of being brought into a place far removed from every creature."[84]

FRENCH MYSTICS OF THE SIXTEENTH AND SEVENTEENTH CENTURIES

While the sixteenth century was the Golden Age of Spanish mysticism, the seventeenth century belongs to the mystics of France. In the early sixteenth century, the French kings Francis I (1515–47) and Henry II (1547–59) were locked in incessant wars against the Holy Roman Emperor Charles V (1519–56) and largely ignored the growing number of Calvinists in their lands. However, by the early 1550s the Protestantism had spread widely among the nobility and even into the royal family, prompting an alarmed Henry II to begin a determined effort to destroy the Protestants in the last years of his reign. The French Calvinists, now called Huguenots, in their turn aspired to eradicate Catholics. The resulting Wars of Religion in France were continued under Henry II's three sons, Francis II (1559–60), Charles IX (1560–74) and Henry III (1574–89). The desultory fighting dragged on to the end of the century with mutual atrocities, crowned by the slaughter of about 20,000 Huguenots throughout France in the St. Bartholomew's Day Massacre on 24 August 1572. Finally Henry IV (1589–1610), the Catholic-turned Protestant-turned Catholic king, halted the wars with his Edict of Nantes in 1598, granting religious freedom and civil rights to the Protestants in the areas under their control, principally in the West and South of the kingdom. An uneasy religious truce reigned for a quarter of a century until the inconsistent enforcement of the Edict of Nantes and the growing authoritarianism of the monarchy led to fresh Huguenot rebellions.

One of the first of the seventeenth-century mystics who gained a great following in France came from just beyond the frontiers of France in the very heart of Calvinism. Francis de Sales (1567–1622) was born to a noble family in the duchy of Savoy, an independent French-speaking region bordering on the kingdom of France and surrounding the Swiss city of Geneva on three sides. As his parents' eldest son he was destined for high position in law and politics and after his basic schooling in Savoy, at the age of eleven, he was sent to the Jesuit Collège de Clermont in Paris for his advanced studies. Here he was trained in Latin, rhetoric, the classics, philosophy and natural sciences, while also learning the *Spiritual Exercises* of Ignatius of Loyola and attending lectures on the mystical interpretation of the Song of Songs. After being exposed to the teachings on predestination by St. Augustine and Thomas Aquinas, he was gripped by a great spiritual crisis, concerned that God had predestined him for damnation. While in great mental anguish in this crisis, he entered the church of St.-Étienne, declared his passionate love for God and vowed perpetual chastity while praying for God's pity. The crisis instantly evaporated. A few years later he rejected the theology of predestination despite its sanction by the two greatest theologians of the Western Church.

After ten years in Paris he studied law at the University of Padua. While there he also continued his theological studies and became well-acquainted with the works of Teresa of Ávila and other sixteenth-century Spanish mystics. During his time in Italy, he visited the shrine of the house of the Holy Family in Loretto, where he had perhaps the first of his many mystical experiences, falling into rapture as his face was transfigured, shining "in an unearthly manner."[85] In 1591, at the age of twenty-four, he earned his doctorate in law.

Francis's father was now ready for his son to return home, marry the wife chosen for him and enter the senate of Savoy. However, Francis was determined to be a priest and he overcame his father's great disappointment to gain approval for his clerical career. He was ordained in 1593, formally renouncing his claims to secular position and lands. However, one of Francis's social rank could never truly begin at the bottom rung of the ecclesiastical ladder and he was promptly appointed provost, or senior priest, of the cathedral of the bishop of Geneva.

The entire region of Geneva and Savoy was in religious turmoil. The theocracy established in Geneva by John Calvin forced the Catholic bishop of that city to flee and he established his seat in exile in the town of Annecy, some twenty miles south of Geneva. Moreover, the Calvinist region of the Chablais, immediately to the east of Geneva, had recently been regained by the duke of Savoy, who wanted to re-establish the Catholic faith there as well. Francis volunteered to undertake the hazardous work of founding a mission there. For four years Francis preached publicly in the Chablais, survived attempts on his life, won over a number of converts to Catholicism, wrote tracts in defense of his faith and even made secret journeys into Geneva to debate with the Protestant leaders of the city. In 1599 he was named coadjutor (designated successor) to the ailing bishop of Geneva.

A few years later the duke of Savoy sent Francis on a diplomatic mission to Paris, where he successfully completed his discussions with King Henry IV. He also preached and met the highest spiritual circles of Paris, including a number of mystics who recognized in Francis a kindred spirit and sought him out as a spiritual director. Francis returned to Savoy, succeeding as bishop of Geneva in 1602. During his consecration ceremony his face again became transfigured, as in Loretto, and he fell into a trance, during which the Trinity placed its hands on him. Francis now became deeply involved in diocesan administrative duties. He reformed the monasteries and the clergy under his supervision, insisting that the clerics live good moral lives and preach to their flocks, while he himself continued his preaching and spiritual direction.

In 1608 he finished his most famous work, *Introduction to the Devout Life*, derived from his years of directing souls and addressed to Philothea, the soul seeking "godly love." In this work he denied that a devout life was confined to contemplatives and monastics: "Wherever we may be, we can and should aspire to a perfect life."[86] He wrote, "Genuine, living devotion presupposes love of God, and hence it is simply true love of God."[87] His guidance in the devout life was commonplace – reject vices, cultivate virtues, read devotional literature, meditate, practice prayer, dedicate oneself to God and love one's fellow human beings – but it was eminently practical, counseling moderation and being spiced with examples and illustrations drawn from everyday life and from nature.

The *Introduction to the Devout Life* is not obviously mystical. Indeed, following John of the Cross, de Sales counseled Philothea against an interest in "ecstasies or raptures, states of insensibility and impassibility, deific unions, levitations, transformations, and similar perfections."[88] But the *Introduction* is certainly not anti-mystical, for it is a primer on laying the foundations for a mystical life, with its program following the mystical progression of purgation, illumination and union with God. The devout soul was guided through a series of meditations beginning with the counsels, "Place yourself in the presence of God. Beseech him to inspire you."[89] While vocal prayer was good, "I especially counsel you to practice mental prayer, the prayer of the heart" and all prayer should begin "in the presence of God."[90] If, while engaged in vocal prayer, "you should feel your heart drawn and invited to interior or mental prayer, don't refuse to take it up."[91] The bishop knew that "few people in our time" knew how to engage in mental prayer, so he offered directions, beginning with "a lively, attentive realization of God's absolute presence, that is, that God is in all things and all places. There is no place or thing in this world where he is not truly present."[92] He also warned his readers of the dryness that sometimes comes to those on the spiritual path: "if you have not received any consolation do not be disturbed, no matter how great the dryness may be, but continue to keep a devout posture before God."[93] Moreover, despite his warnings regarding ecstasies and raptures, he tempted his readers with an enticing prospect: "God generally grants some foretaste of heavenly delight to those who enter his service in order to draw them away from earthly pleasures and encourage them in the pursuit of his love."[94] The *Introduction* was an instant success and was quickly translated into all major European languages. The queen of France sent a copy to King James I of England, who treasured it. Moreover, it was highly recommended by William Laud, the archbishop of Canterbury, while King James II of England had a special edition prepared for use by the royal family.[95]

About ten years later, Francis published his second major work, the *Treatise on the Love of God*, not intended for beginners on the spiritual path like the *Introduction*, but for "souls that are advanced in devotion."[96] This was a thoroughly mystical work: "When the Holy Ghost would express a perfect love, he almost always employs words expressing union or conjunction."[97] Here are no cautions about ecstasies and raptures, for they are natural to those devoted to God, "those angelic men who are ravished in God and heavenly things," who, while in rapture, lose "the use and attention of the senses, movement, and all exterior actions."[98] In addition, concerning God's communication to the soul, he wrote, "When God gives us faith he enters into our soul and speaks to our spirit, not by manner of discourse, but by way of inspiration."[99] The full vision of God can come only in heaven, he wrote, but meanwhile, in one's earthly life, "he gives us some kisses by a thousand feelings of his delightful presence: for unless the soul were kissed she would not be drawn, nor would she run in the odour of the beloved's perfumes."[100]

Books six and seven of the *Treatise* are entirely devoted to mysticism, in which he equated prayer and mystical theology and guided his readers to a detailed discussion of meditation and contemplation while distinguishing between ecstasies and raptures. He also gave a moving and detailed description of how God communicates to the soul:

> Sometimes the soul not only perceives God's presence, but hears him speak, by certain inward illuminations and interior persuasions which stand in place of words. Sometimes she perceives him, and in her turn speaks to him, but so secretly, sweetly and delicately … At other times she hears the beloved speak, but she cannot speak to him, because the delight she has to hear him, or the reverence she bears him, keeps her in silence … But, finally, sometimes she neither hears nor speaks to her well-beloved, nor yet feels any signs of his presence, but simply knows that she is in the presence of her God.[101]

There were some particular "advanced souls" to whom Francis was intending his book, Jeanne de Chantal and her nuns in the new Order of the Visitation. The bishop met Madame de Chantal in 1604 when she, a young widow and mother of four surviving children, heard him preach in Dijon. She did not want to remarry after her husband's death but instead desired a life of prayer, an inclination made difficult by her husband's domineering family. For many years she had been receiving feelings that God was within her, such as a great heat, and she had received visions as well. Francis added her to the other women whose spiritual advisor he was (he seemed drawn to be an advisor to women to such an extent that a Parisian priest criticized him, "You are a bishop, and you spend your whole time with women!"[102]) and soon the two were close friends. He encouraged her desire to found a new monastic order for women like herself, who were too devout for the existing orders that were lax and lukewarm in their religion but who had too many obligations to enter the more austere and ascetic orders. In 1610, in his episcopal capital of Annecy, together they founded the Order of the Visitation of Holy Mary. By now Jeanne was becoming a spiritual leader in her own right, supervising the expansion of the Visitation, which had eighty houses by the time of her death in 1641.

Francis continued his episcopal duties, serving on diplomatic and legal missions for the duke of Savoy, as well as his spiritual guidance and writing works that fill twenty-seven volumes in the modern French edition. He also continued his work as a healer, being especially effective in cases of possession – he was said to have cured over 400 people with this affliction. However, he was somewhat embarrassed by the crowds that came to him for healing. Futilely he extracted promises of silence from those thus cured and he even questioned some rather sharply to determine if indeed they were possessed. The bishop's always fragile health began to fail and on 28 December 1622 he died of a stroke and was buried in Jeanne's convent of the Visitation in Annecy. There was an immediate clamor for recognition of his saintly life and he was canonized in 1665. A further distinction was added in 1877 when he was declared to be a Doctor of the Church, while in 1923 he was made the Church's patron of writers. When Jeanne died in 1641 she was buried near his grave in her convent.

One of the women in Paris who had been directed by Francis de Sales was Angélique Arnaud (1591–1661), the abbess of the convent of Port-Royal in the suburb of Saint-Jacques. She had become abbess at the early age of eleven and for six years enjoyed the relaxed atmosphere of the convent. However, in 1608 she was moved by a sermon of a friar of the Capuchin order (a reformist movement within the Franciscan Order desiring to return to the original austerity of St. Francis) and she undertook a drastic reform of her abbey. She enforced its rules with exactness, even to the point of barring her father and brothers from entering the convent. She was naturally drawn to Francis de Sales, for they agreed on the importance of a serious commitment to live the Christian life. However, the bishop believed that God applied his grace generously to sinners while Abbess Angélique was convinced that only a few could live the rigorous life demanded by God.

De Sales' death in 1622 left Mother Angélique without a strong spiritual advisor until she met Jean Duvergier de Hauranne, the abbot of Saint-Cyran (1581–1643), one of the founders and chief advocates of the doctrine most closely associated with the name of his friend Cornelius Jansen, bishop of Ypres (1585–1638). Jansenism was a reaction to the Jesuit tendency to make Christianity as accommodating to the lives of ordinary people as possible in order to keep them in the church. In contrast, Jansen advocated the strict predestinarianism of St. Augustine, emphasizing the fallen nature of man and the absolute need to have true contrition for one's sins and to do proper penance for them, a teaching that meshed nicely with the rigorist inclinations of Mother Angélique. She became a devoted follower of Saint-Cyran and her convent became a center of Jansenist teaching and practice, attracting crowds of people drawn to Port-Royal's uncompromising stand on morality and the need for the conversion of the inner person.

Among the number of more rigorous Christians who became attached to Port-Royal was the family of Blaise Pascal (1623–62). Pascal's parents belonged to the lower nobility, his father Étienne being a provincial judge in Clermont-Ferrand. The family moved to Paris in 1631, where Étienne Pascal advanced his career and personally supervised the education of his children. The young Blaise was adept in mathematics and geometry and at age sixteen he wrote his first scientific tract. He put his skills to practical use in 1639 when the family moved to Rouen where his father was tax collector for Upper Normandy. To help his father in the complicated calculations required in his duties, Blaise invented a calculating machine, for which he received a royal patent. Pascal continued his scientific work, establishing that a column of mercury in a tube fluctuated in height due to air pressure rather than a vacuum and conducting experiments that led to his inventing the barometer, the hydraulic press and the syringe. He also continued his work in mathematics and geometry and developed a forerunner of calculus.

While Pascal's scientific fame was spreading, the family had come into contact with Port-Royal and adopted the abbey's rigorous brand of Christianity, including Jansenism. Blaise's sister Jacqueline became a nun at Port-Royal but he threw himself into the pleasant attractions of social life in Paris. However, by 1654 Blaise was expressing his distaste for the emptiness of his worldly life. Then, in the midst of his anguish, he experienced his "second conversion," which he kept secret throughout his life. However, he recorded it in his "Memorial" and sewed it into the lining of his jacket, repeating the process as he replaced his clothing until it was found after his death. His note recorded the day, Monday, 23 November 1654, and the time, "From about half past ten in the evening until half past midnight," and then he wrote "Fire," followed by "God of Abraham, God of Isaac, God of Jacob, not of philosophers and scholars. Certitude, certainty, heartfelt joy, peace. God of Jesus Christ. God of Jesus Christ. … Joy, joy, joy, tears of joy."[103] The experience transformed him and he retreated to Port-Royal for three weeks, devoting himself to prayer. He abandoned most of his scientific work as well as thoughts of marriage.

He now employed his formidable intellect and writing skills to defend Port-Royal and Jansenism. Jansenism had originally been directed against the practice of the Jesuits, who were mounting a vigorous counter-attack. In France Saint-Cyran was imprisoned by Cardinal Richelieu, chief minister of King Louis XIII, in 1638 and not released until after the latter's death in 1642. The Jansenists' criticism of royal policies, along with their support of figures prominent in the Fronde, a rebellion against the government of the young Louis XIV, brought intense royal pressure on Rome to condemn Jansenism. In 1653 Pope Innocent X complied. Antoine Arnaud, brother of Abbess Angélique of Port-Royal and a professor at the Sorbonne, came under attack for his books supporting Jansenism and criticizing the Jesuits and he turned to Port-Royal's friend Pascal for assistance in writing a defense.

Arnaud provided the theological concepts and citations which Pascal, writing anonymously, then rendered into magnificent prose in the form of eighteen *Provincial Letters* (1656–57). Pascal defended Jansenism and excoriated the Jesuits for abandoning traditional Christian teachings concerning sin, confession and penance. He used the Jesuits' own writings to warn that they were making Christians complacent in their sins rather than drawing "them away by a genuine conversion which only grace can effect." Of the Jesuits, he warned, "You must realize that it is not their object to corrupt morals; that is not their policy. But their sole aim is not to reform them either." The concessions that the Jesuits made to human nature had, in Pascal's sarcastic view, "dispensed men from the irksome obligation of actually loving God."[104]

The great popularity of the *Provincial Letters* could not save the Jansenists, for the French government, the Jesuits and most of the Sorbonne were united against them, and Arnaud was expelled from the Sorbonne. Undeterred, Pascal began working on an exposition on Christianity. He collected notes and fragments for this purpose but his failing health prevented him from completing his project. He died in August 1662 at the age of thirty-nine, of complications resulting from stomach cancer. The fragments that he gathered for his Christian apology were found tied into twenty-one bundles, which form his posthumous *Pensées* (*Thoughts*). They present no integrated teaching but the aphorisms in the *Pensées* indicate the consistency of Pascal's mystical thinking. Reason was "an absurd God" and he regarded those who attempted to be guided by reason alone as madmen, for "there are an infinite number of things beyond" reason. His approach to God was apophatic, for God is "infinitely beyond our comprehension" and is a hidden God. Moreover, "He is a God who unites himself with [Christians] in the depths of their being," a God who "disclos[es] himself only to those whose hearts are sanctified." [105]

Francis de Sales had advised in the *Introduction to the Devout Life* that the soul seeking God should have a realization of God's absolute presence in all things and places,[106] and two mystics of the mid- and late-seventeenth century seemingly realized this injunction to perfection. While Jansenists, Jesuits and Quietists quarreled in France, a branch of the great century of French mysticism had been grafted to the newly-established French settlement in Canada. Marie of the Incarnation (1599–1672) was one of three Ursuline nuns who arrived at Quebec in 1639, dedicated to win over to Christianity the souls of indigenous inhabitants of Canada who were ignorant of Christ. Marie's career is well documented, for she was a writer. Her almost 300 surviving letters (out of perhaps 3000 originally written) form an important source on life in Quebec in the mid-seventeenth century, while her *Relation of 1654* is a detailed account of her spiritual life.[107] From her writings it is clear that mysticism led Mother Marie from the safety of her convent in France to the frontier outpost of Quebec. She was well-aware that it was highly unusual for one to describe mystical experiences in the detail that she provided, but she had been ordered to do so by her spiritual director. She speculated that previous writers on the interior life preferred to remain silent on their own experiences "either out of reverence for God or because it is beyond human ability to do so. Or better still: although able to speak, they prefer not to, fearing that those who are not led in these ways might be scandalized."[108]

Marie was born Marie Guyart in the city of Tours, southwest of Paris, and was the child of a solidly middle-class baker. Her parents arranged for her marriage to Claude Martin, a young silk merchant in Tours, when she was seventeen. By eighteen she had given birth to a son and by nineteen she was a widow. Marie extricated herself from her husband's tangled business affairs and was fending off proposals of marriage when she had her conversion in 1620. She had always been very devout, tracing her experiences back to the age of seven when she had a dream of herself playing in the schoolyard:

> I was looking upward when I saw the heavens open and Our Lord Jesus Christ in human form emerge and come toward me. … As this most adorable Majesty approached me, my heart felt on fire with love for him and I started to open my arms to embrace him. Then he, the most beautiful of all the children of men, took me in his arms and with a look full of indescribable sweetness and charm, kissed me with great love and asked me, "Will you be mine?" I answered, "Yes!"[109]

Following this dream, Marie became accustomed to discuss her needs with Jesus and to seek seclusion for her prayers. She remembered having "a desire to belong completely" to God and staying for many hours a day in church yearning for such union. Even in this early stage of her spiritual life, she felt united to Jesus in an extraordinary manner. But then on 24 March 1620, while dealing with business matters:

> Suddenly I was brought stock-still, both inwardly and outwardly. Even my thoughts were abruptly brushed aside. Then, in an instant, my inner eyes were opened and all the faults, sins, and imperfections that I had committed since my birth were shown to me in the most vivid detail … At the same moment I saw myself immersed in the blood of the Son of God, shed because of the sin which had been shown to me … These visions and what they evoke penetrate so deeply that in an instant they communicate everything with their own perfect efficacy. At that very moment I felt transported beyond myself and transformed through the mercy of him who had wrought this wonderful grace. … I was plunged in the Precious Blood for the shedding of which I myself was guilty.[110]

She returned home a changed person. She began wearing a hairshirt, felt new urgings for solitude and was convinced that she was constantly speaking to God.

She turned to books of devotion, including works of Teresa of Ávila and Francis de Sales, and followed their instructions on meditation, but she experienced only a profound and lasting headache. Finally her confessor ordered her to end her meditations so that she could return to her natural prayers, which led her back into the constant presence of God in a "continual colloquy with Our Lord."[111] She redoubled her penances and harsh disciplines, which brought her to "a state of abnegation and such profound humility that I expected nothing from self and awaited everything from God. I was sure that I possessed him in that intimate union for which he had given me such a powerful attraction."[112] In her heart she felt a fire, and then,

> I felt that my heart was taken away and enclosed in another heart so that although there were still two hearts, they were so closely fitted together that they were like one. Then an inner voice said to me: "It is thus that a union of our hearts is accomplished." I don't know if I was asleep or awake, but when I came to myself my heart was, for many days, in such a state of union with Our Lord.[113]

Marie was then called away from her parents' house to assist her sister Claude and her husband Pierre Buisson in their cartage business in Tours, working in the warehouses and on the wharfs, managing the workers and supervising the movement of merchandise in a rough atmosphere that at times was harsh on a woman and especially one as spiritually inclined as she. Undaunted, she gave spiritual instruction to her brother-in-law's servants just as she had previously done to her own. Meanwhile, her spiritual life steadily deepened. In May 1625 Marie had the first of her visions of the Trinity, when "my eyes suddenly closed and my spirit was raised and absorbed into the vision of the Most Holy and August Trinity, in a way I cannot express."[114] She was shown the Persons of the Trinity, how they operated, and she understood the gradation of angels: "As I was enlightened, I understood and experienced how I was created in the image of God ... This vision lasted for the duration of several Masses."[115] She was in a new spiritual state and even when engaged in business dealings she felt "in the depths of my soul a kind of heaven, experiencing a movement which bound me to this divine majesty."[116]

About two years later, she had her second Trinitarian vision, which culminated in the summit of mystical experiences, her spiritual marriage with Christ:

> One morning while I was in prayer God drew my spirit into himself by an unusually powerful attraction. I do not know in what position my body remained. The vision of the most August Trinity was once more communicated to me and its movements shown to me in a more exalted and distinct manner than before. ... This time, although my understanding was enlightened even more than before, it was the will which was important ... the Sacred Person of the Divine Word revealed to me that he was in truth the spouse of the faithful soul. ... At that moment, this adorable Person seized my soul and embracing it with indescribable love united it to himself, taking it as his spouse. ... Then for a few moments I returned to myself and saw the Eternal Father and the Holy Spirit, and then the unity of Divine Persons. ... With the spiritual marriage the soul has completely changed its state. ... Now the soul has no further longing because it possesses him whom it loves.[117]

Now, even as she conducted her business, she would be swept away by her Divine Spouse, being in continual ecstasy.

For ten years she had been inclined to become a nun and finally, while in her "usual union," an inner voice told her: "it's time; there's nothing more for you to do in the world."[118] She could have entered one of the contemplative ascetic orders, but instead she applied for admission to the Ursulines, founded a century earlier specifically to educate young girls. In January 1631 Marie went behind the walls of the Ursuline convent in Tours, leaving behind her eleven-year-old son, who would stand at the gate of the monastery crying out, "Give me back my mother!"[119]

Once within the cloister, Marie felt that "Everything I saw in religious life seemed to me to be full of the spirit of God," and she continued to experience a constant state of ecstasy, walking "as though I did not touch the ground."[120] Two years after her entry into the convent, Marie took her vows and adopted the name Marie of the Incarnation. Soon she was appointed assistant to the Mistress of Novices, in which capacity she gave Christian instruction to the novices and wrote an explanation of the Christian faith as well as a commentary on the Song of Songs for those under her tutelage. As she taught, she found that the relevant passages from Scripture would simply come into her mind as she experienced "interiorly that it was the Holy Spirit who had given me the key to the treasures of the Sacred Word Incarnate … although hitherto I had not studied or meditated on them."[121]

She also began having dreams of being in a "vast country, full of mountains and valleys and thick fog which covered everything except a tiny house which was the church for this country, and which alone was free from the mists."[122] She had an "outpouring of apostolic spirit" which took possession of her soul and carried her

in thought to the Indies, to Japan, to America, to the East and to the West, to parts of Canada, to the country of the Hurons – in short, to every part of the inhabited world where there were human souls who belonged by right to Jesus Christ.[123]

At last her spiritual director suggested that her dream could be fulfilled if she were to go to Canada, advice confirmed by God when her spirit was "suddenly absorbed in God" and she was shown that same land, whereupon "this adorable Majesty said to me: 'It is Canada that I have shown you; you must go there to build a house for Jesus and Mary.'"[124]

Powerfully confirmed of her destiny, she worked for several years to overcome the understandable hesitation of her convent to send her to the wilds of Canada, but finally in 1639 she and two of her sister nuns set out with a small party to the settlement around Fort Saint Louis at Quebec. Marie was chosen to be the first superior of their little community, a position she held for the next six years, and she set about organizing the small convent and school while also learning the local Algonquin and Montagnais languages. She supervised the construction of the convent's buildings and the provisioning of the sisters and the students and began writing works for her Indian students – prayers, catechisms, dictionaries and religious works in the Algonquin,

Huron and Iroquois languages. In 1650 a fire destroyed the convent and school and Marie was again chosen superior. Refusing to move the community back to France, she rebuilt the convent on an even larger scale.

In her interior life, Marie suffered from sadness and bitterness and even wished to be cast down into hell "out of contempt for God."[125] Meanwhile, paradoxically, she still enjoyed intimate, habitual union with God. After her bitterness was lifted, she began experiencing "union, love, and constant communication" with the Virgin Mary, which sustained her in the rebuilding after the fire of 1650, for "I also felt her with me, yet without ever seeing her. She accompanied me everywhere in all the comings and goings that were necessary from the beginning of the raising of the walls until the very end of the work."[126]

Although Marie's life would seem to be one of constant visions and other supernatural experiences, she gave no great emphasis to them. On "extraordinary matters," she wrote, "persons of knowledge and virtue are withholding their judgement and remain in doubt, not daring to trust in extraordinary visions of this nature."[127] She also explained that, in the highest state of grace, "there are no visions nor imagination" and she denied that God led her by the means of prophetic visions.[128]

At about the time that Marie of the Incarnation arrived in Quebec and Jansen launched the controversy that bears his name, an ex-soldier from Lorraine entered the Discalced Carmelite monastery in Paris. From his position in the kitchen and the sandal shop of the friary, for more than forty years Brother Lawrence (1614–91) "practiced the presence of God" and remained in constant conversation with God. He was born Nicolas Herman in the duchy of Lorraine, not yet incorporated into France. Little is known about his early life, but at the age of eighteen he experienced an opening, a Zen-like awareness, in which he observed a tree standing leafless in the winter, and, as he related the story to a priest, "he realized that in a little while its leaves would reappear, followed by its flowers and fruit, he received a profound insight into God's providence that has never been erased from his soul."[129] The scene left him feeling free from worldly attachments and with an intense love for God.

Before he could act on this insight, he became a soldier in the Thirty Years' War (1618–48). In the course of his service he was captured, threatened with death on suspicion that he was a spy, rejoined his forces, was injured and returned home. Wracked with guilt for his sins, he was determined to change his ways and to give himself completely to God. For a time he tried the life of a hermit, which, although "excellent for the advanced and the perfect, it is not ordinarily the best way for beginners."[130] In 1640, at the age of twenty-six, he abandoned solitude to enter a community, joining his uncle in the house of the Discalced Carmelites in Paris. Upon entering his novitiate he took the name Brother Lawrence of the Resurrection and was assigned to the kitchen, "to which he had the strongest natural aversion."[131] As a Discalced Carmelite, he became well-acquainted with the works of Teresa of Ávila and John of the Cross and in time he "was familiar with mystical texts."[132]

During his novitiate he apparently experienced visions and revelations, which, in proper Discalced Carmelite tradition, he minimized. Perhaps he progressed beyond them, for he came to attain a life of constant, silent conversation with God which he enjoyed everywhere, even in the kitchen, maintaining a continuous awareness of God. Everything he did was for love of God, whether picking up a straw from the ground or flipping "my little omelette in the frying pan."[133] "We do not always have to be in church to be with God," he wrote, "we can make of our hearts an oratory."[134]

The other friars began coming to him for advice on how they could "practice the presence of God" and his fame spread beyond the monastery. Religious authorities came to see him, including the archbishop of Cambrai, François Fénelon,[135] while sixteen letters of spiritual counsel that he wrote to spiritual directors, nuns and laywomen are extant. Brother Lawrence was well experienced to provide spiritual advice, for his own progress had been slow and arduous. He admitted that in his first years he had difficulty focusing his mind during prayer and for the first ten years he "suffered a great deal … During this period I fell often, but I got back up just as quickly" and it seemed as though "all creatures, reason, and God himself were against me." He persevered until his soul "experienced a deep inner peace as if it had found its center and place of rest."[136] The turning-point came while he was suffering torments as if in hell, horrified by his past sins, fearing self-deception (perhaps in his visions and revelations) and feeling spiritually paralyzed as if he had lost everything. But upon realizing that all of his suffering was for the love of God, he resolved to endure them, "not only for the rest of his life, but even for all eternity if it pleased God so to ordain it." At that point God "opened his eyes all at once. Lawrence saw a ray of divine light that illumined his mind, dissipated his fears, and put an end to his suffering."[137]

Brother Lawrence felt that everyone is capable of having conversation with God to varying degrees, recommending it as "the shortest, easiest way to arrive at Christian perfection,"[138] "the holiest, surest, the easiest, and the most efficacious form of prayer,"[139] and "the holiest, most ordinary, and most necessary practice of the spiritual life."[140] He wrote,

> If I were a preacher, I would preach nothing but the practice of the presence of God; and if I were a spiritual director, I would recommend it to everyone, for I believe there is nothing so necessary or so easy.[141]

Nonetheless, he had to admit that it required great time and effort, that only a few chosen souls would be given the grace of the presence of God.

Brother Lawrence died highly-esteemed by his fellow Carmelites and by ecclesiastics of all ranks. However, within a few years his reputation was tainted when Archbishop Fénelon of Cambrai used his writings in support of his own Quietistic doctrines, then under attack by both Jansenists and Jesuits. Fénelon's condemnation dragged down Brother Lawrence as well and he became largely ignored in France. However, Protestants took a great interest in the controversy and were strongly attracted to Brother Lawrence's simple, intense life in God. His writings were quickly translated, with William Law having a hand in it in England and John Wesley further popularized Brother Lawrence by including his writings in his Christian Library.[142]

The unwilling agent of Brother Lawrence's ignominy was François de Salignac de la Mothe-Fénelon (1651–1715), Francis de Sales's successor as a prince of the church promoting mysticism. However, his fate demonstrated that, as the seventeenth century was ending, the court circle around the French king was aghast at mysticism quite so close to home. Fénelon was born into an aristocratic family in the region of Périgord, in southwestern France, which boasted several prelates of the church among its members. He studied at the University of Cahors before going to Paris to the Collège du Plessis as well as the Saint-Sulpice seminary. Fénelon was ordained a priest around 1675 and was named to be the Superior of the Congrégation des Nouvelles Catholiques, an institution dedicated to the conversion of Protestants to Catholicism, by force if necessary. The façade of religious toleration was crumbling in France and in 1685 King Louis XIV revoked the Edict of Nantes, which had guaranteed freedom of worship for the Protestant Huguenots who were especially numerous in southwestern France. Fénelon directed a mission to his home region for the purpose of converting them while struggling to restrain the less patient ecclesiastics in their penchant for forced conversions. Fénelon used peaceful methods aimed at persuading the population but, as he admitted, "It is no small thing to change the feelings of an entire people."[143]

In Paris he had already written a number of works on theology and education and had established excellent connections. He joined the coterie of friends around Jacques-Bénigne Bossuet, the bishop of Meaux, and even entered the circle of spiritually-minded associates around Madame de Maintenon, the wife of King Louis XIV. As a result, Fénelon was chosen to be educational director (preceptor) of the seven-year-old Duke of Burgundy, the grandson of Louis XIV and heir to the throne, in which capacity he wrote many works for the edification of his young pupil. One of these works was his great didactic epic poem, *Télémaque*, based on Homer's *Iliad*, but forming "one long lesson in the art of kingship"[144] for the young duke. The work became a sensation in France because it was believed, rightly or not, to be a critique of the kingship of Louis XIV. It was at this point that Fénelon met Madame Guyon, who also was connected to Madame de Maintenon.

By the time she met Fénelon, Jeanne Marie Bouvier de la Mothe Guyon (1648–1717) was already a figure of some notoriety in France. An aristocrat, she received her education in a number of convents and grew to be a beautiful young girl much given to lovely clothes and an exciting social life but she was also drawn to a serious religious life and read spiritual works by Thomas à Kempis, Francis de Sales and Madame de Chantal. After her parents arranged a marriage for her, at age sixteen, to a lord more than twice her age she continued her spiritual reading even though she had become a mother and was forced to live with a domineering and cruel mother-in-law. When she was twenty she was pulled away from her self-centered life by a passing Franciscan who told her that she was having difficulty praying because "you seek outside what you have within. Accustom yourself to seek God in your heart, and you will find him there." These words struck her "like an arrow that pierced my heart through and through. I felt in that moment a very deep wound, as delicious, as full of love, a wound so sweet, I desired never to be healed of it." Now her heart was converted, for "God was there, and I had no longer any trouble to find him; for from that moment

I was given an experience of his presence in my central depth … as a thing one possesses really in a very sweet manner."[145]

She now was absorbed in God, feeling a "fire that devoured me,"[146] and abandoned her former way of life. Insatiable in prayer, she continued to experience Christ within her in "operations … so powerful, so sweet, and so concealed at the same time, that I could not explain them to myself. I felt myself burning within, with a continual fire, but a fire so peaceful, so tranquil, so divine, that it is inexplicable."[147] She moved from vocal prayers, which she could say only with difficulty, to being "absorbed in a profound silence and in a peace beyond expression … It made in me, without the sound of words, a continual prayer."[148] She was sustained in her spiritual progress by a chance encounter with a poor man while on her way to church. He told her "it was not enough to avoid Hell, but that the Lord required of me the utmost purity and height of perfection. My heart assented to his reproofs. I heard him with silence and respect, his words penetrated my very soul."[149]

At age twenty-two, Jeanne was stricken with smallpox, which scarred her face severely, but she praised God "in profound silence" for depriving her of that source of pride and distraction. Soon afterwards, her son, father and husband died. She then fell into "a state of total privation … of weakness and entire desertion"[150] for seven years, until the Father La Combe became her spiritual director. In July of 1680, she found God again. "What I possessed was so simple, so immense, that I cannot express it. It was then, O God, that I found again in you ineffably all that I had lost."[151] Madame Guyon and Father La Combe became inseparable despite all the efforts of the priest's superior, her own half-brother, to pull them apart by ordering the priest to Geneva. Not to be thwarted, she followed Father La Combe there and for five years they traveled about together, a scandalous move that generated rumors of immoral acts between them.

The scandal was intensified by Jeanne's belief that she was in an "apostolic state" wherein she preached her method of prayer and wrote about it, first in *The Spiritual Torrents* and then in *A Short and Simple Method of Prayer*, a commentary on the Scriptures, and another on the Song of Songs. It was sufficiently shocking for a woman to teach on religion but it was worse when she was not even in a religious order and, moreover, when she was the center of risqué gossip. However, her teachings themselves were also suspect, smacking of Quietism, recently condemned in the form of the teachings of the Spanish priest Miguel de Molinos (1640–97).

The *Spiritual Guide* of Molinos was innocent enough. It exalted mental prayer and contemplation above vocal prayer and meditation, taught that in the state of perfection the soul must become completely disinterested in itself as it rested in a state of quiet, indifferent to everything, even salvation. In this state, all external religious acts are superfluous. In Italy Molinos gained a virtual cult following, which he headed as a self-declared prophet. His movement began to look very much like the earlier Alumbrados in Spain and the Jesuits were especially incensed that he had deprecated meditation, which they lauded, as appropriate only for beginners in the spiritual life.

All of this was very close to Madame Guyon's teachings. She always minimized the externals of mysticism, disparaging visions, ecstasies, and transports as incapable of producing true union and prone to lead the soul to vanity, and they should be neither emphasized nor relied upon. Nonetheless she was the recipient of prophetic dreams even while warning against "revelations of things to come" and she claimed infallible knowledge of the interior of people's souls.

Quietism was especially opposed by the Jansenists, for while both the Jansenists and the Quietists stressed a deeper spiritual life, they differed greatly on how it was to be accomplished. The Quietists taught a means to God open to all while the Jansenists saw the path to God as being closed to all but a few. Moreover, the Quietists stressed that one ought to be completely unconcerned about one's salvation, which was of great importance to the Jansenists. Although in retreat, the Jansenists remained strong in France, eager to buttress their beleaguered position. The very public Quietist teachings of Madame Guyon provided them with an opportunity to affirm their shaky orthodoxy.

Madame Guyon and Father La Combe reached Paris in 1686 and became part of the spiritual circle of Madame de Maintenon. However, powerful enemies encircled her. Both the Jansenists and Jesuits opposed her Quietism, now condemned by the papacy, while Louis XIV was personally antagonistic towards it. The king may have had reasons of state to be so opposed to mysticism in any form. In southern France, Huguenots were joining mysticism to apocalypticalism, just as Thomas Müntzer had done. Even before he revoked the Edict of Nantes, Louis XIV threw power of the state against the Huguenots, depriving them of legal rights, attacking their schools and churches and forcing them to convert to Catholicism. It was clear that "the king intended to destroy their religion … The crown had shown a mastery of the judicious use of force and terror that contemporary dictators might well emulate."[152] In 1685, the year of the revocation of the Edict of Nantes, the supernatural element surfaced. People heard the singing of psalms in the sky and had visions of angels. Moreover, prophets appeared, sometimes preaching while asleep, proclaiming the imminent end of the world. Soon those who gathered to hear the prophets became possessed by the spirit, shaking, gasping and falling to the ground. At about the time that Fénelon met Guyon, in 1689 the king was ready to take action against the Huguenot ecstatics and ordered his troops against them. Around 300 of them were killed and the movement was driven underground, only to resurface in 1701 fighting against both king and Catholicism. Their uniform was the wearing of white shirts (camisas), thus gaining the collective name "Camisards." After more than a decade of fighting, the movement was crushed and the survivors fled to Germany and also to England, where they were known as the French Prophets.

After reaching Paris in 1687 Madame Guyon was held in detention for eight months. At this point Fénelon met Madame Guyon and, after reading her works, became her most ardent supporter, completely won over by her view of the contemplative life of mental prayer. However, Madame de Maintenon was concerned at the spread of Quietism in her own circle, perhaps being jealous of Guyon's influence on Fénelon as well, and banished Jeanne from her company. Guyon, supported by Fénelon, who was now archbishop of Cambrai, demanded that she receive a proper hearing so that she might defend her orthodoxy. However, the animosity of the royal court preordained the verdict against her while she had an implacable opponent in Fénelon's friend Bishop Bossuet, who understood mysticism poorly and detested what little he understood. In a shocking display of corruption, Bossuet broke the sanctity of the confessional and revealed Jeanne's writings given to him in confidence, suppressed her defense of her orthodoxy and engineered a campaign of forged documents and lies against her as well as against Father La Combe, imprisoned along with her in 1687.

Appalled at Bossuet's vendetta against Madame Guyon, Archbishop Fénelon defended Jeanne's mysticism in his *Explanation of the Maxims of the Saints of the Interior Life*, an appeal to history in which he quoted from the great saints of the church who taught the very doctrines for which she was being questioned. Among those whom he cited in support of Quietism was Brother Lawrence, who indeed had written that he gave no thought to heaven or hell and, "Since I entered religious life, I no longer think about virtue or my salvation."[153] The *Maxims of the Saints* outraged Louis XIV, who exiled Fénelon to his diocese, while Bossuet denounced Fénelon as a heretic. Fénelon appealed to Pope Innocent XII but Louis XIV pursued the case to the Vatican, bullying the pope and demanding that Fénelon be condemned. The pope personally favored the *Maxims of the Saints*, but he retreated in the face of the demands of the powerful French king, but only a few steps. He issued a Brief, not the more formal Bull, that branded some inferences that could be drawn from some of Fénelon's points as "rash, offensive scandalous," but he stopped short of condemning them as heretical. Nonetheless, the damage was done. Fénelon seemed to stand condemned by the papacy, as did Madame Guyon by implication.

Fénelon was confined to his diocese of Cambrai but he remained its bishop until his death in 1714, continuing to write justifications of his views on mysticism, compose works on philosophy, and maintain his opposition to Jansenism. Madame Guyon survived them all. She was imprisoned again in 1695 at the command of Louis XIV and eventually was incarcerated in the infamous prison of the Bastille, being released only after Bishop Bossuet died in 1702. She moved to Blois, completed her autobiography and died in 1717. The unfortunate Father La Combe was never released from his imprisonment, suffering terrible tortures and eventually losing his mind.

By the beginning of the eighteenth century, mysticism was equated with the condemned heresy of Quietism by secular and ecclesiastical officials in France while the Jansenists contributed to the utter discredit of mysticism in French society at large. In 1713 Pope Clement XI issued his anti-Jansenist encyclical *Unigenitus*, which was bitterly opposed both by Jansenists and by others who resented it as interference in the internal affairs of the French Church. When King Louis XV accepted it as French law in 1730 the indefatigable Jansenists responded by touting the miracles performed at the cemetery of the Parisian church of Saint-Médard as evidence that God was on their side. A few years earlier the severely ascetical Jansenist deacon François de Pâris had been buried in the parish cemetery of Saint-Médard. Soon hundreds of healing miracles were reported to have been effected at his tomb, usually accompanied by bodily convulsions, contortions and speaking in tongues by those who sought cures there, very similar to the phenomena exhibited by Quakers[154] and Camisards. Large crowds began gathering at the cemetery, among whom were apocalyptic preachers and others who denounced *Unigenitus* in decidedly anti-royal and anti-ecclesiastical tones. By 1732, fearing the political danger of the gatherings, the king ordered troops to close the cemetery while efforts were undertaken to suppress the cult around de Pâris. The French *philosophes* and Enlightenment thinkers such as Montesquieu and Voltaire viewed the whole matter with scorn. Their "basically hostile treatment of the subject was part of a wide-ranging crusade against irrationality and superstition, part of a general skeptical attack on all allegedly supernatural manifestations."[155] While the cult of de Pâris was not exterminated, the "convulsionary movement was no longer regarded as respectable – or, more importantly, supportable – by any politically-significant or numerically-substantial segment of French society."[156] In the French popular mind, the events at Saint-Médard were firmly wedded to Jansenism, and thus intimately associated with Port-Royal and mysticism. Now all were tainted as products of irrational religious fanaticism. In only a slight exaggeration it could be said that "all general interest in mysticism was absent both within and without the Catholic Church for some two centuries before the twentieth."[157] However, post-Reformation mysticism in England continued with vigor in the eighteenth centuries and was transplanted to its American colonies where it blossomed in the nineteenth and twentieth centuries.

CHAPTER V

POST-REFORMATION MYSTICS IN ENGLAND AND AMERICA

THE TWENTIETH-CENTURY REVIVAL OF MYSTICISM

—— •✦• ——

ENGLISH MYSTICISM

In England the Reformation was a royal enterprise, initiated when King Henry VIII (1509–47) made himself the supreme head of the church in 1534 while maintaining most of the previous ecclesiastical structure with the exception of the monasteries, which were abolished (1536–9). When Henry VIII was succeeded by his nine-year-old son Edward VI (1547–53), the regents around the young king made the creed of the Church of England more clearly Protestant and allowed Protestants from the Continent to enter England. However, when King Edward died at the age of fifteen, his very Catholic sister Mary Tudor, daughter of Henry VIII and Catherine of Aragon, ascended the throne (1553–8) determined to restore Catholicism to England. She repealed the laws of her father and brother and persecuted those who resisted, thus earning her name "Bloody Mary." When Mary died in 1558, her half-sister Elizabeth, the daughter of Henry VIII and Anne Boleyn, succeeded her as queen of England (1558–1603). Thus England had known four monarchs in eleven years, each one representing a change of religious policy.

Under Elizabeth I, those who had gone into exile under Queen Mary, often in Geneva and Zurich, returned home eager to establish a Calvinist theology and form of worship, others in England were proponents of the milder Protestantism of Henry VIII or Edward VI, while Catholics, recently invigorated under Queen Mary, survived in large numbers. Together these factions had irreconcilable aspirations for the religious future of England, leading Elizabeth I to steer a middle ground with the "Elizabethan Settlement" of 1559, restoring the monarch as supreme head of the Church of England and defining faith as broadly as possible. This compromise was unacceptable to extremists on all sides but it did restore a degree of religious peace. For Catholics the calm was shattered in 1570 with the excommunication of Elizabeth by Pope Pius V, who also called upon English Catholics to overthrow her. When his successor Pope Gregory XIII took the lead in organizing the planned invasion of the

Spanish Armada in 1588, Catholicism became synonymous with treason and a series of laws aimed especially at the activity of Catholic clergy in England were enacted.

With the dissolution of the English monasteries and the atmosphere of religious turmoil and strife, the brilliant series of fourteenth and fifteenth-century English mystics came to an end. Among English Catholics mysticism was forgotten even as Catholic Spain enjoyed its remarkable efflorescence of mysticism with Teresa of Ávila, John of the Cross and Ignatius of Loyola. Nonetheless, mysticism did reappear among the beleaguered remnant of English monastics living in exile on the Continent in Augustine Baker (1575–1641), a mystic against all odds. He was a Catholic and a Benedictine monk at a time when Catholicism in England was on the defensive and at times persecuted. Catholics certainly had no wish to reinforce the Reformation propaganda that derided their practices as superstition. In addition, the violence of some of the Anabaptists who emphasized individual inspiration had discredited such communication with God for many Catholics. Moreover, the Benedictine order had no great tradition of mysticism, at least not in the previous four centuries. Cistercians, Franciscans, Dominicans and Carmelites might dabble in mysticism, but not sane, moderate Benedictines.

Baker was a mystic many years in the making. He was born with the Christian name of David in the Welsh town of Abergavenny to a well-to-do family of Catholics who gave lip-service to the Church of England to escape the legal penalties against Catholics while privately practicing Catholic devotions. After a good Protestant education in which he learned Latin, Greek and a better pronunciation of English, Baker went to university at Oxford for two years and then turned to legal studies. During these years he drifted away from both Protestantism and Catholicism while sliding into atheism. At about the age of twenty-five he was turned back to religion when he was miraculously saved from death. Five years later, in 1605, he went to Italy to become a Benedictine monk, adopting the name Augustine, and within ten years he was ordained a priest.

Early in his Benedictine career Baker tried contemplation but he failed to achieve results. Having no spiritual director to counsel him on perseverance, he soon gave it up. About five years later, after considerable reading on contemplation, he made another effort. This time he made some progress, even experiencing "passive contemplation," which for Baker meant "not a state but an actual grace and favour from God, by which He is pleased … to communicate a glimpse of his majesty to the spirits of His servants, after a secret and wonderful manner."[1] He described it as "a speaking of God in his soul; and whether the soul spake anything as in answer to God, he could not tell."[2] It was a brief experience, lasting no more than a quarter of an hour, followed by a return of his spiritual dryness. Again he abandoned contemplation, this time for twelve years. Finally, in 1620, Baker tried contemplation for the third time but now he broke through the dryness and for the rest of his life he was a "professional mystic."[3]

In the meantime, Baker had returned to England to assist in re-establishing the English Benedictine monastic Congregation, a hazardous move, for as a Catholic priest ordained in a foreign country, his mere presence in England constituted treason against the Crown. After about four years, he returned to France to become the spiritual director of English Benedictine nuns in Cambrai, a role in which he could draw upon his own struggles and experiences to provide the nuns with the sort of guidance that would have been so helpful to him in his earlier efforts at mysticism. For their benefit he translated a number of medieval mystical classics, especially those from England, while also writing his own tracts for them. Because he was counseling the nuns who were beginning their mystical lives, Baker's works focused on beginners' problems, with which he was well-acquainted.

A number of the nuns had great success in their contemplation, most famously Dame Gertrude More (1606–33), a descendant of Sir Thomas More. She entered the convent in 1623 but had been unable to become comfortable in her early monastic profession, especially due to her authoritarian and dogmatic spiritual directors. Then Father Baker came to Cambrai. At first she refused to speak to him, but once she came to know him, she followed his gentle and experienced direction to pray so that the Holy Spirit would inspire her to know her path. Fr. Baker himself told her that no single absolute rule could be mandated for all to follow. In only fifteen days her life was transformed, finding herself "so quieted that I wondered at myself. This change took place as soon as I had received from him some general instruction."[4] She continued to progress in her life of contemplation and, in a brief hint at her mystical experiences, she wrote,

> What shall I say of a soul that hath tasted how sweet our Lord is? … And although Thou dost admit her, longing and sighing after Thee alone, to, I know not what, nor can I express the unspeakable joy and delights which Thou sometimes admittest her to.[5]

She developed into a "remarkable mystic"[6] before she died an extremely painful death from smallpox in 1633.

However, not all the nuns were as responsive to Baker's emphasis on mysticism and they gained an ally in Francis Hull, the nuns' official chaplain at Cambrai, a man who "did not understand mysticism."[7] The argument between the two spiritual leaders was taken to the Benedictine chapter, which approved of Baker's writings. However, because of the dispute he was transferred to Douai where he continued to write. Controversy followed him to Douai when he antagonized his superior by claiming that a monk's duty of obedience to his superior extended only to external matters, for purely internal matters, such as one's contemplative life, were private matters. In 1638 Baker's superior gave him an exterior command to return to England in spite of his fragile health and the danger of being arrested and executed. Faithful to his principles, Baker obeyed. Once in England, Baker's health further deteriorated. He gave up writing but he probably continued to progress in the mystical life, and he died in August 1641.

Baker's mystical writings, mostly confined to the period of his spiritual direction of the nuns at Cambrai, are insistent that the call to perfection is given to all Christians and that contemplation, that is, approaching God as directly as possible, is the path to that perfection. Baker was supremely confident of the efficacy of the direct approach to God. In England he won converts to Catholicism, not by engaging in creedal disputes, but rather simply by encouraging the person to pray to God "with pure submission of mind and indifferency, flowing from a soul free from all worldly interests and designs."[8] Baker taught that the path to perfection is open to all, even the unlearned, who are not satisfied with simply meeting the minimum requirements of religion (whom he called "internal livers" or "spiritual livers"), but wanted to abandon "tepidity" in religion, "a bitter poisonous root fixed in the minds of negligent Christians."[9] However, those in religious orders imposed upon themselves an obligation to seek perfection and thus if they did not engage in interior prayer, they failed in their calling. Baker did not dictate the exact path by which such people should find God, for all should follow what was best for them and they should simply progress as far as they could, with God's help. Baker's task was to make them aware of contemplation and, drawing upon mystical writings going back to the Desert Fathers, to guide those under his charge through the difficulties that they would encounter. He felt a spiritual director of "internal livers" could not be satisfied simply with study and reasoning, "but very oft an actual supernatural illumination will moreover be requisite and necessary."[10]

It was no easy task to reintroduce mysticism into English society. Henry VIII's dissolution of monasteries in England destroyed the nurseries of contemplation and English Protestants tended to recoil from mysticism and its attendant manifestations, especially when political and religious extremists appealed to private revelations from God and frequently experienced visions. Baker, like John of the Cross in a similar situation, strongly discouraged visions: "As for extraordinary supernatural inspirations, illuminations, apparitions, voices, conversations with spirits, messages from heaven, etc., a spiritual internal liver is forbidden to pretend to, or so much as desire them; yea, rather to pray against them."[11] However, in the face of constant attacks, he refused to soften his emphasis on divine illumination, for "God alone is our only master and director." All other sources of knowledge must be

> subordinate and comfortable to the internal directions and inspirations of God's Holy Spirit. ... All our light, therefore, is from divine illumination, and all our strength as to these things is from the divine operation of the Holy Ghost on our wills and affections.[12]

Baker's status as a genuine mystic was denied by one of the most influential modern scholars of English mysticism, Dom David Knowles. However, Knowles' judgment, based on a narrow theological definition of mysticism, has not been supported by most others who have studied mysticism and Baker's standing as a mystic received strong support from Thomas Merton. Baker's life demonstrated that mysticism survived in English Catholicism, however narrowly, and that one source of its revival could be exposure to the classical works written by mystics of the past. In addition, his call for the Christian to take seriously the Christian life and not to be content with minimum requirements would be a recurrent theme in England and elsewhere.

Just as Augustine Baker was becoming attracted to monasticism, English history was taking another dramatic turn. The childless Elizabeth I died in 1603 and was succeeded by her cousin King James VI of Scotland (son of Mary Queen of Scots), who was crowned as James I of England (1603–25). The compromise of the Elizabethan Settlement was unravelling, as English Presbyterians (Puritans) sought to move the Church of England in a more Calvinistic direction, which the new king vehemently resisted. Under James's son Charles I (1625–49) the religious and political crises worsened. Charles continued his father's authoritarian style of government, cracked down on the increasingly rebellious Puritans and also, owing to his personal inclinations, fostered the growth of Catholicism in England. In 1640 civil war erupted, with the Parliamentary and Puritan forces in arms against Charles I, backed by royalists and Catholics. In 1649 Charles I was executed by the Parliamentary forces and for the next ten years England was in the hands of Oliver Cromwell and the Parliamentary faction. The Church of England was disestablished and the Puritans could now worship freely, but at the same time the rigid censorship of the royal church disappeared, allowing the proliferation of new sects, the "Independents," including many that were mystical.

The Family of Love, or Familists, emphasized the primacy of the personal experience of God within, providing individual inspiration that took precedence over the Scriptures, which could be understood only with the help of the indwelling Holy Spirit. Other groups shared many of the Familists' ideas, especially concerning the presence of the Spirit within the believers, and their worship services often featured silent waiting for the arrival of the Holy Spirit. All other churches, even that of the Puritans, were considered reprobate. In return, the Puritans scorned them with pejorative labels such as Ranters and Seekers and imagined the existence of an organization where there were simply groups of individuals, thus magnifying the threat represented by the Independents. The radicals' scorn for the Scriptures, touch of antinomianism, talk of overthrowing traditional morality and tendency to purposeful offensiveness to the Puritans led to repressive legislation.

Millenarian expectation was in the air as well. The Levelers argued for complete equality of all classes before the law and complete freedom of religion, while their radical wing, the Diggers, added an eschatalogical fervor while advocating the redistribution of land in England to communities of farmers. More extreme millenarians were the Fifth Monarchy Men, who wished to assist the return of Christ to the earth by overthrowing all earthly governments and establishing God's kingdom themselves. The decade of the 1650s seemed to many of the sober Puritans and Anglicans to be one of religious and social anarchy that threatened to dissolve society into immorality and godlessness and behind it all seemed to be false prophets claiming personal inspiration and indwelling of the Holy Spirit.

Into this strongly anti-mystical attitude on the part of the new establishment in England stepped George Fox (1624–91), who came from a Puritan family in the Midlands. In his early years he apprenticed as a cobbler and a shepherd before leaving his family at age nineteen to find true religion. Fox fit easily into this atmosphere of listening to the guiding voice of God (the inner light) and challenging the institutions of the existing churches. As he related in his *Journal* (a reminiscence he dictated much later), he was constantly given "openings" in which God revealed to him the meaning of the

Scriptures and religious truths. His own turning-point came in 1647, as he felt that no priest, minister or teacher could help him in his zeal to know God's will:

> I heard a voice which said, "There is one, even Christ Jesus, that can speak to thy condition," and when I heard it my heart did leap for joy. Then the Lord did let me see why there was none upon the earth that could speak to my condition, namely, that I might give him all the glory; ... My desires after the Lord grew stronger, and zeal in the pure knowledge of God and Christ alone, without the help of any man, book or writing.[13]

He wrote that later, as he was walking about, "I was taken up in the love of God, so that I could not but admire the greatness of his love. ... Then after this there did a pure fire appear in me." He was granted spiritual discernment and "by this invisible spirit I discerned all the false hearing and the false seeing, and false smelling which was atop, above the Spirit, quenching and grieving it."[14] In addition, he saw "the infinite love of God. I saw also that there was an ocean of darkness and death, but an infinite ocean of light and love, which flowed over the ocean of darkness."[15] Fox did not see himself as being especially blessed in his openings, for "the Lord opened it to me by his invisible power how that every man was enlightened by the divine light of Christ; and I saw it shine through all."[16]

Fox was no quietistic mystic, simply reveling in his experiences. He had a divine mission, nothing less than effecting a religious reform that would lead humankind back to God, "to turn people from darkness to the light that they might receive Christ Jesus, for to as many as should receive him in his light, I saw that he would give power to become the sons of God."[17] With the aid of his revelations Fox began preaching throughout England: "And the Lord's power brake forth; and I had great openings, and prophecies, and spake unto them of the things of God, and they heard with attention and silence, and went away, and spread the fame thereof."[18] Fox preached what had been revealed to him, that church establishments were empty and meaningless, as were their creeds, doctrines, sacraments, rituals, saints, holy days and clergy. Fox's task was to lead people back to the apostolic church founded by Jesus, one led by the constant intervention and inspiration of the Holy Spirit. Fox himself manifested the gifts of the Spirit, just as the apostles had. Some regarded him as a prophet while others sought him out for his ability to cure people's illnesses, and he could discern what was in the hearts and minds of those who came to him.

Like the political radicals, Fox criticized English society, denouncing the injustice of the legal system with its harsh penalties for minor crimes. He rejected the social hierarchy that permeated English life and refused to doff his hat in the presence of his social superiors or to address them with the formal "you," preferring instead the common and familiar "thee" and "thou." Moreover, he refused to take the standard oaths of allegiance and denounced fighting and warfare of any kind.

His powerful preaching gained an immediate following, blending easily with many of the teachings of the Ranters, Diggers, Levelers, Seekers, Fifth Monarchy Men and Familialists. In the early days, Fox was simply one of many preachers dedicated to follow the Inner Light and advocating a revolution in religion and society. At first Fox's followers called themselves Children of Light, which became Friends of Truth and eventually the Society of Friends. However, by 1650 they were being called Quakers, "because we bid [the justices] tremble at the word of God."[19]

Fox and his fellow Quakers were called upon to demonstrate the same confidence in their divine revelations as did their apostolic models. Their teachings alienated the Puritan and Anglican clergies as well as the ruling authorities of England, who easily confused them with the radical groups whom they resembled so strongly. The Quakers were subjected to harsh persecution, as they were beaten, flogged, jailed, sometimes tortured, and frequently subjected to mob violence. Nonetheless they persevered, distancing themselves from the more radical elements, and survived.

The death of Oliver Cromwell in 1658 marked the beginning of the end of Puritan ascendancy and in 1660 the monarchy was restored when Charles II (1660–85), son of the beheaded Charles I, was accepted as king. Within two years the Church of England regained its position as the state church and the Puritans were again persecuted dissenters. By the eighteenth century, the religious storms that had raked England had at last quieted, leaving a nation too exhausted to wish for their return. However, the established Church of England seemed incapable of providing anything more than a kind of religious tepidity that Augustine Baker had decried two centuries earlier. Complacency, torpor, corruption and decay are the words most commonly used to describe the Church of England during this period and the problems ran from top to bottom: "The practical result of the expulsion of genuine spiritual leadership from the Church and of the nearly complete corruption of its administrative hierarchy was a wholesale neglect of the spiritual life at the parish level."[20]

One of the first English spiritual writers to attempt to combat this prevailing spirit of religious complacency was William Law (1686–1761) in two great works, *A Practical Treatise upon Christian Perfection* (1726) and especially in *A Serious Call to a Devout and Holy Life* (1728). Law was born into a prosperous grocer's family in King's Cliffe, Northamptonshire. In 1705 he was able to enter Emmanuel College, Cambridge, already showing his own serious call. Before leaving for university he drew up his "Rules for My Future Conduct" which included his intentions

> To fix it deep in my mind, that I have but one business upon my hands, to seek for eternal happiness, by doing the will of God. … To avoid all concerns with the world, or the ways of it, but where religion and charity oblige me to act. To remember frequently, and to impress it upon my mind deeply, that no condition in this life is for enjoyment, but for trial; … To avoid all excess in eating and drinking. … To be always fearful of letting my time slip away without some fruit. To avoid all idleness. … To think often of the life of Christ, and propose it as a pattern to myself.[21]

As might be expected from so dedicated a student, Law excelled at Emmanuel. After receiving his B.A. in 1708 he was ordained a deacon (although he did not become a priest until 1727), was elected a fellow of the College in 1711 and received his M. A. in

1712. However, his promising church career was cut short by the accession of King George I in 1714 as Law, an outspoken supporter of the hereditary rights of the Stuart claimants to the throne, refused to take the requisite oath of allegiance to the new ruler. As a "nonjuror," Law could hold no university or clerical position. Eventually he became tutor to Edward Gibbon, the father of the historian of the same name who wrote *The Decline and Fall of the Roman Empire.* Law also wrote works on the religious controversies of his day along with practical works like *A Practical Treatise* and *A Serious Call,* and, in his later years, mystical works in which he adapted and promoted the system of Jacob Boehme.

The *Serious Call* won Law a devoted following among serious-minded people in England and, next to the Bible, "contributed more than any other book to the spread of evangelicalism."[22] John Wesley lauded it as having sown the seed of his Methodist movement while Samuel Johnson wrote that he was turned away from religious inattention and indifference and toward earnestness after he picked it up expecting to be amused. Law's message was a challenge to all complacent Christians. Christian life demanded nothing less than "a life given or devoted to God" completely, in "all the ordinary actions of our lives" and required "introducing religion into all the actions of your common life."[23] What was required was to live in opposition to the world, not in conformity with it, for true Christians were those who "have lived contrary to this spirit of the world" and, he warned, "the world become a friend makes it difficult for [Christians] to save their religion."[24]

The *Serious Call* is not overtly mystical but Law had been a self-admitted "diligent reader" of mystical writers "through all ages of the Church,"[25] from Pseudo-Dionysius to Cassian, Tauler, Suso, Ruusbroec and near contemporary mystics like Guyon and Fénelon. Law's mysticism permeates his description of the devout life for all Christians, who are baptized "to live according to [God's] holy inspiration."[26] The method of prayer he recommended would prepare one "for the reception of the Holy Spirit … it will procure the assistance of the Holy Spirit."[27] Law did not encourage the stifling of higher experiences, for if "he finds his heart ready to break forth into new and higher strains of devotion, he should leave his form for a while and follow those fervors of his heart till it again wants the assistance of his usual petitions."[28] At the beginning of one's prayers, "The first thing that you are to do when you are upon your knees is to shut your eyes and with a short silence let your soul place itself in the presence of God."[29]

Law never emphasized claims of his own experiences and he denied having any of the more extreme forms of visions and other phenomena, which were called "enthusiasm" in Law's England, in which "anything approaching fanaticism or even emotion, was a quality equally abhorred and feared in the eighteenth century by philosophers, divines and methodists, indeed, by everyone except mystics."[30] Law warned against using such phenomena as proof of the workings of God within the soul but he accepted the phenomena themselves:

> as a spiritual man or one devoted to the Spirit of God, I am not to look after any
> extraordinaries, any new openings, illuminations, visions, or voices, inward or

outward, from God as proofs of the Spirit of God dwelling and working within me.[31]

He pointed out that the church had always had "extraordinary persons" who had enjoyed "these extraordinary operations of God's Holy Spirit and the wonders of His gifts and graces ... through all the ages of the Church," but which were "not matters of common instruction."[32] His concern was that spiritual writers ought not to discuss "states which ought not to be described"[33] lest they be misunderstood. Nonetheless, one passage in the *Serious Call* reads very much like a personal experience:

> Sometimes our hearts are so awakened, have such strong apprehensions of the divine presence, are so full of deep compunction for our sins, that we cannot confess them in any language but tears. Sometimes the light of God's countenance shines so brightly upon us, we see so far into the invisible world, we are so affected with the wonders of the love and goodness of God that our hearts worship and adore in a language that is higher than that of words, and we feel transports of devotion which only can be felt.[34]

Law's later works became more overtly mystical. In *The Spirit of Love* (1752), he wrote of "perpetual inspiration," which ought not to be branded as non-Scriptural fanaticism and enthusiasm:

> What a mistake it is to confine inspiration to particular times and occasions, to prophets and apostles and extraordinary messengers of God, and to call it enthusiasm when the common Christian looks and trusts to be continually led and inspired by the Spirit of God.[35]

This "perpetual, always-existing operation of the Spirit of God within us is absolutely necessary. For we cannot be inwardly led and governed by a spirit of goodness, but by being governed by the Spirit of God Himself."[36] It is this "inward birth of divine light, goodness, and virtue in our renewed spirit" that can lead one to be "united in heart and spirit with the Light and Word and Spirit of God."[37]

Law was himself led to conclusions that differed from the traditional theology of Christianity in his day. His God was unknowable, "an entire hidden, shut up, unknown, and unknowable abyss," who was "nothing but infinite love," who could not "begin to have any wrath, rage, or anger in Himself ... absolutely free from wrath and rage."[38] All wrath was within humans, not God, and this was hell, "For I know of no Hell either here or hereafter, but the power and working of wrath ... wrath can be no more in God Himself than Hell can be in Heaven."[39] In addition, he utterly rejected the traditional concept of the Atonement as Christ's payment to God of a debt owed by humans for their sins. This view, he affirmed, "has less scripture for it than the infallibility of the Pope ... The whole truth of the matter is plainly this. Christ given for us is neither more nor less than Christ given into us."[40] For Law, there was "no wrath in God, no fictitious Atonement, no folly of debtor and creditor, no suffering in Christ for suffering's sake."[41]

Around 1730 Law came across translations of the works of Jacob Boehme and accepted this extra-biblical search for God who is hidden in nature as an avenue that provided more profound explanations for the deep questions of life than found in the Scriptures and in Christian theology, and his writings from that point begin to expound the essential points of Boehme's system. The more fully that Law became a "Behmenist," the more he alienated many of his former supporters. John Wesley had been a frequent visitor of Law's but Law's attachment to Boehme was too much for Wesley, already concerned that Law's view of Christian life was too perfectionist, who dismissed Boehme's writing as "most sublime nonsense, inimitable bombast, fustian not to be paralleled."[42] In the face of considerable criticism, Law never wavered from his attachment to Boehme's teachings and thus "he suffered his considerable reputation to be eclipsed by his espousal of an uncomprehended and unpopular mysticism."[43]

Law also continued to live out a life of devotion. An admirer, impressed by his reading of Law's *Christian Perfection*, gave him £1000, with which he established a school for girls in his native King's Cliffe. Around 1740 Law retired to his house in King's Cliffe where he lived with two women to whom he had been providing spiritual direction and together they formed a small Christian community. They followed Law's rigorous prayer discipline, pooled their revenues and with all that was not necessary for themselves they practiced Christian charity. He personally distributed milk to poor neighbors, handed out clean clothing to the needy and fed the hungry with soup that he tasted to ensure that it was of good quality. They gave money to the poor without inquiring into the worthiness of the recipients, generosity that, to the distress of many of his neighbors, attracted swarms of eager indigents to the neighborhood. Law and his companions also established a school for boys to complement the school for girls. In 1761 Law was struck by his final illness. According to one of his companions, as he was dying, "He said he had such an opening of the divine life within him, that the fire of divine love quite consumed him."[44]

By the time of Law's death, John Wesley's Methodist movement, which had been so inspired by Law's works, numbered well over 10,000 adherents and had matured to the point that it could engage in internal disputes over its theology and be in the process of separating from the Church of England. Wesley (1703–91) was as serious-minded about religion as Law had been but with a difference – he was an evangelist determined to preach to all the gospel of attaining Christian Perfection, which was nothing less than union with God but expressed in moderate language acceptable to Protestants. Christian Perfection was perfect love, which is loving God completely and, concomitantly, loving one's neighbor as oneself. The path to this state is the familiar mystical path, giving to God all of one's soul, body, and substance, freeing oneself from all self-will, denying and resigning oneself completely to the will of God, stripping oneself and abandoning everything, praying earnestly, fasting, gradually mortifying one's sins (thus dying to sin) and renewing oneself in the image of God. This leads to justification and sanctification, the assurance of which would be given by the Holy Spirit directly to the Christian. This was certainly not an easy path, but after reading Law's *Christian Perfection* and *Serious Call,* Wesley realized "the absolute impossibility of being half a Christian."[45]

Perhaps Wesley could have taken no other path. He was a descendant of several generations of Dissenting clerics with strong Puritan impulses; his father, Samuel Wesley, was a minister in the Church of England, and an interest in mystical writers extended back into his family for several generations. In his father's rectory in Epworth, Lincolnshire, John was taught to be a serious Christian, learning from his mother Susanna that "Religion is not confined to the church, or closet, nor exercised only in prayer and meditation. Everywhere we are in the presence of God, and every word and action is capable of morality."[46] John pursued university studies at Christ Church, Oxford, and, with the help of a patristics student at Oxford, he began studying the Church Fathers of the second and third centuries. He also read widely in the writings of mystics of the seventeenth century, such as Molinos, Pascal, Fénelon, and Guyon, many of whom were Quietists, and they impressed him profoundly with their "noble descriptions of union with God and internal religion" that "made everything else appear mean, flat, and insipid."[47] Wesley was well-acquainted with the mysticism of the early church and in the century before his own, but he was ignorant of almost all the medieval mystical authors of the 1300 intervening years.

In 1724 he received his B.A. degree and became a lecturer at Lincoln College, Oxford. He gained his M.A. in 1727 and was ordained a priest of the Church of England in 1728. The next year he returned to Oxford after a short period of assisting his father in his parish and, with his younger brother Charles, he associated with other young men who met together to study Scripture and encourage each other to cultivate morality and follow the fasts of the ancient church. Their less religious fellows at Oxford derisively referred to them as the Holy Club or Methodists, meaning practitioners of a new and therefore wrong method of spirituality. Wesley had a strongly-developed sense of social action and at this time he began visiting prisoners in jail, attempting to help the poor in any way that he could, including ridding his life of "superfluities" and restricting his expenses as severely as he could.

By 1735 Wesley had developed a solidly mystical approach to his religious life and, seeing the world as his parish, set out for America to minister to the Anglicans in frontier Georgia and to convert the Indians. While at Oxford Wesley had "lived almost like a hermit"[48] and had practiced a serious religion. Now he attempted to impose these same standards on the pioneers in Savannah and failed miserably. Eventually a Savannah jury brought an indictment against him for his severity and at the end of 1737 he fled Georgia in spiritual turmoil. The way of the mystics, as he had understood it, had failed him but it still retained its hold on his heart. The mystical writings with which he was familiar leaned decidedly toward Quietism, which conflicted with many of his own beliefs. Quietism tended to deprecate good works or any other actions on the part of the believer, but he held firmly to good works as essential fruits of belief. The Scriptures remained the touchstone of Wesley's faith but mystics were rarely concerned with demonstrating the conformity of their teachings with the Bible. Moreover, Wesley's Puritan conscience was racked by an awareness of his sins without a real conviction that they had been forgiven.

Once back in England, Wesley kept up contact with Moravians, descendants of the Anabaptists of the sixteenth century,[49] whom he had met in America and on shipboard on his return and they explained to him that one could have an internal, personal experience of forgiveness of sins and the dwelling of the Holy Spirit within. Even better, they could demonstrate that this experience was in agreement with the literal interpretation of Scripture. During this crisis, Wesley related, "I hear a voice (and is it not the voice of God?) saying, 'Believe and thou shalt be saved.'" On the morning of 24 May 1738, he opened his Bible and read that Christians should be "partakers of the divine nature"[50] and then he opened it again to read, "Thou art not far from the kingdom of God."[51] That evening he attended the meeting of the religious society just off Aldersgate Street in London. During a reading of Martin Luther's Epistle to the Romans, "I felt my heart strangely warmed. I felt I did trust in Christ, Christ alone, for salvation; and an assurance was given me that He had taken away *my* sins, even *mine*, and saved *me* from the law of sin and death."[52] Wesley returned home, "much buffeted with temptations," but he "cried out and they fled away." Previously, Wesley wrote, "I was indeed fighting continually, but not conquering." Now, after his Aldersgate Street experience, "I was always the conqueror."[53]

To his firm idea of Christian Perfection was added his doctrine of Assurance of inward holiness, which to Wesley meant "union of the soul with God."[54] Assurance, the key to Wesley's new spirituality, was "an inward impression on the soul, whereby the Spirit of God immediately and directly witnesses to my spirit that I am a child of God." This provided assurance that "all my sins are blotted out, and I, even I, am reconciled to God." This assurance did not come "by any outward voice; no, nor always by an inward voice, although he may do this sometimes." But there was "a sweet calm" as the sinner was satisfied that all his "iniquities are forgiven, and his sins covered."[55] This experience was the direct and immediate testimony of the Holy Spirit, coming "directly from God into the believing soul," which Wesley could experience "in my own breast."[56] Because Wesley was now preaching an experiential religion, he was "roughly attacked in a large company as an enthusiast, a seducer and a setter-forth of new doctrines."[57] The charge of "enthusiasm" was a serious one in eighteenth-century England, throwing Wesley in with the likes of the Quakers, French Prophets and others similarly despised in the mainstream of Anglican religious culture in which Wesley moved.

For the rest of his life Wesley combated the smear of enthusiasm. He relied on Scripture, likening Assurance to the movement of the Holy Spirit on the Apostles on the day of Pentecost and repeatedly cited Scriptural authority to argue that "a *direct testimony* that we are sanctified is necessary in the highest degree" and that "it belongs to all the children of God."[58] Meanwhile, he also denounced "enthusiasm," disassociating his teachings from "dreams, voices, impressions, visions, or revelations [claimed] to be from God." He warned his followers to "beware of *enthusiasm*. Such is the imagining you have the gift of *prophesying*, or of *discernment of spirits*, which I do not believe one of you has."[59] At the same time, in his sermon on *The Nature of Enthusiasm* he attempted to turn the table on his detractors by discussing the "good sense" of the term enthusiasm, which meant "a divine impulse or impression, superior to all the natural faculties, and suspending for the time … both the reason and the outward senses." Under Wesley's definition, the Old Testament prophets the apostles "were proper 'enthusiasts'; being at divers times, so filled with the Spirit." But adopting the pejorative meaning of enthusiasm, Wesley argued that "Every enthusiast then is properly a madman" and found that "the most common of all the enthusiasts of this kind are those who imagine themselves Christian, and are not … [who are] without one grain of true faith in Christ, or of real, inward holiness!"[60]

Almost a year after his Aldersgate Street experience, Wesley began his open-air preaching, "field preaching," which met with spectacular success, drawing as many as 3000 listeners at a time. In this manner the Methodist movement began. Wesley was the driving force behind the movement to adopt a serious Christianity, "genuine Christianity" to Wesley, but he was neither the only preacher nor the best preacher of what was at first a large religious society within the Church of England, for he was far surpassed in preaching by his collaborator George Whitefield. By the time of Wesley's death in 1791, there were more than 70,000 Methodists in Europe and even more in America.

Throughout this period of expansion Wesley clung to his mysticism. He continued to argue that the Assurance he and other Methodists experienced was the same as the New Testament accounts of the coming of the Holy Spirit. He taught concepts commonly found in mystical writings throughout the centuries and he strove to make the essence of those mystical writings known for the edification of his followers. Between 1749 and 1755 he published the fifty volumes of *The Christian Library: Consisting of Extracts from and Abridgements of, the Choicest Pieces of Practical Divinity*, intended to serve the same purpose in the Church of England as the publication of the *Philokalia* did in the Eastern Orthodox churches later that same century. The abridgements and extracts, often Wesley's own translations, ranged from the second and third-century church fathers, largely unknown to the general populace, to Wesley's favorite mystics of the previous century, such as Molinos, Fénelon and Pascal. Clearly Wesley continued to recommend mystical writers to his Methodists, though with caution. Because he felt that perfect love must be manifested in action, he was opposed to any hints of Quietist mysticism – indeed, his concern for action was manifested in his opposition to slavery and smuggling as well as in his establishment of schools and support of the Sunday-school movement. Moreover, because he believed that the only genuine Christianity was a serious Christianity, he was especially aghast at the antinomian tendencies of some of the more enthusiastic forms of mysticism.

In this late eighteenth-century atmosphere of widespread dissatisfaction with the staid and complacent Church of England, the ideas of Emanuel Swedenborg had been eagerly embraced by a circle of admirers. In return, he praised the English as "the best and most sincere of the Christians."[61] Swedenborg made many trips to England, often to circumvent Swedish censorship of his books. He was in London when he died in 1772 and was buried there in the Swedish Church. By 1788 the English Swedenborgians organized the Society for Promoting the Heavenly Doctrines of the New Jerusalem, or the New Jerusalem Church. In April 1789 they held the first session of the general conference of the New Church, attended by sixty or seventy

Swedenborgians who signed their names to a declaration that Swedenborg's theological writings "are genuine Truths, revealed from Heaven." Among those who signed and attended the conference was the engraver, artist and poet William Blake (1757–1827).

Blake was very much like Swedenborg. He too had been a visionary even as a child – he saw a tree filled with angels, angels walking amid haymakers in the morning, the prophet Ezekiel sitting under a tree – which drew both threatened and actual punishments from his parents.[62] Visions continued throughout his life as great personages from the past came to him, the likes of Moses, Homer, David, Julius Caesar, Mark Antony, Dante, Edward III, Shakespeare, Milton, Voltaire, even Mohammed, some of whom Blake recognized as his friends in past lives. During these apparitions he conversed with his spiritual visitors and even drew their portraits. On one occasion he was drawing William Wallace when King Edward I interposed himself between Blake and his old Scots foe. Blake was obliged to draw the king before he could continue with the portraiture of Wallace. Blake was quite open about his supernatural visitors, leading many to the conclusion that Blake was simply unhinged. One who came to know Blake wrote that, at first, "I thought him mad. I do not think so now. I never suspected him of imposture. His manner was too honest for that."[63]

Blake was the son of James Blake, a prosperous London hosier who reared his children as religious dissenters. At age fourteen William was apprenticed to an engraver to learn his life's trade and here, too, his visions intruded. He was assigned to sketch Westminster Abbey and while there, "secluded in the dim vaulted solitude," he saw the great church "suddenly filled with a great procession of monks and priests, choristers and censer-bearers, and his entranced ear heard the chant of plain-song and chorale, while the vaulted roof trembled to the sound of organ music."[64]

In 1782 Blake married Catherine Boucher, the daughter of a market gardener of modest means, and he began his career sketching and painting while also composing verse. Two years later his father died and Blake was left with an inheritance of £100, which he used to establish a business making and selling prints. In the evenings, after hours, he continued to write poetry which he illustrated. In 1787 Blake was present when his favorite brother Robert died and he watched his brother's spirit ascending upward, "clapping its hands for joy."[65] Not long afterwards, Robert's spirit came to Blake and revealed to him a new technique for producing his engraved prints, a method he put to use in 1788 and he continued to apply the spiritually-delivered method for the rest of his life.

Assessing the mysticism of poets is often difficult, for it is often unclear if they wrote from personal experience or they were simply being poetic. Certainly Blake's own words indicate that he was a visionary but he does not provide examples of his experiences with the divine. However, he felt that he wrote in "the Interest of True Religion & Science" while "under the direction of Messengers from Heaven Daily & Nightly."[66] He also wrote in a form of automatic writing, which he called "immediate dictation," during which he might dash out twenty or thirty lines at a time, "without Premeditation & even against my Will, the Time it has taken in writing was thus renderd Non Existent."[67] He wrote of working under inspiration: "I am drunk with intellectual vision whenever I take a pencil or graver into my hand."[68] In his poetry, Blake wrote that his task was "To open the Eternal Worlds, to open the immortal Eyes/ Of Man inwards into the Worlds of Thought: into Eternity/ Ever expanding in the Bosom of God."[69]

However, woven throughout all of his writings are mystical themes and descriptions of mystical experiences. He expressed a transformed perception of nature: "To see a World in a Grain of Sand/ And a Heaven in a Wild Flower/ Hold Infinity in the palm of your hand/ And Eternity in an hour."[70] He inveighed against the traditional enemy of mysticism, the exaltation of reason and the intellect in attempting to understand God, for "none traveling over known lands can find out the unknown."[71] With the mind, Blake wrote, one can only "compare & judge of what he has already perciev'd."[72] Thus with reason alone, one "sees himself only," but "He who sees in the Infinite in all things sees God. … Therefore God becomes as we are, that we may be as he is."[73] Reminiscent of Brother Lawrence and Marie of the Incarnation, Blake proclaimed, "I am in Gods presence night & day/ and he never turns his face away."[74] To Blake, science was "Antichrist" and "the Tree of Death," for Christ did not mean "To teach doubt & experiment."[75] Blake's God was an immanent, in-dwelling God, "All deities reside in the human breast … I am not a God afar off, I am a brother and a friend;/ Within your bosoms I reside, and you reside in me: … Seek not thy heavenly father then beyond the skies."[76] With so many mystics of the past, Blake cried out to God, "Annihilate the Selfhood in me."[77] These are not sentiments confined to Blake's poetry, for he said to a friend, "We are all coexistent with God – Members of the Divine body – we are all partakers of the divine nature." Discussing the divinity of Jesus, he exclaimed, "He is the only God" and he added quickly, "And so am I and so are you."[78]

At least some of the illustrations in his poetic texts came from visions. For his work *Europe a Prophecy*, he drew The Ancient of Days, in which "a mighty, bearded god leans out of the sun to separate the light from the darkness, the land from the sea."[79] This figure (see plate 10), which remained very dear to him, was one that he saw "hovering over his head at the top of his staircase" making "a more powerful impression upon his mind than all he had ever been visited by."[80] Most intriguing as a possible source of his visions and insights is the laconic entry he made in the autograph book of a friend, "William Blake … Born 28 Novr 1757 in London & has died Several times Since."[81]

Blake's marriage was a good one. His wife Catherine assisted him in the production of his works and eventually joined him in visionary experiences as she learned to have visions, "to see processions of figures wending along the river, in broad daylight; and would give a start when they disappeared in the water. As Blake truly maintained, the faculty for seeing such airy phantoms can be cultivated."[82] Blake's life was forever a visionary one. His wife once said, "I have very little of Mr. Blake's company; he is always in Paradise."[83] Blake died as he had lived: "Just before he died His Countenance became fair – His eyes brighten'd and He burst out in Singing of the things he Saw in Heaven."[84]

AMERICAN PROTESTANT MYSTICISM

Britain's amazing variety of religious life was transplanted in its American colonies along with those who willingly settled there or were forced by economic, political or legal circumstances to move across the Atlantic. The entire spectrum of religious beliefs and practices was exported to the new world – Catholics and Anglicans, Baptists and Puritans, Boehmists and occultists, Quakers, Shakers and Methodists, even the French Prophets. At the same time that Britain witnessed the tremendous religious fervor that was manifested in the Methodist movement, in the American colonies there was a related outbreak of religious revivals that now carries the misleading name of The Great Awakening, which is perhaps best understood as "a short-lived Calvinist revival in New England during the early 1740s,"[85] although the revivals were also known in the southern colonies into the 1750s and 1760s. The revivals in England and in America also have a connecting link, the stirring Calvinist preacher George Whitefield, John Wesley's associate in the foundation of the Methodist movement, who made seven revival tours through the colonies between 1738 and 1770. His arrival in New England in 1740 is usually regarded as the beginning of the so-called Great Awakening.

"Enthusiasm" was a prominent feature of the revivals, with prophesying, visions and all manner of ecstasies experienced by many who were swept up in the religious fervor. One who was caught up in the excitement of George Whitefield's preaching in 1740 was Nathan Cole (1711–83), who in 1765 wrote his *Spiritual Travels*, "the guileless autobiography of a common farmer in Farmington, Connecticut."[86] When Cole heard that Whitefield was coming his way, he dropped everything to join a great crowd of people, "3 or 4000 of people Assembled together," in his estimation.[87] Cole was utterly convinced by Whitefield's doctrine of predestination but he was also convinced that he himself was not among heaven's elect. After two years of emotional agony over the prospect of burning in the fires of hell for all eternity:

> God appeared unto me and made me Skringe: before whose face the heavens and the earth fled away; and I was Shrinked into nothing; I knew not whether I was in the body or out, I seemed to hang in open Air before God, and he seemed to Speak to me in an angry and Sovereign way what won't you trust your Soul with God.

Cole hastily affirmed that he did and, "while my Soul was viewing God, my fleshly part was working imaginations and saw many things which I will omitt to tell at this time."[88] When God vanished, Cole found himself freed of his distress over his salvation. He had found that God was "altogether-lovely … now I perfectly felt truth: now my heart talked with God; now everything praised God; the trees, the stone, the walls of the house and every thing I could set my eyes on, they all praised God." He was now weeping and sobbing, "for I was swallowed up in God."[89] Several months later, as he was going to work in his field:

> I fell into a prayer … and then I had a glorious Sight. … It seemed as if I really saw the gate of heaven by an Eye of faith, and the way for Sinners to Get to heaven by Jesus Christ; as plain as ever I saw any thing with my bodily eyes in my life … I saw what free Grace was; I saw how stubborn and willfull man was … I saw I was saved by Christ … what I saw here is unspeakable.[90]

After many more months, this assurance was followed by Cole's own dark night of the soul, "a turn of extreem darkness" as

> God with drew and hid his face from me, and left me in Egyptian darkness … now I had lost God and I could not find him … Once I had a God but now I have lost him; and it is the loss of God that makes hell … them that never had a God know not what it is to loose a God.

After three days this cloud went away and "the Clear light of Gods countenance broke into my Soul again."[91]

Many years later Cole had an early morning dream, in which he heard a great multitude singing praise to the glory of God. They were

> all drinked into one Spirit and oneness … so sweetly conformed to Gods will that his will was theirs and they rejoyced in it … it is impossible for me to tell the thousandth part of what I saw and felt; it is unspeakable.[92]

The farmer became convinced of the power of prayer. He performed a form of "distant healing," for when he prayed for the recovery of those at the point of death, "them persons did get well again beyond their expectation." Moreover, he seemed to know when "Saints some miles from me were distresd, and in the dark about some things, and wanted to converse with other certain Saints … I believe that Saints have been fetched from town to town many a time by the strength of prayer."[93]

Cole's spiritual life of alternating doubts and assurances continued: "God brought me through fire and thro water," as he put it,[94] and he searched one church after another, constantly looking for one that truly followed the will of God. Whitefield's stirring preaching had not converted him instantly but it had put him on a path of striving to follow the will of God and to become a serious Christian. His encounters with God came only after he had "made great Resolutions that I would forsake every thing that was Sinfull; And do to my uttermost every thing that was good."[95]

Phenomena such as visions of God or other examples of enthusiasm were denounced by some of the staid clergy of New England in the manner typical of religious authorities in England and on the Continent but Jonathan Edwards (1703–1758), a figure closely associated with the Great Awakening, was not one of them. Jonathan Edwards has been defined in the American imagination by his sermon of 1741, *Sinners in the Hands of an Angry God*. In this sermon Edwards reiterated in uncompromising terms his Calvinist theology: Humans "*deserve* to be cast into hell … They are *already* under a sentence of condemnation to hell … Therefore let everyone that is out of Christ, now awake and fly from the wrath to come."[96] These sentiments, so harsh to many modern ears, were also preached in similar terms by Catherine of Siena and Francis of Assisi, who, oddly, enjoy much warmer reputations than does Edwards. Surprisingly, in light of his general modern reputation, Edwards strongly defended the enthusiasm prominent in the Great Awakening and was himself, like St. Catherine and St. Francis, a mystic.

In the same year of his *Sinners in the Hands*, Edwards published *The Distinguishing Marks of a Work of the Spirit of God*. "Edwards argued calmly and subtly that, although physical manifestations were not in themselves signs of the working of God's Spirit, neither were they necessarily *not* a sign."[97] He argued that the phenomena should be judged by their effects on the person exhibiting the behaviors, for if they produced a greater regard for the Scriptures and for religion, a more virtuous life and greater love for God and neighbor, then "they plainly shew the finger of God, and are sufficient to outweigh a thousand such little objections."[98] In the next year Edwards published another defense of enthusiasm. In *Some Thoughts Concerning the Revival of Religion in New England*, Edwards summarized the recent experiences of someone he knew, a person not "in the giddy age of youth, nor a new convert, and unexperienced Christian, but in one that was converted above twenty-seven years ago."[99] After describing the person's experiences, Edwards applied the criteria of *The Distinguishing Marks* to show that the person had thereby grown in love of God and man, in humility, in appreciation of the majesty of God and in dedication to accept the will of God. He concluded that the phenomena came from God and one could not discount them without disproving "the whole of the Christian religion."[100] He attacked the issue of enthusiasm directly, "Now if such things are enthusiasm, and the fruits of a distempered brain, let my brain be evermore possessed of that happy distemper!" He declared the experiences to be "the most glorious of God's works," especially manifesting "the glory of God."[101]

The person whom Edwards was discussing was in fact his wife Sarah (1710–1758). Her own account of her experiences, an "exact statement" that she wrote at his request, survives and provides a detailed description of her experiences from 19 January to 4 February 1742. In the midst of a personal crisis, she felt that God "sweetly smiled upon me ... In consequence of this, I felt a strong desire to be alone with God, to go to him, without having any one to interrupt the silent and soft communion."[102] In the days that followed, she had a "delightful sense of the immediate presence and love of God" and

[t]he presence of God was so near, that I seemed scarcely conscious of anything else ... and Christ appeared to me ... my mind was so deeply impressed with the love of Christ, and a sense of his immediate presence, ... with a continual view of God as *nearer*, and as *my God*.[103]

She felt that she was "lifted above heaven and hell ... my soul was drawn so powerfully towards Christ and heaven, that I leaped unconsciously from my chair. I seemed to be drawn upwards, soul and body, from the earth towards heaven." She felt drawn toward heaven so strongly that

> it appeared to me that I must naturally and necessarily ascend thither ... This was accompanied with a ravishing sense of the unspeakable joys of the upper world. They appeared to my mind in all their reality and certainty, and as it were in actual and distinct vision.[104]

She repeated that throughout this time, "My soul remained in a kind of heavenly elysium."[105] She seemed to perceive "a glow of divine love come down from the heart of Christ in heaven, into my heart" and she had "an idea of a shining way, or path of light, between heaven and my soul."[106] She felt "entirely swallowed up in God."[107]

Throughout these experiences, she produced "a great flow of tears" and her bodily strength failed her. But at the same time she felt a tremendous agitation of body and could scarcely refrain from "rising in my seat, and leaping for joy" as she "walked the room for some time, in a kind of transport. ... I could hardly forbear leaping from my chair and singing aloud for joy and exultation."[108] These experiences gave her, much like a Methodist, assurance of having been saved from hell. Moreover, her submission to the will of God was so complete that, reminiscent of the Quietists, she was willing to be kept out of heaven for a thousand years if it were God's will, and to "live a thousand years in horror, if it be most for the honour of God," for she had "an absolute indifference as to all external circumstances."[109]

In her statement, Sarah Edwards specified that these were not the first experiences of that kind that she had known, and indeed they came to her continuously. In his description of her experiences in *Some Thoughts*, her husband explained that the "late great transports" were nothing new to her but were "of the same nature with what was felt formerly, when a little child of about five or six years of age; but only in a vastly higher degree."[110] He never wavered in his belief in the legitimacy of spiritual experiences that produced positive effects, for he had personal knowledge of the validity of such experiences.

Jonathan Edwards was the son and grandson of Congregational pastors. In his *Personal Narrative*, written in 1739, Edwards wrote openly about his own "two seasons of awakening." As a boy he prayed five times a day and spoke of religion with other boys. Desiring solitude, he and some friends "built a booth in a swamp, in a very secret and retired place, for a place of prayer. And besides, I had particular secret places of my own in the woods, where I used to retire by myself."[111] At age thirteen, the young Jonathan moved on to Yale and four years later he graduated at the head of his class. During his later years at Yale, he had his second awakening. He was reading the Bible, 1 Tim. 1.17, and

> there came into my soul, and was as it were diffused through it, a sense of the glory of the divine being; ... I thought with myself ... how happy I should be, if I might enjoy that God, and be wrapt up to God in heaven.

He then "began to have a new kind of apprehension and ideas of Christ … I had an inward, sweet sense of these things … and my soul was led away in pleasant views and contemplations of them."[112] He read in the Song of Songs, and there came to him periodically "an inward sweetness" that carried him away into contemplation. He felt a "sweet abstraction of soul" from worldly concerns, leaving him with "a kind of vision, or fixed ideas and imaginations, of being alone in the mountains, or some solitary wilderness, far from all mankind, sweetly conversing with Christ, and wrapt up and swallowed up in God."[113]

He found nature to be a source of spiritual experiences for him. Once, walking in his father's pasture, he looked up into the sky. There came to him

> so sweet a sense of the glorious majesty and grace of God, that I know not how to express. I seemed to see them both in a sweet conjunction: majesty and meekness joined together: it was a sweet and gentle, and holy majesty; and also a majestic meekness; an awful sweetness; a high, and great, and holy gentleness.[114]

He spent much of his time "in walking alone in the woods, and solitary places, for meditation, soliloquy, and prayer, and converse with God."[115] To Edwards, God "seemed to appear in every thing; in the sun, moon, and stars; in the clouds, and blue sky; in the grass, flowers and trees; in the water, and all nature."[116] It was in nature that Edwards found his image for the soul of a true Christian, which was

> like such a little white flower, as we see in the spring of the year, low, and humble on the ground, opening its bosom to receive the pleasant beams of the sun's glory; rejoicing as it were in a calm rapture; diffusing around a sweet fragrancy; standing peacefully and lovingly, in the midst of other flowers round about; all in like manner opening their bosoms, to drink in the light of the sun.[117]

In 1720, Edwards went to New York as pastor to his first church and his experiences continued there: "I very frequently used to retire into a solitary place, on the banks of Hudson's River, at some distance from the city, for contemplation on divine things, and secret converse with God; and had many sweet hours there."[118] In 1726 he moved on to the First Church in Northampton, Massachusetts, to assist his grandfather, who was pastor there. There, too, "God has appeared to me, a glorious and lovely being, … It has often appeared sweet to me, to be united to Christ."[119] In 1727, Edwards was ordained to the ministry and married Sarah Pierrepont, the descendant of founders of Yale, Harvard and the town of Hartford, Connecticut. She was a very tall woman, a good match for a man who stood over six feet in height, and was strikingly beautiful as well. He had known her for several years and seemed most attracted to her spiritual beauty. He described her at age thirteen as "beloved of the almighty Being" and noted an interest that they shared: "She loves to be alone, and to wander in the fields and on the mountains, and seems to have someone invisible always conversing with her."[120] By all accounts they had a good marriage and she bore eleven children.

In 1729 Edwards succeeded his deceased grandfather as pastor of the Northampton church. The *Personal Narrative* records the continuation of his intense spiritual experiences, In 1737, as he was out riding in the woods, he dismounted

> in a retired place, as my manner commonly has been, to walk for divine contemplation and prayer; I had a view, that for me was extraordinary, of the glory of the Son of God; … The person of Christ appeared ineffably excellent, with an excellency great enough to swallow up all thought and conception. Which continued, as near as I can judge, about an hour; which kept me, the bigger part of the time, in a flood of tears and weeping aloud. I felt withal, an ardency of the soul to be, what I know not otherwise how to express, than to be emptied and annihilated.[121]

The prevailing disbelief in the possibility of personal encounters with the divine led Jonathan Edwards, as it had Symeon the New Theologian and Richard Rolle, to describe mystical experiences in such graphic detail. From his own experiences Edwards knew with absolute assurance that God reveals himself to human beings, that, in his words, "God is a communicative being."[122] Very naturally he regarded the contemporary deists, with their denial of divine revelation, to be his archenemies. His graphic descriptions of his own mystical experiences as well as those of his wife and his written defense of "enthusiasm" were weapons in his arsenal to attack the doubting deists. However, Edwards went far beyond simply affirming the reality of God's revelation to Christians, for he also believed that God had revealed himself to virtually all the cultures and religions of the world. Moreover, among those non-Christians there were individuals who had a "disposition," which was an "inner religious consciousness … that is the only prerequisite to salvation."[123] Salvation, therefore, was not restricted to Calvinists or even to Christians for that matter. In addition, Edwards differed from his fellow American colonials in his favorable view of Indians, whom he told, "We are no better than you in no Respect,"[124] and, unlike most of his contemporary American theologians, he found value in Judaism, a vessel of God's revelation and "a true religion, if under a veil."[125]

Edwards shared much with his contemporary John Wesley. Both were serious Christians who, as young men, were inclined to make repeated resolutions concerning their behavior (both were especially concerned not to waste time) and both lived in a world of experiential religion leading them to defend proper enthusiasm. Wesley was impressed with news of Edwards' preaching in Northampton and published abridgements of a number of Edwards' works. Edwards, however, was far too Calvinist to accept Wesley's advocacy of Christian Perfection and branded him and his followers "high pretenders to spirituality these days."[126] However, Edwards was just as rigorous and uncompromising a pastor as Wesley had been in Georgia. Like Wesley, he aroused the ire of his weary parishioners. Apparently one can be too Calvinistic for

Calvinists and in 1750, after years of wrangling with his church, Edwards was turned out as pastor at Northampton.

The Edwards family moved on to Stockbridge, Massachusetts, where he became a missionary to the Indians of the area and served as pastor to the white settlers. In 1757 Edwards was chosen to be president of the College of New Jersey, now Princeton University, but he died at the age of fifty-four only a few weeks after his inauguration, on 22 March 1758, from faulty serum which he received as a precautionary inoculation against an epidemic of smallpox.

The age of great Christian revivals did not end with the waning of the Great Awakening. After the successful war for American independence, the fires of revival swept through western New York so frequently in the first decades of the nineteenth century that the region came to be called the Burned-Over District. The area, like the neighboring parts of New England, was a religious maelstrom, with competing churches engaging in bitter doctrinal battles, each claiming its own path as the sole means to salvation. Some followed the more esoteric teachings of Swedenborg and others the eclecticism of Jacob Boehme, while waves of intense religious fervor rolled over the population. At the same time, interest in and practice of magic, divination, astrology, alchemy, and all aspects of the occult persisted within all classes of society.

All of these facets of the religious turmoil of the early nineteenth century were manifested in the family of Joseph Smith (1805–44, the founder of the Church of Jesus Christ of Latter-day Saints, popularly called the Mormon Church), which had moved to Palmyra, in western New York, in 1816. His parents and grandparents were wary of religious denominational strife and for most of their lives refused to affiliate with any church. However, the entire family believed in the power of the divine and the occult in everyday life and his mother's brother had received the gifts of the Holy Spirit and preached the belief to others. Both of Joseph's parents received dream visions which they interpreted as forms of divine guidance. In addition, "Joseph Smith's family was typical of many early Americans who practiced various forms of Christian folk magic."[127] They were known to use divining rods, Joseph had a pair of seer stones, and he and his father used both means to hunt for buried treasure.

Joseph's career as a prophet of God began in his fifteenth year, in 1820, when he received his First Vision. While pondering the conflicting claims of the various denominations, he went into the woods seeking wisdom from God to make his way through the confusion. As he knelt in prayer,

> I was seized upon by some power which entirely overcame me, and had such an astonishing influence over me as to bind my tongue so that I could not speak. Thick darkness gathered around me, and it seemed to me for a time as if I were doomed to sudden destruction.

In this state of alarm, he saw, over his head, a pillar of light "above the brightness of the sun, which descended gradually until it fell upon me." In the light he saw two figures, "whose brightness and glory defy all description, standing above me in the air. One of them spake unto me, calling me by name, and said, pointing to the other – '*This is my*

Beloved Son, hear him!" Seizing his opportunity to put his question to Father and Son face to face, Joseph asked which church he should join, but the reply was that they were all an abomination and he should join none of them. "When I came to myself again, I found myself lying on my back, looking upward into heaven."[128] For the rest of his life, throughout the persecutions that followed, he affirmed that the vision was indeed genuine: "For I had seen a vision, I knew it, and I knew that God knew it, and I could not deny it."[129]

Three years later, on the night of 21 September 1823, Joseph received another great vision, as a light began to appear in his room, "until the room was lighter than a noonday, when immediately a personage appeared at my bedside, standing in the air, for his feet did not touch the floor." The personage identified himself as Moroni, a messenger from God, and informed Joseph that God had a mission for him. He was also told of a book, written on gold plates, buried in the ground, containing "an account of the former inhabitants of this continent, and the source from whence they sprang."[130] In addition, there were two seer stones, the Urim and the Thummim, which he should use to translate the plates, and he was shown the place where all the items were deposited.

Joseph found the items as described buried in the Hill Cumorah, between Palmyra and Manchester, New York. It was not until 1827 that he was allowed to have the plates and the stones, whereupon he set about translating the texts, written "in Egyptian characters." After many travails, he completed his task in 1829 and had the work published as *The Book of Mormon*, the story of the descendants of Jews who fled Judea just before the Babylonian conquest of Jerusalem around 600 BC. They came to North America and separated into two groups, the Nephites and the Lamanites, and they continued to worship the god of the Jews. A key moment in their history was the appearance of the resurrected Jesus among them, which led to the establishment of a North American Christian church. About the year AD, 400, the Lamanites destroyed the Nephites in warfare. Mormon, the last Nephite leader, wrote the Book of Mormon while his son Moroni, the personage who had been appearing to Joseph, deposited it and the other books in the hiding place on Hill Cumorah.

The purpose of the *Book of Mormon* was not to call for belief in its historical contents but rather to establish the credentials of Joseph Smith as a prophet of God chosen to give the world new divine revelations to accompany and complement the Christian Bible, for Smith's principal task was to establish a restored church that followed the commandments of God rather than of men. After completing his translation, Smith and his scribe, Oliver Cowdery, went down to a river to pray when another heavenly messenger appeared, John the Baptist, who laid his hands on their heads and ordained them into the priesthood of Aaron. Smith and Cowdery then baptized each other. In Smith's words, "Immediately on our coming up out of the water, after we had been baptized, we experienced great and glorious blessings from our heavenly Father." Moreover, both men were given the gift of prophecy, "We were filled with the Holy Ghost, and rejoiced in the God of our salvation."[131] With enlightened minds they understood "the true meaning" of the more mysterious passages of the Scriptures.

On 6 April 1830 the new church was organized and counted among its members most of Joseph Smith's relatives and a few neighboring families that had accepted Smith's revelations. There was much work to be done, for the return of Christ to earth was imminent and the New Jerusalem had to be constructed for the gathered-in righteous ones. For some, the gift of a new revelation of Scripture and the miraculous healings that Smith worked were convincing evidence of the authenticity of his role as God's prophet. Moreover, Smith was constantly guided by fresh revelations from God, given to "Joseph, the Seer,"[132] and the distinctive Mormon doctrines and practices began to take shape. Moreover, from the first the new church stressed the reception of the gifts of the Holy Spirit, with visions and revelations, divine healings and speaking in tongues.

However, others viewed the appearance of new Scripture as pure blasphemy and denounced them as fraudulent. Some remembered Smith as occultist treasure-hunter and were determined to get their hands on the gold plates, unaware that they had been retrieved by Moroni upon the completion of the translation. Opposition and violence were constant in the lives of Smith and his followers from the beginning even as the number of their converts in the Burned-Over District grew. However, the new church was actively evangelical and soon there were converts in Ohio and Missouri. Eventually Nauvoo, Illinois, on the Mississippi river, was chosen as the site of New Jerusalem. Mormons began converging there and the construction of a temple was begun. By 1844, Nauvoo had a population of about 10,000, surpassed in Illinois only by Chicago.

In the Mormon city of Nauvoo, Smith, as prophet and president of the church, established his theocracy. Revelations that provided elaborate ceremonies at the temple in Nauvoo and authorized polygamy, along with Smith's soaring ambitions for political power, provoked bitter disputes among the Mormons while the issue of polygamy and Smith's use of violence against his opponents led to concern by the neighboring non-Mormon population and intervention by the Illinois government. Smith and other leaders were arrested but a mob stormed the jail and murdered Joseph and his brother Hyrum in June 1844. The leadership of the Mormon Church fell to Brigham Young, who led the Latter-day Saints across the western desert to the territory of Utah, then part of Mexico, to reestablish the temple.

At the same time that western New York was being "burned over" by revivals, the same phenomenon spread into the Appalachian regions by 1800. "In a six-month period in the central counties of Kentucky, the five to seven-day communions, with a growing number of families camped on the grounds, attracted a cumulative attendance of over 100,000 people."[133] The most famous of the Appalachian revivals was held at Cane Ridge, Kentucky, in August 1801, which was primarily a Presbyterian meeting but also attended by Methodists and Baptists. Those in attendance witnessed and experienced a tremendous manifestation of "enthusiasm," perceived as a great outpouring of the Holy Spirit, an American Pentecost. The enthusiasts at Cane Ridge manifested symptoms like those of Sarah Edwards. Some of them fell to the floor as though dead, the bodies of others would receive the "jerks" while others danced, being filled with the Spirit.

The revivals continued over the next several years and created a great crisis for the

Presbyterians, who tended to be wary of such enthusiasm, but for the Methodists they signaled a time of rapid growth as settlers continued their inexorable expansion beyond the Appalachians. Methodists in America had firmly embraced John Wesley's doctrine of Christian perfection, which taught that justification, the first stage, was followed by sanctification, that is, the inward experience of the Spirit of God. Sometimes called the "second blessing," it often led to what critics denounced as enthusiasm, prompting Wesley to write in defense of "good enthusiasm."[134] In the 1770s, those in attendance at Methodist religious services found their bodies shaking and trembling and fell into profuse tears with joyful shouting, much to the disapproval of ministers in other denominations. Enthusiastic states were easily incorporated into the Wesleyan system and as the frontier steadily rolled westward in the nineteenth century, Methodism drew in those attracted to a more experiential religion.

After the cataclysmic American Civil War, a great rift appeared in Methodism. During the war much of the severe Wesleyan penitential system had been dropped, along with the revivals and after the war many of the congregations disdained reviving what now seemed to be antiquated, primitive practices. However, others were intent on reviving "old-time religion" and formed associations "for the promotion of holiness, … and make common supplication for the descent of the Spirit upon ourselves, the church, the nation, and the world."[135] The second half of the nineteenth century saw the growth of this Holiness Movement, especially among enthusiastic Methodists, but Baptists and others were also in their numbers, along with some Quakers who recognized the similarity of the doctrines of George Fox and John Wesley. The leaders of the Holiness Movement, arising out of the Wesleyan tradition and thus familiar with Wesley's *Christian Library*, were well aware that their second blessing was essentially a mystical experience and they acknowledged Tauler, John of the Cross and Ruusbroec as their spiritual ancestors. However, they especially identified themselves with Quietists like Molinos, Madame Guyon, and Fénelon, whose lives and works they abridged and published.[136]

One aspect of the Holiness Movement was Keswick spirituality, which grew out of a series of conferences held in England, at Keswick, beginning in 1875. Also called "higher life spirituality," its teachings were in agreement with what most of the Desert Fathers and mystics of the Western Middle Ages had taught. Humans must first acknowledge that "our individual self is entirely and completely under the power of sin" and have a "deep conviction of the entire corruption of our nature." The believer must then "consent to die to every fleshly desire" and to "hand over the fleshly deeds of the body to the Spirit for mortification." Thus God becomes the "all-in-all" in the life of the believer, who now obeys the Holy Spirit in all things. This "dethronement of self" and "saying 'No' to self" leads to sanctification, which in turn unites the believer with Christ, becoming "a man 'in Christ.'" Keswick spirituality taught that sanctification resulted in one's being filled with the Holy Spirit although the exact nature of this varied according to the person. The Keswickians traced their teaching back to the New Testament and the Apostolic Church, affirming that "there have always been saints who have seen it clearly," although they spurned the medieval period and its "prevailing ignorance." The Medieval Church was equated with the

Roman Catholic Church and was thus rejected in the same spirit that led them to hail Madame Guyon for her holiness teaching, but to publish her autobiography with such modifications to the text that one might never know that she was Roman Catholic.[137]

By the latter nineteenth century, however, Methodism was divided into two factions. Some, especially those in the northern United States, were becoming more urban, modern and mainstream in their religion and began to separate from what they regarded to be the fanaticism of their more rural brethren in the South and West. By the last two decades of the nineteenth century, the Holiness Movement began to cut a great divide in Methodism and the denomination was forced either to accept or reject the Holiness Movement. At its 1894 General Conference, the southern Methodist Church repudiated the movement, prompting perhaps up to 100,000 to decamp to form twenty-three separate Holiness denominations by 1900, in addition to independent congregations.[138]

However, just as the Holiness churches were in the process of coalescing after their ouster from Methodism, a movement emerged elaborating Wesley's second blessing, making it explicit that after sanctification there was the third blessing of the baptism of the Holy Spirit. Prominent in their services were all of the ecstatic features of the Cane Ridge revival. Moreover, just after the turn of the twentieth century, some began to emphasize one particular grace given to those who were baptized in the Holy Spirit – glossolalia, or speaking in tongues. Glossolalia had appeared in London in 1831 when members of the Edward Irving's Presbyterian Church began speaking in tongues, evidence that they had received that baptism. Irving praised speaking in tongues as the primary and "standing sign" of having received the Holy Spirit. This charismatic gift was also evident in services at the YMCA meetings held in Victoria Hall by Dwight Moody as well as in the great Welsh Revival of Evan Roberts in 1904, which was widely publicized within the Holiness Movement.[139]

Glossolalia had already appeared among some Holiness groups in the 1890s, but it was one of the ejected Holiness Methodist ministers, Charles Fox Parham in Topeka, Kansas, who began to single out speaking in tongues as the initial and distinguishing mark of having received the baptism of the Holy Spirit. At a service on the evening of 31 December 1900 to see in the new century, Parham's own students began speaking in foreign tongues and a few days later he did as well. As he described it, he was praying to receive the blessing of tongues and God

> distinctly made it clear to me that He raised me up and trained me to declare this mighty truth to the world, and if I was willing to stand for it, with all the persecutions, hardships, trials, slander, scandal that it would entail, He would give me the blessing. And I said "Lord I will, if You will just give me this blessing." Right then there came a slight twist in my throat, a glory fell over me and I began to worship God in the Sweedish tongue, which later changed to other languages and continued till morning.[140]

Newspapers spread reports of the events and crowds of the curious descended on Parham in Topeka. He embarked on a great revival tour and by 1905 had settled in

Houston, Texas, where he opened his Bible Training School and continued teaching the speaking of tongues as the essential gift of the Holy Spirit.

One of the students who came to Parham's school was William J. Seymour. After leaving his native Louisiana, Seymour settled for a time in Indianapolis and joined Holiness churches there, attracted by their rigorous form of Christianity, and was eventually ordained. While in Jackson, Mississippi, in 1905, Seymour met Lucy Farrow, a woman who had worked as a servant in Parham's house in Kansas and had there received the gift of tongues. The news of the Welsh Revival was running through the Holiness groups and Seymour took himself to Houston for study under Parham himself. Parham was far from being a racial egalitarian but he agreed to take on the African-American Seymour as a student. Texas law at that time prohibited blacks and whites attending classes together, so Seymour audited the lectures by sitting in a chair in the hallway outside the open door of the classroom.

Several months later Seymour was invited to Los Angeles to become pastor of a fledgling Holiness mission. Upon his arrival he began teaching Parham's doctrine on the necessity of glossolalia and was promptly barred from the church by the authorities of the Holiness Association to which it belonged. Undeterred, Seymour moved his preaching into a private home, where, on the night of 12 April 1906, after a long bout of fervent prayer,

> a sphere of white hot brilliance seemed to appear, draw near, and fall upon [Seymour]. Divine love melted his heart; he sank to the floor seemingly unconscious. Words of deep healing and encouragement spoke to him. As from a great distance he heard unutterable words being uttered – was it angelic adoration and praise? Slowly he realized the indescribably lovely language belonged to him, pouring from his innermost being. A broad smile wreathed his face.[141]

At last Seymour had received his own Pentecost experience, which many others shared. Reports spread and crowds began gathering at the home, forcing a move to larger quarters, to an abandoned church on Azusa Street in downtown Los Angeles.

Led by Seymour's preaching, the rehabilitated church was packed with worshippers of all races who fell into ecstasy and spoke in tongues. For Seymour, this was the second Pentecost awaited by many in the Holiness movement, a recreation of the first Pentecost, including its international and multi-racial witnesses and participants in this fresh manifestation of the Holy Spirit. Local newspapers published sensational accounts of the happenings on Azusa Street while Seymour disseminated his own interpretation within the Holiness movement by means of his mission newspaper. For the next three and a half years, the continuing revival received visitors from around the world. Parham himself came to observe what his student had wrought and was appalled. He detested highly emotional services, with "all the chattering and jabbering, wind-sucking, holy-dancing-rollerism"[142] and at Azusa Street he found ample evidence of what he termed "the unintelligent, crude negroisms of the Southland, and laying it on the Holy Ghost."[143] Of special significance to him was his belief that the gift of tongues was manifested by speaking in known foreign languages (xenoglossia), not in speaking unknown tongues, which he deemed "babbling" done by "working of the chin, or the message of the throat."[144] He believed that the vast majority of "the people professing Pentecost are either hypnotized or spook-driven."[145] Parham thus lost all credibility with those who had been baptized by the Holy Spirit on Azusa Street and relations between Parham and Seymour were forever ruptured. However, the two men remain forever associated as the joint founders of the organized Pentecostal movement, for Parham supplied the distinctive doctrine that was followed by Seymour's energizing spark.

The Azusa Street Revival galvanized Americans awaiting the second Pentecost as well as the glossolalists who strove to take their churches over to Parham's teaching. Failing this, they defected from resistant Holiness congregations and formed their own churches, usually bearing the word Pentecostal somewhere in their names. Before long they formed themselves into clusters and associations in various parts of the United States and in 1914 the largest of the predominantly white Pentecostal denominations, the Assemblies of God, was formed by ministers from various denominations and congregations. What emerged as the largest black American Pentecostal church, the Church of God in Christ, was originally a Holiness denomination that predated the Azusa Street revival by nine years. However, the Azusa Street events forced it to take a stand on the question of Parham's doctrine of glossolalia. Opponents of tongue-speaking lost and departed, leaving the church firmly Pentecostal.

TWENTIETH-CENTURY CATHOLIC MYSTICISM

As a result of the suppression of mysticism in Spain and France, the nineteenth century was "singularly barren"[146] of mysticism among Catholics but as the century drew to a close mystics again became prominent. In France, Elizabeth of the Trinity (1880–1906) was born not far from Bourges to a military family. Her father, Captain Joseph Catez, was a veteran of the Franco-Prussian war of 1870 and had been taken captive by the Prussians, later being named Chevalier of the Légion d'Honneur. In 1879 he married Marie Rolland, the daughter of a retired army officer. After Elizabeth was born to them the family moved to Dijon, in Burgundy. Elizabeth's father died not long after she celebrated her seventh birthday, leaving Mme. Catez to manage for her two daughters alone.

The little Elizabeth of that age was remarkable to her friends for "her recollection when at prayer, the purity of her ardent gaze, and a truly remarkable energy in overcoming her impressions" and she had already proclaimed that "I am going to be a nun."[147] At the age of ten she emerged from church after having received her first Communion and declared, "I am no longer hungry; Our Lord has fed me," and often after prayer she would exclaim, "Oh, how He has fed me!"[148] By the age of twelve, she was hearing God talk to her at church and around fourteen, she was certain that she would be a Carmelite, declaring, "I am thinking how happy I shall be when Carmel opens its doors to me." Elizabeth herself stated that one day, after she had received

Communion, "it seemed to be that I heard pronounced in my soul the word: *Carmel*, and I no longer thought of anything but of shutting myself up behind its grilles." It was about this time that she vowed her virginity to Jesus.[149]

Her mother gave grudging permission for Elizabeth to enter the Carmelite convent in Dijon once she was twenty-one and in August 1901 Elizabeth became a Carmelite postulant in Dijon, receiving her monastic name, Elizabeth of the Trinity. Even before she entered the convent, Elizabeth was hearing God's voice "in the depths of her heart"[150] and when she began reading her spiritual mother, St. Teresa of Ávila, on prayer and interior mortification, she recognized the experience of sublime ecstasy that God had given her, in which "the soul forgets everything and sees only its God."[151]

Life in Carmel was everything she expected. In the more than 250 letters that she wrote from the cloister she poured out her joy: "I have found my Heaven on earth in my dear solitude in Carmel, where I am alone with God alone."[152] At Carmel she found all the things she craved, silence, solitude and God: "In silence and solitude, we live here alone with God alone. Everything speaks of Him here, we feel Him everywhere, so living, so present."[153] In the same manner as Brother Lawrence, Sister Elizabeth was constantly in the presence of God: "Oh, you see, everything is delightful in Carmel, we find God at the wash just as at prayer. Everywhere there is only Him. We live Him, breathe Him."[154] She wrote to her aunts that she "spent a whole day at the stove. I didn't go into ecstasy while holding the handle of the frying pan … but I believed in the divine presence of the Master who was in the midst of us."[155] God was equally present in her cell, "which I call my 'little paradise' because it is entirely filled with Him for whom all live in Heaven."[156] For Elizabeth, God was truly everywhere: "All nature seems so full of God to me: the wind blowing in the tall trees, the little birds singing, the beautiful blue sky, everything speaks to me of Him."[157]

For Elizabeth, this union, this same experience of living constantly in the presence of God, of being filled with God, could be found by everyone, not just a cloistered Carmelite, and she encouraged her correspondents that they, too, could attain it. She exhorted her sister, "Oh! let yourself be wholly caught, wholly invaded by His divine life." To her friend Françoise she wrote, "Ah, if you only knew [Jesus] a little as your Sabeth does! He *fascinates*, He sweeps you away; under His gaze the horizon becomes so beautiful, so vast, so luminous." She added, "Since you need to live beyond yourself, live in Him; it's so simple. And then be good."[158] Françoise, even though not in the cloister, could still create her own interior Carmel: "You must build a little cell within your soul as I do. Remember that God is there and enter it from time to time."[159] She wrote to another friend that one who had this communion was indeed a Carmelite whether in the cloister or out: "You carry this heaven within your soul, my little Germaine, you can be a Carmelite already, for Jesus recognizes the Carmelite from *within*, by her soul."[160] Elizabeth came to believe this sort of exhortation was her mission once she entered heaven, "to [help souls] go out of themselves to cling to God by a wholly simple and loving movement, and to keep them in this great silence within that will allow God to communicate Himself to them and transform them into Himself."[161]

Sister Elizabeth had little time to enjoy her Carmelite heaven on earth. She contracted tuberculosis and then developed Addison's disease, leaving her scarcely able to eat or drink. In her final months, her interior knowledge of God sustained her: "it is this intimacy with Him 'within' that has been the beautiful sun illuminating my life, making it already an anticipated Heaven; it is what sustains me today in my suffering."[162] In letters written in her last few days of life, she continued her teaching: "How serious this life is: each minute is given us in order to 'root' us deeper in God ... I wish I could make souls understand, tell them the vanity, the emptiness of anything not done for God."[163] Elizabeth's prioress recorded her last moments on the morning of 6 November 1906, "Sister Elizabeth of the Trinity seemed in ecstasy rather than in her death agony. The expression of her face was wonderfully beautiful, so that we could not take our eyes off her as she seemed already gazing at the eternal hills."[164]

In Poland the mystical life of Sister Faustina Kowalska (1905–38) is almost a return to the fourteenth century, for she lived almost constantly in the presence of God and communicated freely with Jesus Christ, who not only revealed to her her great mission in life but also guided her in her daily life. Like Catherine of Siena, she was given the invisible stigmata and she, too, was led to the religious life at a very early age. She experienced the spiritual espousal and was even allowed to hold the tiny infant Jesus in her arms. At the command of Jesus and of her spiritual directors and superiors, she wrote the remarkably detailed record of her spiritual life in her diaries, which comprises over 1800 entries on more than 600 pages of the English translation.[165]

She was born Helena Kowalska in the small village of Glogowiec near the manufacturing city of Łodz in central Poland. She was only seven years old when she first heard God's voice in her soul calling her to enter the religious life. As the poorly educated third of ten children born to parents of modest means, her prospects for entering a convent were not promising. When she was born, her part of Poland belonged to the Russian Empire and schools opened only just before Poland's independence in 1919. Her education lasted a mere three terms before she was turned out to make room for the younger students now crowding into the schools and she began working as a maid.

Helena could not escape her vocation, however, for Jesus appeared to her at a dance, asking her how long she was going to keep putting him off and directing her to go to Warsaw to enter a convent there. She was led to the congregation of Our Lady of Mercy, which agreed to admit her without a dowry but she still had to pay for her wardrobe. Utterly confident in her calling, she worked as a maid and saved for a year until she had the necessary sum, and was able to enter that convent in August 1925. The lack of time for prayer distressed her and she considered leaving for a more ascetic order but Jesus appeared to her and stopped her. In April 1926, as Sister Maria Faustina, she received the habit and in 1933 she took her perpetual vows as a nun. In her order Faustina worked as gardener, cook and gatekeeper in fourteen different houses in both Poland and Lithuania. In 1936 she had contracted tuberculosis and died in October 1938, just past the age of thirty-three.

Faustina's diary reveals her almost constant contact and communication with the world of the divine: "My spirit communicates with God without any word being spoken. I am aware that He is living in me and I in Him."[166] Normally she heard the voice of Jesus speaking to her but she also frequently discerned the presence of the three persons of the Trinity within her. The Virgin Mary came to her often both as a voice and in visions, as did other saints and angels, especially St. Michael. Her constant theme is feeling completely immersed in the presence of God, pervaded by the presence of God, drowned in God, "extraordinarily fused with God."[167] She struggled to describe the ineffable, writing "No one will understand what I experience in that splendid palace of my soul where I abide constantly with my Beloved. No exterior thing hinders my union with God."[168] On another occasion, she began, "God descends to the soul and unites it to himself in a way that ... here, I must be silent, for I cannot describe what the soul experiences."[169] She was most desirous to "know and fathom who God is," but a voice told her, "Who God is in His Essence, no one will fathom."[170] In one moment in union with God, "I learn more than during long hours of intellectual inquiry and meditation. These are sudden lights which permit me to know things as God sees them, regarding matters of both the interior and the exterior world."[171] Her most common description of her union is fire: "I was all afire, but without burning up ... I felt some kind of fire in my heart ... I was so enveloped in the great interior fire of God's love ... I feel I am all aflame. ... Today, a living flame of divine love entered my soul."[172]

Sister Faustina had lessons regarding mysticism for her readers. Silence was fundamental, "in order to hear the voice of God, one has to have silence in one's soul and to keep silence; not a gloomy silence, but an interior silence ... A talkative soul is empty inside."[173] Like with so many other mystics, she said that a "noble and delicate soul, even the most simple, but one of delicate sensibilities, sees God in everything, finds Him everywhere, and knows how to find Him in even the most hidden things."[174] At the same time, "I have never sought God in some far-off place, but within myself. It is in the depths of my own being that I commune with my God."[175]

Sister Faustina's visions were not given to her simply for her spiritual enjoyment, for God called her to a mission, to be his Apostle of Mercy. On the evening of 22 February 1931, while in her cell, she saw Jesus: "One hand (was) raised in the gesture of blessing, the other was touching the garment at the breast. From beneath the garment, slightly drawn aside at the breast, there were emanating two large rays, one red, the other pale." Jesus then commanded her to have a picture made of what she had seen, with the signature, "Jesus, I trust in You." His wish was that "this image be venerated, first in your chapel, and (then) throughout the world,"[176] as well as that a Feast of Mercy be instituted, to be celebrated on the first Sunday after Easter. On a later occasion, after she had directed the painting of the image, it was revealed to her that "the two rays denote Blood and Water. The pale ray stands for the Water which makes souls righteous. The red ray stands for the Blood which is the life of souls."[177] She also came to understand that there should be a new religious order, "a group of souls who would beg for His mercy," or as the Virgin Mary told her, "Your lives must be like mine: quiet and hidden, in unceasing union with God, pleading for humanity and preparing the world for the second coming of God."[178]

Sister Faustina also received numerous revelations of God's displeasure with Poland in which he threatened destruction of Warsaw as well as of the country. She died 5 October 1938, less than a year before the German and Soviet invasions of Poland that led to the outbreak of the Second World War. Moreover, in 1978 the devotion to the Divine Mercy was announced by the Polish pope, John Paul II, who also beatified Sister Faustina in 1993 and declared her canonization as a saint of the church in 2000. There is now in existence a group of contemplatives following the devotion to the Divine Mercy.

If the life of Faustina Kowalska is reminiscent of female mystics of the thirteenth or fourteenth century, the career of the French Jesuit priest Pierre Teilhard de Chardin (1881–1955) is imaginable only in the twentieth century. Teilhard blended an ebullient pantheistic nature mysticism, his personal mystical experiences, firm Christian faith and devotion to modern science to produce a unique view of a dynamic universe steadily evolving in the direction of greater complexity and greater consciousness, ultimately arriving at the Omega point, which is Christ, the Cosmic Christ.

Teilhard was born in the Auvergne region of central France, the son of aristocratic and devout parents. He was educated at home before being sent to a Jesuit boarding school at age ten, which led him to enter the novitiate of that order at age eighteen. He took his initial vows in 1901 and then had to continue his theological training on the English Channel Island of Jersey because of newly-enacted French laws restricting religious orders. From his earliest days Teilhard had been fascinated with nature and matter, or "what 'shone' at the heart of Matter." He contemplated his "Iron God," for iron seemed so hard, heavy, tough, durable. He became fascinated with geology, which is "the primacy of material matter, 'Matter-Matter', expressed in Mineral and Rock." He admitted that, "like the pagan I worship a God who can be touched; and I do indeed touch him" and he wished to "touch God in the world of matter."[179] During World War I, he wrote, "my taste for the earth is strange, and, at first sight, most anti-Christian," for he was caught "between two passions I really believe to be to some degree united in me, and which in any case I certainly experience – a passion for the world, and a passion for God."[180] In the end, Teilhard could say, "I looked around and I saw, as though in an ecstasy, that *through all nature I was immersed in God.*"[181]

After teaching chemistry and physics at the Jesuit school in Cairo for three years, he tore himself away from the monuments of Egypt to return to theological studies in England, where he was ordained a priest in 1911. During this time Teilhard also studied paleontology while heartily embracing the theory of evolution and was involved in scientific expeditions regarding early humans in Spain. In England he was excited to have a role in the finds in Sussex in 1913 that produced Piltdown Man, one of the great scientific hoaxes. Indeed, some have pointed to Teilhard himself as being partly responsible for the hoax, either as a prank or as an effort to plant clearly bogus evidence that would expose what he himself believed to have been a hoax, but there is no definitive evidence to support either contention.

Teilhard's studies came to an end with the outbreak of the First World War. He was called to military duty and served as a stretcher-bearer in a front-line unit from January 1915 to the end of the war. He was in the heart of the fighting on the Western Front, at Ypres, the Marne, and Verdun. During the almost four years of service on the front, Teilhard was awarded several military citations, including one for having "deliberately entered a trench under heavy bombardment to bring back a casualty," and after the war he was appointed a Chevalier de la Légion d'Honneur.[182]

Teilhard was certainly no mountain-top mystic, for even in the midst of the war, he found God: "more than ever I believe that life is beautiful in the grimmest circumstances – when you look around God is always there."[183] In October of 1917, he wrote to his cousin, "I have an almost physical sensation of God catching me up and clasping me more closely … it is unbelievably good to bury oneself deep in God."[184] Even under the extreme circumstances of war, he took himself to nature whenever possible for solitary walks in the woods and fields, often at night to avoid drawing fire (during one "noctambulation" he remarked, "I was favoured by a wonderful moon"[185]).

In the midst of the carnage of war he formulated his pantheistic-mystical vision of a cosmos evolving towards God, which appeared in short works such as *Cosmic Life* and *The Mystical Milieu*.[186] In *Christ in the World of Matter* he described three mystical experiences of a priest, ostensibly a friend of Teilhard's but almost certainly it was the author himself. On one occasion, in a church, "a picture representing Christ offering his heart to men," which he was contemplating appeared to be transformed, with Christ being surrounded by "a vibrant atmosphere," and indeed "the entire universe was vibrant!" He found himself gazing into the eyes of Christ;

> the pupils of Christ's eyes, which had become abysses of fiery, fascinating life, suddenly I beheld rising up from the depths of those same eyes what seemed like a cloud, blurring and bending all that variety I have been describing to you. Little by little an extraordinary expression, of great intensity, spread over the diverse shades of meaning which the eyes revealed, first of all permeating them and then finally absorbing them all … And I stood dumbfounded.[187]

On another occasion he observed a consecrated communion host displayed in a church. The host appeared to expand as it

> enveloped me, passed over me, overran everything … it penetrated objects at the core of their being, at a level more profound even than their own life. … So, through the mysterious expansion of the host the whole world had become incandescent, had itself become like a single giant host.[188]

The third vision was one in which the priest was carrying the consecrated host in a small box, a pyx. He ate the host, which seemed to become part of his own flesh while yet remaining outside of him. He wanted to possess the host but it withdrew from him, always ahead of him. "By my withdrawal into myself and my continual purification of my being I was penetrating ever more deeply into it," yet "I was losing myself in it without ever being able to grasp it" as "its centre was *receding from me as it drew me on*." When he was able to put his hands on it, he found that he was not holding the host itself but rather "one or other of the thousand entities which make up our lives: a suffering, a joy, a task, a friend to love or to console." He wrote, "I will not dwell on the feeling of rapture it produced in me by this revelation of the universe placed between Christ and myself like a magnificent prey."[189]

During the war, Teilhard came to understand his task in life, "to impart it as much as possible to others – the sort of mysticism that makes one seek passionately for God in the heart of every substance and every action." He understood "how much the world demands that 'those who see' should commit themselves integrally, whatever they may sometimes experience themselves or learn by hearsay, to the side of primacy of spirit."[190]

With the war over, Teilhard continued his scientific studies. He graduated from the Sorbonne with certificates in geology, zoology and botany, and gained his doctorate from the same institution in 1922. He began teaching geology at the Institut Catholique in Paris and accompanied a paleontological expedition to China in 1923. However, by the time he returned from the East his academic career was in ruins. Teilhard's ecclesiastical superiors in Rome and in the Jesuit Order had become increasingly concerned about his ardent defense of evolution and their patience with him snapped in 1922 when he wrote a piece attempting to explain the theological conception of original sin in the light of recent scientific discoveries that cast doubt on the historical existence of Adam, Eve and the Garden of Eden, in which he laid out "new possible ways of conceiving original sin." He concluded, "The earthly paradise never existed."[191] Bound by his vow of obedience, Teilhard did what was demanded of him, promising never again to disseminate his views on that topic. Nonetheless, his license to teach at the Institut Catholique was revoked and never restored. As a Jesuit, he was required to submit any manuscript to his superiors for permission to publish and the necessary permission was withheld for almost all of his philosophical works.

Teilhard's scientific career continued, however, and his scientific writings fill ten volumes. He made repeated trips to China, served as the geologist on the team that discovered Sinanthropus ("Peking Man") and for a time he headed the Chinese Geological Survey. In 1937 Villanova University in the United States awarded him the prestigious Mendel Medal for his accomplishments in science and in 1947 he was promoted to the position of Officer in the Légion d'Honneur as recognition that he "may now be regarded, in the fields of palaeontology and geology, as one of the chief ornaments of French science."[192] After Teilhard's death his philosophical works on Christ, the cosmos and humanity could at last be published freely and the entire world could finally read of the vision that he saw so clearly even in the trenches of the Western Front.

It is not hard to understand the reluctance of his superiors to approve the publication of works wherein he revealed his pantheism, "properly understood," arguing that humans are naturally "drawn to the One, that is the Whole" and lamented that "the great mass of those who follow the religion of the Whole have abandoned Christianity." Christianity had no choice, in his judgment, but to take that religion and "overcome it, take possession of it, and assimilate it."[193] Teilhard's ability to see God everywhere and in all things gave him a pantheistic love of matter. Out of his reverence for "holy matter"[194] he attacked the typical mystical contrast between matter and spirit, for he felt that he could touch God in the world of matter. In *The Spiritual Power of Matter* he wrote of a man's experience of the overwhelming "Thing," in which he had an "irresistible rapture." The Thing identified itself as "matter" and commanded the man to "steep yourself in the sea of matter ... bathe yourself in the ocean of matter," and told him, "Never, if you work to live and to grow, will you be able to say to matter: 'I have seen enough of you,'" adding, "Purity does not lie in separation from, but in a deeper penetration of the universe." At the end, "God was shining forth from the world of matter whose waves were carrying up to him the world of spirit."[195]

TWENTIETH-CENTURY MYSTICAL WRITERS ON MYSTICISM

In addition to the reappearance of prominent Catholic mystics in the twentieth century, the early years of the century also witnessed the rise of serious studies on mysticism in the main stream of Christianity in the English-speaking world. William Ralph Inge published *Christian Mysticism* in 1899, William James delivered his Gifford Lectures, published as *The Varieties of Religious Experience,* in 1901–2 and Baron Friedrich von Hügel's *The Mystical Element of Religion as Studied in Saint Catherine of Genoa and Her Friends* appeared in 1908. However, the book credited by a contemporary reviewer with having "done more to popularise the subject [of mysticism] than any other single work"[196] was *Mysticism* (1911), the work of Evelyn Underhill (1875–1941), remembered by a friend as "slight and thin she was … and not very tall, her body carrying her spirit with as little fuss about it as possible."[197] While lacking the authority of high academic credentials, by dint of her intelligence, determination and spirituality she came to dominate the study of mysticism in England in the first two decades of the twentieth century. Michael Ramsey, Archbishop of Canterbury, regarded her as one who did as much as anyone in the Church of England to "help people to grasp the priority of prayer in the Christian life and the place of contemplative prayer within it."[198]

Underhill's literary production is staggering, for "in thirty-nine years she produced forty books, editions, and collections, and more than three hundred and fifty articles, essays, and reviews."[199] Equally amazing is her list of "firsts":

> [S]he was the first woman to lecture in theology at an Oxford college, the first woman to lecture Anglican clergy, and one of the first women to be included in Church of England commissions. These accomplishments, along with her work as a retreat leader, made Evelyn Underhill a prominent figure in her day.[200]

Evelyn's early life gave no hint that she would achieve such renown as a mystic and spiritual leader. She was the only child of the London barrister Sir Arthur Underhill and his wife Lucy and she received only a nominal religious upbringing (although the Church of England could claim her uncle and cousin among its priests and bishops). By age seventeen Underhill declared herself a Socialist, admired Jesus for his ethics and care for "the weak ones," denied the inspiration of the Bible and questioned the need to "worry" an omniscient God with prayers. When she married it was to another barrister, Hubert Stuart Moore, whose disinterest in religion matched that of her parents.

Study at King's College for Women expanded her knowledge of languages, literature and philosophy, in particular the Neoplatonic mystic Plotinus, and in the last few years of the nineteenth century Underhill had passed from her period of "very comfortable"[201] agnosticism into a philosophical theism. For a brief time she dabbled in the occult and for a year was a member of the Hermetic Society of the Golden Dawn, which sought experiential contact with Ultimate Reality.

However, when her experience came, in February 1907, it was a powerful one that convinced her of the truth of Roman Catholicism and prompted in her a desire to convert to that faith. The objections of her husband Hubert, whom she married in July of that same year, caused her to delay her conversion, which was then obviated by the publication of a papal encyclical that same year condemning in absolute terms Modernism (the effort to reinterpret Christianity to conform with modern scientific notions), a movement to which she was devoted. Unable to become a Catholic and unwilling to embrace the Anglican Church, Underhill remained aloof from the organized religions which had gained little regard in her eyes.

However, her spiritual encounters with the divine continued unabated. She later reported that during the next twenty years she had "what seemed to be vivid experiences of God"[202] and "several vivid calls-back."[203] Her letters of spiritual advice in the years following her "conversion" experience of the truth of Catholicism hint at some of these revelations. One of the first was of "the exalted and indescribable beauty in the most squalid places," which left so strong an after-flavor that even several years later its memory was still so real that she felt "to look upon it as wrong would be an unthinkable absurdity."[204] It is not surprising that during these years she exalted personal religious experience: "Direct personal experience is the only possible basis [of religion]; and if you will trust yours absolutely you are safe."[205]

Underhill's "conversion" experience came as she had just begun her career as a novelist (1904–9) and her three novels published during these years all concerned themes of mysticism. That experience also set her to work on *Mysticism*, her masterful treatment of the subject published in 1911, which reflected her own theocentric and Neoplatonic spiritual state and in which she relied on her own mystical experiences for an understanding of the mystics of the past. The work brought her fame as well as the spiritual direction of more souls who, inspired by her views, sought her guidance in their spiritual quests. She continued her work as a "populariser and defender of mysticism"[206] in the years before the First World War with *The Mystic Way* (1913), a vigorous presentation of her belief that Jesus was the greatest of mystics and that earliest Christianity was essentially a mystical religion, and *Practical Mysticism* (1914), an encouragement to all to embrace contemplation. For about fifteen years after the publication of *Mysticism* Underhill also produced a number of works on her favorite mystics (Ruusbroec, especially dear to her, Jacopone da Todi and Angela of Foligno, Richard Rolle, Walter Hilton and Julian of Norwich, the *Cloud of Unknowing* and Marguerite Porete, the Indian mystic Kabir and the Neoplatonist Plotinus) as well as translations of some of their works.

During the war Underhill used her linguistic skills as a translator while working in Naval Intelligence and by war's end her own continuing spiritual evolution was evident. Her pronounced anti-institutional bias began to wane and she was coming to see Christianity as a religion that functioned best in community. By 1921 she quietly had become an active member of the Church of England, had joined the Spiritual Entente founded by the Italian Franciscan nun Sorella Maria (an ecumenical body whose members sought the presence of God within their own religious homes), and she had found a spiritual director in Friedrich von Hügel.

Underhill had known von Hügel, the foremost Catholic theologian in England, for more than a decade and now, under his direction, her spiritual life took a decided Christocentric turn. Somehow von Hügel "compelled me to experience Christ" and then her "whole religious life and experience seem centered with increasing vividness on our Lord … Sometimes the sense of His Presence is so vivid, I wonder what will happen next."[207] In October 1922 Evelyn had one of her most profound experiences when a voice spoke "one short thing" to her (unfortunately she provided no further details), in both English and Latin, whose "effect on me was terrific. Sort of nailed me to the floor for half-an-hour, which went in a flash. I felt definitely called-out and settled, once for all."[208] Seven months later she wrote, "Thou has shown thyself to me, O Christ," adding, "It all goes back to the day I heard the Voice."[209] Underhill, a student of the psychology of religion fully aware of the phenomenon of auto-suggestion, was in constant self-doubt concerning her experiences, fearful that they were the creations of her own mind – as she asked von Hügel's advice on the matter of "the Voice," in exasperation she added, "There are times when I wish I had never heard of psychology."[210] Von Hügel assured her that he believed her experience to be genuine but she remained unsure of how much reliance could be placed in experiences and even wrote to a correspondent, "You have been relying too much on experience, and not enough on the facts of faith."[211] Nonetheless Underhill's personal notebooks of the mid-1920s are filled with references to her experiences – her constant awareness of being in the presence of God, of being plunged into an ocean of love and of a golden glow that forced its way into her prayer, "and within this glow of God one sees Jesus."[212]

Underhill's life as a very public advocate of mysticism was closing. She published her last work on the subject, *Mystics of the Church*, in 1925 and for the next ten years she was devoted to directing spiritual retreats and publishing her retreat notes as well as other works on prayer. This phase of her life culminated with her last major book *Worship* (1936), a scholarly investigation of the history of the development of the Christian liturgy, that is, an expression of Christian communities' collective prayer to God.

Underhill's activities in the last years of her life were limited by increasingly poor health, especially asthma, but they were also marked by her last conversion, this time to pacifism, which she viewed as the ultimate expression of Christian love. She never swerved from its principles even after the outbreak of the Second World War in September 1939 or as German bombs fell around her during the early days of the Blitz. She died in June 1941, remembered as a mystic who "seemed to radiate such a calm,"[213] whose face glowed with a discernible aura as "light simply streamed from her face."[214]

Her friend and biographer assessed her life by stating, "She was experiencing all the time what it meant to bring people into communion with God ... primarily her greatest gift to us was her sense of God."[215]

In the same year that Evelyn Underhill died, the American Trappist monastery of Gethsemeni, Kentucky, welcomed a new postulant, Thomas Merton, who in many ways was Underhill's continuator as an acclaimed promoter of mysticism, contemplation and prayer. Merton (1915–68) is an ideal coda for an examination of Christian mystics. As a Trappist monk in twentieth-century America, he was a member of a contemplative monastic order who had available to him all the modern means of communication with the world and in his own lifetime gained international recognition as both a mystic and a writer on mysticism. Moreover, he was well-informed on Christian history and equally well-acquainted with the writings of the principal writers on mysticism in the Catholic tradition, from the New Testament and the Desert Fathers through the Middle Ages and the Modern period, including the mystics of the Eastern Orthodox Church.

There are no typical hagiographical stories from Merton's youth to indicate that he would become either monk or mystic. As Merton told his own story in his autobiography, *The Seven Storey Mountain*, he was born in France to an artist father from New Zealand and an American mother. Soon after his birth in 1915 the family moved to America but in 1921 his mother died of stomach cancer. His father then led Merton and his younger brother on an odyssey, to Bermuda, to Long Island and to France, where he began his formal schooling in a lycée. In 1928 they all packed off to England and Merton entered public school in Oakham in Leicestershire. However, in 1931 his father died of brain cancer and Merton found himself

> without a home, without a family, without a country, without a father, apparently without any friends, without any interior peace or confidence or light or understanding of my own – without God, too, without God, without heaven, without grace, without anything.[216]

After a poorly-spent year at Clare College, Cambridge, Merton took ship to America, possibly distancing himself from a recently resolved paternity suit,[217] and enrolled at Columbia University. He received his B.A. degree in 1938 and then began work on his M.A. degree in English Literature. Merton, who had not received a religious education of any depth, although he had occasionally attended Quaker services enjoying the silence and peace, now found that his reading was taking him into religion and especially mysticism. His introduction to the Catholic Church and its mystics came from reading medieval philosophy and his love of William Blake, on whom he wrote his Master's thesis at Columbia, led him more deeply into mysticism.

By 1938 the foundation for Merton's conversion to the Catholic Church and mystical religion had been laid. He was prompted to begin his conversion by a strong urge to go to Mass: "It was something quite new and strange, this voice that seemed to prompt me, this firm, growing interior conviction of what I needed to do."[218] This was followed by another prompting that led him to contact a priest to begin taking

Catholic instruction. He converted and, as he took his first Communion, "[God] called out to me from His own immense depths."[219] Merton later recalled, "my conversion to Catholicism began with the realization of the presence of God *in this present life*, in the world and in myself."[220]

As he began to feel a call to become a monk and a priest, he went on holiday in Cuba. In the church of San Francisco in Havana, as the Creed was begun,

> something went off inside me like a thunderclap and without seeing anything or apprehending anything extraordinary through any of my senses (my eyes were open on only precisely what was there, the church), I knew with the most absolute and unquestionable certainty that before me, between me and the altar, somewhere in the center of the church, up in the air (or any other place because in no place), but directly before my eyes, or directly present to some apprehension or other of mine which was above that of the sense, was at the same time God in all His essence, all His power, God in the flesh and God in Himself and God surrounded by the radiant faces of the thousand million uncountable numbers of saints contemplating His glory and Praising His Holy Name. And so the unshakeable certainty, the clear and immediate knowledge that heaven was right in front of me, struck me like a thunderbolt and went through me like a flash of lightning and seemed to lift me clean up off the earth.[221]

The experience left Merton saying, "Heaven is right here in front of me: Heaven, Heaven!"[222]

After a failed postulancy as a Franciscan he taught English at St. Bonaventure College in New York and adopted a simple, ascetic way of life. From a friend he learned of the Trappist monastery of Gethsemani in Kentucky and in 1941 he decided to make an Easter retreat there, attracted to that reformed Cistercian Order and its characteristic contemplation and silence. On Merton's arrival, "I felt the deep, deep silence! I had entered into a solitude that was an impregnable fortress. And the silence that enfolded me, spoke to me, and spoke louder and more eloquently than any voice."[223]

Merton knew that monastic silence and contemplation would allow him to continue his arduous mystical path leading to the knowledge of God and on 10 December 1941, he entered his Trappist novitiate as Brother Louis, taking his simple vows in 1944, making his solemn vows in 1947 and fulfilling his old dream of becoming a priest two years later. At the abbey of Gethsemani he was master of students from 1951 to 1955, when he was appointed master of novices. By this time, however, Merton was no longer a simple monk, for he had become a celebrity. The publication of *The Seven Storey Mountain* in 1948 brought him renown and wide communication with the outside world.

With the encouragement of his monastic superiors, Merton's literary career flourished. The coordinating theme of all of his books and articles was contemplation. He admitted that, "if prayer, meditation and contemplation were once taken for granted as central realities in human life everywhere, they are no longer,"[224] even among monastics. This was a great loss to the Church and to the souls of human beings that

Merton hoped to remedy, for contemplation is "the union of our mind and will with God in an act of pure love that brings us into obscure contact with Him as He really is … it knows God by seeming to touch Him."[225]

Merton's most important work on contemplation is *Seeds of Contemplation*, revised as *New Seeds of Contemplation*, in which he covered the entire subject by means of a series of short essays and aphorisms that were drawn from his extensive reading and his own mystical experiences: "remember that in this book the author is talking about spiritual things from the point of view of experience rather than in the concise terms of dogmatic theology or of metaphysics."[226] Here he followed the classic spiritual texts in defining and describing contemplation, the means by which one attained it: self-emptying, detachment, freeing oneself from the "desires and cares and attachments of an existence in time and in the world,"[227] ascetic self-discipline, and solitude. However, Merton did not believe that this was possible only for secluded monastics, for "it must not be thought that no man can be a contemplative unless his whole life is always externally miserable and disgusting."[228] Everyone can find solitude, in a room or corner where one would not be disturbed or in a "quiet, dark church."[229] Merton's mysticism was decidedly apophatic, for God is

> unknown in his intimate essence, for he is beyond merely human vision. … Since God cannot be imagined, anything our imagination tells us about Him is ultimately misleading and therefore we cannot know Him as He really is unless we pass beyond everything that can be imagined and enter into an obscurity without images and without the likeness of any created thing.[230]

Merton's works discuss the roster of the mystics of the Christian tradition and he was never wanting for an opinion. Jacob Boehme's writing, he wrote, "is so full of abstruse terminology borrowed from alchemy, etc., that I find it hard to follow him. But when I do make contact with his mind, I like his spirit very much indeed."[231] Marguerite Porete was "an unfortunate Beguine who was burned for some very innocent statements."[232] Julian of Norwich was "a true theologian with greater clarity, depth, and order than St. Theresa," while Fénelon "is sometimes quite dull. Whoever got the idea that he was *dangerous?*"[233] On the other hand, Merton dismissed Madame Guyon as "unoriginal and rather neurotic … so sick and so discredited."[234] John of the Cross was "the greatest of Catholic mystical theologians,"[235] who was the subject of Merton's book *The Ascent to Truth*.

In the last decade of his life, Merton's former narrow Roman Catholic sectarianism began to dilate. Without compromising his devout Catholicism, he studied the mysticism of the Asian tradition, in Buddhism, Taoism, and Hinduism, and he also found that the Muslim Sufi mystics could be read with profit:

> I will be a better Catholic, not if I can *refute* every shade of Protestantism, but if I can affirm the truth in it and still go further. So, too, with the Muslims, the Hindus, the Buddhists, etc. … There is much that one cannot "affirm" and "accept," but first one must say "yes" where one really can.[236]

He wrote on Taoism and Zen in *Mystics and Zen Masters* and published his version of the poems of the Taoist Chuang Tzu in *The Way of Chuang Tzu*. Merton was in Bangkok in December 1968 attending an international monastic gathering when he died on 9 December, apparently from electrocution when he touched a fan with faulty wiring. Unfortunately his death was "investigated in such a bungled and amateurish fashion"[237] that many were led to believe that conspiracy and murder were involved.

Merton left a legacy of fifty books, over 4000 letters and a thousand pages of poetry that extol mysticism and contemplation as an answer to the aridity of religion that "remains content with the bare externals of worship, with 'saying prayers' and 'going to church,' with fulfilling one's external duties and merely being respectable."[238] In its place one could have the utter happiness of the direct experience of God, known for two millennia in Christianity:

> Sometimes these tides of joy are concentrated into strong touches, contacts of God that wake the soul with a bound of wonder and delight, a flash of flame that blazes like an exclamation of inexpressible happiness and sometimes burns with a wound that is delectable although it gives pain. God cannot touch many with this flame, or touch even these heavily. But nevertheless it seems that these deep movements of the Spirit of His Love keep striving, at least lightly, to impress themselves on every one that God draws into this happy and tranquil light.[239]

The message and writings of Thomas Merton prove that one may apply to the mystics in particular the observation of Teilhard de Chardin concerning those who have seen the truth in the religion of the Whole:

> In the great stream of past mankind, poets, philosophers, and mystics – the long procession of those who have been initiated into the vision and cult of the Whole – have left behind them a central wake which we can follow unmistakably from our own days right back to the most distant horizons of history.[240]

For Merton, reading the works of the mystics of the Christian tradition was just as useful and even necessary for promoting the deeper spiritual life as it had been for those who compiled and translated the *Philokalia* and for Wesley and his *Christian Library*.

EPILOGUE

———— •◦• ————

Attempting to make generalizations concerning these almost one hundred mystics whose lives stretch over the two thousand years of the existence of Christianity can easily lead to the invention of a false uniformity that obliterates the myriad individual experiences of diverse people living in quite different cultures and historical circumstances. Many were monks or cloistered nuns, some were priests living in the world while others were highly spiritual laypeople. Moreover, it is extremely difficult to be well-informed of the inner mystical life of any of these figures before the beginning of the twelfth century owing to the lack of surviving historical sources and a prevailing bias against drawing attention to oneself by an immodest description of a personal mystical encounter. Many of the figures made no claims for themselves and, strictly speaking, must be considered mystical writers rather than mystics (for example, most of the representatives of the early centuries of Christianity, Gregory the Great, Meister Eckhart) although it is generally agreed that indeed they were writing from their own experiences. In addition, many of them, particularly women mystics of the Middle Ages, are known only through the accounts written about them by others, especially male priests, which provide us with secondary accounts that often are suspected of having been shaped to serve the purposes of the intermediaries who sifted through their subjects' original information. "Any sifter changes what it sifts"[1] and the result is often hagiography rather than biography. In spite of these limitations, several conclusions can be reached concerning Christian mystics.

Perhaps the archetypal image of the mystic is that of the hermit, sitting on a mountain top withdrawn from contact with the world while lost in private communion with God. Yet very few of the mystics examined here were true hermits and even those who lived "in solitude" typically lived within shouting distance of other "solitaries" and, like the Russian *startzi*, found their lives occupied in providing spiritual guidance to their fellow monastics and even to great numbers of the laity. These mystics demonstrate a remarkable involvement in the affairs of the church and the world. Many of these mystics were founders and reformers of monastic orders (Anthony, Cassian, Francis of Assisi, Dominic, Birgitta of Sweden, Ignatius of Loyola, Teresa of Ávila, John of the Cross, Francis de Sales and Jeanne de Chantal, and Faustina Kowalska), or were abbots, abbesses and superiors of monastic houses (Anthony, Symeon the New Theologian, Sergius of Radonezh, Paisius Velichkovsky, Athanasia, Thaisia, Bernard of Clairvaux, Hildegard of Bingen, Marie of the Incarnation). Some carried on the heavy administrative burdens of high ecclesiastical office as bishops (Gregory of Nyssa, Tikhon of Zadonsk, Theophan the Recluse, Augustine, Francis de Sales), archbishops (Gregory Palamas, Fénelon) and even pope (Gregory I).

One third of the individuals presented here have been acclaimed as saints by either the Eastern Church or the Western Church or by both, and eight of them are among the élite group of the thirty-three Doctors of the Church.[2] The two greatest medieval theologians of the West were mystics (Augustine and Thomas Aquinas), as were the first two theologians of the Christian Church after the apostolic age (Clement of Alexandria and Origen) and many of the most revered theologians of the Eastern Church (Gregory of Nyssa, Macarius, John Climacus, Symeon the New Theologian and Gregory Palamas). Moreover, among Protestants, many of these mystics were founders of or inspirations for religious movements (Emanuel Swedenborg, George Fox, John Wesley, Joseph Smith, Charles Parham and William Seymour). John of Kronstadt and Catherine of Genoa dedicated their lives to easing human suffering, Blaise Pascal and Emanuel Swedenborg are important in the history of science, technology and mathematics, Teilhard de Chardin received international recognition for his accomplishments in paleontology and biology and Thomas Merton was a renowned figure on the stage of world religion. Thus, taken in the aggregate, mystics have often been recognized by their contemporaries as able, accomplished and responsible people and were considered to be leaders of their local communities and sometimes were the most prominent figures of their society.

Moreover, these figures frequently displayed a firmness of resolve that belies any association of mystics with meekness and a retiring nature. Marguerite Porete and Joan of Arc refused to waver from absolute confidence in their revelations and were burnt at the stake for their steadfastness while Joseph Smith was murdered by those who opposed his new Mormon movement. Margery Kempe withstood repeated trials for the heresy of Lollardy and upbraided the courtiers of bishops for their immorality, while Ignatius of Loyola seemed always to be one step ahead of the Inquisition. Teresa of Ávila and John of the Cross were persecuted for their efforts to reform the Carmelites and St. John even endured an excruciating imprisonment at the hands of his own order. Augustine Baker endured the hostility of his non-mystical fellow Benedictines and repeatedly risked the death penalty by returning to England to promote Catholicism and George Fox endured severe persecution as he established the Quaker movement. Symeon the New Theologian, Meister Eckhart, Jacopone da Todi, Bishop Fénelon and Teilhard de Chardin suffered degrees of ecclesiastical censure and Madame Guyon was imprisoned for her Quietism. Origen, Hildegard of Bingen and Margaret Ebner defied their ecclesiastical superiors in order to do what they were convinced was right, Catherine of Siena and Birgitta of Sweden lectured popes on their duties and Blaise Pascal wielded his pen to attack the powerful Jesuits.

A study of mystics in the aggregate also mitigates the popular image that specific mystical phenomena are unique to particular individuals. Teresa of Ávila is especially associated with levitation, but Jesus can be seen as the prototypical Christian mystical levitator and the phenomenon is also recorded for Seraphim of Sarov, the author of *The Way of a Pilgrim*, Lutgard of Aywières, Christina Mirabilis, Henry Suso, Catherine of Siena, Catherine of Genoa and Marie of the Incarnation. Richard Rolle is most associated with the "fire of love" and sensory mysticism, but fire, warmth and heat is one of the most frequently recorded of mystical phenomena, having been affirmed by Macarius, Symeon the New Theologian, Theophan the Recluse, John of Kronstadt, Augustine, Bernard of Clairvaux, Hildegard of Bingen, almost all of the Beguines reviewed here, Tauler, Angela of Foligno, Birgitta, Margery Kempe, Catherine of Genoa, Francisco de Osuna, Marie of the Incarnation, Madame Guyon, George Fox, William Law, Faustina Kowalska, and of course Pascal with his exclamation "Fire!" Indeed, other sensory impressions have been a constant accompaniment of descriptions of mystical experiences, especially that of sweetness, as with Richard Rolle as well as Symeon the New Theologian, Seraphim of Sarov, Augustine, Gregory the Great, the Beguines, Margaret Ebner, Jean Gerson, Angela of Foligno, Birgitta, Francisco de Osuna, Francis de Sales, Marie of the Incarnation, Madame Guyon, and Sarah and Jonathan Edwards. Margery Kempe has a reputation as a great weeper, yet tears and loud crying is also found among many of the other Christian mystics, for St. Dominic's "roaring and crying" could be heard some distance away, Marie d'Oignies and Catherine of Siena disrupted church services with their loud weeping, Ignatius of Loyola reported his own frequent visitation of tears, while Nilus of Sora, Gregory the Great and Francisco de Osuna affirmed tears as one of the essential gifts of the Holy Spirit and not to be discouraged. Even the extreme phenomena of erratic physical movements that today are especially associated with the Pentecostal movement (whence its members are often derisively termed "Holy Rollers") were also reported by Ruusbroec, witnessed among the Camisards and the enthusiasts at the cemetery of St. Médard and defended by Wesley and Jonathan Edwards (whose wife Sarah experienced agitation of her body and felt compelled to leap about). In fact, it is difficult to identify any manifestation of mystical experience that is unique to a particular individual mystic.

It is evident that there is no single path by which a person becomes a mystic. Some of the individuals began receiving divine visions when they were quite young (Hildegard of Bingen, Birgitta of Sweden, Marie of the Incarnation, Blake, Jonathan and Sarah Edwards, Thaisia) while others were much older. Some were put on the mystical path by extraordinary experiences that transformed their lives (Richard Rolle and Margery Kempe), others came into contact with the divine during health crises (Francis of Assisi and Ignatius of Loyola) and even near-death-experiences (Christina Mirabilis and Julian of Norwich), while others gained the direct experience of God only after much study and repeated failures (Teresa of Ávila and Augustine Baker). Some mystics lived their lives aware of the constant presence of God (Brother Lawrence and Catherine of Siena) while others may have had only a singular mystical experience that transformed their lives (Thomas Aquinas and Julian of Norwich). Because these mystics manifest such a great variety in the nature of their mystical lives, it seems clear that while a single definition can comprise them all (direct experiences of God), it is in a sense an inadequate general reference term to apply to those who see visions and hear voices which they attribute to the divinity as well as to those who receive prophecies, are given divinely infused knowledge or understanding of the Scriptures, or feel themselves constantly to be in the presence of God.

Without postulating a mystical dogma, there are many recurring themes in the teachings of these mystics. An emphasis on the incomprehensibility of God runs through the writings of these mystics from Clement of Alexandria ca. 200 on, along with a consciousness of the intellect's inability to understand or to find God ("God may be loved but not thought" in the *Cloud of Unknowing*) and insistence on the insufficiency of the Scriptures alone to provide a means of finding God. Accordingly mystics have often emphasized the Godhead rather than God (as Meister Eckhart pled for God to free him from God) and have frequently appreciated the feminine and maternal aspects of the divine (not only Julian of Norwich but also Clement of Alexandria, Symeon the New Theologian and Catherine of Siena).

Repeatedly one finds mystics expressing an awareness that God is in all of creation, even plants and trees as Catherine of Genoa proclaimed, with Blake seeing the world in a grain of sand and heaven in a flower and Angela of Foligno exclaiming that the whole world is pregnant with God. Concurrently there is the recurring awareness of the smallness of the whole of creation (Gregory I, Angela, and Julian of Norwich). It is common for mystics to transcend the standard theology of their day, as Origen taught that all of creation could be saved, Macarius no longer condemned non-Christians, Nilus of Sora opposed burning the Judaizers, Christina Mirabilis saw a place that was neither heaven, hell nor purgatory and Meister Eckhart said that in union with God we become God in spite of the very pagan sound of that statement. Julian of Norwich saw neither hell nor purgatory, saw no Jews in eternal torment and taught the salvation of all of humankind, Catherine of Genoa saw heaven and hell as states of the soul rather than places (for hell is where rebellion is). Johann Arndt decried useless denominational disputations, Jacob Boehme had no patience with creedal disputes and taught friendship with Jews, Turks and heathens, Augustine Baker advocated prayer rather than engaging in doctrinal polemics, William Law found no wrath in God and rejected hell and the doctrine of the Atonement, Jonathan Edwards believed that all the world's religions had received God's revelation and that salvation was possible for non-Christians, and Thomas Merton came to understand that he would be a better Catholic not by refuting other faiths but by affirming their beliefs when he could.

For those who seek union with God there has been a consistent message put forward in the teachings of mystics: to become united with God one must overcome the body and its appetites so that one is unmoved by the passions; vices must be vanquished and the virtues must be promoted; and all that is not God must be eradicated so that all that remains is divine. The two key scriptural passages for the Christian mystics, especially in the Eastern Church, that exemplify the mystical life are Luke 17.21 ("the kingdom of God is within you") and 1 Thessalonians 5.17 ("pray without ceasing").

This view of mysticism makes it clear that historically mystics have not occupied an odd corner of Christianity. In fact Jesus can be seen as a mystic as well as mystagogue and, from its inception, just as in the Greco-Roman mystery religions and in contemporary movements in Judaism, Christianity was a mystical religion whose purpose was to lead its adherents to an experience of God. However, by the second generation of Christians there was a growing fissure between mystical Christianity with its emphasis on the direct reception of the Holy Spirit and non-mystical Christianity with its emphasis on hierarchical authority. Clement of Alexandria and Origen made it clear that by around the year 200 there were really two Christian churches, that of the mystics and that of the non-mystics, a situation acknowledged overtly or tacitly throughout Christian history – stated harshly by Marguerite Porete but less confrontationally by the Friends of God. Despite the Eastern Church's theological recognition that divinization was indeed the goal of every Christian and the fact that almost all of its theologians were mystics, mysticism there, just as in the West, was often confined to the monastics who were able to lead the lives of asceticism that was seen as the necessary precondition for union with God.

Frequently mystics critiqued the dominant church for its efforts to bring more souls into the church by accommodating itself to those not ready for onerous demands being placed on them, and likewise were dismayed by clergy who sought to direct the church even though lacking a personal experience of God but relying instead on the surface meaning of the Scriptures. The Friends of God, Augustine Baker, William Law and John Wesley all urged Christians to take seriously the demands of the faith that they professed and not be content with mere outward compliance with the minimal demands of the church (and Symeon the New Theologian lamented that "among thousands and tens of thousands you will scarcely find one who is Christian in word and deed."[3]). Moreover, even monastic orders were prone to complacency and ignoring the mystical basis of Christianity. It is remarkable how frequently mysticism has been rediscovered after such periods of dormancy and the vehicle for the rediscovery has usually been the same, by means of an awareness of the mystics of the Christian tradition and their writings, whether in the *Philokalia*, in Augustine Baker's study of mystical literature, John Wesley's *Christian Library* or the works of Evelyn Underhill and Thomas Merton.

A survey of mystical Christianity illustrates the presence of the mystics throughout the two thousand years of Christian history when, for long periods, mysticism was exalted as the highest form of Christian life. While Christianity is commonly regarded as a religion based on the acceptance of an established theology or creed and the performance of certain external acts, at the same time it is also a living religion based on a personal experience of God. Over the past two millennia its mystics have proven that Christianity is indeed a mystical religion. For those who would agree with Thomas Merton that "Real Christian living is stunted and frustrated if it remains content with the bare externals of worship, with 'saying prayers' and 'going to church,' with fulfilling one's external duties and merely being respectable,"[4] the way of the mystics offers an authentic alternative derived from the essence of Christianity. In common with Buddhism, Hinduism, the Sufis of Islam, Kabbalistic Judaism, and shamanism, Christianity, too, is a spirituality of the direct apprehension of the Absolute.

NOTES

—•—

PROLOGUE

1 *Memories and Reflections*, London, Darton, Longman & Todd, 1998, p. 109.
2 Evelyn Underhill, *The Mystics of the Church*, Cambridge, James Clarke, 1925; repr. Wilton, CN, Morehouse-Barlow, p. 10.
3 Paul Crook, "W. R. Inge and Cultural Crisis, 1899–1920," *Journal of Religious History*, 1997, vol. 16, p. 413.
4 New York, Charles Scribner's Son, and London, Methuen, 1899, p. 3.
5 William James, *Varieties of Religious Experience*, New York, Longmans, Green & Co., 1902; repr. New York, London, Ringwood, Markham, ON, Auckland, Penguin, 1982, pp. 379–80.
6 Ibid., p. 30.
7 Harvey D. Egan, S.J., *What Are They Saying About Mysticism?*, New York and Ramsey, NJ, Paulist Press, 1982, p. 3, and see pp. 6–31 for a review of scholars who have approached mysticism from a psychological basis.
8 Christopher J. R. Armstrong, *Evelyn Underhill (1875–1941), An Introduction to Her Lilfe and Writings*, London and Oxford, Mowbrays, 1975, p. 126.
9 Underhill, *Mystics of the Church*, p. 9.
10 Adolf Deissmann, *Paul, A Study in Social and Religious History*, William E. Wilson (trans.), New York, Harper & Row, 1957, p. 149.
11 For example, see Denise Lardner Carmody and John Tully Carmody, *Mysticism, Holiness East and West*, New York and Oxford, Oxford University Press, 1996, p. 10, "what do we suggest as a working description of mysticism? We suggest: 'direct experience of ultimate reality.'" And see F. C. Happold, *Mysticism, A Study and an Anthology*, rev. ed., Harmondsworth, New York, Ringwood, Markham and Auckland, Penguin, 1970, p. 19, "In the religious mystic there is a direct experience of the Presence of God."
12 Vol. 1, *The Foundations of Mysticism*, New York, Crossroad, 1992; vol. 2, *The Growth of Mysticism*, New York, Crossroad, 1994; vol. 3, *The Flowering of Mysticism*, New York, Crossroad–Herder, 1998.
13 See above, n. 6.
14 F. C. Happold, *Mysticism, A Study and an Anthology*, Harmondsworth, New York, Victoria, Markham, Auckland, Penguin Books, 1963, rev. ed. 1970, p. 121.
15 Joan Halifax, *Shaman, the Wounded Healer*, New York, Crossroad, 1982, p. 5.
16 Åke Hultkrantz, *Native Religions of North America*, San Francisco, Harper & Row, 1987, p. 30.
17 Sidney Spencer, *Mysticism in World Religion*, South Brunswick, NJ, A. S. Barnes, 1963, p. 18.
18 Geoffrey Parrinder, Mysticism in the World's Religions, New York, Oxford University Press, 1976, p. 55.
19 Spencer, Mysticism, p. 78.
20 Huston Smith, *The World's Religions*, San Francisco, HarperSanFrancisco, 1991 (originally published as *The Religions of Man*, New York, Harper, 1958), p. 136.

21 Martin P. Nilsson, *Greek Folk Religion*, Philadelphia, University of Pennsylvania Press, 1987 (originally published as *Greek Popular Religion*, New York, Columbia University Press, 1940), p. 132.

22 Carl W. Ernst, preface, *Early Islamic Mysticism, Sufi, Qu'ran, Mi'raj, Poetic and Theological Writings*, Michael A. Sells (trans. and ed.), New York and Mahwah, Paulist Press, 1996, p. 1.

23 Thomas Merton in his unpublished manuscript "The Inner Experience," p. 110, cited in William H. Shannon, *Thomas Merton's Dark Path*, rev. ed., New York, Farrar, Straus, Giroux, 1987, pp. 132–3.

I ORIGINS

1 Proclus, *In Platonis Rem Publicam Commentarii*, G. Kroll (ed.), 2 vols, Leipzig, Teubner, 1901, repr. Amsterdam, Adolf M. Hakkert, 1965, 2:108, ll. 17–24; trans. in Walter Burkert, *Ancient Mystery Cults*, Cambridge, MA, and London, Harvard University Press, 1987, p. 114. Burkert notes that although Proclus wrote in the fifth century, "what he writes about mysteries should be taken seriously as containing authentic tradition," ibid.

2 11.5, in Apuleius of Madauros, *The Isis-Book (Metamorphoses, Book XI)*, J. Gwyn Griffiths (ed. and trans.), Leiden, Brill, 1975, pp. 75–7.

3 Ibid., 11.23, p. 99.

4 S. Angus, *The Mystery-Religions, A Study in the Religious Background of Early Christianity*, London, John Murray, 1925 [as *The Mystery-Religions and Christianity*]; repr. NY, Dover, 1975, p. 102.

5 Corpus Hermeticum, *Poimandres*, 4, in *Hermetica*, Brian P. Copenhaver (trans.), Cambridge, University Press, 1992, p. 1.

6 Clement of Alexandria, Excerpta ex Theodoto, 78.2, in *Clément d'Alexandre, Extraits de Théodote*, F. Sagnard, OP (ed.), Sources Chrétiennes, vol. 23, Paris, Éditions du Cerf, 1948, p.203.

7 *Corpus Hermeticum, Poimandres*, 26, in *Hermetica*, p. 6.

8 Plato, *Theaetetus*, 155e, in Myles Burnyeat, *The Theaetetus of Plato*, M. J. Levett (trans.), rev. Myles Burnyeat, Indianapolis and Cambridge, Hackett Publishing, 1990, p. 277.

9 Plato, *Seventh Letter*, 341, in *Plato, Phaedrus and the Seventh and Eighth Letters*, Walter Hamilton (trans.), London, New York, Victoria, Toronto, Auckland, Penguin Books, 1973, p. 136.

10 Gen. 40.8; all biblical quotations are from *The Jerusalem Bible*, Garden City, NJ, Doubleday, 1966, unless otherwise indicated.

11 1 Sam. 3.1.

12 1 Kgs. 19.13.

13 2 Kgs. 2.11.

14 Isaiah 6.1–4.

15 Ezek. 1.4–5, 13-4, 19, 28.

16 April D. De Conick, *Seek to See Him, Ascent and Vision Mysticism in the Gospel of Thomas*, Leiden, New York and Cologne, E. J. Brill, 1996, p. 32.

17 4Q491, fragment 11 I 4b–11, trans. James Davila, "Heavenly Ascent Literature in the Dead Sea Scrolls," in *The Dead Sea Scrolls After Fifty Years, A Comprehensive Assessment*, Peter W. Flint and James C. Vandekam (eds), vol. 2, Leiden, Boston and Cologne, Brill, 1999, p. 474.

18 De Conick, *Seek to See Him*, p. 33. As is so often the case in matters of mysticism, there is no scholarly agreement about whether this ascent literature concerned actual mystical

visions or was "imaginative literary" productions, see Davila, "Heavenly Ascent Literature," 2:480–2, esp. 481, n. 55.

19 John J. Collins, "Apocalypticism and Literary Genre in the Dead Sea Scrolls," in *Dead Sea Scrolls After Fifty Years*, p. 426.
20 See below, pp. 22–7.
21 *Quis Rerum Divinarum Heres Sit*, 70, in Philo of Alexandria, *The Contemplative Life, The Giants, and Selections*, David Winston (trans.), New York, Ramsey, and Toronto, Paulist Press, 1981, p. 169.
22 *De Migratione Abrahami*, 35, ibid., p. 76.
23 *Quis Rerum Divinarum Heres*, 265, ibid., p. 154.
24 Andrew Louth, *The Origins of the Christian Mystical Tradition, From Plato to Denys*, Oxford, Clarendon Press, 1981, p. 31.
25 See below, pp. 17–9.
26 Angus, *Mystery-Religions*, p. 111.
27 For a convenient although hostile review of recent Jesus scholarship, see Luke Timothy Johnson, *The Real Jesus*, San Francisco, HarperSanFrancisco, 1966, pp. 29–56.
28 Mk. 1.9; Lk. 3.22; see also Mt. 3.16, Jn. 1.34.
29 Lk. 4.14, 18, 21; cf. Isaiah 61.1.
30 Mt. 12.18; cf. Isaiah 42.1.
31 Stevan L. Davies, *Jesus the Healer: Possession, Trance, and the Origins of Christianity*, New York, Continuum, 1995, p. 66.
32 Morton T. Kelsey, *Psychology, Medicine & Christian Healing*, San Francisco, Harper & Row, 1988, p. 42.
33 Mt. 12.24–32.
34 Davies, *Jesus the Healer*, p. 77.
35 Jn. 1.48.
36 Mt. 9.4, 12.15.
37 Jn. 4.16.
38 Mt. 14.25–6; Mk. 6.48; Jn. 6.19.
39 Lk. 17.21; Mt. 4.17; Mk. 1.14.
40 Craig A. Evans, "Jesus and the Dead Sea Scrolls," in *Dead Sea Scrolls After Fifty Years*, pp. 584–5.
41 Mt. 13.3, 10; Mk. 4.11, 33; Lk. 8.9–10.
42 John Dominic Crossan, *The Historical Jesus*, San Francisco, HarperSanFrancisco, 1992, p. 19.
43 Morton Smith, "Two Ascended to Heaven – Jesus and the Author of 4Q491," in *Jesus and the Dead Sea Scrolls*, James H. Charlesworth (ed.), New York, London, Toronto, Sydney, and Auckland, Doubleday, 1992, p. 291.
44 L. William Countryman, *The Mystical Way in the Fourth Gospel*, Valley Forge, PA, Trinity Press International, 1994, p. 8.
45 8.28.
46 8.40.
47 8.26, 28.
48 12.45.
49 14.11.
50 15.15.
51 17.16.
52 14.16–7, 23, 15.15, 16.13.
53 14.23.
54 Acts 2.2–4.
55 Acts 10.3–11.18.
56 Alan F. Segal, *Paul the Convert*, New Haven and London, Yale University Press, 1990, p. 34.
57 Acts 19.6.

58 1 Cor. 2.7; Eph. 3.3; Col. 1.26.
59 1 Cor. 12.11.
60 2 Cor. 12.5.
61 Gal. 2.20
62 2 Cor. 13.5.
63 See below, ch. II, p. 41.
64 Mt. 28.20, 18.20.
65 Gal. 1.8.
66 James D. G. Dunn, *Baptism in the Holy Spirit: A Re-examination of the New Testament Teaching on the Gift of the Holy Spirit in Relation to Pentecostalism Today*, London, SCM Press, 1970, p. 66; James D. G. Dunn, *Jesus and the Spirit: A Study of the Religious and Charismatic Experience of Jesus and the First Christians as Reflected in the New Testament*, London, SCM Press, 1975, p. 194. This latter work has been described as "essential reading for anyone interested in a broad-ranging, sympathetic but scholarly discussion of religious experience in the New Testament," L. W. Hurtado, "Religious Experience and Religious Innovation in the New Testament," *Journal of Religion*, 2000, vol. 80, p. 186.
67 Dunn, *Baptism in the Holy Spirit*, p. 225.
68 Montanist Oracles 1, 2, Robert M. Grant, *Second-Century Christianity, A Collection of Fragments*, London, SPCK, 1946, p. 95.
69 Montanist Oracles 13, in ibid., p. 96.
70 Montanist Oracles 16, in ibid.
71 Eusebius, *The History of the Church*, G. A. Williamson (trans.), Harmondsworth, New York, Victoria, Ontario, Auckland, Penguin Books, 1965, 5.16.8, p. 218.
72 Elaine Pagels, *The Gnostic Gospels*, New York, Vintage Books, 1981, pp. 72–3.
73 *On the Soul*, 9, Edwin A. Quain (trans.), in Tertullian, *Apologetical Works and Minucius Felix: Octavius*, Fathers of the Church, vol. 10, New York, Fathers of the Church, 1950, p. 197.
74 I. M. Lewis, *Ecstatic Religion, an Anthropological Study of Spirit Possession and Shamanism*, Harmondsworth, Baltimore, Victoria, Markham, Ontario, Auckland, Penguin, 1971, p. 34.

II THE EASTERN CHURCH

1 Clement of Alexandria, *Miscellanies*, 7.7.47, in *Alexandrian Christianity, Selected Translations of Clement and Origen*, introduction and notes by John Ernest Leonard Oulton and Henry Chadwick, Philadelphia, Westminster Press, 1954, pp. 122–3.
2 Ibid., 6.15, in Clement, *The Ante-Nicene Fathers*, Alexander Robert and James Donaldson (eds), vol. 2, Buffalo, Christian Literature Publishing, 1887; repr. Grand Rapids, MI, Wm. B. Eerdmans, 1962, p. 509.
3 Clement, *Stromateis, Books One to Three*, John Ferguson (trans.), The Fathers of the Church, vol. 85, Washington, DC, Catholic University of America Press, 1991, 1.20.98, p. 97.
4 *Miscellanies*, 6.15, in *Ante-Nicene Fathers*, 2:507.
5 *Stromateis*, 2.16, p. 206.
6 *Miscellanies*, 5.10, in *Ante-Nicene Fathers*, 2:460.
7 Ibid., 5.11, 2:461.
8 Ibid., 1.24, 5.1, 6.1, 2:337, 445, 460.
9 Ibid., 5.12, 2:463.
10 Ibid., 5.12, 2:464.
11 *Who Is the Rich Man That Shall Be Saved?*, 37, in *Ante-Nicene Fathers*, 2:601.
12 *Stromateis*, 2.2.5, p. 160.
13 *Miscellanies*, 7.10.55, in *Alexandrian Christianity*, p. 128.
14 *Miscellanies*, 6.9, in *Ante-Nicene Fathers*, 2:497.
15 Ibid., 7.7.49, in *Alexandrian Christianity*, p. 536.

16 Ibid., 3.5.43, in *Alexandrian Christianity*, pp. 59–60.
17 Ibid., 6.13, in *Ante-Nicene Fathers*, 2:504.
18 Joseph W. Trigg, *Origen*, London and New York, Routledge, 1998, p. 5.
19 Origen, *De Principiis*, 1.1.5, in *The Ante-Nicene Fathers*, Alexander Robert and James Donaldson (eds), vol. 4, New York, Charles Scribner's Sons, 1926; repr. Grand Rapids, MI, Wm. B. Eerdmans, 1956, p. 243.
20 Origen, *Commentary on John, Book 2*, 23, in *Ante-Nicene Fathers*, 4:339.
21 *Origen: Contra Celsum*, Henry Chadwick (trans.), Cambridge University Press, Cambridge, London, New York, New Rochelle, Melbourne, Sydney, 1965, 6.68, p. 382.
22 *Commentary on John, Book 13.3–19*, 5.30, in Trigg, *Origen*, p. 154.
23 Ibid., 6.34, p. 155.
24 Ibid., 6.37, p. 155.
25 *De Principiis*, 4.2.7, in *Origen, An Exhortation to Martyrdom, Prayer, First Principles: Book IV, Prologue to the Commentary on the Song of Songs, Homily XXVII on Numbers*, Rowan A. Greer (trans.), New York, Ramsey, Toronto, Paulist Press, 1979, p. 186.
26 *Contra Celsum*, 7.42, p. 430.
27 Clement, *On Prayer*, 11.2, in *Alexandrian Christianity*, p. 259.
28 *Contra Celsum*, 6.70, p. 384.
29 *Homily XXVII on Numbers*, 12, in *Origen* (Greer), p. 266.
30 *Commentary on the Song of Songs*, Prologue, in *Origen* (Greer), p. 235.
31 *Exhortation to Martyrdom*, 3, in *Alexandrian Christianity*, p. 395.
32 *Contra Celsum*, 6.17, p. 330.
33 Matt. 19.12, Revised Standard Version.
34 Ibid., 7.41, p. 429.
35 Ibid., 3.60, p. 169.
36 *De Principiis*, 4.3.8, in *Origen* (Greer), p. 195.
37 *Homily XXVII on Numbers*, 12, in *Origen* (Greer), p. 264.
38 *Homily XXVII on Numbers*, 11, in *Origen* (Greer), p. 261.
39 Johannes Quasten, *Patrology*, vol. 2, The Ante-Nicene Literature After Irenaeus, Westminster, MD, Newman Press, Utrecht-Antwerp, Spectrum Publishers, 1962, p. 98.
40 Athanius, *Athanasius, The Life of Anthony and the Letter to Mercellinus*, Robert C. Gregg (trans.), New York, Ramsey and Toronto, Paulist Press, 1980, 84, p. 92.
41 Ibid., 30, p. 54.
42 Ibid., 14, p. 42.
43 Ibid., 66, p. 80.
44 Ibid., 25, p. 50.
45 Ibid., 39, p. 60.
46 Ibid., 38, p. 60.
47 Ibid., 67, p. 81.
48 *The Lives of the Desert Fathers*, Norman Russell (trans.), London and Oxford, Mowbray, Kalamazoo, MI, Cistercian Publications, 1981, VIII.20, p. 67.
49 Ibid., I.26, p. 56.
50 Ibid., I.45, p. 59.
51 Ibid., I.22–8, p. 146.
52 Ibid., I.63, p. 62.
53 Ibid., I.58, p. 56.
54 Ibid., II.15, p. 72.
55 Palladius, *The Lausiac History*, Robert T. Meyer (trans.), Westminster, MD, Newman Press, and London, Longmans, Green and Co., 1965, Foreword, 1, p. 17.
56 Ibid., 29.5, p. 90.
57 Ibid., 11.5, p. 47.
58 Ibid., 41.4, p. 118.
59 Ibid., 45.4, p. 123.

60 Ibid., 58.4, p. 139.

61 *Lives of the Desert Fathers*, II.10, p. 64; see also *The Sayings of the Desert Fathers*, Benedicta Ward (trans.), London and Oxford, Mowbray, Kalamazoo, MI, Cistercian Publications, 1975, Arsenius, 33, p. 15.

62 This was the doctrine of the Alexandrian priest Arius that God the Son was not eternally co-existent with God the Father, nor was he of identical substance with the Father.

63 Homily Six: On the Beatitudes, in Anthony Meredith, S.J., *Gregory of Nyssa*, London and New York, Routledge, 1999, p. 94.

64 Gregory of Nyssa, *The Life of Moses*, Abraham J. Malherbe and Everett Ferguson (trans.), New York, Ramsey and Toronto, Paulist Press, 1978, 2.163, p. 95.

65 Gregory of Nyssa, *Commentary on the Canticle of Canticles*, sermon 6, in *From Glory to Glory, Texts From Gregory of Nyssa's Mystical Writings*, Jean Daniélou, S.J. (ed.), Herbert Musurillo, S.J. (trans.), New York, Charles Scribner's Sons, 1961, p. 201.

66 *On His Brother Basil*, 812C, in *Glory to Glory*, p. 28.

67 *Life of Moses*, 2.24, p. 60.

68 Exodus 20.21.

69 *Life of Moses*, 2.163, p. 95.

70 Gregory of Nyssa, Ch. 3, in *Gregory of Nyssa: Dogmatic Treatises, Etc.*, in *A Select Library of Nicene and Post-Nicene Fathers of the Christian Church*, 2nd ser., vol. 5, Philip Schaff and Henry Wace (trans.), New York, Christian Literature Company, 1893; repr. Grand Rapids, Wm. B. Eerdmans, 1994, p. 345.

71 Ibid.

72 Homily 6, in Meredith, *Gregory of Nyssa*, p. 91.

73 Gregory of Nyssa, *Commentary on the Canticle*, sermon 10, in *From Glory to Glory*, pp. 239–40.

74 See below, pp. 41–2.

75 See below, pp. 75–6, 184–7.

76 *Pseudo-Macarius, The Fifty Spiritual Homilies and the Great Letter*, George A. Maloney, S.J. (trans.)., New York and Mahwah, NJ, Paulist Press, 1992, p. 269.

77 Ibid., 8.3, p. 82.

78 Ibid., 8.6, p. 83.

79 Ibid., 15.10, p. 112.

80 Ibid., 11.1, p. 90.

81 Ibid., 11.15, p. 97.

82 Ibid., 18.10–1, p. 145.

83 Ibid., 18.10, p. 145.

84 Ibid., 4.11–3, pp. 55–6.

85 Ibid., 15.21, pp. 115–6.

86 Ibid., 39.1, p. 213.

87 Ibid., 18.5, p. 143.

88 Ibid.

89 Ibid., 17.10, p. 139.

90 *John Climacus, The Ladder of Divine Ascent*, Colm Luibheid and Norman Russell (trans.), New York, Ramsey and Toronto, Paulist Press, 1982, 29, pp. 282, 284.

91 Ibid., p. 264

92 Ibid., p. 289.

93 Ibid., p. 291.

94 Ibid., 23, p. 209.

95 Ibid., 26, p. 249

96 Ibid., 28, p. 276

97 Ibid., 27, p. 268.

98 1.1, *Pseudo-Dionysius, The Complete Works*, Colm Luibheid (trans.), New York and Mahwah, NJ, Paulist Press, 1987, p. 135.

99   Ibid., 1.3, p. 137.
100 Ibid., 4, p. 141.
101 Ibid., 5, p. 141.
102 Ibid., 3, p. 139.
103 *Celestial Hierarchy* 2.3, in *Pseudo-Dionysius, The Complete Works*, p. 150.
104 Maximus, *Maximus Confessor, Selected Writings*, George C. Berthold (trans.), New York and Mahwah, NJ, Paulist Press, 1985, The Four Hundred Chapters on Love, First Century, 10, Second Century, 6, pp. 36, 47.
105 Ibid., Chapters on Knowledge, Second Century, 39, p. 156.
106 Ibid., Chapters on Knowledge, Second Century, 73–4, pp. 163–4.
107 Symeon the New Theologian, *St. Symeon the New Theologian, On the Mystical Life: The Ethical Discourses*, vol. 2, *On Virtue and Christian Life*, Alexander Golitzin (trans.), Crestwood, NJ, St. Vladimir's Seminary Press, 1996, p. vii.
108 Symeon, *Symeon the New Theologian, the Discourses*, C. J. deCatanzaro (trans.), New York, Ramsey and Toronto, Paulist Press, 1980, 22.91–103, pp. 245–6.
109 Ibid., 16.84–9, p. 200.
110 Ibid., introduction by George A. Maloney, p. 2.
111 Ibid., p. 4.
112 Ibid., 29, p. 312.
113 Ibid., 17.35–41, 22.91–103.
114 Symeon, *St. Symeon the New Theologian, On the Mystical Life: The Ethical Discourses*, vol. 1, *The Church and Last Things*, Alexander Golitzin (trans.), Crestwood, NJ, St. Vladimir's Seminary Press, 1995, Third Ethical Discourse, p. 123.
115 Ibid., Ninth Ethical Discourse, p. 127.
116 Symeon, *Symeon the New Theologian, The Practical and Theological Chapters and The Three Theological Discourses*, Paul McGuckin, C. P. (trans.), Kalamazoo, MI, Cistercian Publications, 1982, 3.100, p. 103.
117 Symeon, *Hymns of Divine Love by St. Symeon the New Theologian*, George A. Maloney, S. J. (trans.), Denville, NJ, Dimension Books, 1975, 25, pp. 135–6.
118 Symeon, *Discourses*, 13.39–40, 52–5.
119 Symeon, *Hymns*, 30, p. 169.
120 Ibid., 15, pp, 54–5, adapted. Symeon's intent was to shock his readers and listeners with the realization of the complete identification between Christ and the Christian mystic, and he still does. Maloney's translation discretely renders penis, βάλανον (line 161), as "this organ," p. 54; the standard French translation, *Syméon le nouveau théologien, Hymnes*, Joseph Paramelle (trans.), Paris, Cerf, 1969, does the same, "en cet organe," p. 291.
121 Symeon, *Symeon the New Theologian, On the Mystical Life*, vol. 2, Sixth Ethical Discourse, p. 68.
122 Symeon, *The Practical and Theological Chapters and The Three Theological Discourses*, McGuckin (trans.), Third Theological Discourse, p. 138.
123 Ibid., Fourth Ethical Discourse, p. 20.
124 Gregory Palamas, *Gregory Palamas, The Triads*, Nicholas Gendle (trans.), Mahwah, NJ, Paulist Press, 1983, 1.2.8, p. 46.
125 Mt 17.1–6, Mk 9,1-8, Lk 9.28–36.
126 On the Messalians, see above, p. 32.
127 Palamas, *Triads*, 1.3.21.
128 Ibid., 2.3.8.
129 Ibid., 2.3.9.
130 Ibid., 2.3.11.
131 Ibid., 2.3.66, pp. 38, 39, 57, 58, 68.
132 Timothy Ware, *The Orthodox Church*, Harmondsworth, Baltimore and Victoria, Penguin, 1963; repr. 1964, p. 79.

133 Nicholas Cabasilas, *The Life in Christ*, Carmino J. deCatanzaro (trans.), Crestwood, NJ, St. Vladimir's Seminary Press, 1998, 6.9, pp. 173–4.

134 1 Thess. 5.17.

135 Cabasilas, *Life in Christ*, 6.13, p. 192.

136 Ibid., 7.1, p. 196.

137 Ibid., 2.1, p. 65.

138 Ibid., 4.3, p. 116.

139 Ibid., 6.14, p. 193.

140 Ibid., 2.20–2, pp. 98, 101.

141 Ibid., 6.5, pp. 166–7.

142 See above, pp. 38

143 George P. Fedotov, *The Russian Religious Mind,* vol. 1, *Kievan Christianity, the Tenth to the Thirteenth Century,* Cambridge, MA, Harvard University Press, 1946; repr. New York, Harper & Brothers, 1960, p. 388.

144 Ibid., p. 153.

145 On cenobia, see above, p. 28.

146 Fedotov, *The Russian Religious Mind,* vol. 2, *The Middle Ages, The Thirteenth to the Fifteenth Centuries,* Cambridge, MA, Harvard University Press, 1956, p. 196.

147 Ibid.

148 *Treasury of Russian Spirituality,* George P. Fedotov (ed.), Gloucester, MA, Peter Smith, 1969, p. 59.

149 Ibid., p. 54.

150 Ibid.

151 See below, p. 87.

152 Ibid., p. 61.

153 Ibid., p. 82.

154 Ibid., p. 73.

155 Ibid., pp. 80–1.

156 Ibid., pp. 76–7.

157 Ibid., p. 78.

158 Pierre Kovalevsky, *Saint Sergius and Russian Spirituality*, Crestwood, NY, St. Vladimir's Seminary Press, 1976, p. 156.

159 See below, p. 91.

160 Sergius Bolshakoff, *Russian Mystics*, Kalamazoo, MI, Cistercian Publications, London, A. R. Mowbray, 1977, p. 18.

161 However, in the Russian Church "Laura" is an honorary title given only to four Russian monasteries. On the laura and cenobia of the Desert Fathers, see above, p. 27–8.

162 *The Monastic Rule*, introduction, in Fedotov, *Treasury of Russian Spirituality*, p. 95.

163 Fedotov, *Russian Religious Mind*, 2:272.

164 *Monastic Rule*, ch. 2, in Fedotov, *Treasury*, pp. 103–4.

165 Ibid., pp. 104–5.

166 Ibid., ch. 9, p. 129.

167 Ibid., ch. 3, p. 108.

168 Ibid., ch. 3, pp. 107–8, ch. 2, p. 102.

169 Ibid., ch. 8, p. 127.

170 Ibid., p. 128.

171 The Judaizers had arisen around 1470 and were outward Christians who believed that Jesus was only a human, not the Messiah, and that one had to become a Jew in order to be saved.

172 George A. Maloney, S.J., *Russian Hesychasm, the Spirituality of Nil Sorskij*, The Hague and Paris, Mouton, 1973, p. 204.

173 Bolshakoff, *Russian Mystics*, p. 62.

174 *Memoirs by Chebotarev on the Life of St. Tychon of Zadonsk*, in Fedotov, *Treasury*, p. 190.

175 Ibid., p. 191.
176 Ibid., p. 195.
177 *From the Memoirs of Ivan Yefimov*, in Fedotov, *Treasury*, p. 210.
178 Ibid., p. 208.
179 Fedotov, *Memoirs by Chebotarev*, ibid., p. 193.
180 Fedotov, *Memoirs of Ivan Yefimov*, ibid., p. 209.
181 Nadeja Gorodetzky, *Saint Tikhon of Zadonsk, Inspirer of Dostoevsky*, Crestwood, NY, St. Vladimir's Seminary Press, 1976, p. 7.
182 Ibid., p. 221.
183 Cited by George S. Bebis in the introduction, *Nicodemus of the Holy Mountain, A Handbook of Spiritual Counsel*, Peter A. Chamberas (trans.), New York and Mahwah, NJ, Paulist Press, 1989, p. 23.
184 Velichkovsky, *Saint Paisius Velichkovsky*, Fr. Seraphim Rose (trans.), *Little Russian Philokalia*, vol. 4, Platina, CA, St. Herman Press, 1994, p. 21.
185 Ibid., p. 30.
186 Ibid., p. 51.
187 Quoted in Fr. Sergii Chetverikov, *Starets Paisii Velichkovskii, His Life, Teachings, and Influence on Orthodox Monasticism*, Vasily Lickwar and Alexander I. Lisenko (trans.), Belmont, MA, Nordland Publishing, 1980, p. 279.
188 Ibid., p. 320.
189 Bolshakoff, *Russian Mystics*, p. 273.
190 However, the Greek title had the meaning of "anthology."
191 Ibid., p. 90.
192 Ibid., p. 122.
193 Seraphim, *Saint Seraphim of Sarov*, Fr. Seraphim Rose (trans.), 4th ed., *Little Russian Philokalia*, vol. 1, Platina, CA, St. Herman of Alaska Brotherhood, 1996, p. 14.
194 Valentine Zander, *St Seraphim of Sarov*, Sister Gabriel Anne (trans.), Crestwood, NY, St. Vladimir's Seminary Press, 1975, p. 20.
195 Seraphim, *The Spiritual Instructions*, 38, in *Little Russian Philokalia*, 1:55.
196 Quoted in Bolshakoff, *Russian Mystics*, p. 126.
197 *St. Seraphim of Sarov*, by A. F. Dobbie-Bateman, in Fedotov, *Treasury*, p. 253.
198 Seraphim, *The Acquisition of the Holy Spirit*, 3, in *Little Russian Philokalia*, 1:79.
199 Ibid., 4, pp. 88–9.
200 Ibid., 5, p. 94.
201 Ibid., 7, p. 99.
202 Ibid., p. 100.
203 Ibid., p. 103
204 Ibid., p. 104.
205 Ibid., p. 106, referring to Jeremiah 23.23.
206 Seraphim, *Little Russian Philokalia*, 1:128–9.
207 Fr. Alexander Priklonsky, *Blessed Athanasia & the Desert Ideal*, 2nd ed., Platina, CA, St. Herman of Alaska Brotherhood, 1993, pp. 51–2.
208 Ibid., p. 63.
209 Ibid., p. 69.
210 Ibid., p. 73.
211 Ibid., p. 74.
212 Ibid., p. 81.
213 Ibid., p. 82.
214 Ibid., p. 97.
215 St. Theophan the Recluse, *The Path to Salvation, A Manual of Spiritual Transformation*, Fr. Seraphim Rose (trans.), Platina, CA, St. Herman of Alaska Brotherhood, 1996, p. 191.
216 Ibid., p. 257.
217 Ibid., pp. 314–5.

218 Ibid., p. 325.
219 Ibid., p. 314.
220 Bolshakoff, *Russian Mystics*, p. 215.
221 See below, p. 160.
222 Bolshakoff, *Russian Mystics*, p. 218.
223 R. A. Hodges, introduction, in *Unseen Warfare, 'The Spiritual Combat' and 'Path to Paradise' of Lorenzo Scupoli*, as edited by Nicodemus of the Holy Mountain and revised by Theophan the Recluse, E. Kadloubovsky and G. E. H. Palmer (trans.), Crestwood, NY, St. Vladimir's Seminary Press, 1995, p. 59.
224 Fr. Clement Sederholm, *Elder Leonid of Optina*, Platina, CA, St. Herman of Alaska Brotherhood, 1990, p. 75.
225 Ibid., p. 80.
226 Ibid.
227 Ibid., p. 100.
228 Ibid., p. 95.
229 Ibid., p. 161.
230 Bolshakoff, *Russian Mystics*, p. 182.
231 Sederholm, *Elder Leonid*, p. 102.
232 Ibid., p. 103.
233 Fr. Sergius Chetverikov, *Elder Ambrose of Optina*, Platina, CA, St. Herman of Alaska Brotherhood, 1997, p. 93.
234 Fr. Leonid Kavelin, *Elder Macarius of Optina*, Valentina V. Lyovina (trans.), Platina, CA, St. Herman of Alaska Brotherhood, 1995, p. 73.
235 Ibid., pp. 115, 138.
236 Bolshakoff, *Russian Mystics*, p. 186.
237 Kavelin, *Elder Macarius*, p. 157.
238 Ibid., p. 230.
239 Chetverikov, *Elder Ambrose*, p. 53.
240 Ibid., p. 54.
241 Ibid., pp. 26–9.
242 Ibid., pp. 140–1.
243 Ibid., p. 143.
244 Ibid., p. 373.
245 Ibid., p. 406.
246 Ibid., p. 334.
247 Ibid.
248 Ibid., p. 337.
249 *The Way of a Pilgrim and The Pilgrim Continues His Way*, R. M. French (trans.), New York, Harper, 1954; repr. San Francisco, HarperSanFrancisco, 1991, p. 5.
250 Ibid., pp. 43–4.
251 Ibid., p. 5.
252 Ibid., pp. 7–10.
253 Ibid., pp. 50–1.
254 Ibid., pp. 38–9.
255 Ibid., p. 93.
256 Ibid., pp. 78–9.
257 Ibid., p. 30.
258 Ibid., p. 17.
259 Ibid., p. 47.
260 Ibid., pp. 36, 29.
261 Ibid., p. 91.
262 John B. Dunlop, *Staretz Amvrosy, Model For Dostoevsky's Staretz Zosima*, Belmont, MA, Nordland Publishing, 1972, p. 162.

263 Ibid., p. 163.
264 Archimandrite Constantine, *A Spiritual Portrait of Saint John of Kronstadt*, Liberty, TN, St. John of Kronstadt Press, 1982, p. 89.
265 John of Kronstadt, *The Spiritual Counsels of Father John of Kronstadt*, Select Passages from *My Life in Christ*, W. Jardine Grosbrooke (ed.), Crestwood, NY, St. Vladimir's Seminary Press, 1989, p. 9.
266 Constantine, *Spiritual Portrait*, p. 60.
267 Bishop Alexander Semenoff-Tian-Chansky, *Father John of Kronstadt: A Life*, London and Oxford, Mowbrays, 1955, p. 166.
268 Constantine, *Spiritual Portrait*, p. 72.
269 John of Kronstadt, *Spiritual Counsels*, pp. 27, 17.
270 Ibid., p. 31.
271 John of Kronstadt, *My Life in Christ*, E. E. Goulaeff (trans.), 4th ed., London, Paris and Melbourne, Cassell, 1897; repr. Jordanville, NY, Holy Trinity Monastery, 1994, pp. 25–6.
272 Ibid., pp. 103–4.
273 Ibid., p. 448.
274 Ibid., p. 451.
275 *Spiritual Counsels*, p. 48.
276 Ibid., p. 16.
277 Fedotov, *Treasury*, p. 349.
278 Semenoff-Tian-Chansky, *Father John*, p. 174.
279 Nadieszda Kizenko, *A Prodigal Saint, Father John of Kronstadt and the Russian People*, University Park, PA, Pennsylvania State University Press, 2000, p. 146.
280 Thaisia, *Abbess Thaisia of Leushino, The Autobiography of a Spiritual Daughter of St. John of Kronstadt*, Platina, CA, St. Herman of Alaska Brotherhood, 1989, p. 290.
281 Ibid., p. 291.
282 Bolshakoff, *Russian Mystics*, p. 115.
283 Thaisia, *Abbess Thaisia of Leusino*, p. 206.
284 Ibid., preface, p. 12.
285 Ibid., p. 27.
286 Ibid., p. 38.
287 Ibid., pp. 41–3.
288 Ibid., p. 44.
289 Ibid., p. 127.
290 Ibid., p. 148.
291 Ibid., p. 158.
292 Ibid., p. 172.
293 Ibid., pp. 171–2.
294 Ibid., p. 179.
295 Ibid., pp. 188–9.
296 Ibid., p. 194.
297 Ibid., p. 229.
298 Ibid.
299 Staretz Silouan, *Wisdom From Mount Athos, The Writings of Staretz Silouan, 1866–1938*, Archimandrite Sophrony (ed.), Rosemary Edmonds (trans.), Crestwood, NY, St. Vladimir's Seminary Press, 1975, p. 65.
300 Archimandrite Sophrony, *The Monk of Mount Athos, Staretz Silouan, 1866–1938*, Rosemary Edmonds (trans.), Crestwood, NJ, St. Vladimir's Seminary Press, 1973, p. 14.
301 Ibid., p. 14.
302 Ibid., p. 17.
303 Ibid., pp. 19–20.
304 Silouan, *Wisdom From Mount Athos*, p. 113.
305 Ibid., p. 88.

306 Sophrony, *Monk of Mount Athos*, p. 59.
307 Ibid., p. 80.
308 Ibid., p. 29.
309 Ibid., p. 50.
310 Ibid., p. 32.
311 Ibid., p. 71.
312 Ibid., p. 87.
313 Ibid., pp. 69, 70.
314 Bolshakoff, *Russian Mystics*, p. 275.

III THE WESTERN CHURCH IN THE MIDDLE AGES

1 *John Cassian, Conferences*, Colm Luibheid (trans.), New York, Mahwah, NJ, Toronto, Paulist Press, 1985, Conf. 10.11.
2 Ibid., 3.7.
3 Ibid., 1.8.
4 Benedict of Nursia, *St. Benedict's Rule for Monasteries*, Leonard J. Doyle (trans.), St. Louis, Herder Book Co., 1935; repr. Collegeville, MN, Liturgical Press, 1948, ch. 73, p. 100.
5 Mary T. Clark, introduction to *Augustine of Hippo, Selected Writings*, Mary T. Clark (trans.), New York, Ramsey, Toronto, Paulist Press, 1984, p. 37.
6 Ibid., pp. 35–42; Bernard McGinn, *The Foundations of Mysticism*, New York, Crossroad, 1992, pp. 230–31.
7 Cuthbert Butler, *Western Mysticism*, New York, E. P. Dutton, 1924, p. 24.
8 Augustine of Hippo, Sermon 52.16, *Sermons*, Edmund Hill (trans.), New York, New City Press, vol. 3, p. 57.
9 On the apophatic approach, see above, p. 36.
10 Augustine, Letter 120, *Saint Augustine, Letters*, Wilfrid Parsons (trans.), Washington, DC, Catholic University of America Press, 1953, vol. 2, p. 311.
11 Augustine, *De ordine*, 2.16.44, in *Corpus Scriptorum Ecclesiasticorum Latinorum*, Pius Knöll (ed.), Vienna and Leipzig, Hölder-Pichler-Tempsky, 1922, vol. 63, p. 177.
12 Ibid., 2.18.47, p. 180.
13 Augustine, *On Christian Doctrine*, 1.6, J. F. Shaw (trans.), in *A Select Library of Nicene and Post-Nicene Fathers of the Christian Church*, Philip Schaff (ed.), 1st series, vol. 2, Edinburgh, T & T Clark, repr. Grand Rapids, Wm. B. Eerdmans, 1993, p. 524.
14 Augustine, *St. Augustine, Confessions*, Henry Chadwick (trans.), Oxford and New York, Oxford University Press, 1991, 7.9.14, p. 121.
15 Ibid., pp. xxi–xxii.
16 E. I. Watkin, "The Mysticism of St. Augustine," *Saint Augustine*, New York, Meridian Books, 1957, p. 116
17 Augustine, *Confessions*, trans. Chadwick, 9.10.24, p. 171.
18 Ibid., 3.6.11, p. 43.
19 Ibid., 7.10.16–11.17–18., 16.23, pp. 123–7.
20 Augustine, *Homily on the First Epistle of St. John*, 7.8, in *Augustine of Hippo, Selected Writings*, p. 305.
21 On this point, related to the teachings of St. Paul and Martin Luther, see Rudolf Otto, *The Idea of the Holy*, John W. Harvey (trans.), 2nd ed., London, Oxford and New York, Oxford University Press, 1950, pp. 88–93.
22 Augustine, *Confessions*, trans. Chadwick, 10.40.65, p. 218.
23 Ibid., 13.9.10, p. 278.
24 Augustine, *The City of God*, Marcus Dods (trans.), New York, Modern Library, 1950, 9.16.

25 The Istrian, or Three Chapters Schism.

26 Gregory the Great, *Moralia*, 23.41, in *Morals on the Book of Job by Gregory the Great*, Members of the English Church (trans.), vol. 3, part 1, Oxford, John Henry Parker, and London, F. and J. Rivington, 1847, p. 36.

27 Bernard McGinn, *The Growth of Mysticism*, New York, Crossroad, 1994, p. 71.

28 Gregory the Great, *Saint Gregory the Great, Dialogues*, trans. Odo John Zimmerman, New York, Fathers of the Church, 1959, 2.35, p. 105.

29 Ibid., p. 106.

30 Ibid., 1, prologue, pp. 3–5.

31 Gregory the Great, *Dialogues*, 2.36.

32 Virginia G. Berry, "The Second Crusade," *A History of the Crusades*, Marshall W. Baldwin (ed.), vol. 1, Madison, Milwaukee and London, University of Wisconsin Press, 1969, pp. 472–3.

33 Otto of Freising, *The Deeds of Frederick Barbarossa, Otto of Freising and His Continuator*, Charles Christopher Mierow (trans.), New York, W. W. Norton, 1953, 1.40, p. 75.

34 See above, p. 30.

35 See below, p. 85.

36 The symbol of mystical union, drawn from the Song of Songs 1.2.

37 Bernard, Sermons on the Song of Songs, 3.1, in *Bernard of Clairvaux, Selected Works*, G. R. Evans (trans.), New York and Mahwah, NJ, Paulist Press, 1987, p. 221.

38 Ibid., 74:2.4–7, pp. 254–6.

39 Ibid., 1.1, p. 210.

40 Gottfried, *The Life of the Saintly Hildegard by Gottfried of Disibodenberg and Theoderic of Echternach*, Hugh Feiss, OSB (trans.), Toronto, Peregrina Publishing, 1996, book 3, pp. 73–97.

41 Henry-Coüannier, *Hildegard of Bingen, Scivias*, Mother Columba Hart and Jane Bishop (trans.), New York and Mahwah, NJ, Paulist Press, 1990, Declaration, pp. 59, 61.

42 Henry-Coüannier, *Scivias*, Declaration, pp. 59–60.

43 Henry-Coüannier, Letter to Guibert of Gembloux, *Hildegard of Bingen, an Anthology*, p. 143. This letter is also in *Hildegard of Bingen's Book of Divine Works*, Matthew Fox (ed.), Santa Fe, Bear & Co., 1987, pp. 348–51.

44 Ibid., p. 145.

45 Ibid.

46 Barbara Newman, *Sister of Wisdom, St. Hildegard's Theology of the Feminine*, Berkeley, Los Angles, London, University of California Press, 1987, p. 4.

47 See *The Life of Christina of Markyate: A Twelfth Century Recluse*, C. H. Talbot (ed. and trans.), Oxford, Oxford University Press, 1959; repr. Toronto and Buffalo, University of Toronto Press, 1998, pp. v–ix. See also Christopher J. Holdsworth, "Christina of Markyate," in *Medieval Women*, Derek Baker (ed.), Oxford, Blackwell, 1978, pp. 185–204.

48 Ibid., p. 103.

49 Ibid., p. 105.

50 Ibid., pp. 109–11.

51 Ibid., p. 119.

52 Ibid., p. 139.

53 Ibid., p. 155.

54 Ibid., p. 171.

55 On the new mysticism, see Bernard McGinn, *The Flowering of Mysticism*, New York, Crossroad Herder, 1998, pp. 12–69, and idem, "The Changing Shape of Late Medieval Mysticism," *Church History*, 1996, vol. 65, pp. 197–219.

56 See the life of St. Francis, the Legenda Maior, 2.1, in *Bonaventure*, Ewert Cousins (trans.), New York, Ramsey, Toronto, Paulist Press, 1978, p. 191.

57 Ibid., 12.8, p. 298.

58 *Francis and Clare, The Complete Works*, Regis J. Armstrong and Ignatius C. Brady (trans.), New York, Ramsey and Toronto, Paulist Press, 1982, pp. 70, 127.
59 Legenda Maior, 10.2, in *Bonaventure*, p. 273.
60 Ibid., 2.8, 11.14, pp. 215, 289.
61 Ibid., 8.9, 12.3, pp. 258, 295.
62 See above, pp. 46, 54, 57.
63 For a convenient text of this canticle, see *Bonaventure*, pp. 27–8; see also *Francis and Clare*, pp. 38–9.
64 Life of St. Francis, 5.9, in *Bonaventure*, pp. 224–5.
65 Angela of Foligno, *Angela of Foligno, Complete Works*, Paul Lachance (trans.), New York and Mahwah, NJ, Paulist Press, 1993, *Memorial*, ch. 1, p. 124.
66 Ibid., ch. 1, p. 126.
67 Ibid.
68 Ibid., ch. 2, pp. 139–40.
69 Ibid., p. 141.
70 Ibid., p. 142.
71 Ibid., ch. 3, p. 140; ch. 5, p. 164.
72 Ibid., ch. 2, p. 134.
73 Ibid., ch. 4, p. 149.
74 Ibid., ch. 6, pp. 169–70.
75 Ibid., ch. 9, p. 212.
76 Ibid., p. 205.
77 Ibid., ch. 7, p. 186, ch. 4, p. 151.
78 See above, pp. 81–2.
79 Angela of Foligno, *Memorial*, ch. 7, pp. 187–9.
80 Ibid., ch. 9, p. 214.
81 Ibid., ch. 1, p. 131.
82 Ibid., ch. 9, p. 213.
83 Ibid., ch. 3, p. 147.
84 Ibid., ch. 1, p. 128.
85 Ibid., ch. 7, p. 182.
86 Ibid., ch. 7, p. 186.
87 Ibid., ch.9, p. 215.
88 See below, pp. 102, 111.
89 Lachance, ibid., Introduction, pp. 98–9.
90 Angela of Foligno, *Memorial*, ch. 9, p. 212.
91 Jacopone da Todi, *Jacopone da Todi, the Lauds*, Serge and Elizabeth Hughes (trans.), New York, Ramsey, Toronto, Paulist Press, 1982, Laud 68, p. 213, "What life is left for me to live/ Will be a life of solitude."
92 Ibid., no. 34, p. 128.
93 Ibid., no. 79, p. 231.
94 Ibid., no. 90, pp. 267–8.
95 Ibid., no. 90, pp. 264–5.
96 Ibid., no. 84, pp. 241–2.
97 Ibid., no. 85, p. 243.
98 The Cathars followed a dualistic theology of competing and opposite forces of Good and Evil, Light and Darkness, Spirit and Matter.
99 *Dominic*, Vladimir J. Koudelka, OP (ed.), Consuelo Fissler, OP, and Simon Tugwell, OP (trans.), London, Darton, Longman and Todd, 1997, 1, p. 56.
100 Ibid., 174, p. 160.
101 Ibid., 81, p. 88.
102 Ibid., 91, p. 112.

103 *Early Dominicans, Selected Writings*, Simon Tugwell (trans.), Ramsey, NJ, Paulist Press, 1982, p. 97.

104 *Dominic*, 5, p. 58.

105 Ibid., 82, p. 92.

106 Ibid., 75, p. 86; n. 1, p. 174.

107 Ibid., 81, p. 88,

108 Ibid., 82, p. 105.

109 His biographer Bernard Gui described him as "tall and stout," *The Life of Saint Thomas Aquinas, Biographical Documents*, Kenelm Foster, OP (trans. and ed.), London, Green and Co., Baltimore, Helicon, 1959, p. 53.

110 *Albert & Thomas, Selected Writings*, Simon Tugwell (trans.), New York and Mahwah, NJ, Paulist Press, 1988, pp. 230, 282–3, 290.

111 Ibid., p. 277.

112 Simon Tugwell, "The Spirituality of the Dominicans," in *Christian Spirituality II, High Middle Ages and Reformation*, Jill Raitt (ed.), New York, Crossroad, 1977, p. 28.

113 *Life of Saint Thomas Aquinas*, pp. 109–10, 46.

114 Ibid., p. 248.

115 Miriam Marsolais, "Jacques de Vitry and the Canons of St. Victor," in *Two Lives of Marie d'Oignies: The Life by Jacques de Vitry*, Toronto, Peregrina, 1998, pp. 13–36.

116 *The Life of Marie d'Oignies by Jacques de Vitry*, Margot H. King (trans.), in ibid., 1.11A–13, ibid., pp. 53–6.

117 Ibid., 2.45, p. 88.

118 Ibid., 1.16–17, pp. 58–9.

119 Ibid., 1.25, 2.90, pp. 165, 33.

120 Ibid., 2.72, 87–8, 92, pp. 130, 136, 225.

121 Ibid., 1.21, 33, 37, pp. 63, 75, 37.

122 Ibid., 2.55, 77, 82, 86, 106, pp. 98–9, 119, 125, 129, 149.

123 Ibid., 2.109, p. 153.

124 Thomas of Cantimpré, *The Life of Lutgard of Aywières by Thomas of Cantimpré*, Margot H. King (trans.), rev. ed., Toronto, Peregrina, 1991, pp. 17–18.

125 Ibid., 1.1.10–13, pp. 29–32.

126 Ibid., 1.2.14, pp. 33–4.

127 Ibid., 1.2.19, p. 38.

128 Ibid., 3.2.9, p. 96.

129 Ibid., p. 97.

130 Thomas of Cantimpré, *The Life of Christina Mirabilis by Thomas of Cantimpré*, Margot H. King (trans.), Toronto, Peregrina, 1997, 1.4, p. 11.

131 Ibid., 1.5, p. 12.

132 Ibid., 1.5-6, pp. 12–13.

133 Ibid., 2.22, p. 21.

134 Ibid., 3.35, p. 28.

135 Ibid., 4.39, p. 30.

136 Ibid., 2.34, p. 27.

137 Ibid., 5.52–3, pp. 37–8.

138 Thomas of Cantimpré, *The Life of Margaret of Ypres by Thomas of Cantimpré*, Margot H. King (trans.), 2nd ed., Toronto, Peregrina, 1996, 16, p. 31.

139 Ibid., 19, pp. 35–6.

140 Ibid., 30.33, pp. 45, 47.

141 Ibid., 11, 21, 23, pp. 25, 37–8.

142 Ibid., 42, p. 55.

143 Richard Kieckhefer, *Unquiet Souls: Fourteenth-Century Saints and Their Religious Milieu*, Chicago and London, University of Chicago Press, 1984, p. 14.

144 *Mechthild of Magdeburg, The Flowing Light of the Godhead*, Frank Tobin (trans.), New York and Mahwah, NJ, Paulist Press, 1998, 4.2, p. 139.

145 Ibid., 1.29, p. 54.

146 Ibid., 1.44, p. 62.

147 Gertrude of Helfta, *Gertrude of Helfta, The Herald of Divine Love*, Margaret Winkworth (ed. and trans.), New York and Mahwah, NJ, Paulist Press, 1993, 2.1, p. 95.

148 Ibid., Prologue, p. 49.

149 Ibid., 2.4, p. 100.

150 Mechthild of Hackeborn, *Liber specialis gratiae*, 5.30, trans. in Caroline Walker Bynum, *Jesus as Mother*, Berkeley, Los Angeles and London, University of California Press, 1982, p. 225.

151 Brenda M. Bolton, "Mulieres Sanctae," in *Sanctity and Secularity: The Church and the World, Studies in Church History* vol. 10, Derek Baker (ed.), New York, Barnes & Noble, 1973, p. 80.

152 Robert E. Lerner, *The Heresy of the Free Spirit in the Later Middle Ages*, Berkeley, Los Angeles and London, University of California Press, 1972, pp. 46–7, 81–2.

153 Norman Cohn, *The Pursuit of the Millennium*, rev. ed., New York, Oxford University Press, 1970, pp. 152–6; Malcolm Lambert, *Medieval Heresy*, 2nd ed., Oxford and Cambridge, MA, Blackwell, 1992, pp. 99–100.

154 See above, p. 91.

155 *Albert & Thomas*, pp. 236–40.

156 Rudolf Otto, *Mysticism East and West*, Bertha L. Bracey and Richenda C. Payne (trans.), New York, Collier, 1960; Daisetz T. Suzuki, *Mysticism Christian and Buddhist*, London, Sydney, Wellington, Unwin, 1979.

157 *Meister Eckhart, Selected Writings*, Oliver Davies (trans.), London, New York, Victoria, Toronto, Auckland, Penguin, 1994, pp. 61, 182, 258, 171.

158 *Meister Eckhart, a Modern Translation*, Raymond Bernard Blakney (trans.), New York, Harper & Row, 1941, p. 142.

159 *Meister Eckhart, Selected Writings*, pp. 236–7.

160 Ibid., p. 129.

161 Ibid., p. 244.

162 Ibid., p. 207.

163 Ibid., p. 224.

164 Ibid., p. 149.

165 Ibid., p. 176.

166 Ibid., p. 189.

167 Tauler, Josef Schmidt, Introduction, in *Johannes Tauler, Sermons*, Maria Shrady (trans.), New York and Mahwah, NJ, Paulist Press, 1985, p. 31.

168 Ibid., Sermon 1, p. 37.

169 Ibid., Sermon 11, 24, pp. 55, 86

170 Ibid., Sermon 19, p. 72.

171 Ibid., Sermons 19, 29, 24, 40, pp. 71, 104, 89, 137.

172 Suso, *The Life of the Servant*, in *Henry Suso, The Exemplar, With Two German Sermons*, Frank Tobin (ed. and trans.), New York and Mahwah, NJ, Paulist Press, 1989, p. 63.

173 *Johannes Tauler, Sermons*, no. 24, p. 85.

174 Suso, *The Life of the Servant*, p. 64.

175 Ibid., 1.2, p. 66.

176 Ibid.

177 Ibid., 2.50, p. 188.

178 Ibid., 1.14, p. 88.

179 Ibid., 1.18, p. 97.

180 Ibid., 2.35, pp. 139–40.

181 See Tauler's comment above, p. 105, that union with God was unlikely before one's fortieth birthday.

182 Ibid., 1.19, p. 98.

183 On Suso, ibid., 2.41, p. 161; on Tauler, *Sermons*, no. 10, p. 51.

184 Sermon 76, p. 170; Sermon 39, p. 132.

185 See Anna Groh Seesholtz, *Friends of God, Practical Mystics of the Fourteenth Century*, New York, Columbia University Press, 1934; repr. New York, AMS Press, 1970; Rufus M. Jones, *The Flowering of Mysticism, The Friends of God in the Fourteenth Century*, New York, Macmillan, 1939; repr. New York, Hafner Publishing, 1971.

186 Ebner, *Margaret Ebner, Major Works*, Leonard P. Hindsley (ed. and trans.), New York and Mahwah, NJ, Paulist Press, 1993, *Revelations*, p. 125.

187 Ibid., pp. 100, 126.

188 Ibid., p. 111.

189 Ibid., p. 108.

190 Ibid., p. 157.

191 Rosemary Hale, "*Imitatio Mariae*: Motherhood Motifs in Devotional Memoirs," *Mystics Quarterly*, 1990, vol. 16, pp. 193–203, esp. 196–7 for Margaret.

192 Ebner, *Revelations*, p. 132. Margaret's "doll" of Jesus is still in the convent of Maria Medingen, see Ulinka Rublack, "Female Spirituality and the Infant Jesus in Late Medieval Dominican Convents," *Gender & History*, 1994, vol. 6, pp. 37–57, esp. p. 38 for a photograph of it.

193 *Revelations*, pp. 165–6.

194 Ibid., p. 104.

195 Ibid., p. 168.

196 Merswin, *Mystical Writings of Rulman Merswin*, Thomas S. Kepler (ed.), Philadelphia, Westminster Press, 1960, p. 40.

197 Ibid., pp. 41–2.

198 Ibid., p. 51.

199 Ibid., p. 119.

200 Ibid., pp. 123–4.

201 The bodhisattva is one who gains enlightenment but postpones entry into Nirvana to remain in the world in order to assist others escape suffering.

202 Ibid., p. 134.

203 See above, p. 102.

204 Porete, *Marguerite Porete, The Mirror of Simple Souls*, Ellen L. Babinsky (trans.), New York and Mahwah, NJ, Paulist Press, 1993, ch. 63, p. 140.

205 Ibid., ch. 2, p. 81.

206 Ibid., p. 79.

207 Ibid., ch. 122, p. 200.

208 Ibid., ch. 18, p. 101.

209 Ibid., ch. 43, p. 122.

210 Ibid., ch. 66, p. 142.

211 Ibid., ch. 134, p. 217.

212 Ibid., ch. 9, p. 86.

213 Ibid., ch. 85, p. 160.

214 Ibid., ch. 118, pp. 191–2.

215 Ibid., ch. 118, p. 193

216 Ibid., ch. 118, p. 193.

217 See Lerner, *Heresy of the Free Spirit*, pp. 7, 73 n. 32.

218 See Lerner, *Heresy of the Free Spirit*, pp. 76–7; *Marguerite Porete, The Mirror of Simple Souls*, p. 24.

219 Lerner, *Heresy of the Free Spirit*, p. 190.

220 Jan van Ruusbroec, *The Spiritual Espousals*, J. Alaerts (ed.), H. Rolfson (trans.), Collegeville, MN, Liturgical Press, 1995, 2.b2083–8, p. 110.

221 *Mirror of Eternal Blessedness*, in *John Ruusbroec, The Spiritual Espousals and Other Works*, James A. Wiseman, OSB (trans.), Mahwah, NJ, Paulist Press, 1985, p. 231.

222 Paul Verdeyen, SJ, *Ruusbroec and His Mysticism*, André Lefevere (trans.), Collegeville, MN, Liturgical Press, 1994, pp. 146–55, esp. 146, 151.

223 Ruusbroec, *The Little Book of Enlightenment*, in *Corpus Christianum, Continuatio Mediaeualis*, vol. 101, Dr. G. De Baere (ed.), Ph. Crowley and Dr. H. Rolfson (trans.), Turnholt, Brepols, 1989, p. 150.

224 Ruusbroec, *De vita et miraculis fratris Johannis Ruusbroec*, in *Analecta Bollandiana*, vol. 4, Paris, Brussels and Geneva, Société Générale de Librairie Catholique, 1885, chs 14, 9, p. 289.

225 Ruusbroec, *The Spiritual Espousals*, c53–6, p. 115.

226 See below, pp. 173–4, 199.

227 Ruusbroec, *Spiritual Espousals*, b338–55, p. 68; *Little Book of Enlightenment*, p. 134; see also *Mirror of Eternal Blessedness*, p. 196.

228 Ruusbroec, *Little Book of Enlightenment*, p. 152.

229 Ruusbroec, *Mirror of Eternal Blessedness*, p. 196.

230 Ruusbroec, *Sparkling Stone*, p. 241; *Little Book of Enlightenment*, p. 130; *Mirror of Eternal Blessedness*, p. 213.

231 C28–30, p. 114.

232 Gerson, *Jean Gerson, Early Works*, Brian Patrick McGuire (trans.), New York and Mahwah, NJ, Paulist Press, 1998, Letter 13, pp. 202–3.

233 Ibid., p. 204.

234 Ibid.

235 Gerson, *On Distinguishing True From False Religion*, in *Jean Gerson, Early Works*, p. 349.

236 Ibid., pp. 348–9, 362–3.

237 Brian Patrick McGuire, "Late Medieval Care and Control of Women: Jean Gerson and His Sisters," *Revue d'Histoire Ecclésiastique*, 1997, vol. 92, p. 8.

238 See below, pp. 152–5, 159–62.

239 Gerson, *Jean Gerson, Early Works*, 3, pp. 77–8.

240 Ibid., 23, p. 96.

241 Ibid., 35, p. 109.

242 Ibid., 44, pp. 123–4.

243 Ibid., 45, pp. 124–5.

244 Gerson, Letter 21, in *Jean Gerson, Early Works*, p. 233.

245 Gerson, *On Distinguishing True From False Revelations*, in ibid., p.338.

246 Ibid., p. 354.

247 Régine Pernoud, *Joan of Arc By Herself and Her Witnesses*, Edward Hyams (trans.), Lanham, New York and London, Scarborough House, 1982, pp. 23–4.

248 Ibid., p. 58.

249 Ibid., pp. 62–3.

250 Ibid., pp. 142–3.

251 Ibid., p. 275.

252 Ibid., p. 209.

253 Ibid., p. 269.

254 See below, p. 175.

255 Richard Rolle, *The Fire of Love*, Clifton Wolters (trans.), Harmondsworth, Baltimore and Victoria, Penguin, 1972, ch. 15, pp. 91–5.

256 Ibid., Prologue, p. 45.

257 Ibid., ch. 14, pp. 88–9.

258 See above, p. 39–40.

259 Rolle, *The Form of Living*, ch. 2, pp. 157–8, in *Richard Rolle, The English Writings*, Rosamund S. Allen (trans.), London, SPCK, 1989.

260 Rolle, *The Fire of Love*, Prologue, p. 46.

261 Ibid., ch. 5, p. 61.

262 Ibid., ch. 29, p. 136.

263 Ibid., ch. 12, p. 81.

264 Hope Emily Allen, *Writings Ascribed to Richard Rolle, Hermit of Hampole, and Materials for His Biography*, New York, D. C. Heath, and London, Oxford University Press, 1927, pp. 335, and pp. 527–37, for the text of the "Defence Against the Detractors of Richard" by the hermit Thomas Basset.

265 Michael Sargent, "Contemporary Criticism of Richard Rolle," *Analecta Cartusiana*, 1981, vol. 55, pp. 160–87, esp. 182–7; Sargent published the Latin text of Basset's text in an appendix to this article, "A Diplomatic Transcript of Thomas Basset's *Defense* of Richard Rolle," pp. 188–205.

266 Dom David Knowles, *The English Mystical Tradition*, New York, Harper & Brothers, 1961, p. 64; see also Allen, *Richard Rolle, The English Writings*, p. 2.

267 Wolters in *The Fire of Love*, pp. 26–7; Thomas Merton, *Mystics and Zen Masters*, New York, Farrar, Straus and Giroux, 1967, pp. 147–50; McGinn, "The English Mystics," p. 196; and see above, pp. 33–5, 40, 56, 58, 66–8, 73.

268 Adolar Zumkeller, "The Spirituality of the Augustinians," in Raitt, ed., *Christian Spirituality II*, p. 64.

269 C. H. Lawrence, *Medieval Monasticism*, 2nd ed., London and New York, Longman, 1989, pp. 166–7.

270 Paul De Jaegher, *An Anthology of Christian Mysticism*, Springfield, IL, Templegate, 1977, p. 70.

271 Walter Hilton, *The Scale of Perfection*, John P.H. Clark and Rosemary Dorward (trans.), New York and Mahwah, NJ, Paulist Press, 1991, 1.9, p. 83.

272 Ibid., 1.22, p. 96; 72, pp. 144–5; 76, p. 148.

273 Ibid., 1.60–61, pp. 131–3.

274 Ibid., 2.31, p. 258; 32, p. 259; 34, p. 263; 46, p. 301.

275 Ibid., 2.30, p. 236.

276 Ibid., 1.10, pp. 83–4.

277 Ibid., 1.26, p. 98.

278 Ibid., introduction, p. 51.

279 Ibid., 1.37, p. 108.

280 Bernard McGinn, "The English Mystics," in *Christian Spirituality II*, Raitt, ed., p. 197.

281 *The Cloud of Unknowing and Other Works*, Clifton Wolters (trans.), Harmondsworth, New York, Victoria, Ontario, Auckland, Penguin, 1978, *The Cloud of Unknowing*, ch. 45, p. 114, ch. 57, p. 130.

282 Ibid., pp. 205–18.

283 *The Cloud of Unknowing*, in ibid. ch. 12, p. 76.

284 Ibid., ch. 26, p. 95.

285 *The Cloud of Unknowing*, chs 5, 8, pp. 68, 73.

286 *Epistle of Privy Counsel*, in ibid., ch. 12, pp. 198–9.

287 Ibid., ch. 9, p. 185.

288 *The Cloud of Unknowing*, ch. 39, p. 107.

289 Ibid., ch. 21, p. 89; and see ch. 18, p. 84.

290 *The Commandment*, in *Richard Rolle, The English Writings*, p. 150; see also *The Form of Living*, in ibid., ch. 9, p. 173.

291 *The Cloud of Unknowing*, ch. 7, pp. 69–70.

292 On anchoresses, see above, p. 84–5, 122.

293 As did her younger contemporary and fellow mystic Margery Kempe, who recorded at least one visit to Julian in her *Book*, 1.18, *The Book of Margery Kempe, A New Translation*, John Skinner (trans.), New York, London, Toronto, Sydney, Auckland, Image Books , 1998, pp. 73–5.

294 Short Text 4, Long Text 5, *Julian of Norwich, Showings*, Edmund Colledge and James Walsh (trans.), New York, Ramsey and Toronto, Paulist Press, 1978, pp. 130–1, 183–4.

295 Ibid., pp. 166, 137, 192, 197–9 (Short Text 8, 23; Long Text 9, 11).

296 Ibid., p. 288 (Long Text 56).

297 Ibid., pp. 166 (Short Text 23).

298 Ibid., pp. 262–3 (Long Text 48–9).

299 Ibid., pp. 137, 166, 236 (Short Text 8, 23; Long Text 34).

300 Ibid., p. 225 (Long Text 27).

301 Ibid., p. 151 (Short Text 15).

302 Ibid., pp. 231–3 (Long Text 32).

303 Ibid., p. 293 (Long Text 58).

304 Ibid., p. 294 (Long Text 58).

305 Ibid., p. 295 (Long Text 59).

306 Bynum, *Jesus as Mother*, pp. 110–69; Grace M. Jantzen, *Julian of Norwich, Mystic and Theologian*, New York and Mahwah, NJ, Paulist Press, 1988, pp. 115–24; Frances Beer, *Women and Mystical Experience in the Middle Ages*, Woodbridge, Suffolk, and Rochester, Boydell, 1992, pp. 151–7.

307 Ibid., p. 234 (Long Text 33).

308 See above, p. 121; and see Knowles, *English Mystical Tradition*, pp.146–7; on this topic, see also Eluned Bremner, "Margery Kempe and the Critics: Disempowerment and Deconstruction," in *Margery Kempe: A Book of Essays*, Sandra J. McEntire (ed.), New York and London, Garland, 1992, pp. 117–35.

309 Underhill, *Mysticism*, 12th ed., London and New York, Methuen and E. P. Dutton, 1930; repr. New York, Meridian, 1974, p. 466.

310 See above, n. 293.

311 Kempe, *The Book of Margery Kempe*, trans. Skinner, 1.18, pp. 73–5.

312 Ibid., 1.1, p. 27.

313 Ibid., pp. 27–8.

314 Ibid., 1.3, p. 31.

315 Ibid., 1.36, p. 134.

316 Ibid., 1.35, p. 130.

317 Ibid., 1.89, p. 296.

318 Ibid., 1.35, p. 131.

319 Ibid., 1.72, p. 242.

320 Ibid., 1.35, p. 130.

321 Ibid., 1.64, p. 224.

322 Clarissa W. Atkinson, *Mystic and Pilgrim, The Book and the World of Margery Kempe*, Ithaca and London, Cornell University Press, 1983, pp. 50–1.

323 Kempe, *The Book of Margery Kempe*, 1.67, p. 232.

324 Ibid., 1.62, pp. 217–19.

325 See below, p. 130.

326 Kempe, *The Book of Margery Kempe*, Introduction, p. 16.

327 Beginning in 1309, popes had been in residence in Avignon, in Provence, rather than in Rome due to the political instability in the Papal States.

328 See below, pp. 155–6.

329 Raymond, *The Life of St Catherine of Siena by Blessed Raymond of Capua*, George Lamb (trans.), New York, P. J. Kennedy & Sons, 1960, 1.2, p. 25.

330 On tertiaries, see above, p. 88.

331 *Life of St Catherine.*, 1.7, p. 61.

332 Ibid., 2.2, p. 113.

333 Ibid., 2.6, p. 164.

334 Ibid., 1.12, pp. 99–100.

335 Ibid., 2.6, pp. 165–6.

336 Ibid., 2.6, p. 170.
337 Ibid., pp. 174–6.
338 Ibid., pp. 192–3.
339 See above, n. 327.
340 Raymond, *Life of St Catherine*, 2.4, pp. 138–9.
341 *The Letters of St. Catherine of Siena*, vol. I, Suzanne Noffke, OP (trans.), Binghamton, NY, State University of New York at Binghamton, 1988, no. 71, p. 222.
342 On Jean Gerson and the Great Schism, see above, p. 116.
343 *Letters of St. Catherine of Siena*, no. 65, pp. 207–8.
344 Raymond, *Life of St Catherine*, 2.6, pp. 168–9.
345 Catherine of Siena, *Catherine of Siena, the Dialogue*, trans. Suzanne Noffke, OP (trans.), New York and Mahwah, NJ, Paulist Press, 1980, 124, p. 239, 127, p. 249.
346 Ibid., 23, 51, pp. 60, 105; 43, p. 88.
347 Ibid., 151, p. 323.
348 Ibid., 96, p. 181.
349 Ibid., 112, p. 211; note that Raymond of Capua reported that as Catherine received Communion, "it seemed to her as though her soul entered into the Lord and the Lord into her, as the fish enters into the water and the water surrounds it; and she felt so absorbed in God that she could hardly get to her cell," *Life of St Catherine*, 2.6, p. 173.
350 Raymond, *Life of St Catherine*, 1.10, p. 86.
351 Ibid., 3.4, p. 344.
352 Bridget, *Birgitta of Sweden*, Marguerite Tjader Harris (ed.), Albert Ryle Kezel (trans.), New York and Mahwah, Paulist Press, 1990, *The Life of Blessed Birgitta*, 9, p. 73.
353 Ibid., 26, p. 78.
354 Ibid., *Seventh Book of Revelations*, prologue, p. 160.
355 Ibid., 4, p. 161.
356 Ibid., 19, p. 196.
357 Ibid., 3–4, p. 101.
358 Bridget, *Revelations*, 6.63, in *Sancta Birgitta, Revelaciones*, Book VI, Birger Bergh (ed.), Stockholm, Almqvist & Wiksell International, 1991, p. 208.
359 *Extrauagancium* 44, 1–7, quoted in Helen M. Redpath, *God's Ambassadress*, Milwaukee, Bruce, 1947, p.91.
360 *Revelations*, 4.45; 8.51; quoted in Redpath, *God's Ambassadress*, p. 112.
361 *Seventh Book of Revelations*, 21.7, p. 203.
362 *Life of Blessed Birgitta*, 95, p. 98.
363 On Margery, see above, pp. 126–8.
364 *The Book of Margery Kempe*, 1.39, pp. 139–40.
365 Catherine of Genoa, *The Spiritual Dialogue*, I, in *Catherine of Genoa: Purgation and Purgatory, The Spiritual Dialogue*, Serge Hughes (trans.), New York, Paulist Press, 1979, pp. 109–10.
366 Two vols, London and New York, J. M. Dent & Sons.
367 Catherine, *The Spiritual Dialogue*, III, p. 143.
368 *Treatise on Purgatory*, retitled *Purgation and Purgatory* in *Catherine of Genoa: Purgation and purgatory, The Spiritual Dialogue*, p. 71.
369 Ibid., p. 84.
370 Von Hügel, *Mystical Element of Religion*, 1:160.
371 Catherine, *The Spiritual Dialogue*, II, p. 133.
372 Catherine, *The Life and Doctrine of St. Catherine of Genoa*, in *The Spiritual Doctrine of St. Catherine of Genoa*, Rockford, IL, Tan Books, 1989 [first published as *Life and Doctrine of St. Catherine of Genoa*, New York, Christian Press Association Publishing Co., 1874], ch. 25, p. 93.
373 Catherine, *The Spiritual Dialogue*, III, p. 143.
374 Ibid., pp. 140–1.

375 Columbus, *The Libro de las profecías of Christopher Columbus*, Delno C. West and August Kling (trans. and commentary), Gainesville, FL, University of Florida Press, 1991.
376 Ibid., p. 105.
377 Ibid., pp. 54–5.
378 It has been estimated that between 1500 and 1650, approximately 181 tons of gold and 16,000 tons of silver reached Europe from America through official channels, J. H. Elliott, *Spain and Its World, 1500–1700, Selected Essays*, New Haven, Yale University Press, 1989, p. 19.

IV MYSTICS IN EARLY MODERN EUROPE

1 See above, p. 102, 110.
2 Abraham Friesen, *Thomas Muentzer, a Destroyer of the Godless*, Berkeley, Los Angeles, Oxford, University of California Press, 1990, p. 32.
3 See above, pp. 108.
4 Thomas Müntzer, *Prague Manifesto*, in *The Collected Works of Thomas Müntzer*, Peter Metheson (ed. and trans.), Edinburgh, T. & T. Clark, 1988, p. 377.
5 *Prague Manifesto*, p. 358.
6 Ibid., p. 378.
7 Johann Arndt, *True Christianity*, Peter Erb (trans.), New York and Mahwah, NJ, Paulist Press, 1979, 6.3.2, pp. 276–7.
8 Ibid., Preface, p. 23.
9 Ibid., 6.3.2, p. 280.
10 Ibid., 1, Foreword, pp. 21–2.
11 Ibid., 1.11, p. 69.
12 Ibid., 1.4, p. 42.
13 Ibid., 1.19, p. 103.
14 Ibid., 1.21, p. 112.
15 Ibid., 5.2.7, p. 256.
16 Ibid., 1.6, p. 40.
17 *De Vita et Scriptis* 11, cited in John Joseph Stoudt, *Jacob Boehme: His Life and Thought*, New York, Seabury Press, 1968, p. 50.
18 *Libri Apologetici, wieder Balthasar Tilken*, preface, 26, in Jacob Böhme, *Sämtliche Schriften*, 11 vols, Will-Erich Peuckert (ed.), F. Frommanns, Stuttgart, 1955–61, 5:5; trans. Stoudt, *Jacob Boehme*, p. 60.
19 Letter 12, dated 1621, in Jacob Böhme, *Jacob Boehme, Essential Readings*, Robin Waterfield (ed.), Wellingborough, Northamptonshire, Crucible, 1989, p. 64.
20 Böhme, *The Aurora*, John Sparrow (trans.), London, John M. Watkins and James Clarke & Co., 1960, 18.9, 19.11, 13, pp. 453, 488, in *Sämtliche Schriften* 1:246, 266.
21 Böhme, Letter 12 in *Essential Readings*, p. 64.
22 Böhme, *Libri Apologetici wieder Tilken*, preface, 31,7, in *Sämtliche Schriften* 5:6; trans. Stoudt, *Jacob Boehme*, p. 60.
23 Böhme, *Mysterium Magnum*, 40.94, 98, in *Sämtliche Schriften* 7:408–9, trans. Stoudt, ibid., p. 292.
24 Böhme, *Of The Incarnation of Jesus Christ*, John Rolleston Earle (trans.), London, Constable and Co., 1934, 3.1.2, p. 237.
25 Andrew Weeks, *Boehme, An Intellectual Biography of the Seventeenth-Century Philosopher and Mystic*, Albany, NY, State University of New York Press, 1991, p. 174.
26 See below, ch. 5, pp. 181–4, 187–9.
27 See Signe Toksvig, *Emanuel Swedenborg, Scientist and Mystic*, London, Faber & Faber, 1948, pp. 578–8.

28 Emanuel Swedenborg, *Swedenborg's Journal of Dreams, 1743–1744*, G. E. Klemming and William Ross Woofenden (eds), J. J. G. Wilkinson (trans.), 2nd ed., Bryn Athyn, PA, Swedenborg Scientific Association, and London, Swedenborg Society, 1989.

29 Ibid., 51, p. 22.

30 Ibid., 52-7, pp. 22–4.

31 Ibid., 65, p. 27.

32 Ibid., 81, p. 33.

33 Ibid., 80, p. 33.

34 Cyriel Odhner Sigstedt, *The Swedenborg Epic*, New York, AMS Press, 1952, repr. New York, AMS Press, 1971, p. 198.

35 Swedenborg, *Arcana Coelestia* 68, in *Conversations with Angels, What Swedenborg Heard in Heaven*, Leonard Fox and Donald L. Rose (eds), David Gladish and Jonathan Rose (trans.), West Chester, PA, Chrysalis Books, 1996, p. 3.

36 Sigstedt, *Swedenborg Epic*, p. 280.

37 *Journal of the American Society for Psychical Research*, quoted in Toksvig, *Emanuel Swedenborg*, p. 332.

38 Sigstedt, *Swedenborg Epic*, p. 404.

39 Alastair Hamilton, *Heresy and Mysticism in Sixteenth-Century Spain: The Alumbrados*, Cambridge, James Clarke & Co., 1992, p. 20.

40 See below, p. 153.

41 Osuna, *Francisco de Osuna, The Third Spiritual Alphabet*, Mary E. Giles (trans.), New York and Mahwah, NJ, Paulist Press, 1981, 6.2, p. 164.

42 Ibid., 21.3, pp. 556–7.

43 Ibid., 3.3, 13.3, pp. 105, 347.

44 Ibid., 6.4, p. 171.

45 Ibid., 1.1, p. 48.

46 Ibid., 12.7, p. 335.

47 Ibid., 5.2, p. 154, 9.6, p. 265, 16.9, p. 442.

48 Ignatius of Loyola, *Autobiography*, 1, Parmanandar R. Divarkar (trans.), in *Ignatius of Loyola, The Spiritual Exercises and Selected Works*, George E. Ganss (ed.), New York and Mahwah, NJ, Paulist Press, 1991, p. 68.

49 Ibid., 10, p. 71.

50 Ibid., 30, pp. 80–1.

51 Ibid., 48, p. 88.

52 Ibid., 71, p. 99.

53 Ibid., 85, p. 104.

54 Ibid., 96, p. 109.

55 Ignatius, *Spiritual Diary*, 8, Edward J. Malatesta (trans.), in *Ignatius of Loyola, The Spiritual Exercises and Selected Works*, p. 240.

56 Ibid., 10, p. 241.

57 Ibid., 62, p. 247.

58 Ibid., 74, p. 250.

59 Ignatius, *Autobiography*, 99, p. 111.

60 Ignatius, *Spiritual Exercises*, George E. Ganss (trans.), in *Ignatius of Loyola, The Spiritual Exercises and Selected Works*, 104, 15, pp. 148, 125.

61 Ignatius, *Autobiography*, 98, p. 110.

62 Teresa, *The Life of Saint Teresa of Ávila by Herself*, J. M. Cohen (trans.), London, New York, Victoria, Markham, Ontario, Auckland, Penguin, 1957, ch. 4, p. 35.

63 Ibid., p. 36.

64 Ibid.

65 Ibid., ch. 25, p. 175.

66 Ibid., p. 177.

67 Ibid., ch. 10, p. 71.

68 Ibid., ch. 20, p. 137.

69 Ibid., p. 142.

70 Ibid., ch. 28, p. 202.

71 Ibid., ch, 38, p. 285.

72 Ibid., ch 22, pp. 153–4.

73 Teresa, *Teresa of Ávila, The Interior Castle*, Kieran Kavanaugh and Otilio Rodriguez (trans.), New York and Ramsey, NJ, Paulist Press, 1979, 7.2.9, p. 181.

74 John of the Cross, *The Spiritual Canticle*, in *The Collected Works of St. John of the Cross*, Kieran Kavanaugh, OCD, and Otilio Rodriguez, OCD (trans.), rev. ed., Washington, D.C., ICS Publications, 1991, Prologue, 2, 4, pp. 470–1.

75 John, *The Ascent of Mount Carmel*, in *Collected Works*, Theme, p. 113; Prologue, 9, p. 118.

76 Ibid., 2.29.4, p. 257.

77 John, *The Dark Night*, in *Collected Works*, 2.2.3, p. 397.

78 John, *Ascent of Mount Carmel*, 2.11.5.

79 On apophaticism, see above, p. 36.

80 John, *The Ascent of Mount Carmel*, 1.4.5.

81 Ibid., 2.4.4.

82 Ibid., 1.10.1.

83 Ibid., 1.8.3, p. 376.

84 Ibid., 2.17.6, p. 437.

85 Maurice Henry-Coüannier, *Saint Francis de Sales and His Friends*, Veronica Morrow (trans.), Staten Island, NY, Alba House, 1964, p. 45.

86 Francis de Sales, *Introduction to the Devout Life*, John K. Ryan (trans.), New York, London, Toronto, Sydney, Auckland, Image Books, 1972, 1.3, p. 45.

87 Ibid., 1.1, p. 40.

88 Ibid., 3.2, pp. 126–7.

89 For example, see ibid., 1.9, p. 52.

90 Ibid., 2.1.2,5, pp. 81–2.

91 Ibid., 2.1.8, p. 83.

92 Ibid., 2.2., pp, 83–4.

93 Ibid., 2.9, p. 93.

94 Ibid., 4.23, p. 268.

95 Ibid., p. 19.

96 Francis de Sales, *St. Francis de Sales, Treatise on the Love of God*, Henry Benedict Mackey, OSB, (trans.), Westminster, MD, Newman Bookshop, 1945; repr. Westport, CT, Greenwood Press, 1971, preface, p. 15.

97 Ibid., 1.9, p. 39.

98 Ibid., 1.10, pp. 42–3.

99 Ibid., 2.14, p. 101.

100 Ibid., 3.6, p. 145.

101 Ibid., 6.11, p. 262.

102 Ibid., p. 352.

103 Blaise Pascal, *Pensées*, A. J. Krailsheimer (trans.), rev. ed., London, New York, Ringwood, Toronto, Auckland, Penguin, 1995, p. 285.

104 Pascal, *Pascal, The Provincial Letters*, A. J. Krailsheimer (trans.), Harmondsworth, Middlesex, Baltimore, Victoria, Penguin Books, 1967, letters nine, p. 134; five, p. 75; ten, p. 160.

105 Ibid., 172, pp. 149–50; 305, p. 208.

106 See above, p. 160.

107 This work was styled *The Autobiography of Venerable Marie of the Incarnation, O.S.U., Mystic and Missionary*, trans. John J. Sullivan, SJ, Chicago, Loyola University Press, 1964.

108 Marie, *Marie of the Incarnation, Selected Writings*, Irene Mahoney, OSU (ed.), New York and Mahwah, NJ, Paulist Press, 1989, Relation of 1654, 20, p. 78.

109 Ibid., 1, pp. 41–2.
110 Ibid., 6, pp. 49–50.
111 Ibid., 10, p. 58.
112 Ibid., 12, p. 63.
113 Ibid., 16, p. 71.
114 Ibid., 18, p. 74.
115 Ibid., p. 75.
116 Ibid., 19, p. 76.
117 Ibid., 22–23, pp. 81–3.
118 Ibid., 29, p. 93.
119 Ibid., 31, p. 96.
120 Ibid., 34, p. 102.
121 Ibid., 38, p. 111.
122 Ibid., 37, p. 109.
123 Ibid., 39, p. 112.
124 Ibid., 41, p. 116.
125 Ibid., 52, p. 143.
126 Ibid., 64, p. 168.
127 Marie, *Words From New France, The Selected Letters of Marie de l'Incarnation*, Joyce Marshall (ed. and trans.), Toronto, Oxford University Press, 1967, p. 366.
128 Ibid., pp. 368, 343.
129 Lawrence, First Conversation, 1, in *Brother Lawrence of the Resurrection, OCD, Writings and Conversations on the Practice of the Presence of God*, Conrad De Meester, OCD (ed.), Salvatore Sciurba, OCD (trans.), Washington, DC, ICS Publications, 1994, p. 89.
130 Eulogy, 15, ibid., p. 8.
131 Second Conversation, 18, ibid., p. 93.
132 Letter of Joseph de Beaufort, ibid., p. 147.
133 *The Ways of Brother Lawrence*, 10, ibid., p. 116.
134 Letter 9, ibid., p. 69.
135 See below, pp. 169.
136 Letter 2, ibid., pp. 52–3.
137 Eulogy, 26-7, ibid., p. 11.
138 Eulogy, 32, ibid., p. 13.
139 *Spiritual Maxims*, 6.31, ibid., p. 41.
140 Ibid., 2.6, p. 36.
141 Letter 3, ibid., p. 57.
142 See below, pp. 181–7.
143 Quoted in James Herbert Davis, Jr., *Fénelon*, Boston, Twayne Publishers, 1979, p.18.
144 Ibid., p. 106.
145 Guyon, *Autobiography of Madame Guyon*, Thomas Taylor Allen (trans.), 2 vols, London, Kegan Paul, Trench, Treubner & Co., 1897, 1.8, 1:66–7. .
146 Ibid., 1.10, 1:76; 1.12, 1:96.
147 Ibid., 1.12, 1:92.
148 Ibid., 1.13, 1:100.
149 Ibid., p. 107.
150 Ibid., 1.21, 1:165.
151 Ibid., 1.28, 1:216.
152 Clarke Garrett, *Spirit Possession and Popular Religion From the Camisards to the Shakers*, Baltimore and London, Johns Hopkins University Press, 1987, pp. 16–17.
153 Lawrence, The Second Conversation, 12, in *Brother Lawrence of the Resurrection*, pp. 92, 116.
154 On the Quakers, see below, ch. 5, pp. 179–81.
155 B. Robert Krieser, *Miracles, Convulsions, and Ecclesiastical Politics in Early Eighteenth-Century Paris*, Princeton, Princeton University Press, 1978, p. 398.

156 Ibid., p. 390.
157 David Knowles, *What Is Mysticism?*, London, Burns & Oats, 1967; repr. London, Sheed and Ward, 1988, p. 9.

V POST-REFORMATION MYSTICS IN ENGLAND AND AMERICA

1 Fr. Augustine Baker, *Holy Wisdom or Directions for the Prayer of Contemplation* Wheathampstead, Hertfordshire, Anthony Clarke, 1964, repr. 1972, 3.4.1, p. 452.
2 Fr. Serenus Cressy, *The Life of the Venerable Father Augustine Baker*, in *The Life of Father Augustine Baker, O.S.B. (1575–1641)*, Justin McCann (ed.), London, Burns, Oates & Washbourne, 1933, 40, p. 76.
3 Anthony Low, *Augustine Baker*, New York, Twayne Publishers, 1970, p. 7.
4 Gertrude More, *The Writings of Dame Gertrude More*, Dom Benedict Weld-Blundell (ed.), Manchester, Birmingham, Glasgow, R. & T. Washbourne, 1910, *Apology*, 60, p. 274.
5 Ibid., *Confession* 18, p. 64.
6 Evelyn Underhill, *Mysticism*, 12th ed., London and New York, Methuen and E. P. Dutton, 1930; repr. New York, Meridian, 1974, p. 88.
7 Ibid., p. 43.
8 Cressy, *Life*, in McCann, ed., *Life*, 67, p. 93.
9 Baker, *Holy Wisdom*, 1.1.5, p. 27.
10 Ibid., 1.2.2, pp. 48, 50.
11 Ibid., 1.2.2, p. 45.
12 Ibid., 1.2.1, p. 41.
13 George Fox, *The Journal of George Fox*, John L. Nickalls (ed.), Cambridge, University Press, 1952, p. 11.
14 Ibid., pp. 14–15.
15 Ibid., p. 19.
16 Ibid., p. 33.
17 Ibid., p. 34.
18 Ibid., p. 21.
19 Ibid., p. 58.
20 *English Spirituality in the Age of Wesley*, David Lyle Jeffrey (ed.), Grand Rapids, MI, William. B. Eerdmans, 1987, p. 6.
21 A. Keith Walker, *William Law, His Life and Thought*, London, SPCK, 1973, pp. 3–4.
22 Caroline F. E. Spurgeon, "William Law and the Mystics," ch. 12 in *The Cambridge History of English Literature*, A. W. Ward and A. R. Waller (eds), vol. 9, New York, G. P. Putnam's Sons, Cambridge, University Press, 1913, p. 350.
23 William Law, *A Serious Call*, in *William Law, A Serious Call to a Devout Life and Holy Life, The Spirit of Love*, Paul G. Stanwood (trans.), New York, Ramsey and Toronto, Paulist Press, 1981, ch. 1, pp. 47–8, ch. 4, p. 86.
24 Ibid., ch. 17, pp. 237, 246.
25 Law, *Two Answers to Dr. Trapp*, in *Selected Mystical Writings of William Law*, Stephen Hobhouse (ed.), London, C.W. Daniel Company Ltd, 1938, p. 33.
26 Law, *Serious Call*, ch. 4, p. 82.
27 Ibid., ch. 14, p. 196.
28 Ibid., ch. 14, p. 197.
29 Ibid., ch. 14, p. 198.
30 Spurgeon, "Law and the Mystics," p. 365.
31 Law, *The Spirit of Prayer*, in *Selected Mystical Writings*, p. 114.
32 Ibid., p. 115.

33 John Byrom, *Selections from the Journal & Papers of John Byrom, Poet-Diarist-Shorthand Writer 1691–1763*, Henri Talon (ed.), London, Rockliff, 1950, 19 April 1737, p. 175.
34 Law, *Serious Call*, ch. 14, p. 197.
35 Law, *First Dialogue*, in *William Law, A Serious Call ... and the Spirit of Love*, pp. 402–3.
36 Ibid., p. 403.
37 Law, *Spirit of Love, Third Dialogue*, in *William Law, A Serious Call ... and the Spirit of Love*, p. 468.
38 Law, *Spirit of Love, First Dialogue*, in *William Law, A Serious Call ... and the Spirit of Love*, pp. 418, 413, 392, 422.
39 Ibid., pp. 394, 398.
40 Law, *Spirit of Love, Second Dialogue*, pp. 432, 435.
41 Ibid., p. 450.
42 See Wesley's journal for 4 June 1742, in *The Works of John Wesley*, vol. 19, *Journal and Diaries II*, W. Reginald Ward and Richard P. Heitzenraters (eds), Nashville, Abingdon Press, 1990, p. 272.
43 Spurgeon, "Law and the Mystics," p. 359.
44 Walker, *William Law*, p. 229.
45 Wesley, *A Plain Account of Christian Perfection*, in *John and Charles Wesley, Selected Prayers, Hymns, Journal Notes, Sermons, Letters and Treatises*, Frank Whaling (ed.), Mahwah, NJ, Paulist Press, 1981, p. 299.
46 Quoted in John A. Newton, *Susanna Wesley and the Puritan Tradition in Methodism*, London, Epworth Press, 1968, p. 133.
47 John Wesley's *Journal*, Tuesday, January 24, 1738, in Whaling, ed., *John and Charles Wesley*, p. 102.
48 His letter to Mrs. Bennis, January 10, 1777, in *John and Charles Wesley*, p. 167.
49 See above, p. 140–1.
50 2 Pet. 1.4.
51 Mark 12.34.
52 Journal, May 24, 1738, 13, in *John Wesley*, Albert C. Outler (ed.), New York, Oxford University Press, 1964, p. 66.
53 Ibid., 10, 16, pp. 64, 67.
54 Ibid., 7, p. 63.
55 *The Witness of the Spirit, Discourse II*, II.2, in ibid., pp. 211–12.
56 Wesley, *A Plain Account of Genuine Christianity*, II.12, III.1, in *John and Charles Wesley*, pp. 129.
57 Journal, May 28, 1738, *John Wesley*, Outler, ed., p. 58.
58 Wesley, *A Plain Account of Christian Perfection*, Q. (18, 19), in *John and Charles Wesley*, pp. 353–4.
59 Ibid., Q (33), pp. 362–3.
60 8, 12, 16, in *The Works of John Wesley*, vol. 2, *Sermons II 34–70*, Albert C. Outler (ed.), Nashville, Abingdon Press, 1985, pp. 48, 50–2.
61 Toksvig, *Emanuel Swedenborg*, p. 304.
62 G. E. Bentley, Jr., *Blake Records*, Oxford, Clarendon Press, 1969, pp. 7, 519; *The Complete Poetry and Prose of William Blake*, David V. Erdman (ed.), rev. ed., Berkeley and Los Angeles, University of California Press, 1982, *The Marriage of Heaven and Hell*, pl. 12, "The Prophets Isaiah and Ezekiel dined with me," p. 38.
63 Bentley, *Blake Records*, p. 222.
64 Ibid., p. 13.
65 Ibid., p. 32.
66 Blake, *Complete Poetry and Prose*, ed. Erdmann, letter to Thomas Butts of 30 January 1803, p. 724.
67 Ibid., letter to Thomas Butts of 25 April 1803, p. 728.
68 Ibid., letter to William Hayley, 23 October 1804, p. 757.

69 Ibid., *Jerusalem*, pl. 5, ch. 1, p. 147.
70 Ibid., *Auguries of Innocence*, ll. 1–4, p. 490.
71 Ibid., *All Religions Are One*, Principle 4, p. 1.
72 Ibid., *There Is No Natural Religion [a]*, II, p. 2.
73 Ibid., *There Is No Natural Religion [b]*, p. 3.
74 Ibid., *Songs and Ballads*, ll. 13–14.
75 Ibid., *The Laocoön*, p. 274; *The Everlasting Gospel*, l. 45.
76 Ibid., *The Marriage of Heaven and Hell*, pl. 11, p. 38; *Jerusalem*, pl. 4, ch. 1, ll. 18–20; *Milton*, 1, pl. 20 (22), p. 114.
77 Ibid., *Jerusalem*, pl. 5, ch. 1, p. 147.
78 *Blake Records*, p. 310.
79 G. E. Bentley, *Blake Records Supplement*, Oxford, Clarendon Press, 1988, p. xxxi.
80 *Blake Records*, pp. 470–1 and Plate LII.
81 *Blake Records Supplement*, p. xx; a photograph of the signature is in Peter Ackroyd, *Blake*, New York, Knopf, 1996, following p. 64.
82 *Blake Records*, p. 237.
83 Ibid., p. 222.
84 Ibid., p. 347.
85 Jon Butler, "Enthusiasm Described and Decried: The Great Awakening as Interpretative Fiction," *Journal of American History*, 1982, vol. 69, p. 309.
86 *The Great Awakening, Documents on the Revival of Religion, 1740–1745*, Richard L. Bushman (ed.), New York, Atheneum, 1970, p. 66.
87 See the text in Michael J. Crawford, "The Spiritual Travels of Nathan Cole," *William and Mary Quarterly*, 1976, 3rd ser., vol. 33, pp. 89–126, esp. p. 93.
88 Ibid., p. 96.
89 Ibid., p. 97.
90 Ibid., p. 99.
91 Ibid., pp. 99–100.
92 Ibid., pp. 109–10.
93 Ibid., pp. 105–6.
94 Ibid., p. 116.
95 Ibid., p. 94.
96 Jonathan Edwards, *A Jonathan Edwards Reader*, John E. Smith, Harry S. Stout, and Kenneth P. Minkema (eds), New Haven and London, Yale University Press, 1995, pp. 91, 95, 102, 105.
97 David S. Lovejoy, *Religious Enthusiasm in the New World, Heresy to Revolution*, Cambridge, MA, and London, Harvard University Press, 1985, p. 190.
98 In Jonathan Edwards, *Works of Jonathan Edwards*, vol. 4, *The Great Awakening*, C. C. Goen (ed.), New Haven and London, Yale University Press, 1972, pp. 258–9.
99 In ibid., p. 334.
100 Ibid., p. 341.
101 Ibid., p. 344.
102 Edwards, *The Works of Jonathan Edwards*, vol. 1, London, 1834; repr. Peabody, MA, Hendrickson Publishers, 1998, p. civ.
103 Ibid., pp. cv–vi, cviii.
104 Ibid., pp. cv–vii.
105 Ibid., pp. cvii–viii.
106 Ibid., pp. cvii–viii.
107 Ibid., pp. cvii.
108 Ibid., pp. cv, cvi, cx.
109 Ibid., pp. cviii, cx.
110 Edwards, *Works of Jonathan Edwards*, vol. 4, *The Great Awakening*, p. 335.

111 Edwards, *Personal Narrative*, in Jonathan Edwards, *Works of Jonathan Edwards*, vol. 16, *Letters and Personal Writings*, George S. Claghorn (ed.), New Haven and London, Yale University Press, 1998, p. 791.

112 Ibid., p. 793.

113 Ibid.

114 Ibid.

115 Ibid., p. 794.

116 Ibid.

117 Ibid., p. 796.

118 Ibid., p. 797.

119 Ibid., p. 799.

120 *On Sarah Pierpont*, ibid., pp. 789–90.

121 Ibid., p. 801.

122 Jonathan Edwards, *The "Miscellanies" (Entry Nos. a–z, aa–zz, 1–500)*, Thomas A. Schafer (ed.), vol. 13 in *Works of Jonathan Edwards*, New Haven and London, Yale University Press, 1994, no. 332, p. 410.

123 Gerald R. McDermott, *Jonathan Edwards Confronts the Gods, Christian Theology, Enlightenment Religion, and Non-Christian Faiths*, Oxford and New York, Oxford University Press, 2000, p. 134.

124 Ibid., p. 202.

125 Ibid., p. 154.

126 *Some Thoughts Concerning the Revival of Religion*, p. 341.

127 D. Michael Quinn, *Early Mormonism and the Magic World View*, rev. ed., Salt Lake City, Signature, 1998, p. 30.

128 Joseph Smith, *Joseph Smith's Own Story*, written in 1842, in *Murder of an American Prophet*, Keith Huntress (ed.), San Francisco, Chandler Publishing Co., 1960, pp. 5–6.

129 Ibid., p. 7.

130 Ibid., p. 8.

131 Joseph Smith and Heman C. Smith, *History of the Church of Jesus Christ of Latter-Day Saints*, 4 vols, 8th ed., Lamoni, IO, Reorganized Church of Jesus Christ of Latter-Day Saints, 1908, 1:36.

132 The revelations are contained in *The Doctrine and Covenants of the Church of Jesus Christ of Latter-Day Saints*, Salt Lake City, Desert News, 1880; repr. Westport, CN, Greenwood Press, 1971.

133 Paul R. Conkin, *Cane Ridge, America's Pentecost*, Madison, University of Wisconsin Press, 1990, p. 115.

134 See above, pp. 186–7.

135 Delbert R. Rose, *A Theology of Christian Experience*, Minneapolis, Bethany Fellowship, 1965, p. 52; and see Vinson Synan, *The Holiness–Pentecostal Tradition, Charismatic Movements in the Twentieth Century*, 2nd ed., Grand Rapids, MI, and Cambridge, William B. Eerdmans Publishing Co., 1997, p. 25.

136 See Patricia W. Ward, "Madame Guyon and Experiential Theology in America," *Church History*, 1998, vol. 67, pp. 484–98.

137 Steven Barabas, *So Great Salvation, The History of the Message of the Keswick Convention*, Westwood, NJ, Fleming H. Revell Company, 1953, pp. 139, 106–7, 117, 103.

138 Synan, *Holiness–Pentecostal Tradition*, p. 43.

139 See Synan, *Holiness-Pentecostal Tradition*, pp. 86–8.

140 Sarah E. Parham, *The Life of Charles F. Parham, Founder of the Apostolic Faith Movement*, Birmingham, AL, Commercial Printing, p. 54; and see James R. Goff, Jr., *Fields White Unto Harvest, Charles F. Parham and the Missionary Origins of Pentecostalism*, Fayetteville, AK, and London, University of Arkansas Press, 1988, p. 68.

141 Douglas J. Nelson, *For Such a Time as This: the Story of Bishop William J. Seymour and the Azusa Street Revival*, unpubl. Ph.D. dissertation, University of Birmingham, May 1981,

p. 31, cited in Iain MacRobert, *The Black Roots and White Racism of Early Pentecostalism in the USA*, New York, St. Martin's Press, 1988, p. 53.

142 Joe Creech, "Visions of Glory, The Place of the Azusa Street Revival in Pentecostal History," *Church History*, 1996, vol. 65, p. 412.

143 MacRobert, *Black Roots*, p. 60.

144 Parham, *Life*, p. 169.

145 Goff, *Fields White Unto Harvest*, p. 130.

146 John Chapman, "Mysticism (Christian, Roman Catholic)," *Encyclopædia of Religion and Ethics*, James Hastings (ed.), vol. 9, New York, Charles Scribner's Sons, Edinburgh, T. & T. Clark, 1922, p. 101.

147 Elizabeth of the Trinity, *Reminiscences of Sister Elizabeth of the Trinity, Servant of God, Discalced Carmelite of Dijon*, a Benedictine of Stanbrook Abbey (trans.), Westminster, MD, Newman Press, 1952, pp. 3, 11.

148 Ibid.

149 Ibid., pp. 10–11.

150 Elizabeth, Élisabeth de la Trinité, *Œuvres Complètes*, Conrad de Meester (ed.), Paris, Cerf, 1991, Journal 1, p. 811.

151 Ibid., 14, pp. 816–17.

152 Elizabeth of the Trinity, *I Have Found God, Complete Works*, vol. II, Letters from Carmel, Anne Englund Nash (trans.), Washington, DC, ICS Publications, 1995, 139, p. 70.

153 Ibid., 142, p. 73.

154 Ibid., 89, p. 17.

155 Ibid., 235, p. 208.

156 Ibid., 246, p. 226.

157 Ibid., 236, p. 210.

158 Ibid., 128, p. 56.

159 Ibid., 123, p. 52.

160 Ibid., 142, p. 73.

161 Ibid., 335, p. 360.

162 Ibid., 333, p. 358.

163 Ibid., 333, 340, pp. 358, 363.

164 Elizabeth, *Reminiscences*, p. 165.

165 Kowalska, *Divine Mercy in My Soul, The Diary of the Servant of God, Sister M. Faustina Kowalska*, Stockbridge, MA, Marian Press, 1987.

166 Ibid., 560, p. 237.

167 Ibid., 137, p. 76.

168 Ibid., 582, p. 245.

169 Ibid., 768, p. 307.

170 Ibid., 30, p. 17.

171 Ibid., 733, p. 295.

172 Ibid., 142, 432, 745, 1776, pp. 78, 191, 299, 629.

173 Ibid., 118, p. 66.

174 Ibid., 148, p. 83.

175 Ibid., 1302, p. 468.

176 Ibid., 47, p. 24.

177 Ibid., 299, p. 139.

178 Ibid., 623, 625, pp. 260–1.

179 Pierre Teilhard de Chardin, *The Heart of Matter*, René Hague (trans.), New York and London, Harcourt Brace Jovanovich, 1979, pp. 17, 21, 125.

180 Pierre Teilhard de Chardin, *The Making of a Mind, Letters From a Soldier-Priest, 1914–1919*, René Hague (trans.), New York, Harper & Row, 1965, p. 165.

181 Pierre Teilhard de Chardin, *Cosmic Life*, in his *Writings in Time of War*, René Hague (trans.), New York and Evanston, Harper & Row, 1968, p. 60.

182 Teilhard, *Making of a Mind*, p. 41.

183 Ibid., p. 56.

184 Ibid., pp. 207, 209.

185 Ibid., p. 89.

186 Teilhard, *Writings in Time of War*, pp. 14–71, 115–49.

187 In Pierre Teilhard de Chardin, *Hymn to the Universe*, Simon Bartholomew (trans.), New York and Evanston, IL, Harper & Row, 1965, p. 46.

188 Ibid., p. 48.

189 Ibid., pp. 52–3.

190 Ibid., pp. 190, 239.

191 Teilhard, *Note on Some Possible Historical Representations of Original Sin*, in *Christianity and Evolution*, René Hague (trans.), New York, Harcourt Brace Jovanovich, 1971, p. 47, 54.

192 Robert Speaight, *The Life of Teilhard de Chardin*, New York and Evanston, IL, Harper & Row, 1967, p. 282.

193 Teilhard, *Pantheism and Christianity*, in *Christianity and Evolution*, pp. 57, 64–5.

194 Teilhard, *The Divine Milieu*, Harper & Row, New York, Cambridge, Philadelphia, San Francisco, London, Mexico City, São Paolo, Singapore, Sydney, 1960, p. 106.

195 Teilhard, *Hymn to the Universe*, pp. 61, 63–5, 68.

196 Christopher J. R. Armstrong, *Evelyn Underhill (1875–1941), An Introduction to her Life and Writings*, London and Oxford, Mowbrays, 1975, p. 155.

197 Margaret Cropper, *Life of Evelyn Underhill*, New York, Harper & Brothers, 1958, p. 157.

198 Introduction, in Armstrong, *Evelyn Underhill*, p. x.

199 Dana Greene, *Evelyn Underhill, Artist of the Infinite Life*, New York, Crossroad, 1990; repr. London, Darton, Longman and Todd, 1991, p. 37.

200 Todd E. Johnson, "Evelyn Underhill's Pneumatology: Origins and Implications," *Downside Review*, 1998, 116, no. 403, p. 109.

201 Underhill, *Fragments From an Inner Life, The Notebooks of Evelyn Underhill*, Dana Greene (ed.), Harrisburg, PA, Morehouse Publishing, 1993, letter to Friedrich von Hügel (December 1921), p. 108.

202 Underhill, *The Letters of Evelyn Underhill*, Charles Williams (ed.), London, New York, Toronto, Longmans, Green & Co., 1943; repr. 1944, letter of 1926, p. 79.

203 Underhill, *Fragments*, p. 108.

204 Underhill, *Letters* (December 1909), p. 80.

205 Ibid. (October 1907), p. 69.

206 Greene, *Underhill*, p. 57.

207 Underhill, *Fragments* (letter of 1926), p. 79.

208 Ibid. (letter of June 1923), p. 122.

209 Ibid. (May 1923), pp. 41–2.

210 Ibid., p. 124.

211 Underhill, *Letters* (November 1923), pp. 33–4.

212 Ibid. (January 1924), p. 57.

213 Cropper, *Life*, p. 234.

214 Underhill, *Letters*, p. 37.

215 Cropper, *Life*, pp. 143, 158.

216 Thomas Merton, *The Seven Storey Mountain*, New York, Harcourt, Brace, 1948; repr. New York and London, Harcourt Brace Jovanovich, 1978, pp. 71–2.

217 Michael Mott, *The Seven Mountains of Thomas Merton*, Boston, Houghton Mifflin, 1984, pp. 82–3.

218 Ibid., p. 206.

219 Ibid., p. 225.

220 Thomas Merton, *Conjectures of a Guilty Bystander*, Garden City, NY, Image, 1968, p. 320.

221 Thomas Merton, *Run to the Mountain: The Story of a Vocation*, The Journals of Thomas Merton, vol. 1, 1939–1941, San Francisco, HarperSanFrancisco, 1995, p. 218.

222 Merton, *Seven Storey Mountain*, p. 285.
223 Ibid., p. 321.
224 Thomas Merton, *Contemplation in a World of Action*, rev. ed., Notre Dame, IN, University Press of Notre Dame, 1998, p. 155.
225 Thomas Merton, *New Seeds of Contemplation*, New York, New Directions, 1961; repr. 1972, pp. 214, 2.
226 Thomas Merton, *Seeds of Contemplation*, Norfolk, CN, New Directions, 1949, p. xii.
227 Merton, *New Seeds*, p. 84.
228 Ibid., p. 252.
229 Ibid., p. 82.
230 Merton, *Contemplation in a World of Action*, p. 167; *New Seeds*, p. 131.
231 Merton, *The Hidden Ground of Love*, the Letters of Thomas Merton on Religious Experience and Social Concerns, William H. Shannon (ed.), New York, Farrar, Straus, Giroux, 1985, p. 60.
232 Ibid., p. 341.
233 Merton, *Conjectures*, pp. 211, 282.
234 Ibid., p. 282.
235 Thomas Merton, *The Ascent to Truth*, New York, Harcourt, Brace, 1951, p. 70.
236 Merton, *Conjectures*, p. 144.
237 Mott, *Seven Mountains*, p. 568.
238 Merton, *Contemplation in a World of Action*, p. 160.
239 Merton, *New Seeds*, p. 277.
240 Teilhard de Chardin, *Christianity and Evolution*, p. 60.

EPILOGUE

1 Caroline Walker Bynum in *Gendered Voices, Medieval Saints and Their Interpreters*, Catherine M. Moody (ed.), Philadelphia, University of Pennsylvania Press, 1999, p. xi.
2 See Bernard McGinn, *The Doctors of the Church*, New York, Crossroad Publishing, 1999.
3 *Symeon the New Theologian, The Discourses*, C. J. deCantanzaro (trans.), New York, Ramsey and Toronto, Paulist Press, 1980, 22.8, p. 250.
4 Thomas Merton, *Contemplation in a World of Action*, rev. ed., Notre Dame, IN, University Press of Notre Dame, 1998, p. 160.

GLOSSARY

— •◆• —

Albigensians (Cathars) – heretics especially numerous in southern France in the twelfth and thirteenth centuries, following a Dualistic theology of contrast and opposition between good and evil, spirit and matter; the Albigensian Crusade was preached against them in 1208 and they disappeared after the creation of the Inquisition to discover them and correct their errors.

Allegorical interpretation of Scripture – when what is written is understood to refer symbolically to a different matter.

Amalricians – twelfth and thirteenth-century followers of the teachings of Amalric of Bène, a scholar in Paris; they blended together neoplatonic, gnostic, pantheistic, and antinomian teachings; attaining the state of sinlessness was dependent upon one's having the Holy Spirit dwelling within and they were given to ecstatic raptures.

Anabaptists – collective name for groups of Christians during the Reformation who rejected infant baptism and rebaptized those who had been baptized as children.

Antinomians – those who believe they are freed from the necessity to follow moral laws.

Apatheia – passionlessness.

Apophatic – the approach to understanding God through denial, by affirming what God is not rather than the cataphatic approach of affirmations of the nature and attributes of God.

Arianism – fourth-century heresy, named for its founder the Alexandrian priest Arius, which taught that God the Son was not co-eternal with the God the Father and was not of exactly the same substance, or essence, as the Father.

Ascesis – literally "athletic training," in religion the training of the body that will lead to deification; see asceticism.

Asceticism – the exercise of rigorous self-discipline, austerity and self-denial in order to overcome bodily passions and to promote the virtues.

Atonement – the Western Christian doctrine that Christ died as a vicarious payment for the sins of humans in order to satisfy God's requirement that sin must be paid for by death, thus permitting God to save sinners.

Bridal Mysticism – an emphasis on mystical union seeing the human soul as the bride of Jesus.

Calvinism – followers of the theology of John Calvin, stressing the Bible as the source of faith, stressing the lack of free will in humans, and divine predestination of some for salvation and others for damnation.

Cathars, see Albigensians.

Cenobium (adj. cenobitic) – a monastery where monks live a communal life, as opposed to those who live as hermits or in a laura.

Charisms (adj. charismatic) – the divine gifts given to humans, especially those mentioned in 1 Cor. 12 (speaking in tongues, prophecy, healing) and thus referring to possession by the Holy Spirit.

Christocentrism – worship or devotion that focuses on Christ rather than God or the Godhead (see Theocentrism).

Deification (theosis) – the teaching of the Eastern Church that a human is transformed into God (or united with divine energies) through divine grace, often seen in a mystical sense of union with God.

Deists – those in the seventeenth and eighteenth centuries who declared that God, and thus religion, must be reasonable and rational; thus they rejected the miraculous and mysterious in religion and denied that God intervenes in the world, precluding the possibility of divine revelation.

Dobrotolyubie – the Slavonic name of the Philokalia.

Doctors of the Church – those officially proclaimed by the Roman Catholic Church as "doctors" ("teachers") of the Church on the basis of the exceptional worth of their teaching of the faith (although not necessarily possessing inerrancy).

Dualism – the religious viewpoint of the division, separation and hostility between spirit and matter, light and dark, good and evil; dualists tend to argue for two gods, a good god of spirit and light and an evil god (or very powerful being) of matter and darkness.

Ecstasy (rapture) – a mystical state of being taken out of oneself and a state of obliviousness to one's surroundings.

Essenes – an ascetical and contemplative Jewish sect known from the mid-second century BC to the first century AD thought to have had a community at Qumran; many scholars believe that the Dead Sea Scrolls, discovered near Qumran, were part of an Essene library.

Free Spirit – a term used for antinomian mystics in the thirteenth and fourteenth centuries; considered heretical by the established Medieval Church.

Gnosticism – various sects found in paganism, Judaism and Christianity, stressing *gnosis*, revealed knowledge of God, as the source of their teachings.

Hellenistic period – the age between the conquests of Alexander the Great (d. 323 BC) and conquest of the Mediterranean by the Roman Empire (completed 31 BC), referring especially to the eastern Mediterranean, whose states were marked by a high degree of uniformity of culture based on Greek civilization.

Hellenized Jews – those who dispersed from Palestine and Judea in the period from Alexander the Great to the early first century AD and adopted much of the culture of the Hellenistic world, even to the point of abandoning the Hebrew language for the Greek, without, however, losing their religion.

Hesychia – (Greek "quietness") the state of passionlessness that leads to mystical union with God.

Huguenots – French Calvinists.

Ineffability – in mysticism, the aspect of the mystical experience making it inexpressible in human language because of its transcendent quality.

Jansenism – the seventeenth and eighteenth-century reaction against Catholicism's emphasis on individual responsibility for one's actions by stressing the doctrine of original sin and thus human sinfulness which created the necessity of divine grace for salvation.

Jesus Prayer – the prayer in the Eastern Church, dating from the sixth and seventh centuries, which in its most common form runs "Lord Jesus Christ, Son of God, have mercy on me."

Josephites – in Russia in the fifteenth and sixteenth centuries, followers of Joseph of Volokolamsk in accepting the ownership of property by monasteries (thus they were "Possessors") and in stressing observance of the traditional formalism of Russian monastic life.

Judaizers – as used in this work, the group in Russia in the fifteenth and sixteenth centuries who stressed monotheism and thus denied the Trinity.

Laura (adj. lauritic) – monks who live in individual cells but with a group of other monks under the authority of an abbot and having a single church for the performance of services.

Lollards – the movement in fourteenth and fifteenth century England begun by the theologian John Wyclif; which attacked the celibacy of the clergy and the doctrine of Transubstantiation while arguing for the supreme authority of the Scriptures.

Manicheans – adherents of a religious sect, sometimes considered to be a Christian heresy, especially prominent in the Roman Empire in the third, fourth and fifth centuries; Manicheanism originated in Persian dualism (see Dualism) but adopted many elements of Judeo-Christian views of the origin of the world and of humans.

Messalians – a Christian sect of the fourth century, believing that because of Adam's sin, all humans had a demon within them that could be expelled only by the elimination of passion and desire, which would lead to perfection and an immediate vision of God.

Monotheletism – the teaching promoted by the Roman emperor Heraclius in the seventh century, intended to reconcile Monophysites to the Church, that while Christ had both human and divine natures, he had but a single will, the divine; it was condemned as heretical in 681.

Montanism – the second-century Christian movement, named for Montanus, whose members received the Holy Spirit and the attendant charismatic gifts.

Mother Mysticism – the visions of female mystics in which they behave in a maternal manner towards the infant Jesus, especially in suckling him.

Mystagogue – a teacher of mystical doctrines leading others into the mystical life.

Paraclete – literally, "the Comforter," a name for the Holy Spirit.

Pelagianism – the belief that humans can, by the freedom of the will, lead a sinless life and thus merit salvation without an infusion of divine grace; named for its leading proponent, Pelagius (c. 360 to c. 420), a monk from Ireland or Britain.

Philokalia – the seventeenth-century compilation of ascetical and mystical writings of Eastern Christianity dating from the third century to the fifteenth century.

Pneumatic – concerning the spirit (Greek *pneuma*), specifically the Holy Spirit; thus often referring to the coming of the Holy Spirit into a person.

Pythagoreanism – the philosophy and manner of life attributed to Pythagoras (c. 550 to c. 500 BC), stressing the transmigration of souls and the separation of body and soul.

Quietism – in the seventeenth and eighteenth centuries, stress on the inability of humans to bring about the direct experience of God; instead, a person should achieve complete passionlessness, even to the point of abandoning concern over one's own salvation.

Quietness, see hesychia.

Qumran – a site on the western shore of the Dead Sea which is thought to have housed a community of Essenes.

Skete – a small monastic community with the monks living in separate cells, similar to a laura.

Spiritual Franciscans – the Franciscans who tried to follow St Francis's prohibition against the order's ownership of property despite the majority of Franciscan opinion and papal condemnation of their position.

Staretz (pl. startzi) – literally "elder(s)," a spiritually gifted and experienced monk who served as spiritual director to other monks and often to laypeople.

Synoptic Gospels – in the Bible, the gospels of Matthew, Mark and Luke.

Theocentrism – worship or devotion that focuses on God or the Godhead rather than on Christ (see Christocentrism).

Theosis – see deification.

Therapeutae – an ascetical and contemplative Jewish sect of the first century whose members lived in communities withdrawn from society, perhaps related to the Essenes; they are known only in the writings of Philo of Alexandria.

Waldensians – followers of Valdes (sometimes known as Peter Waldo), who translated the Scriptures into the vernacular, criticized clerical wealth and corruption, and allowed laypeople to preach and administer sacraments; after being condemned in 1184, Valdes and his followers formed their own church; despite persecution they continue to exist today, especially in Italy.

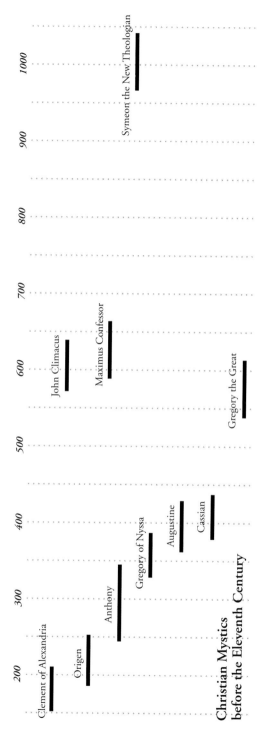

Christian Mystics before the Eleventh Century

Clement of Alexandria

Origen

Anthony

Gregory of Nyssa

Augustine

Cassian

Gregory the Great

John Climacus

Maximus Confessor

Symeon the New Theologian

200   300   400   500   600   700   800   900   1000

Timeline 1 Timeline of mystics before the eleventh century

Eastern/Russian Churches

Bernard of Clairvaux
Hildegard of Bingen
Christina Markyate
Christina Mirabilis
Dominic
Marie d'Oignies
Francis of Assisi
Liutgard
Mechthild of Magdeburg
Margaret of Ypres
Thomas Aquinas

Gregory Palamas
Sergius of Radonezh
Nicholas Cabasilas

Meister Eckhart
Margaret Ebner
Jan van Ruusbroec
Henry Suso
Richard Rolle
John Tauler
Birgitta of Sweden
Rulman Merswin
Julian of Norwich
Catherine of Siena

Nilus of Sora

Catherine of Genoa
Christopher Columbus
Thomas Müntzer
Francisco de Osuna
Ignatius of Loyola
Teresa of Avila
John of the Cross
Johann Arndt

Paisius Velichkovsky
Tikhon of Zadonsk

Ambrose of Optina
Theophan the Recluse
Seraphim of Sarov John of Kronstadt
Thaisia
Leonid of Optina Silouan
Macarius of Optina
Anastasia

Brother Lawrence
Blaise Pascal
George Fox
François Fénelon
Mme Guyon
Emanuel Swedenborg
William Law
John Wesley
Jonathan Edwards
Sarah Edwards
Nathan Cole

Charles F. Parham
Elizabeth of the Trinity
Evelyn Underhill
Teilhard de Chardin
Faustina Kowalska
Thomas Merton

Jacopone da Todi
Angela of Foligno
Gertrude the Great
Jean Gerson
Margery Kempe
Joan of Arc

Jacob Boehme
Augustine Baker
Francis de Sales
Jeanne de Chantal
Marie of the Incarnation
Gertrude More

Joseph Smith
William J. Seymour

Western Churches

| 1100 | 1200 | 1300 | 1400 | 1500 | 1600 | 1700 | 1800 | 1900 | 2000 |

Timeline 2 Timeline of mystics, eleventh to twentieth centuries

258

BIBLIOGRAPHY

———— •◆• ————

Ackroyd, P. (1996) *Blake*, New York: Knopf.

Albert and Thomas (1988) *Albert & Thomas, Selected Writings*, S. Tugwell (trans.), New York and Mahwah, NJ: Paulist Press.

Allen, H. E. (1927) *Writings Ascribed to Richard Rolle, Hermit of Hampole, and Materials for His Biography*, New York, D. C. Heath, and London: Oxford University Press.

An Anthology of Christian Mysticism (1977) P. De Jaegher (ed.), Springfield, IL: Templegate.

Angela of Foligno (1993) *Angela of Foligno, Complete Works*, P. Lachance (trans.), New York and Mahwah, NJ: Paulist Press.

Angus, S. (1925) *The Mystery-Religions, A Study in the Religious Background of Early Christianity*, London: John Murray (1975) as *The Mystery-Religions and Christianity* repr. NY: Dover.

Apuleius of Madauros (1975) *The Isis-Book (Metamorphoses, Book XI)*, J. G. Griffiths (ed. and trans.), Leiden: Brill.

Armstrong, C. J. R. (1975) *Evelyn Underhill (1875–1941), An Introduction to her Life and Writings*, London and Oxford: Mowbrays.

Arndt, J. (1979) *True Christianity*, P. Erb (trans.), New York and Mahwah, NJ: Paulist Press.

Athanasius of Alexandria (1980) *Athanasius, The Life of Anthony and the Letter to Mercellinus*, R. C. Gregg (trans.), New York, Ramsey and Toronto: Paulist Press.

Atkinson, C. W. (1983) *Mystic and Pilgrim, The Book and the World of Margery Kempe*, Ithaca and London: Cornell University Press.

Augustine of Hippo (1922) *De ordine*, in *Corpus Scriptorum Ecclesiasticorum Latinorum*, P. Knöll (ed.), Vienna and Leipzig: Hölder-Pichler-Tempsky.

—— (1950) *The City of God*, M. Dods (trans.), New York: Modern Library.

—— (1953) *Saint Augustine, Letters*, 2, W. Parsons (trans.), Washington, DC: Catholic University of America Press.

—— (1984) *Augustine of Hippo, Selected Writings*, M. T. Clark (trans.), New York, Ramsey, Toronto: Paulist Press.

—— (1990) *Sermons*, 3, E. Hill (trans.), New York: New City Press.

—— (1991) *St. Augustine, Confessions*, H. Chadwick (trans.), Oxford and New York: Oxford University Press.

—— (1993) *On Christian Doctrine*, J. F. Shaw (trans.), in *A Select Library of Nicene and Post-Nicene Fathers of the Christian Church*, 1st series, 2, P. Schaff (ed.), Edinburgh:T & T Clark, repr. Grand Rapids: Wm. B. Eerdmans.

Baker, Fr. A. (1964, repr. 1972) *Holy Wisdom or Directions for the Prayer of Contemplation*, Wheathampstead, Hertfordshire: Anthony Clarke.

Barabas, S. (1953) *So Great Salvation, The History of the Message of the Keswick Convention*, Westwood, NJ: Fleming H. Revell Company.

Bebis, G. S. (1989) Introduction, *Nicodemus of the Holy Mountain, A Handbook of Spiritual Counsel*, P. A. Chamberas (trans.), New York and Mahwah, NJ: Paulist Press.

Beer, F. (1992) *Women and Mystical Experience in the Middle Ages*, Woodbridge, Suffolk, and Rochester: Boydell.

Benedict of Nursia (1935) *St. Benedicts's Rule for Monasteries*, L. J. Doyle (trans.), St. Louis: Herder Book Co.; repr. (1948) Collegeville, MN: Liturgical Press.

Bentley, G. E. Jr. (1969) *Blake Records*, Oxford: Clarendon Press.

—— (1988) *Blake Records Supplement*, Oxford: Clarendon Press.

Bernard of Clairvaux (1987) *Bernard of Clairvaux, Selected Works*, G. R. Evans (trans.), New York and Mahwah, NJ: Paulist Press.

Berry, V. G. "The Second Crusade," (1969) *A History of the Crusades*, 1: 463–512, M. W. Baldwin (ed.), Madison, Milwaukee and London: University of Wisconsin Press.

Blake, W. (1982) *The Complete Poetry and Prose of William Blake*, D. V. Erdman (ed.), rev. ed., Berkeley and Los Angeles: University of California Press.

Böhme, J. (1934) *Of The Incarnation of Jesus Christ*, J. R. Earle (trans.), London: Constable and Co.

—— (1955–61) *Sämtliche Schriften*, 11 vols., W.-E. Peuckert, F. Frommanns (ed.), Stuttgart.

—— (1960) *The Aurora*, J. Sparrow (trans.), London, John M. Watkins and James Clarke & Co.

—— (1989) *Jacob Boehme, Essential Readings*, R. Waterfield (ed.), Wellingborough, Northamptonshire: Crucible.

Bolshakoff, S. (1977) *Russian Mystics*, Kalamazoo, MI: Cistercian Publications; London: A. R. Mowbray.

Bolton, B. M. (1973) "Mulieres Sanctae," in *Sanctity and Secularity: The Church and the World, Studies in Church History*, 10:77–95, D. Baker (ed.), New York: Barnes & Noble.

Bonaventure (1978) *Bonaventure*, E. Cousins (trans.), New York: Ramsey; Toronto: Paulist Press.

Bremner, E. (1992) "Margery Kempe and the Critics: Disempowerment and Deconstruction," in *Margery Kempe: A Book of Essays*, 117–35, S. J. McEntire (ed.), New York and London: Garland.

Bridget of Sweden (1990) *Birgitta of Sweden*, M. T. Harris (ed.), A. R. Kezel (trans.), New York and Mahway: Paulist Press.

—— (1991) *Sancta Birgitta, Revelaciones*, Book VI, B. Bergh (ed.), Stockholm: Almqvist & Wiksell International.

Burkhert, W. (1987), *Ancient Mystery Cults*, Cambridge, MA, and London, Harvard University Press.

Butler, C. (1924) *Western Mysticism*, New York: E. P. Dutton.

Butler, J. (1982) "Enthusiasm Described and Decried: The Great Awakening as Interpretative Fiction," *Journal of American History*, 69:305–25.

Bynum, C. W. (1982) *Jesus as Mother: Studies in the Spirituality of the High Middle Ages*, Los Angeles and London: University of California Press.

Byrom, J. (1950) *Selections from the Journal & Papers of John Byrom, Poet-Diarist-Shorthand Writer 1691–1763*, H. Talon (ed.), London: Rockliff.

Cabasilas, N. (1998) *The Life in Christ*, C. J. deCatanzaro (trans.), Crestwood, NJ: St. Vladimir's Seminary Press.

Carmody, D. L. and Carmody, J. T. (1996) *Mysticism, Holiness East and West*, New York and Oxford: Oxford University Press.

Catherine of Genoa (1979) *Catherine of Genoa: Purgation and Purgatory, The Spiritual Dialogue*, S. Hughes (trans.), New York: Paulist Press.

Catherine of Siena (1980) *Catherine of Siena, the Dialogue*, S. Noffke OP (trans.), New York and Mahwah, NJ: Paulist Press.

—— (1988) *The Letters of St. Catherine of Siena*, I, S. Noffke, OP (trans.), Binghamton, NY: State University of New York at Binghamton.

Chapman, J. (1922) "Mysticism (Christian, Roman Catholic)," *Encyclopædia of Religion and Ethics*, 9:90–101, J. Hastings (ed.), New York: Charles Scribner's Sons; Edinburgh: T. & T. Clark.

Chetverikov, Fr. S. (1980) *Starets Paisii Velichkovskii, His Life, Teachings, and Influence on Orthodox Monasticism*, V. Lickwar and A. I. Lisenko (trans.), Belmont, MA: Nordland Publishing.

—— (1997) *Elder Ambrose of Optina*, Platina, CA: St. Herman of Alaska Brotherhood.

Christian Spirituality II, High Middle Ages and Reformation (1977) J.Raitt (ed.), New York: Crossroad.

Clement of Alexandria (1887) *The Ante-Nicene Fathers*, 2, A. Robert and J. Donaldson (eds), Buffalo: Christian Literature Publishing, repr. (1962) Grand Rapids, MI: Wm. B. Eerdmans.

—— (1948) *Clément d'Alexandre, Extraits de Théodote*, 23, F. Sagnard, OP, (ed.), Sources Chrétiennes, Paris: Éditions du Cerf.

—— (1954) *Alexandrian Christianity, Selected Translations of Clement and Origen*, with introduction and notes by J. E. L. Oulton and H. Chadwick, Philadelphia: Westminster Press.

—— (1991) *Stromateis, Books One to Three*, J. Ferguson (trans.), The Fathers of the Church, 85, Washington, DC: Catholic University of America Press.

The Cloud of Unknowing and Other Works (1978) C. Wolters (trans.), Harmondsworth, New York, Victoria, Ontario, Auckland: Penguin.

Cohn, N. (1970) *The Pursuit of the Millennium*, rev. ed., New York: Oxford University Press.

Collins, J. J. "Apocalypticism and Literary Genre in the Dead Sea Scrolls," in *The Dead Sea Scrolls After Fifty Years*, 403–30.

Columbus, C. (1991) *The Libro de las profecías of Christopher Columbus*, D. C. West and A. Kling (trans. and commentary), Gainesville, FL: University of Florida Press.

Conkin, P. R. (1990) *Cane Ridge, America's Pentecost*, Madison: University of Wisconsin Press.

Constantine, A. (1982) *A Spiritual Portrait of Saint John of Kronstadt*, Liberty, TN: St. John of Kronstadt Press.

Countryman, L. W. (1994) *The Mystical Way in the Fourth Gospel*, Valley Forge, PA: Trinity Press International.

Crawford, M. J. (1976) "The Spiritual Travels of Nathan Cole," *William and Mary Quarterly*, 3rd ser., 33:89–126.

Creech, J. (1996) "Visions of Glory, The Place of the Azusa Street Revival in Pentecostal History," *Church History*, 65:405–24.

Cressy, Fr. S. (1933) *The Life of the Venerable Father Augustine Baker*, in *The Life of Father Augustine Baker, O.S.B. (1575–1641)*, J. McCann (ed.), London: Burns, Oates & Washbourne.

Crook, P. (1997) "W. R. Inge and Cultural Crisis, 1899–1920," *Journal of Religious History*, 16:410–32.

Cropper, M. (1958) *Life of Evelyn Underhill*, New York: Harper & Brothers.

Crossan, J. D. (1992) *The Historical Jesus*, San Francisco: HarperSanFrancisco.

Davies, S. L. (1995) *Jesus the Healer: Possession, Trance, and the Origins of Christianity*, New York: Continuum.

Davila, J. "Heavenly Ascent Literature in the Dead Sea Scrolls," in *The Dead Sea Scrolls After Fifty Years*, 461–85.

Davis, J. H. Jr. (1979) *Fénelon*, Boston: Twayne Publishers.

The Dead Sea Scrolls After Fifty Years, A Comprehensive Assessment, 2 (1999) P. W. Flint and J. C. Vandekam (eds), Leiden, Boston and Cologne: Brill.

De Conick, A. D. (1996) *Seek to See Him, Ascent and Vision Mysticism in the Gospel of Thomas*, Leiden, New York and Cologne: E. J. Brill.

Deissmann, A. (1957) *Paul, A Study in Social and Religious History*, W. E. Wilson (trans.), New York: Harper & Row.

de Sales, F. (1945) *St. Francis de Sales, Treatise on the Love of God*, H. B. Mackey OSB (trans.), Westminster, MD: Newman Bookshop; repr. (1971) Westport, CT: Greenwood Press.

—— (1972) *Introduction to the Devout Life*, J. K. Ryan (trans.), New York, London, Toronto, Sydney, Auckland: Image Books.

De vita et miraculis fratris Johannis Ruusbroec, in *Analecta Bollandiana*, 4 (1885) Paris, Brussels and Geneva: Société Générale de Librairie Catholique.

de Vitry, J. *The Life of Marie d'Oignies* in *Two Lives of Marie d'Oignies*.

The Doctrine and Covenants of the Church of Jesus Christ of Latter-Day Saints (1880) Salt Lake City: Deseret News; repr. (1971) Westport, CN: Greenwood Press.

Dominic (1977) V. J. Koudelka (ed.), C. F., OP, and S. Tugwell, OP (trans.), London: Darton, Longman and Todd.

Dunlop, J. B. (1972) *Staretz Amvrosy, Model For Dostoevsky's Staretz Zosima*, Belmont, MA: Nordland Publishing.

Dunn, J. D. G. (1970) *Baptism in the Holy Spirit: A Re-examination of the New Testament Teaching on the Gift of the Holy Spirit in Relation to Pentecostalism Today*, London: SCM Press.

—— (1975) *Jesus and the Spirit: A Study of the Religious and Charismatic Experience of Jesus and the First Christians as Reflected in the New Testament*, London: SCM Press.

Early Dominicans, Selected Writings (1982) S. Tugwell (trans.), Ramsey, NJ: Paulist Press.

Early Islamic Mysticism, Sufi, Qu'ran, Mi''aj, Poetic and Theological Writings (1996) M. A. Sells (trans. and ed.), New York and Mahwah: Paulist Press.

Ebner, M. (1993) *Ebner, Margaret, Major Works*, L. P. Hindsley (trans. and ed.), New York and Mahwah, NJ: Paulist Press.

Eckhart, Meister (1941) *Meister Eckhart, a Modern Translation*, R. B. Blakeney (trans.), New York: Harper & Row.

—— (1994) *Meister Eckhart, Selected Writings*, O. Davies (trans.), London, New York, Victoria, Toronto, Auckland: Penguin.

Edwards, J. (1834) *The Works of Jonathan Edwards*, 1, London, repr. (1998) Peabody, MA: Hendrickson Publishers.

—— (1972) *Works of Jonathan Edwards*, 4, *The Great Awakening*, C. C. Goen (ed.), New Haven and London: Yale University Press.

—— (1994) *Works of Jonathan Edwards*, 13, *The "Miscellanies" (Entry Nos. a–z, aa–zz, 1–500)*, T. A. Schafer (ed.), New Haven and London: Yale University Press.

—— (1995) *A Jonathan Edwards Reader*, J. E. Smith, H. S. Stout, and K. P. Minkema (eds), New Haven and London: Yale University Press.

—— (1998) *Works of Jonathan Edwards*, 16, *Letters and Personal Writings*, G. S. Claghorn (ed.), New Haven and London: Yale University Press.

Egan, H. D. SJ (1982) *What Are They Saying About Mysticism?*, New York and Ramsey, NJ: Paulist Press.

Elizabeth of the Trinity (1952) *Reminiscences of Sister Elizabeth of the Trinity, Servant of God,*

Discalced Carmelite of Dijon, a Benedictine of Stanbrook Abbey (trans.), Westminster, MD: Newman Press.

—— (1991) *Élisabeth de la Trinité, Œuvres Complètes*, C. de Meester (ed.), Paris, Cerf.

—— (1995) *I Have Found God, Complete Works*, II, Letters from Carmel, A. E. Nash (trans.), Washington, DC: ICS Publications.

Elliott, J. H. (1989) *Spain and Its World, 1500–1700, Selected Essays*, New Haven: Yale University Press.

English Spirituality in the Age of Wesley (1987) D. L. Jeffrey (ed.), Grand Rapids, MI: William B. Eerdmans.

Ernst, C.W. (1996) Preface, *Early Islamic Mysticism, Sufi, Qu'ran, Mi'raj, Poetic and Theological Writings*, 1, M. A. Sells (trans. and ed.), New York and Mahwah: Paulist Press,

Eusebius of Caesarea (1965) *The History of the Church*, G. A. Williamson (trans.), Harmondsworth, New York, Victoria, Ontario, Auckland: Penguin.

Evans, C. A. "Jesus and the Dead Sea Scrolls," in *The Dead Sea Scrolls After Fifty Years*, 573–98.

Fedotov, G. P. (1946) *The Russian Religious Mind*, 1, *Kievan Christianity, the Tenth to the Thirteenth Century*, Cambridge, MA: Harvard University Press; repr. New York (1960): Harper & Brothers.

—— (1956) *The Russian Religious Mind*, 2, *The Middle Ages, The Thirteenth to the Fifteenth Centuries*, Cambridge, MA: Harvard University Press.

Fox, G. (1952) *The Journal of George Fox*, J. L. Nickalls (ed.), Cambridge: University Press.

Francis and Clare (1982) *Francis and Clare, The Complete Works*, R. J. Armstrong and I. C. Brady (trans.), New York, Ramsey and Toronto: Paulist Press.

Friesen, A. (1990) *Thomas Muentzer, a Destroyer of the Godless*, Berkeley, Los Angeles, Oxford: University of California Press.

Garrett, C. (1987) *Spirit Possession and Popular Religion From the Camisards to the Shakers*, Baltimore and London: Johns Hopkins University Press.

Gerson, J. (1998) *Jean Gerson, Early Works*, B. P. McGuire (trans.), New York and Mahwah, NJ: Paulist Press.

Gertrude of Helfta (1993) *Gertrude of Helfta, The Herald of Divine Love*, M. Winkworth (trans. and ed.), New York and Mahwah, NJ: Paulist Press.

Goff, J. R. Jr. (1988) *Fields White Unto Harvest, Charles F. Parham and the Missionary Origins of Pentecostalism*, Fayetteville, AK, and London: University of Arkansas Press.

Gorodetzky, N. (1976) *Saint Tikhon of Zadonsk, Inspirer of Dostoevsky*, Crestwood, NY: St. Vladimir's Seminary Press.

Gottfried of Disibodenberg and Theoderic of Echternach (1996) *The Life of the Saintly Hildegard by Gottfried of Disibodenberg and Theoderic of Echternach*, H. Feiss, OSB (trans.), Toronto: Peregrina Publishing.

Grant, R. M. (1946) *Second-Century Christianity, A Collection of Fragments*, London: SPCK.

The Great Awakening, Documents on the Revival of Religion, 1740–1745 (1970) R. L. Bushman (ed.), New York: Atheneum.

Greene, D. (1990) *Evelyn Underhill, Artist of the Infinite Life*, New York: Crossroad; repr. (1991) London: Darton, Longman and Todd.

Gregory of Nyssa (1893) *Gregory of Nyssa: Dogmatic Treatises, Etc., A Select Library of Nicene and Post-Nicene Fathers of the Christian Church*, 2nd ser., 5, P. Schaff and H. Wace (trans.), New York: Christian Literature Company; repr. (1994) Grand Rapids: Wm. B. Eerdmans.

—— (1961) *From Glory to Glory, Texts From Gregory of Nyssa's Mystical Writings*, J. Daniélou, SJ (ed.), H. Musurillo, SJ (trans.), New York: Charles Scribner's Sons.

——(1978) *The Life of Moses*, A. J. Malherbe and E. Ferguson (trans.), New York, Ramsey and Toronto: Paulist Press.

Gregory I, the Great (1847) *Morals on the Book of Job by Gregory the Great*, Members of the English Church (trans.), 3(1), Oxford: John Henry Parker; and London: F. and J. Rivington.

——(1959) *Saint Gregory the Great, Dialogues*, O. J. Zimmerman (trans.), New York: Fathers of the Church.

Guyon, J. M. Bouvier de la Mothe (1897) *Autobiography of Madame Guyon*, T. T. Allen (trans.), 2 vols, London: Kegan Paul, Trench: Treubner & Co.

Hadewijch of Antwerp (1980) *Hadewijch, The Complete Works*, Mother C. Hart (trans.), New York, Ramsey, Toronto: Paulist Press.

Hale, R. (1990) "*Imitatio Mariae*: Motherhood Motifs in Devotional Memoirs," *Mystics Quarterly*, 16:193–203.

Halifax, J. (1982) *Shaman, the Wounded Healer*, New York: Crossroad.

Hamilton, A. (1992) *Heresy and Mysticism in Sixteenth-Century Spain: The Alumbrados*, Cambridge: James Clarke & Co.

Happold, F. C. (1963) *Mysticism, A Study and an Anthology*, rev. ed. (1970) Harmondsworth, New York, Ringwood, Markham and Auckland: Penguin.

Henry-Coüannier, M. (1964) *Saint Francis de Sales and His Friends*, V. Morrow (trans.), Staten Island, NY: Alba House.

——(1992) *Hermetica*, B. P. Copenhaver (trans.), Cambridge: University Press.

Hildegard of Bingen (1987) *Hildegard of Bingen's Book of Divine Works*, M. Fox (ed.), Santa Fe: Bear & Co.

——(1990) *Hildegard of Bingen, an Anthology*, F. Bowie and O. Davies (eds), London: SPCK.

——(1990) *Hildegard of Bingen, Scivias*, Mother C.Hart and J. Bishop (trans.), New York and Mahwah, NJ: Paulist Press.

Hilton, W. (1991) *The Scale of Perfection*, J. P.H. Clark and R. Dorward (trans.), New York and Mahwah, NJ: Paulist Press.

Hodges, R. A. (1995) Introduction, in *Unseen Warfare, 'The Spiritual Combat' and 'Path to Paradise' of Lorenzo Scupoli*, as edited by Nicodemus of the Holy Mountain and revised by Theophan the Recluse, E. Kadloubovsky and G. E. H. Palmer (trans.), Crestwood, NY: St. Vladimir's Seminary Press.

Holdsworth, C. J. (1978) "Christina of Markyate," in *Medieval Women*, 185–204, D.Baker (ed.), Oxford: Blackwell.

Hultkrantz, Å. (1987) *Native Religions of North America*, San Francisco: Harper & Row.

Hurtado, L. W. (2000) "Religious Experience and Religious Innovation in the New Testament," *Journal of Religion*, 80:183–205.

Ignatius of Loyola (1991) *Ignatius of Loyola, The Spiritual Exercises and Selected Works*, G.E. Ganss (ed.), P. R. Divarkar, SJ, E. J. Malatesta, SJ, and M. E. Palmer, SJ (trans.), New York and Mahwah, NJ: Paulist Press.

Inge, W. R. (1899) *Christian Mysticism*, New York: Charles Scribner's Sons; London: Methuen.

Jacopone da Todi (1982) *Jacopone da Todi, the Lauds*, S. and E. Hughes (trans.), New York, Ramsey, Toronto: Paulist Press.

James, W. (1902) *Varieties of Religious Experience*, New York: Longmans, Green, & Co., repr. (1982) New York, London, Ringwood, Markham, ON, Auckland: Penguin.

Jantzen, G. M. (1988) *Julian of Norwich, Mystic and Theologian*, New York, Mahwah, NJ: Paulist Press.

The Jerusalem Bible (1966) Garden City, NJ: Doubleday.

John Cassian, Conferences (1985) C. Luibheid (trans.), New York, Mahwah, NJ, Toronto: Paulist Press.

John Climacus, The Ladder of Divine Ascent (1982) C. Luibheid and N. Russell (trans.), New York, Ramsey and Toronto: Paulist Press.

John of the Cross (1991) *The Collected Works of St. John of the Cross*, K. Kavanaugh, OCD (trans.), O. Rodriguez, OCD, rev. ed., Washington, DC: ICS Publications.

John of Kronstadt (1897) *My Life in Christ*, 4th ed., E. E. Goulaeff (trans.), London, Paris and Melbourne: Cassell; repr. (1994) Jordanville, NY: Holy Trinity Monastery.

—— (1989) *The Spiritual Counsels of Father John of Kronstadt, Select Passages from My Life in Christ*, W. J. Grosbrooke (ed.), Crestwood, NY: St. Vladimir's Seminary Press.

Johnson, L. T. (1997) *The Real Jesus*, San Francisco: HarperSanFrancisco.

Johnson, T. E. (1998) "Evelyn Underhill's Pneumatology: Origins and Implications," *Downside Review*, 116, (403)109–36.

Jones, R. M. (1939) *The Flowering of Mysticism, The Friends of God in the Fourteenth Century*, New York: Macmillan; repr. (1971) New York: Hafner Publishing.

Jorgensen, K. S. J. (1991) "'Loves Conquers All,' the Conversion, Asceticism and Altruism of St. Caterina of Genoa," in *Renaissance Society and Culture, Essays in Honor of Eugen F. Rice, Jr.*, 87–106, J. Monfasani and R. G. Musto (eds), New York: Italica Press.

Julian of Norwich (1978) *Julian of Norwich, Showings*, E. Colledge and J. Walsh (trans.), New York, Ramsey and Toronto: Paulist Press.

Kavelin, Fr. L. (1995) *Elder Macarius of Optina*, V.V. Lyovina (trans.), Platina, CA: St. Herman of Alaska Brotherhood.

Kelsey, M. T. (1988) *Psychology, Medicine & Christian Healing*, San Francisco: Harper & Row.

Kempe, M. (1998) *The Book of Margery Kempe, A New Translation*, J. Skinner (trans.), New York: Image Books.

Kieckhefer, R. (1984) *Unquiet Souls: Fourteenth-Century Saints and Their Religious Milieu*, Chicago and London: University of Chicago Press.

Kizenko, N. (2000) *A Prodigal Saint, Father John of Kronstadt and the Russian People*, University Park, PA: Pennsylvania State University Press.

Knowles, Dom D. (1961) *The English Mystical Tradition*, New York: Harper & Brothers.

—— (1967) *What Is Mysticism?*, London: Burns & Oates; repr. (1988) London: Sheed and Ward.

Kovalevsky, P. (1976) *Saint Sergius and Russian Spirituality*, Crestwood, NY: St. Vladimir's Seminary Press.

Kowalska, Sister F. (1987) *Divine Mercy in My Soul, The Diary of the Servant of God, Sister M. Faustina Kowalska*, Stockbridge, MA: Marian Press.

Krieser, B. R. (1978) *Miracles, Convulsions, and Ecclesiastical Politics in Early Eighteenth-Century Paris*, Princeton: Princeton University Press.

Lambert, M. (1992) *Medieval Heresy*, 2nd ed., Oxford and Cambridge, MA: Blackwell.

Law, W. (1938) *Two Answers to Dr. Trapp*, in *Selected Mystical Writings of William Law*, S. Hobhouse (ed.), London: C.W. Daniel Company Ltd.

—— (1981) *William Law, A Serious Call to a Devout Life and Holy Life, The Spirit of Love*, P. G. Stanwood (ed.), New York, Ramsey and Toronto: Paulist Press.

Lawrence, Brother (1994) *Brother Lawrence of the Resurrection, OCD, Writings and Conversations on the Practice of the Presence of God*, C. De Meester, OCD (ed.), S. Sciurba (trans.), OCD, Washington, DC: ICS Publications.

Lawrence, C. H. (1989) *Medieval Monasticism*, 2nd ed., London and New York: Longman.

Lerner, R. E. (1972) *The Heresy of the Free Spirit in the Later Middle Ages*, Berkeley, Los Angeles and London: University of California Press.

Lewis, I. M. (1971) *Ecstatic Religion, an Anthropological Study of Spirit Possession and Shamanism*, Harmondsworth, Baltimore, Victoria, Markham, Ontario, Auckland: Penguin.

The Life of Christina of Markyate: A Twelfth Century Recluse (1959) C. H. Talbot (ed. and trans.), Oxford: Oxford University Press; repr. (1998) Toronto and Buffalo: University of Toronto Press.

The Life of Saint Thomas Aquinas, Biographical Documents (1959) K. Foster, OP (trans. and ed.) London: Green and Co.; Baltimore: Helicon.

The Lives of the Desert Fathers (1981) N. Russell (trans.), London and Oxford: Mowbray; Kalamazoo, MI: Cistercian Publications.

Llewelyn, R. (1998) *Memories and Reflections*, London: Darton, Longman & Todd.

Louth, A. (1981) *The Origins of the Christian Mystical Tradition, From Plato to Denys*, Oxford: Clarendon Press.

Lovejoy, D. S. (1985) *Religious Enthusiasm in the New World, Heresy to Revolution*, Cambridge, MA, and London: Harvard University Press.

Low, A. (1970) *Augustine Baker*, New York: Twayne Publishers.

McDermott, G. R. (2000) *Jonathan Edwards Confronts the Gods, Christian Theology, Enlightenment Religion, and Non-Christian Faiths*, Oxford and New York: Oxford University Press.

McGinn, B. "The English Mystics," in *Christian Spirituality II*, 194–207.

—— (1992) *The Foundations of Mysticism*, New York: Crossroad.

—— (1994) *The Growth of Mysticism*, New York: Crossroad.

—— (1996) "The Changing Shape of Late Medieval Mysticism," *Church History*, 65:197–219.

—— (1998) *The Flowering of Mysticism*, New York: Crossroad Herder.

—— (1999) *The Doctors of the Church*, New York: Crossroad Publishing.

McGuire, B. P. (1997) "Late Medieval Care and Control of Women: Jean Gerson and His Sisters," *Revue d'Histoire Ecclésiastique*, 92:5–37.

MacRobert, I. (1988) *The Black Roots and White Racism of Early Pentecostalism in the USA*, New York: St. Martin's Press.

Maloney, G. A. SJ. (1973) *Russian Hesychasm, the Spirituality of Nil Sorskij*, The Hague and Paris: Mouton.

Marie of the Incarnation (1964) *The Autobiography of Venerable Marie of the Incarnation, O.S.U., Mystic and Missionary*, J. J. Sullivan, SJ (trans.), Chicago: Loyola University Press.

—— (1967) *Words From New France, The Selected Letters of Marie de l'Incarnation*, J. Marshall (ed. and trans.), Toronto: Oxford University Press.

—— (1989) *Marie of the Incarnation, Selected Writings*, I. Mahoney, OSU (ed.), New York and Mahwah, NJ: Paulist Press.

Marsolais, M. "Jacques de Vitry and the Canons of St. Victor," in *Two Lives of Marie d'Oignies*, 13–36.

Maximus the Confessor (1985) *Maximus Confessor, Selected Writings*, G. C. Berthold (trans.), New York and Mahwah, NJ: Paulist Press.

Mechthild of Magdeburg, The Flowing Light of the Godhead (1998) F. Tobin (trans.), New York and Mahwah, NJ: Paulist Press.

Meredith, A. SJ. (1999) *Gregory of Nyssa*, London and New York: Routledge.

Merswin, R. (1960) *Mystical Writings of Rulman Merswin*, ed. and interpreted by T. S. Kepler, Philadelphia: Westminster Press.

Merton, T. (1948) *The Seven Storey Mountain*, New York: Harcourt Brace; repr. (1978) New York and London: Harcourt Brace Jovanovich.

—— (1949) *Seeds of Contemplation*, Norfolk, CN: New Directions.

—— (1951) *The Ascent to Truth*, New York: Harcourt Brace.

—— (1961) *New Seeds of Contemplation*, New York: New Directions; repr. (1972).

—— (1967) *Mystics and Zen Masters*, New York: Farrar, Straus & Giroux

—— (1968) *Conjectures of a Guilty Bystander*, Garden City, NY: Image.

—— (1985) *The Hidden Ground of Love, the Letters of Thomas Merton on Religious Experience and Social Concerns*, W. H. Shannon (ed.), New York: Farrar, Straus, Giroux.

—— (1995) *Run to the Mountain: The Story of a Vocation*, The Journals of Thomas Merton, 1, 1939–1941, San Francisco: Harper.

—— (1998) *Contemplation in a World of Action*, rev. ed., Notre Dame, IN: University Press of Notre Dame.

More, Dame G. (1910) *The Writings of Dame Gertrude More*, D. B. Weld-Blundell (ed.), Manchester, Birmingham, Glasgow: R. & T. Washbourne.

Mott, M. (1984) *The Seven Mountains of Thomas Merton*, Boston: Houghton Mifflin.

Müntzer, T. (1988) *The Collected Works of Thomas Müntzer*, P. Metheson (ed. and trans.), Edinburgh: T. & T. Clark.

Nelson, D. J. (1981) *For Such a Time as This: the Story of Bishop William J. Seymour and the Azusa Street Revival*, unpubl. Ph.D. dissertation, University of Birmingham.

Newman, B. (1987) *Sister of Wisdom, St. Hildegard's Theology of the Feminine*, Berkeley, Los Angeles, London: University of California Press.

Newton, J. A. (1968) *Susanna Wesley and the Puritan Tradition in Methodism*, London: Epworth Press.

Nilsson, M. P. (1987) *Greek Folk Religion*, Philadelphia: University of Pennsylvania Press, [originally published as (1940) *Greek Popular Religion*, New York: Columbia University Press].

Origen, works, in (1926) *The Ante-Nicene Fathers*, 4, A. Robert and J. Donaldson (eds), New York, Charles Scribner's Sons; (1956) repr. Grand Rapids, MI: Wm. B. Eerdmans.

—— (1965) *Origen: Contra Celsum*, H. Chadwick (trans.), Cambridge, London, New York, New Rochelle, Melbourne, Sydney: Cambridge University Press.

—— (1979) *Origen, An Exhortation to Martyrdom, Prayer, First Principles: Book IV, Prologue to the Commentary on the Song of Songs, Homily XXVII on Numbers*, R. A. Greer (trans.), New York, Ramsey, Toronto: Paulist Press.

Osuna, F. de. (1981) *Francisco de Osuna, The Third Spiritual Alphabet*, M. E. Giles (trans.), New York and Mahwah, NJ: Paulist Press.

Otto of Freising (1953) *The Deeds of Frederick Barbarossa, Otto of Freising and His Continuator*, C. C. Mierow (trans.), New York: W. W. Norton.

Otto, R. (1950) *The Idea of the Holy*, J. W. Harvey (trans.), 2nd ed., London, Oxford and New York: Oxford University Press.

—— (1960) *Mysticism East and West*, B. L. Bracey and R. C. Payne (trans.), New York: Collier.

Pagels, E. (1981) *The Gnostic Gospels*, New York: Vintage Books.

Palamas, G. (1983) *Gregory Palamas, The Triads*, N. Gendle (trans.), Mahwah, NJ: Paulist Press.

Palladius (1965) *The Lausiac History*, R. T. Meyer (trans.), Westminster, MD: Newman Press; and London: Longmans, Green & Co.

Parham, S. (1950) *The Life of Charles F. Parham, Founder of the Apostolic Faith Movement*, Birmingham, AL: Commercial Printing.

Parrinder, G. (1976) *Mysticism in the World's Religions*, New York: Oxford University Press.

Pascal, B. (1967) *Pascal, The Provincial Letters*, A. J. Krailsheimer (trans.), Harmondsworth, Middlesex, Baltimore, Victoria: Penguin Books.

—— (1995) *Pensées*, A. J. Krailsheimer (trans.), rev. ed., London, New York, Ringwood, Toronto, Auckland: Penguin.

Pernoud, R. (1982) *Joan of Arc By Herself and Her Witnesses*, E. Hyams (trans.), Lanham, New York, London: Scarborough House.

Philo of Alexandria (1981) *The Contemplative Life, The Giants, and Selections*, D. Winston (trans.), New York, Ramsey, and Toronto: Paulist Press.

Plato (1973) *Plato, Phaedrus and the Seventh and Eighth Letters*, W. Hamilton (trans.), London, New York, Victoria, Toronto, Auckland: Penguin.

—— (1990) *The Theaetetus of Plato*, M. J. Levett (trans.), rev. M. Burnyeat, Indianapolis and Cambridge: Hackett Publishing.

Porete, M. (1993) *Marguerite Porete, The Mirror of Simple Souls*, E. L. Babinsky (trans.), New York and Mahwah, NJ: Paulist Press.

Priklonsky, Fr. A. (1993) *Blessed Athanasia & the Desert Ideal*, 2nd ed., Platina, CA: St. Herman of Alaska Brotherhood.

Proclus (1901) *In Platonis Rem Publicam Commentarii*, G. Kroll (ed.), 2 vols, Leipzig: Teubner; repr. (1965) Amsterdam: Adolf M. Hakkert.

Pseudo-Dionysius, The Complete Works (1987) C. Luibheid (trans.), New York and Mahwah, NJ: Paulist Press.

Pseudo-Macarius, The Fifty Spiritual Homilies and the Great Letter (1992) G. A. Maloney, SJ (trans.), New York and Mahwah, NJ: Paulist Press.

Quasten, J. (1962) *Patrology*, 2, The Ante-Nicene Literature After Irenaeus, Westminster, MD: Newman Press; Utrecht-Antwerp: Spectrum Publishers.

Quinn, D. M. (1998) *Early Mormonism and the Magic World View*, rev. ed., Salt Lake City: Signature.

Raymond of Capua (1960) *The Life of St Catherine of Siena by Blessed Raymond of Capua*, G. Lamb (trans.), New York: P. J. Kennedy & Sons.

Redpath, H. M. (1947) *God's Ambassadress*, Milwaukee: Bruce.

Rolle, R. (1972) *The Fire of Love*, C. Wolters (trans.), Harmondsworth, Baltimore and Victoria: Penguin.

—— (1989) *The English Writings*, R. S. Allen (trans.), London: SPCK.

Rose, D. R. (1965) *A Theology of Christian Experience*, Minneapolis: Bethany Fellowship.

Rublack, U. (1994) "Female Spirituality and the Infant Jesus in Late Medieval Dominican Convents," *Gender & History*, 6:37–57.

Ruusbroec, J. (1985) *John Ruusbroec, The Spiritual Espousals and Other Works*, J. A. Wiseman, OSB (trans.), Mahwah, NJ: Paulist Press.

—— (1989) *The Little Book of Enlightenment*, in *Corpus Christianum, Continuatio Mediaeualis*, 101, Dr. G. De Baere (ed.), Ph. Crowley and Dr. H. Rolfson (trans.), Turnholt: Brepols.

—— (1995) *The Spiritual Espousals*, J. Alaerts (ed.), H. Rolfson (trans.), Collegeville, MN: Liturgical Press.

Sargent, M. (1981) "Contemporary Criticism of Richard Rolle," *Analecta Cartusiana*, 55:160–87.

The Sayings of the Desert Fathers (1975) B. Ward (trans.), London and Oxford: Mowbray; Kalamazoo, MI: Cistercian Publications.

Schmidt, J. Introduction, in *Johannes Tauler, Sermons*, 1–34.

Sederholm, Fr. C. (1990) *Elder Leonid of Optina*, Platina, CA: St. Herman of Alaska Brotherhood.

Seesholtz, A. G. (1934) *Friends of God, Practical Mystics of the Fourteenth Century*, New York: Columbia University Press; repr. (1970) New York: AMS Press.

Segal, A. F. (1990) *Paul the Convert*, New Haven and London: Yale University Press.

Semenoff-Tian-Chansky, Bishop A. (1955) *Father John of Kronstadt: A Life*, London and Oxford: Mowbray.

Seraphim of Sarov (1996) *Saint Seraphim of Sarov*, Fr. S. Rose (trans.), *Little Russian Philokalia*, 1, 4th ed., Platina, CA: St. Herman of Alaska Brotherhood.

Shannon, W. H. (1987) *Thomas Merton's Dark Path*, rev. ed., New York: Farrar, Straus, Giroux.

Sigstedt, C. O. (1952) *The Swedenborg Epic*, New York: AMS Press; repr. (1971) New York: AMS Press.

Silouan, Staretz (1975) *Wisdom From Mount Athos, The Writings of Staretz Silouan, 1866–1938*, A. Sophrony (ed.), R. Edmonds (trans.), Crestwood, NY: St. Vladimir's Seminary Press.

Smith, H. (1991) *The World's Religions*, San Francisco, HarperSanFrancisco [originally published as (1958) *The Religions of Man*, New York: Harper].

Spencer, S. (1963) *Mysticism in World Religion*, South Brunswick, NJ: A. S. Barnes.

Smith, J. (1960) *Joseph Smith's Own Story, Murder of an American Prophet*, K. Huntress (ed.), San Francisco: Chandler Publishing Co.

Smith, J. and Smith, H. C. (1908) *History of the Church of Jesus Christ of Latter Day Saints*, 4 vols, 8th ed., Lamoni, IO: Reorganized Church of Jesus Christ of Latter Day Saints.

Smith, M. (1992) "Two Ascended to Heaven–Jesus and the Author of 4Q491," in *Jesus and the Dead Sea Scrolls*, J. H. Charlesworth (ed.), New York, London, Toronto, Sydney, and Auckland: Doubleday.

Sophrony, Archimandrite (1973) *The Monk of Mount Athos, Staretz Silouan, 1866–1938*, R. Edmonds (trans.), Crestwood, NJ: St. Vladimir's Seminary Press.

Speaight, R. (1967) *The Life of Teilhard de Chardin*, New York and Evanston, IL: Harper & Row.

The Spiritual Doctrine of St. Catherine of Genoa (1989) Rockford, IL: Tan Books [first published (1874) as *Life and Doctrine of St. Catherine of Genoa*, New York: Christian Press Association Publishing Co.].

Spurgeon, C. F. E. (1913) "William Law and the Mystics," ch. 12 in *The Cambridge History of English Literature*, 341–67, A. W. Ward and A. R. Waller (eds), 9, New York: G. P. Putnam's Sons; Cambridge: University Press.

Stewart, C. (1998) *Cassian the Monk*, New York and Oxford: Oxford University Press.

Stoudt, J. J. (1968) *Jacob Boehme: His Life and Thought*, New York: Seabury Press.

Suso, H. (1989) *The Exemplar, With Two German Sermons*, F. Tobin (trans. and ed.), New York and Mahwah, NJ: Paulist Press.

Suzuki, D. T. (1979) *Mysticism Christian and Buddhist*, London, Sydney, Wellington: Unwin.

Swedenborg, E. (1989) *Swedenborg's Journal of Dreams, 1743–1744*, G. E. Klemming and W. R. Woofenden (eds), J. J. G. Wilkinson (trans.), 2nd ed., B. Athyn, PA: Swedenborg Scientific Association; and London: Swedenborg Society.

—— (1996) *Conversations with Angels, What Swedenborg Heard in Heaven*, L. Fox and D. L. Rose (eds), D. Gladish and J. Rose (trans.), West Chester, PA: Chrysalis Books.

Symeon the New Theologian (1969) *Syméon le nouveau théologien, Hymnes*, J. Paramelle (trans.), Paris: Cerf.

—— (1975) *Hymns of Divine Love by St. Symeon the New Theologian*, G. A. Maloney, SJ (trans.), Denville, NJ: Dimension Books.

—— (1980) *Symeon the New Theologian, The Discourses*, C. J. deCatanzaro (trans.), New York, Ramsey and Toronto: Paulist Press.

—— (1982) *Symeon the New Theologian, The Practical and Theological Chapters and The Three Theological Discourses*, P. McGuckin, C. P. (trans.), Kalamazoo, MI: Cistercian Publications.

—— (1995) *St. Symeon the New Theologian, On the Mystical Life: The Ethical Discourses*, 1, *The Church and Last Things*, A. Golitzin (trans.), Crestwood, NJ: St. Vladimir's Seminary Press.

—— (1996) *St. Symeon the New Theologian, On the Mystical Life: The Ethical Discourses*, 2, *On Virtue and Christian Life*, A. Golitzin (trans.), Crestwood, NJ: St. Vladimir's Seminary Press.

Synan, V. (1997) *The Holiness-Pentecostal Tradition, Charismatic Movements in the Twentieth Century*, 2nd ed., Grand Rapids, MI, and Cambridge: William B. Eerdmans Publishing Co.

Tauler, J. (1985) *Johannes Tauler, Sermons*, M. Shrady (trans.), New York and Mahwah, NJ: Paulist Press.

Teilhard de Chardin, P. (1960) *The Divine Milieu*, New York, Cambridge, Philadelphia, San Francisco, London, Mexico City, São Paolo, Singapore, Sydney: Harper & Row.

—— (1965) *Hymn to the Universe*, S. Bartholomew (trans.), New York and Evanston, IL: Harper & Row.

—— (1965) *The Making of a Mind, Letters From a Soldier-Priest, 1914–1919*, R. Hague (trans.), New York: Harper & Row.

—— (1968) *Writings in Time of War*, R. Hague (trans.), New York and Evanston: Harper & Row.

—— (1971) *Christianity and Evolution*, R. Hague (trans.), New York: Harcourt Brace Jovanovich.

—— (1979) *The Heart of Matter*, R. Hague (trans.), New York and London: Harcourt Brace Jovanovich.

Teresa of Ávila. (1957) *The Life of Saint Teresa of Ávila by Herself*, J. M. Cohen (trans.), London, New York, Victoria, Markham, Ontario, Auckland: Penguin.

—— (1979) *Teresa of Ávila, The Interior Castle*, K. Kavanaugh and O. Rodriguez (trans.), New York and Ramsey, NJ: Paulist Press.

Tertullian (1950) *Apologetical Works and Minucius Felix: Octavius*, E. A. Quain (trans.), Fathers of the Church, 10, New York: Fathers of the Church.

Thaisia, Abbess (1989) *The Autobiography of a Spiritual Daughter of St. John of Kronstadt*, Platina, CA: St. Herman of Alaska Brotherhood.

Theophan the Recluse (1996) *The Path to Salvation, A Manual of Spiritual Transformation*, Fr. S. Rose (trans.), Platina, CA: St. Herman of Alaska Brotherhood.

Thomas of Cantimpré (1991) *The Life of Lutgard of Aywières by Thomas of Cantimpré*, M. H. King (trans.), rev. ed., Toronto: Peregrina.

—— (1996) *The Life of Margaret of Ypres by Thomas of Cantimpré*, M. H. King (trans.), 2nd ed., Toronto: Peregrina.

—— (1997) *The Life of Christina Mirabilis by Thomas of Cantimpré*, M. H. King (trans.), Toronto: Peregrina.

Toksvig, S. (1948) *Emanuel Swedenborg, Scientist and Mystic*, London: Faber & Faber.

A Treasury of Russian Spirituality (1969) G. P. Fedotov (ed.), Gloucester, MA: Peter Smith.

Trigg, J. W. (1998) *Origen*, London and New York: Routledge.

Tugwell, S. "The Spirituality of the Dominicans," in *Christian Spirituality II*, 15–31.

Two Lives of Marie d'Oignies (1998) M. H. King (trans.), Toronto: Peregrina.

Underhill, E. (1913) *The Mystic Way, A Psychological Study in Christian Origins*, London and Toronto: J. M. Dent & Sons; New York: E. P. Dutton; repr. (1998) Kila, MT: Kessinger Publishing.

—— (1925) *The Mystics of the Church*, Cambridge: James Clarke; repr. (1988) Wilton, CN: Morehouse-Barlow.

—— (1930) *Mysticism*, 12th ed., London and New York: Methuen and E. P. Dutton; repr. (1974) New York: Meridian.

—— (1943) *The Letters of Evelyn Underhill*, C. Williams (ed.), London, New York, Toronto: Longmans, Green & Co., repr. (1944).

—— (1993) *Fragments From an Inner Life, The Notebooks of Evelyn Underhill*, D. Greene (ed.), Harrisburg, PA: Morehouse Publishing.

Velichkovsky, P. (1994) *Saint Paisius Velichkovsky*, Fr. S. Rose (trans.), *Little Russian Philokalia*, 4, Platina, CA: St. Herman Press.

Verdeyen, P. SJ (1994) *Ruusbroec and His Mysticism*, A. Lefevere (trans.), Collegeville, MN: Liturgical Press.

von Hügel, Baron F. (1909) *The Mystical Element of Religion as Studied in Saint Catherine of Genoa and Her Friends*, two vols., London and New York: J. M. Dent & Sons; (1999) repr. in one volume, New York: Crossroad.

Walker, A. K. (1973) *William Law, His Life and Thought*, London: SPCK.

Ward, P. W. (1998) "Madame Guyon and Experiential Theology in America," *Church History*, 67:484–98.

Ware, T. (1963) *The Orthodox Church*, Harmondsworth, Baltimore and Victoria: Penguin; repr. (1964).

Watkin, E. I. (1953) *Poets and Mystics*, London and New York: Sheed and Ward.

—— (1957) "The Mysticism of St. Augustine," *Saint Augustine*, New York: Meridian Books, 103–19.

The Way of a Pilgrim and The Pilgrim Continues His Way (1954) R. M. French (trans.), New York: Harper; repr. (1991) San Francisco: HarperSanFrancisco.

Weeks, A. (1991) *Boehme, An Intellectual Biography of the Seventeenth-Century Philosopher and Mystic*, Albany, NY: State University of New York Press.

Wesley, J. (1964) *John Wesley*, A. C. Outler (ed.), New York: Oxford University Press.

—— (1981) *John and Charles Wesley, Selected Prayers, Hymns, Journal Notes, Sermons, Letters and Treatises*, F. Whaling (ed.), Mahwah, NJ: Paulist Press.

—— (1985) *The Works of John Wesley*, 2, *Sermons II 34–70*, A. C. Outler (ed.), Nashville: Abingdon Press.

—— (1990) *The Works of John Wesley*, 19, *Journal and Diaries II*, W. R. Ward and R. P. Heitzenrater (eds), Nashville: Abingdon Press.

Zander, V. (1975) *St. Seraphim of Sarov*, Sister G. Anne (trans.), Crestwood, NY: St. Vladimir's Seminary Press.

Zumkeller, A. "The Spirituality of the Augustinians," in *Christian Spirituality II*, 63–74.

INDEX

——— ·•· ———